Best Bay Area
BARGAINS

THE INSIDER'S GUIDE TO SMART SHOPPING FOR ALMOST EVERYTHING!

Best Bay Area
BARGAINS

THE INSIDER'S GUIDE TO SMART SHOPPING FOR ALMOST EVERYTHING!

By the editors of SAN FRANCISCO FOCUS

KQED, INC. / SAN FRANCISCO

KQED Inc., San Francisco, CA 94110
© 1994 by KQED Inc.

Distributed to the trade by Publishers Group West.

Best Bay Area Bargains: The Insider's Guide to Smart Shopping for Almost Everything! / by the editors of *San Francisco Focus*.

     p. cm.
     Includes index.
     ISBN 0-912333-46-4: $11.95
     1. Shopping—California—San Francisco Bay Area—Guidebooks.
     2. Discount houses—California—San Francisco Bay Area—Guidebooks.
I. Focus (San Francisco, Calif.)
TX336.5.C22S4 1994
380.1'45'000257946—dc20   94-15341
                           CIP

ISBN 0-912333-46-4

98 97 96 94 5 4 3 2

TABLE OF CONTENTS

CONTRIBUTORS

CHARLENE AKERS is the author of *Never Buy Anything New—Except This Book* (Heyday Books), the definitive guide to secondhand shopping in the Bay Area. Her latest book, *Open to the Public: A Complete Guide to Northern California's 500 Astounding Museums* (Heyday Books) was published this spring.

CLARY ALWARD is a former editorial intern at *San Francisco Focus.* She is a recent graduate of UC Davis and currently lives in Aptos. Her work has appeared in the *California Aggie* and in *San Francisco Focus* magazine.

MIA AMATO is a University of California–accredited Master Gardener and a journalist specializing in gardening and landscaping. Her column "Yardscapes" appears in the *San Francisco Examiner.*

JENNY ANDRUS writes often for *San Francisco Focus.* The mother of two, she coauthored the second edition of *Bay Area Baby: The Essential Guide to Local Resources for Pregnancy, Childbirth, and Parenting* (Spirit Press).

KEVIN BERGER is the coauthor of *Where the Road and the Sky Collide: America Through the Eyes of Its Drivers* (Henry Holt), and *Zen Driving* (Ballantine), which has been translated into six language. His articles on transportation and popular culture have appeared in *San Francisco Focus* and other publications.

CAROL BLACKMAN is a columnist for the *San Jose Mercury News,* the Northern California correspondent for *California Apparel News,* and coauthor of the book *Way to Go! Shopping in San Francisco* (Buy the Book Enterprises). Her articles have appeared in *San Francisco Focus* magazine's *Insider Guide.*

SANDRA BRAVERMAN has written about consumer products and business for the *Boston Globe,* and contributes regular articles on real estate and other subjects to the *Contra Costa Times.* Her articles have appeared in the *San Francisco Chronicle, Marin Independent Jounal,* and *San Francisco Focus.*

PETER CALLAHAN is a freelance writer and editor, the former research editor at *Women's Sports and Fitness* magazine, and the former ski editor at *Travel Age West.* He has skied many mountains, from Jackson Hole to Japan, and has been an avid runner and cyclist for more years than he would like to admit.

JULIE CARLSON is an associate editor at *San Francisco Focus* magazine. Previously, she worked at the *New Yorker,* and her work has appeared in the *Washington Post*, the *Stanford Business School* magazine, and *British W.*

LESLIE CLAGETT is an Oakland-based writer and habitué of summer street fairs, regional produce festivals, and the more eclectic flea markets throughout the Golden State.

SUSANNAH CLARK is a writer and editor specializing in design and the home. A former editor of *Northern California Home & Garden*, Clark has also written for *Elle Decor*, *SF Magazine*, *Garden Design*, *Travel & Leisure*, *Image*, *Diablo*, and *California Horse Review*.

LESLIE CRAWFORD writes for *San Francisco Focus* and the *San Francisco Examiner*, among other publications. She has been managing editor of *Frisko* magazine, helped to launch *Frisko Kids* magazine (which included her column, "Smart Shopping for Kids"), and edited *Fast Forward*, a Bay Area publication for teens.

SHARON EPEL is the editor of the *KQED Family Learning Guide*. A frequent contributor to *San Francisco Focus*, she has written extensively about health, psychology, and consumer issues for *Parents* magazine.

GINNY GRAVES has written about sports for a variety of magazines, including *Parenting*, *Outside*, and *City Sports*. She is an avid runner, scuba diver, skier, and tennis player.

DIANE GREEN currently heads the Fashion Merchandising and Image Consulting program at City College of San Francisco. She travels to Paris twice a year to attend the haute couture collections.

JUDY JACOBS has traveled from the jungles of Borneo to the oases of the Gobi Desert. The author of *Indonesia: A Nation of Islands* (Dillon/Macmillan), her travel writing has appeared in magazines and newspapers around the world.

LAURA JAMISON is the calendar editor for *San Francisco Focus* and a theater columnist for *SF Weekly*. She has written about theater, performance, and music for *VIBE*, *The Village Voice*, *American Theater*, and *High Performance* magazine.

PEGGY KNICKERBOCKER is a writer and chef. A frequent contributor to *San Francisco Focus*, she has written for *Gourmet*, *Saveur*, *Playboy*, *House and Garden*, *Countryside*, *Metropolitan Home*, *Australian Gourmet Traveler*, the *Los Angeles Times*, and the *San Francisco Chronicle* and the *San Francisco Examiner*.

ROBERT KRUGHOFF is publisher of *Bay Area Consumers' Checkbook*, a nonprofit magazine that rates auto repair shops, hospitals, roofers, banks, and other service firms in Northern California.

PAUL LUKES teaches English at San Jose City College, and has also taught journalism from seventh grade to the university level. He free-lances on a variety of topics, including retail, shopping, and the home, in order "to show my students that I can write, too."

MYRIAM WEISANG MISRACH is an award-winning Bay Area journalist whose work has appeared in *Elle, Condé Nast Traveler, Redbook,* and *San Francisco Focus* magazine.

MICHAEL SHARON is a political and consumer affairs writer who has worked with Jack Anderson, the Center for Investigative Reporting, and *Frontline* on PBS. His work has appeared in *San Francisco Focus, San Francisco Downtown,* and the *Bay Guardian.* He is the staff writer for *In Flight USA* magazine.

SHARON SILVA is a food writer who has covered the ethnic cultures and cuisines of the Bay Area for fifteen years. A three-time winner of the William Allen White Award for restaurant criticism, Silva has been a contributing writer to *San Francisco Focus* since 1985. She is also the coauthor of *Exploring the Best Ethnic Restaurants of the Bay Area* (San Francisco Focus Books).

SUZANNE STEFANAC traded her first career in chemistry for another in journalism thirteen years ago. She has covered the computer industry since 1984, first as an editor at *Another Room* magazine (the first magazine to be desktop-published on the Macintosh), then as senior feature editor at *Macworld* magazine. She now freelances, focusing primarily on the emerging realm of interactive media.

SANDRA STEWART is currently the editor of *San Francisco Downtown* magazine. Previously, she served as an editor for six years at *Travel Age West.* She has taught classes in travel writing and copy-editing at Media Alliance. Her work has appeared in *San Francisco Focus* and *Tour and Travel News.*

BARBARA TANNENBAUM is an associate editor at *San Francisco Focus.* She also served as the managing editor on the book *Smart Health* (San Francisco Focus/KQED). Her articles on culture, politics, business, and technology have appeared in the *Advocate, Macworld,* and the *San Jose Mercury News.* She recently won the William Allen White award for public service journalism for her story on Yosemite National Park, which appeared in the January 1993 issue of *Focus.*

S. IRENE VIRBILA is the restaurant critic for the *Los Angeles Times.* She has previously been a contributing editor at *San Francisco Focus.* Virbila has trained as a sommelier in France and has written on food, wine, and travel for the *Wine Spectator, Travel and Leisure,* and the *New York Times.* She has written two books, *Cook's Marketplace: San Francisco* and *Cook's Marketplace: Los Angeles* (101 Publications). She is currently working on a book about the food and wine of the Piedmont region of northern Italy.

CREDITS

KQED PRESIDENT AND CEO
Mary G.F. Bitterman

KQED CHAIRMAN OF THE BOARD
Charlene C. Harvey

VICE PRESIDENT FOR PUBLISHING
& NEW VENTURES
Mark K. Powelson

PUBLISHER, KQED BOOKS AND TAPES
Pamela Byers

EDITOR IN CHIEF
Amy Rennert

CONSULTING EDITOR
Rick Clogher

MANAGING EDITOR
Barbara Tannenbaum

SENIOR EDITOR
Heidi Benson

ASSOCIATE EDITOR
Teresa Wann

SENIOR COPY EDITOR
Marjorie Baer

COPY EDITOR
Eva Spring

RESEARCH EDITOR
JoAnn Cabello

RESEARCH ASSOCIATE
Karen Hutchinson

RESEARCH ASSISTANT
Clary Alward

ART DIRECTOR
Laura H. Martin

PRODUCTION ARTISTS
Alexander Lyon
Jamie Mirabella

ASSOCIATE PUBLISHER/
DIRECTOR OF OPERATIONS
Bradford C. Stauffer

DATABASE CONSULTANT
Leah Brooks

COVER PHOTOGRAPHS
**Stuffed Bear: Courtesy Basic Brown Bear
Factory, photographed by Troy Staten
Candy: Courtesy of Joseph Schmidt Con-
fections, photographed by Leslie Flores
Automobile: Courtesy of Valley Auto Center
Garden Chair: Courtesy of the Gardener,
photographed by Monica Lee
Women's Fashion: Courtesy of Esprit
PowerBook: Courtesy of Apple Computer**

LETTER FROM THE PRESIDENT OF KQED

For more than forty years KQED has delivered one of the best educational and entertainment bargains found in the Bay Area—high-quality broadcasting and first-rate print journalism. Following in that tradition—and more specifically joining in *San Francisco Focus* magazine's long history of being a source to find unique opportunities and experiences—*Best Bay Area Bargains* is just what the educated shopper ordered.

Publishing excellent informational and educational material is as much a part of KQED as is radio and television broadcasting. Helping people learn, grow, and take full advantage of the delightful part of the world in which we live is at the heart of KQED's mission. I hope you find the information in the following pages valuable and enjoyable. Here's to good reading and smart shopping.

Sincerely yours,

Mary G. F. Bitterman
President & CEO
KQED Inc.

INTRODUCTION

Quality for a price. That's the motto of every successful bargain shopper we know. And that's our mission with the first edition of *San Francisco Focus* magazine's new book, *Best Bay Area Bargains*. Each year, the magazine has produced a special January issue with just that title—we think it's a great way to get the year off to a good, money-saving start. In fact, those editions of the magazine are so popular that they have become collectors' items. We got the message and decided to marshal our special expertise to create this book.

Inside, just follow in the footsteps of our reporters—all specialists in their field—to get great deals on everything you need. From major household appliances to housewares and home renovation resources, from furniture and floor coverings to electronics and computers, from clothing, shoes, and jewelry to sports gear and luggage, from gardening equipment to food on the table—you name it, and we'll tell you where to get a great price.

And that's not all. There is useful information in this book that you just won't find in any other bargain book. We've included a guide to those baffling members'-only superstores and an entire chapter on Factory Outlet Centers (and why they're worth a special trip). Plus tips for saving money when you buy a car, how to get great travel bargains, and discounts on cruises, hotels, and airfare. We also include entertainment bargains, such as where to find half-price tickets, bargains on activities for kids, and where to dine out for less than $20!

Since so many people are renovating their homes today, we've included a section on restoration and home renovation resources—a guide to dealers and architectural salvage yards.

We hope you'll find many uses for this book, and we hope you'll have fun reading it, too. It's packed with the kinds of tips, surprises, personality, and information about the region that only a city magazine can accumulate over years of reporting. And lucky for all of us, though the Bay Area is rich in beauty and luxuries of all kinds, it's also rich in bargain shopping options. We think the insider information between these covers will quickly make you an expert at shopping the Bay Area.

—The editors of *San Francisco Focus*

CHAPTER 1

APPAREL

APPAREL

The Bay Area has always been a fabulous place to shop for clothes. Now, looking terrific is also affordable. Read on to find great bargains on high-quality clothing for men, women, and children, plus shoes, jewelry, luggage, and more.

CLOTHING

ADOLFO II

South Bay: Pacific West Outlet Center, 8155 Arroyo Circle (Leavesley Rd at Hwy 101), Gilroy (408) 848-6313.
Mon–Fri 10 am–9 pm, Sat 9 am–9 pm, Sun 10 am–6 pm.
MasterCard, Visa
Parking: Lot on premises

This is an outlet for the licensees of designer Adolfo, now retired. Adolfo fans will instantly recognize his versions of the cardigan-jacketed knit suit. This store also carries more casual clothes such as jogging suits, sweaters, and pants. A Rafael-label three-piece jogging suit retailing for $150 was seen for $90 here. Private dressing rooms. —*PL*

AHC OUTLET

San Francisco: 625 Second St, SF (415) 957-1983.
Mon–Sat 10 am–5 pm.
American Express, MasterCard, Visa.
Other Stores: Go Silk Outlet Store, Village Outlets of Napa Valley, 3111 North St. Helena Hwy, St. Helena (707) 963-5698.
Parking: Street

This is the home of Go Silk, a manufacturer known for upscale washable silk sportswear at designer prices. Savings here on past-season and some current merchandise (usually overruns) are 40 to 50 percent below the original retail prices. To give you an idea: A man's quilted silk parka that was originally $600 was selling recently for $360, and a women's silk jacket in rich fall colors was $192, down from $320. The silk sweaters priced from $98 to $108 were another good value. The selection is limited, so if you find something you like, grab it. —*DG*

AILEEN

South Bay: Pacific West Outlet Center, 8155 Arroyo Circle (Leavesley Rd at Hwy 101), Gilroy (408) 847-3534.
Mon–Fri 10 am–9 pm, Sat 9 am–9 pm, Sun 10 am–6 pm.
MasterCard, Visa
Other Stores: Factory Stores at the Nut Tree, Vacaville (707) 449-3650.
Parking: Lot on premises

This is a great source for basic cotton knits. The line is aimed at older women, and though price reductions aren't necessarily dramatic, if you're a fan of Aileen, you'll be pleased to see a jacket that retails for $64

 ALPHABETICAL STORE LISTING

priced at $40 here. The best bargains are on the clearance racks, where you'll find items as low as $5. Petite and large sizes available. Private dressing rooms. —PL

ANNE KLEIN FACTORY STORE

South Bay: American Tin Cannery, 125 Ocean View Blvd #121, Pacific Grove (408) 647-8804.
Sun–Thur 10 am–6 pm, Fri and Sat 10 am–8 pm.
Discover, MasterCard, Visa
Other Stores: Pacific West Outlet Center, Gilroy (408) 842-7660.
Parking: Lot on premises

This two-floor shop reflects the relaxed yet elegant attitude of Anne Klein clothing. You'll find the same quality and styles sold in department stores, but at great prices. On current season's merchandise, expect up to 50 percent off; clothing from previous seasons can be up to 70 percent off. Women can easily put together a refined business wardrobe here, and pick up a few casual sportswear items. On our last visit, we saw a luxurious, three-piece textured-silk suit that cost about $300 (camisole $49, jacket $159, skirt $89); the same three pieces would have set us back more than $500 retail. A generous offering of Anne Klein's petite line included a wool and cashmere jacket for $189, compared to $392 retail. The best bargains are on the sale racks, where we saw a peach cable-knit silk sweater marked down to $30 (originally $80 at the outlet), and an understated slim silk skirt reduced to $60. —SE

BABETTE

San Francisco: 28 South Park, SF (415) 267-0280.
Mon–Fri 9 am–6 pm, Sat 10 am–5 pm.
MasterCard, Visa
Parking: Street

This is a sophisticated little boutique with wholesale prices on some of the most gorgeous clothes around. Babette is known for her Fortuny pleating on polyester chiffon and microfiber, which she makes into blouses, skirts, pants, jackets, and raincoats that sell in stores such as Bendel's in New York. Samples and ends wholesale for $40 to $100. There's also a rack of bargain merchandise that starts at $20. Recently, for $130 you could pick up an unusual two-layer pleated poly-chiffon skirt with an asymmetrical hemline that would be an asset to any wardrobe. If you can't find what you want in your size, Babette even takes special orders on raincoats (at full retail). —DG

BALLERINI ITALIAN CLOTHING

North Bay: Northgate Mall, 3680 Northgate Dr, San Rafael (415) 499-8812.
Mon–Fri 10 am–8 pm, Sat 11 am–6 pm, Sun 11 am–6 pm.
Major credit cards
Parking: Lot on premises

ALPHABETICAL STORE LISTING

If you like European quality and elegance in your suits but don't want to pay a $1200 price, Ballerini is for you. Ballerini specializes in high-quality, contemporary clothing for men at good prices.

Unlike many stores whose "Italian" suits are made in Hong Kong or Korea, Ballerini's Italian suits are the real thing, made in Italy by manufacturers such as Zanetti, Luigi Gardini, and others. On our last visit, suits ranged from $398 to $598 (for top-of-the-line 100 percent merino wool). Sports coats were going for $150 to $400, while lightweight slacks in wool and blends ranged from $98 to $128.

You can often buy three pairs of slacks and receive one free. Italian 100 percent cotton dress shirts went for $35 to $58, and silks from $37 to $49. Expect to find stylish woolblend sweaters priced from $98 to $298, as well as good values on ties, belts, and socks.

Another plus: Ballerini often discounts selected items 20 to 25 percent, and even more on end-of-season merchandise. Suit sizes range from 34 to 54, short, regular, and long; pants 28 to 44; 14¹/₂ to 18¹/₂ in shirts; and sweaters small to extra-large. On a recent visit, it was hard to keep our hands off a luxurious camel-colored Zanetti cashmere and lamb's wool blend jacket marked down to $321 from $428. Truly bellisimo! —*SB*

BARBIZON LINGERIE

South Bay: American Tin Cannery, 125 Ocean View Blvd #306, Pacific Grove (408) 372-6138.
Sun–Thur 10 am–6 pm, Fri and Sat 10 am–8 pm.
Discover, MasterCard, Visa
Other Stores: Factory Stores at the Nut Tree in Vacaville (707) 447-0482; Pacific West Outlet Center in Gilroy (408) 842-6608.
Parking: Lot on premises

You'll find no seconds or irregulars at this outlet store for Barbizon, the seventy-five-year-old lingerie company now owned by Vanity Fair. Instead, the crowded racks of robes, bras, nightgowns, and slips offer reduced prices on first-quality factory overruns. We discovered an array of basic slips in white, ivory, and black selling for $7 to $12 as well as Vanity Fair nylon-Lycra camisoles at $9 to $12.

There was also a small selection of Eileen West and Vanity Fair bras and panties, but the best selection and prices were in the nightwear department. A romantically old-fashioned white lace nightie in 100 percent cotton was marked $22, while a more sensible flannel gown was selling for $15. —*SE*

BERNIE BERNARD HOTEL ROBES

San Francisco: 1525 Tennessee (at 26 St off Third), SF (415) 550-1188.
Mon–Fri 8 am–4 pm; some Sat (call first).
Checks accepted
Parking: Lot on premises

If you have ever coveted those plush, luxurious bathrobes that hang in your hotel room,

Bernie Bernard's factory outlet is the place to go. Scoop up a dazzling array of slightly irregular, heavyweight terry robes that range from $25 to $50. If perfect, these same styles in white and assorted colors with shawl or sailor collar, or no collar at all would sell in hotel gift shops for $80 to $115.

The most fun is finding robes with logos such as George V, Beverly Hills Hotel, the Savoy, and the Plaza. We got lucky and happened on some cotton piqué robes for $29— a savings of $35, all because someone in the factory used pink thread instead of blue for the Plaza Hotel logo. —DG

BERT SCHROEDER

South Bay: Vallco Fashion Park, 10123 N. Wolfe Road, Cupertino (408) 996-9966. Mon–Fri 10 am–9 pm, Sat 10 am–7 pm, Sun 11 am–6 pm. American Express, MasterCard, Visa Parking: Lot on premises

Many men whose style calls for custom-made shirts with monogrammed cuffs have them made at Bert Schroeder, and have done so for twenty years. Schroeder's casual look features a St. Croix placket shirt, cardigan sweater, or zippered velour top with a crew collar coordinated with 100 percent cotton-fleece slacks with Sansabelt waistband, an accommodation to the retired lifestyle.

For Sunday afternoon dinner at the country club, Baumler's classic blazer is set off with a tie by Portofino or Serica. A traveling wardrobe might feature soft red plaid wool, lime-green hopsack, and off-white linen sportcoats. Bert Schroeder is the source for reasonable prices and excellent service for the top-notch garb that suits the Peninsula good life. —PL

BOSTON TRADER

South Bay: The Outlets at Gilroy, 8300 Arroyo Circle (Leavesley Rd at Hwy 101), Gilroy (408) 842-3454. Mon–Fri 10 am–9 pm, Sat 9 am–9 pm, Sun 10 am–6 pm. Major credit cards Other Stores: Factory Stores at the Nut Tree, Vacaville (707) 447-0587. Parking: Lot on premises

This outlet features factory overrun sportswear (no second-quality merchandise) at least 25 percent below retail. For example, we saw a $40 crewneck sweater for $30. For the big and tall outdoorsman, sizes run to 4x. Boston Trader also carries women's clothing. Mailings to preferred customers (membership is free) announce clearance sales and provide coupons for an additional 20 percent savings. Accessories include fishing hats, coffee mugs, and cedar blocks for protecting stored woolens. —PL

BROOKS BROTHERS OUTLET STORE

North Bay: Village Outlets of Napa Valley, 3111 North St. Helena Hwy, St. Helena (707) 963-9296.

ALPHABETICAL STORE LISTING

Mon–Fri 10 am–6 pm, Sat 10 am–7 pm, Sun 11 am–6 pm.
American Express, MasterCard, Visa, and Visa/JCB
Other stores: The Outlets at Gilroy (408) 847-3440.
Parking: Lot on premises

Although Brooks Brothers is primarily devoted to men, about a third of the store space is set aside for women. Even so, some of the best deals for ladies can be found in the men's section. There's no better example than the B.B. cashmere sweater. At $199, "cheap" is not the operative word, but it's a classic, and for the quality and longevity, it's a smart bargain.

As Assistant Manager Maya Rodriguez notes, "Since Brooks Brothers is conservative, it's never out of style." Another find: Due to hard-to-detect flaws, navy wool blazers that were selling for $295 in retail stores went for $199 at this outlet. Other fashionable offerings we saw included heavy winter overcoats with black velvet collars, priced down from $475 to $399, and irregular blouses at $19. Generally, merchandise is discounted 30 to 70 percent off original prices, and clearance sales following holidays ensure even greater discounts. —*LC*

BUGLE BOY

South Bay: The Outlets at Gilroy, 8300 Arroyo Circle (Leavesley Rd at Hwy 101), Gilroy (408) 847-3422.
Mon–Fri 10 am–9 pm, Sat 9 am–9 pm, Sun 10 am–6 pm.
Major credit cards
Other Stores: Factory Stores at the Nut Tree, Vacaville (707) 446-9291.
Parking: Lot on premises

Men's sizes in these casual styles run 32 to 44 in the waist, with inseams up to 34. Kids' sizes run 4 to 7, boys' 8 to 20, and young men's are 28 to 38—all offered at 20 to 50 percent off regular retail prices. Clearance-rack items are up to 70 percent off. Women's casual clothes run in sizes 4 to 16. We saw a $34 sweatshirt with the Bugle Boy logo for $18. —PL

BUM EQUIPMENT

South Bay: Pacific West Outlet Center, 8155 Arroyo Circle (Leavesley Rd at Hwy 101), Gilroy (408) 848-1660.
Mon–Fri 10 am–9 pm, Sat 9 am–9 pm, Sun 10 am–6 pm.
Major credit cards
Other Stores: Factory Stores at the Nut Tree, Vacaville (707) 448-5050.
Parking: Lot on premises

This outlet's merchandise is current season and first quality with a look that is difficult to miss: The BUM logo appears on everything the company sells, from infantwear to stadium coats. Hats, shirts, and sweats are part of the look. Recently, shirts regularly priced at $42 went for $28, and pants regularly $36 sold for $20. —*PL*

BURLINGTON COAT FACTORY

South Bay: Westgate Mall, 1600 Saratoga

ALPHABETICAL STORE LISTING

Ave, San Jose (408) 378-2628.
Mon–Fri 10 am–9 pm, Sat 10 am–7 pm, Sun 11 am–6 pm.
Major credit cards
Other stores: 899 Howard St, SF (415) 896-6721; Westlake Shopping Ctr, Daly City (415) 997-0733; 1000 La Playa, Hayward (510) 782-7073.
Parking: Lot on premises

First-quality, same-season merchandise and a lot of it, is the story of this department store. They carry clothing for infants and toddlers, boys' sizes 8 to 14, girls' 7 to 14, petite, juniors, misses, big and tall for men, and plus sizes for women.

As the name suggests, coats are featured, but the range of merchandise extends from underwear and lingerie to tuxedo shirts and maternity clothes. When we visited, full-length leather overcoats with the Burlington label were reduced by 60 percent and sold for $199. —DG

BYER FACTORY OUTLET

South Bay: 2118 B El Camino Real, Santa Clara (408) 244-8180.
Mon–Wed 10 am–7 pm, Thur–Fri 10 am–9 pm, Sat 10 am–6 pm, Sun 11 am–6 pm.
MasterCard, Visa
Other Stores: 1300 Bryant, SF (415) 626-1228.
Parking: Lot on premises

San Francisco–based Byer of California is popular among juniors and women seeking fashion trends at good prices. This outlet, which opened in fall 1993, carries all the Byer and Pacquette labels. Unlike the San Francisco outlet, the Santa Clara store has no seconds or irregulars. In fact, the friendly staff says close to 60 percent of the merchandise is current, sometimes arriving there before it pops up in Macy's or Emporium.

Discounts are at least 30 percent off regular retail and on the sales racks may be as high as 70 percent. A panne velvet top that retails at $23 sold for $16 here. Styles range from prom and party dresses to career dresses to casual sportswear. There's also a good selection of party and school clothes for girls' sizes 4 to 6x and 7 to 14. Check out the sample racks for especially good buys. Private dressing rooms. —PL

CALIFORNIA BIG AND TALL

San Francisco: 822 Mission, SF (415) 495-4484.
Mon–Sat 10 am–6 pm (Thur until 7pm), Sun noon–5 pm.
American Express, MasterCard, Visa
Parking: Fifth and Mission Garage

At California Big and Tall, a clearance center for Rochester Big and Tall, everything is marked 20 to 50 percent off retail. Expect more savings, often an extra 20 percent off or better on Manager Specials. Rochester's clothing has become more upscale in recent years, which means big guys can find bargains here by high-end clothing manufacturers such as Adolfo, Mondo, Perry Ellis, Bill

Robinson, and Hart Schaffner & Marx. The selection, which runs from casual to workday clothing, is mostly from previous seasons. Suits are priced from $140 to $440; sport coats from $96 to $300; sweaters from $24 to $195; slacks (wool and poly blends) from $30 to $70. Sizes: suits 42 short to 60 x-tall and x-big; dress shirts to size 22; some shoes to size 17. All sales final with extra charges for alterations. On our last visit, we saw $18 washable-silk shirts, $10 silk ties, and a handsome Bill Robinson wool suit marked down from $725 to $363, a 50 percent savings. If you want savings on Rochester's clothing before it arrives at the clearance center, don't miss Rochester's twice-yearly sales every July and December, when merchandise is discounted 20 to 40 percent off retail. —*SB*

CAPE ISLE KNITTERS

South Bay: Pacific West Outlet Center, 8155 Arroyo Circle (Leavesley Rd at Hwy 101), Gilroy (408) 842-3696.
Mon–Fri 10 am–9 pm, Sat 9 am–9 pm, Sun 10 am–6 pm.
Major credit cards
Other stores: American Tin Cannery, Pacific Grove (408) 655-0115; Factory Stores at the Nut Tree, Vacaville (707) 449-4093.
Parking: Lot on premises

This manufacturer achieved a certain degree of notoriety when President Bill Clinton's mother announced she's bought sweaters for both her son and the First Lady at a Cape Isle outlet. Sweaters are the most plentiful item here, rounded out with a good selection of basic turtlenecks, polo shirts, and tank tops. The key word here is classic. Men's piqué knit polo shirts that retail at $28 are $18 here, while a woman's sweater that retails at $110 is $90. Always check the sales racks—you may find some incredibly good deals on sweaters. Private dressing rooms. —*PL*

CAROLE LITTLE OUTLET

South Bay: Pacific West Outlet Center, 8155 Arroyo Circle (Leavesley Rd at Hwy 101), Gilroy (408) 847-4411.
Mon–Fri 10 am–9 pm, Sat 9 am–9 pm, Sun 10 am–6 pm.
Major credit cards
Other stores: American Tin Cannery, Pacific Grove (408) 655-0160.
Parking: Lot on premises

Los Angeles–based Carole Little is such a prolific designer that even an expert has problems identifying the latest patterns as opposed to ones that are six months old. Merchandise here is a mix of relatively new and older pieces, with a dress that retailed at $148 priced at $89, and a cardigan jacket that retailed at $168 here for $101 when we visited. Little's designs are flattering to most figures, and the outlet includes some large sizes. Best buys are on irregulars and on clearance-rack items, but check carefully before buying. Private dressing rooms. —*PL*

ALPHABETICAL STORE LISTING

CHAMPION HANES

South Bay: Pacific West Outlet Center, 8155 Arroyo Circle (Leavesley Rd at Hwy 101), Gilroy (408) 847-4872.
Mon–Fri 10 am–9 pm, Sat 9 am–9 pm, Sun 10 am–6 pm.
Major credit cards
Other Stores: American Tin Cannery, Pacific Grove (408) 372-4627; Factory Stores at the Nut Tree, Vacaville (707) 448-5081.
Parking: Lot on premises

This factory outlet features prior-season closeouts and a clearance rack with 40 percent off men's and women's underwear, plus lingerie, socks, stockings, and baseball hats. Frequent Buyer Club membership gets you extra savings and advance notice on special sales. —*PL*

CHAUS

South Bay: Pacific West Outlet Center, 8155 Arroyo Circle (Leavesley Rd at Hwy 101), Gilroy (408) 847-1396.
Mon–Fri 10 am–9 pm, Sat 9 am–9 pm, Sun 10 am–6 pm.
American Express, MasterCard, Visa
Parking: Lot on premises

The Chaus label is aimed at the adult women's market, not juniors. Here you'll find a mix that ranges from career separates and dresses to casual jeans. A black lace top with a matching camisole that retailed at $56 was $40 here, while $40 blouses could be found for $20. Good selection of petite and large sizes. Private dressing rooms. —*PL*

CLOTHING BROKER

South Bay: 3280 Victor, Santa Clara (408) 748-7637.
Fri 10 am–7 pm, Sat 10 am–6 pm, Sun 11 am–5 pm.
MasterCard, Visa
Parking: Lot on premises

Limited hours and an out-of-the-way location enable owner Chuck Crow to maintain a pricing structure in which goods are reduced nearly 40 percent below retail. On our visit, for example, a $250 American Trend all-wool sport coat sold here for $99, and in the International Collection of Italian-made clothing, a $600 silk suit was $249, about 60 percent off retail. Stuart Jones cowboy boots went for $60, and Bill Blass tuxedo shirts that retail for $40 were $25. The Clothing Broker has in-store alteration services, with charges based on the amount of adjustment required. Big and tall sizes are also available at the same discount pricing. —*PL*

CM DESIGNS

San Francisco: 3001 Nineteenth St (says John Logvy Company on the door), SF (415) 826-6220.

Mon–Fri 8 am–3:30 pm.
MasterCard, Visa
Parking: Street

This manufacturer's outlet has great buys on previous-season and end-of-season separates in nubby silk noil and coordinating rayon prints. You won't find any high styling here—just classic basics in sizes 4 to 16 with prices ranging from $15 to $60. You'd pay double for these separates in speciality and department stores. There's a communal dressing room for trying on blazers, pants, blouses, skirts, and walking shorts. —*PL*

COLOURS BY ALEXANDER JULIAN

South Bay: 125 Ocean View Blvd #117, Pacific Grove (408) 372-1771.
Sun–Thur 10 am–6 pm, Fri and Sat 10 am–8 pm.
Major credit cards
Other Stores: Factory Stores at the Nut Tree in Vacaville (707) 448-8396.

Parking: Lot on premises

This elegant store looks like a boutique, but the bargain prices will convince you that it is, indeed, a factory-direct outlet. The company cuts out the middleman and offers the same sweater you might see at a department store on the very same day—here for 20 to 40 percent less. As new seasonal merchandise rolls in, the outlet cuts prices on the older stock, so you could find button-down striped shirts for $10, or richly colored chamois workshirts for $20. On a recent trip we discovered pleated trousers in 100 percent cotton for $20, heavy cotton rugby shirts for $30, and the best buy of the day, beautifully dyed, hand-framed, linen-cotton sweaters for $50. —*SE*

COLUMBIA SPORTSWEAR

South Bay: Outlets at Gilroy, 8300 Arroyo Circle (Leavesley Rd at Hwy 101), Gilroy (408) 848-3740.
Mon–Fri 10 am–9 pm, Sat 9 am–9 pm, Sun 10 am–6 pm.

Major credit cards
Parking: Lot on premises

This store specializes in outerwear, including parkas, gloves, and hats. The merchandise is a mix of closeout, past-season, and irregular items, discounted 30 to 50 percent. For example, a parka that retails at $172 was $87 here. Private dressing rooms. —*PL*

CONTEMPO CASUALS OUTLET

North Bay: 108 Vintage Way, Novato (415) 892-5706.
Mon–Sat 10 am–9 pm, Sun 11 am–6 pm.
Major credit cards
Other stores: Woodside Plaza, Woodside Rd and Massachusetts St, Redwood City (415) 365-9835.
Parking: Lot on premises

Contempo has long been a popular retail chain offering fashions for the younger woman. Only quite recently has Contempo opened two outlets—one in Novato and the other in Redwood City. The Novato location

ALPHABETICAL STORE LISTING

is at a new shopping complex brimming over with other outlet shops, but Contempo has the local market cornered for stylish fashions.

The most upscale merchandise is placed up front, where the Pastille line of clothing is stocked. Depending on the day you go, you might luck upon a real find. We did—a beautiful coffee-color rayon blazer originally priced at $119 was reduced because of minor imperfections to $29. Palazzo pants, romper suits, dresses, and blouses in cotton and rayon are also plentiful.

Most everything here is discounted at least 25 percent, and usually more. Tops that sell retail at $29 were $12; some were stylish, some were not. At the back of the store, there are $2, $4, and $6 racks stocked with samples, irregulars, and past-season merchandise. —*LC*

CUT LOOSE FACTORY OUTLET

**San Francisco: 690 Third St, SF
(415) 495-4581.**

**Mon–Sat 10 am–5:30 pm.
MasterCard, Visa, checks accepted
Parking: Street**

Cut Loose prides itself on offering casual-wear made of 100 percent cotton in more than twenty colors. The range of items goes from sweat clothes to dresses, with tops, skirts, pants, jackets, and even socks also in the line. All of the stock is manufactured locally. Prices range from $5 to $50. When we checked, a cotton dress was selling for $20, which was more than 50 percent off retail. You may see many past-season over-runs, so be sure to check dye lots for matches. Sizes range from small to large, with some extra-large. —*CB*

DEJA VU A PARIS

**San Francisco: 400 Brannan, second floor,
SF (415) 541-9177.
Mon–Thur by appointment, Fri 11 am–5
pm, Sat 10:30 am–5 pm.
American Express, MasterCard, Visa**

Parking: Street

This could be San Francisco's best-kept secret. The light-filled showroom on the second floor is filled with beautiful clothes created in European fabrics by a transplanted Parisian who prefers to keep the name on the label out of print. The bolts of European fabrics, with many woven designs, are stored below the cutting table. We saw business suits with feminine flair that sell in the designer's retail operation for $325, marked down to $160. Jackets, skirts, and pants are available. The designer likes to cater to petites. Jackets come in sizes petite through large. Suits are also made and sold in American sizes 4 through 12. —*CB*

DESIGNER'S CO-OP

**San Francisco: 625 Third St, SF
(415) 777-3570.
Mon–Sat 10 am–6 pm, Sun noon–5 pm.
American Express, MasterCard, Visa
Parking: Nearby lot**

A designer emporium for the whole family, Designer's Co-Op recently moved to a spanking new location that even boasts an espresso café. The Co-Op features only California designers—at remarkable discounts. How do owners Susan and David Beugen do it? They slip into a factory and scoop up leftovers (not all sizes) that the manufacturer can't ship to regular accounts. What you see is what you get, and most of the merchandise is current season. A Nina K jacket that was originally $185 was selling for $90; a stunning Duna chenille sweater that originally retailed for $220 was $109. Fans of hip local designers Work Wear, Frank et Gertie, and the contemporary sportswear of Nomadic Traders, Axis, and Raw Edge will find a good selection. The best find? The buttery-soft leather jackets from Ka Uomo that retail in the city's upscale boutiques for $500 to $1500. Here they were selling for $240.

DONNA KARAN COMPANY STORE

North Bay: Village Outlets of Napa Valley, 3111 North St. Helena Hwy, St. Helena (707) 963-8755.
Mon–Fri 10 am–6 pm, Sat 10 am–7 pm, Sun 11 am–6 pm.
American Express, Mastercard, Visa
Parking: Lot on premises

DKNY jean jackets are a steal since this outlet began carrying DKNY Kids' and DKNY Men's collections. Men and tots aren't the only ones who profit either. Women have been flocking to the second floor's far-right corner to purchase extra-large kids' clothes or extra-small mens wear. For example, a navy jean jacket, originally $70, sells here for $40 in the Kids' lines.

For women who want to stick to classic Donna Karan, there's the more formal couture downstairs and the less-expensive Jeans line upstairs. Past-season (one or two seasons) merchandise is imported from their New Jersey factory, and reduced at least 40 percent. You might chance upon a rare find, like a dark violet blazer with satin trim we spotted, marked down from $514 to $235.

One drawback: The outlet carries primarily large or smaller sizes; mediums are rare. Another drawback: dressing rooms, though elegant, are door-less. Accessory tip: DKNY hose, located on the first floor, sell three to a packet for $20. —*LC*

DRESS MARKET

San Francisco: Six Sixty Center, 660 Third St, SF (415) 495-6768.
Mon–Sat 10 am–5:30 pm, Sun noon–5 pm.
MasterCard, Visa
Parking: Lot on premises

You will find more than dresses, but the owner prides herself on having sample Phoebe career dresses that usually sell in large department stores here for wholesale prices. She also stocks gauze dresses and skirts from India and Indonesia, resort wear, and some special-occasion clothes in sizes 4 through 16. During our visit, we saw Ken Done–designed casual clothes from Australia. The T-shirt marked $45 retail sold for $23 at the Dress Market.

While you are browsing, look over the selection of fragrances from Western Fragrances, which shares space with the Dress Market. The owner said her discounts start at 20 percent off retail for major brands like Giorgio. —CB

EDDIE BAUER OUTLET

South Bay: Pacific West Outlet Center, 8155 Arroyo Circle (Leavesley Rd at Hwy 101), Gilroy (408) 842-4445.
Mon–Fri 10 am–9 pm, Sat 9 am–9 pm, Sun 10 am–6 pm.
American Express, Eddie Bauer credit card, MasterCard, Visa
Other Stores: San Leandro (510) 895-1484; Citrus Heights (916) 922-6322.
Parking: Lot on premises

Discontinued and out-of-season items for men and women from Bauer's famous active-wear catalog and retail stores at 30 percent off regular prices are the big attraction here. Overstocked current merchandise from the retail stores is also featured. You can save an additional 40 percent on end-of-season goods. For example, a winter dress will close out for as little as $20 as the spring lines appear. —PL

ESPRIT FACTORY OUTLET

San Francisco: 499 Illinois (at Sixteenth and Third streets), SF (415) 957-2550.
Mon–Fri 10 am–8 pm, Sat 10 am–7 pm, Sun 11 am–5 pm.
American Express, MasterCard, Visa
Parking: Lot on premises

The complexion of the Esprit Store is changing to reflect a maturing clientele. Don't worry, you'll still find Esprit's trademark junior styles, still as vibrant and casual as ever. But now the Susie Tompkins line of

sportswear is added to the mix, offering a sophisticated twist on creative career dressing. How about a caramel-colored suede vest with knitted sleeves for $299 (originally $498), or a fitted, forties-inspired beige wool jacket for $150 that was originally $250? Shoes are a good buy, too, with a good-looking lug-sole platform Oxford in brown or black suede selling for $32. Prices for kids' clothes seem high—we saw a jean bomber jacket for $41. —DG

EXECUTIVE SUITE

South Bay: Pacific West Outlet Center, 8155 Arroyo Circle (Leavesley Rd at Hwy 101), Gilroy (408) 842-2555.
Mon–Fri 10 am–9 pm, Sat 9 am–9 pm, Sun 10 am–6 pm.
Major credit cards
Parking: Lot on premises

This is an outlet for the upper end of the Jones New York line—the "executive at the top" look. The prices are higher here than what you'll find at the nearby Jones New York outlet, but the styles have subtle differences that some working women are willing to pay for. Discounts are not dramatic: A suit that retails for $280, for example, was $210 here. One plus is the small collection of special-occasion clothes designed for the executive who needs to maintain a business image while socializing. End-of-season sales bring even greater savings when the fall line moves out in March. Additional savings come from multiple purchases; we saw men's 100 percent wool suits selling at $210 for one and $375 for two. A Jones of New York tuxedo regularly priced at $400 was selling for $230. Private dressing rooms. —*PL*

FASHION BIN

San Francisco: 615 Third St, SF
(415) 495-2264.
Mon–Sat 10 am–5:30 pm, Sun 11 am–5 pm.
MasterCard, Visa
Parking: Street

There are no designer fashions here, and no designer prices. Dresses, sportswear, separates, weekend wear, and some fashion jewelry make up the stock. The young working woman who wants to find a conservative look for a little money can find a variety of choices. A knockoff of a pricey red short-sleeved coat dress, with gold-tone buttons, was selling for $49. There are plenty of casual separates to choose from. Sizes range from junior 3/4 to plus sizes. —*CB*

FILA

South Bay: Pacific West Outlet Center,
8155 Arroyo Circle (Leavesley Rd at Hwy 101), Gilroy (408) 848-3452.
Mon–Fri 10 am–9 pm, Sat 9 am–9 pm, Sun 10 am–6 pm.
American Express, MasterCard, Visa
Parking: Lot on premises

Fila's outlet sells sample, discontinued, and overrun men's and women's tennis and golf wear. Prices are reduced about 40 percent,

bringing an out-of-season golf sweater we saw down to $25. A rack full of defective merchandise had prices knocked down 50 percent, but look out for serious flaws and tears. —*PL*

FRITZI FACTORY OUTLET

San Francisco: 218 Fremont, SF
(415) 979-1399.
Mon–Thur 9 am–5 pm, Fri–Sat 8 am–5 pm.
Discover, MasterCard, Visa
Parking: Street

This is one of the grande dames of bargain outlets. Fritzi California maufactures many lines, from children's clothes to pre-teens (You Babes and My Michelle), to juniors, and women, including larger sizes and petites. And at one time or another, all of these lines are represented here. On Friday mornings, from 8 am to 10 am, there are "Early Bird Sales" at which selected merchandise can be discounted an additional 20 to 70 percent. Even at regular discount prices, most Fritzi merchandise that could be up to $70 north of Market Street is less than $20 here. It is not designer quality, but many items can be fun for summer or resort wear. We found an entire rack of women's casual pants priced at $4. —*CB*

GEOFFREY BEENE WOMAN

South Bay: Outlets at Gilroy, 8300 Arroyo Circle (Leavesley Rd at Hwy 101), Gilroy (408) 848-8001.
Mon–Fri 10 am–9 pm, Sat 9 am–9 pm, Sun 10 am–6 pm.
Major credit cards
Other Stores: Pacific West Outlet Center, 8155 Arroyo Circle (Leavesley Rd at Hwy 101), Gilroy (408) 842-4747.
Parking: Lot on premises

This outlet carries some of the licensees of respected designer Geoffrey Beene. The selection ranges from casual sportswear such as sweaters and pants to career separates. A silk blazer retailing for $188 was here for $100; a white blouse that was ordinarily $80 went for $50. Merchandise is current season. The best deals are found on the clearance racks in the back of the store. Private dressing rooms. —*PL*

GO SILK OUTLET STORE

North Bay: Village Outlets of Napa Valley, 3111 North St. Helena Hwy, St. Helena (707) 963-5698.
Mon–Fri 10 am–6 pm, Sat 10 am–7 pm, Sun 11 am–6 pm.
American Express, MasterCard, Visa
Other Stores: AHC Outlet, San Francisco (415) 957-1983.
Parking: Lot on premises

True, you can find flashier items in the same fabric at Go Silk, but in terms of simple perfection, none match the white silk blouse. For the price—precisely half what you'll find in retail—none match the economy. On a recent visit, blouses (in many hues) were $110, silk blazers about $275 (down from $460), and silk sweaters that were originally $184 were $84. Like Go Silk's South of Market discount store, the Napa outlet is well stocked with both women's and men's apparel. The markdown is anywhere between 40 and 50 percent, and the majority of clothing is in season and unflawed. Past-season items promise the best discounts, although the selection of these is spotty. Go Silk now carries wonderful jackets, like the thigh-length, raccoon-collared winter coat we spotted for $410 (originally $684). —*LC*

GUESS OUTLET

South Bay: Outlets at Gilroy, 8300 Arroyo Circle (Leavesley Rd at Hwy 101), Gilroy. (408) 847-3400.
Mon–Fri 10 am–9 pm, Sat 9 am–9 pm, Sun 10 am–6 pm.
MasterCard, Visa
Parking: Lot on premises

Fans of Guess already know the name is synonymous with denim separates. This is particularly true at the outlet. What's appealing here is a small selection of the Georges Marciano line of bridge sportswear for women. We saw a blazer that was $196 retail here for $70. Men's $80 silk shirts were marked down to $35. The selection includes sportswear in men's and women's sizes, as well as juniors and a small amount of children's clothing—presumably for people who don't want to stroll down to the Baby Guess outlet ten stores away. Private dressing rooms. —PL

GUNNE SAX OUTLET

San Francisco: 35 Stanford (between Second and Third streets), SF
(415) 495-3326.
Mon–Sat 9 am–5:30 pm, Sun 11 am–5 pm.
American Express, MasterCard, Visa
Parking: Street

For us, a visit to the Gunne Sax outlet is like dying and going to party-dress heaven. There is no other factory outlet quite like it in the Bay Area—racks and racks of out-of-season merchandise that manages to look exactly like the Gunne Sax and Jessica McClintock goods that currently sell in retail stores for double and triple the price. Aficionados of McClintock's feminine designs will find brocade cocktail suits, and lace-and-velvet cocktail dresses for around $69. Long gowns in similar fabrics were also only $69. How about bridal gowns for $99 to $276 (white cotton, lace-embellished, Victorian-styled gowns) in sizes up to 22? There was a terrific assortment of black, rich burgundy, and forest green bridesmaid's dresses for $75 that could also double as formal gowns. Black velvet bustiers from Scott McClintock were only $29. For girls, the flowergirl, communion, and party dresses in sizes 7 to 14 were only $53. Don't forget to drag yourself up the concrete stairs to the second floor (this is no-frills shopping at its best) for the clearance department, where you might snatch a slightly soiled wedding gown for $30. —DG

HARVE BENARD

South Bay: Pacific West Outlet Center, 8155 Arroyo Circle (Leavesley Rd at Hwy 101), Gilroy (408) 848-5152.
Mon–Fri 10 am–9 pm, Sat 9 am–9 pm, Sun 10 am–6 pm.
Discover, MasterCard, Visa
Parking: Lot on premises

Women seeking good career clothes and nice sportswear will feel very comfortable here. Recently blazers that retailed at $182 were $80, and a heavy navy coat that retailed at $340 was marked at $200. If you're in the market for conservative but stylish work clothes, this is the place to shop. There's also a nice selection of accessories; trouser socks that retail at $6 were a good buy here for $2. Private dressing rooms. —PL

HE-RO GROUP OUTLET

South Bay: Pacific West Outlet Center,

ALPHABETICAL STORE LISTING

8155 Arroyo Circle (Leavesley Rd at Hwy 101), Gilroy (408) 847-3632.
Mon–Fri 10 am–9 pm, Sat 9 am–9 pm, Sun 10 am–6 pm.
Major credit cards
Parking: Lot on premises

Glittery eveningwear is one of the most difficult categories for discount hunters to find, which makes this a particularly appealing store. A black-sequinned Oleg Cassini dress that retails for $460 was here recently for $290. For the best deal on evening clothes, check out the sale area in back. Separates and dresses there are divided into racks marked at $60, $100, and $150. While black-tie events are the main impetus for a visit, you'll also find some career clothes such as J.G. Hook suits that retail at $180 marked to $80. Private dressing rooms. —PL

HEADSAIL

North Bay: 67 Liberty Ship Way, Sausalito (415) 331-2739.

Mon–Sun 8 am–8 pm, appointments suggested.
Checks accepted, no credit cards
Parking: Lot on premises

Headsail is a small, quality manufacturer of outerwear and technical performance foul-weather gear for the yacht-racing community whose merchandise is sold in several Bay Area sports stores. Although you may not know starboard from port, you'll appreciate Headsail's unisex collection of durable fleece wear and jackets made from top-of-the-line materials designed to keep the wearer warm and dry. All items, comparable in quality but not price to merchandise made by high-end outerwear manufacturers such as Patagonia and North Face, are 25 to 30 percent below standard retail prices and sometimes even more. Sizes from S to XL. Since Headsail is a small operation, it does business to the public out of its office, located near the Bay Model north of Sausalito's bustling main shopping area. On our last visit, we saw thick fleece pullovers in many colors for $49 and a Supplex fleece-lined jacket for $60. —SB

THE HEAT

San Francisco: 447 Beach St (between Taylor and Jones), SF (415) 931-9398.
Daily 10 am–6 pm.
MasterCard, Visa
Parking: Street

The Heat may not merit a special trip to Fisherman's Wharf, but if you should find yourself down there, stop by this open-air schlock shop to check out the Chinese silk bomber, blouson, and toggle jackets. Priced around $27 to $40, they're just the ticket for throwing over sweats or exercise gear. These come direct to The Heat from the manufacturer. —DG

HIT OR MISS

South Bay: Westgate Mall, 1600 Saratoga Ave, San Jose
(408) 379-6990.
Mon–Fri 9:30 am–9 pm, Sat 10 am–7 pm,

Sun 11 am–6 pm.
Major credit cards
Other stores: Check telephone directory for nearest store.
Parking: Lot on premises

Hit or Miss discount stores feature career women's clothing for at least 25 percent off department store prices. This chain is part of the T. J. Maxx company and carries its own labels, plus Ellen Ashley and Epogee. All merchandise in the Chadwick catalog is also available at Hit or Miss stores. Sizes are mostly 4 to 14 with a few 16 to 18 and petite sizes, too. Avoiding trendy styles, these stores feature mix-and-match wardrobes that customers can use to build on a basic, traditional look. A $40 Hit or Miss dress would cost $53 in a department store. At three pairs for $10, the Hit or Miss pantyhose has a loyal following. —*PL*

I.B. DIFFUSION

South Bay: Pacific West Outlet Center,
8155 Arroyo Circle (Leavesley Rd at Hwy 101), Gilroy (408) 842-4335.
Mon–Fri 10 am–9 pm, Sat 9 am–9 pm, Sun 10 am–6 pm.
American Express, MasterCard, Visa
Parking: Lot on premises

The I.B. Diffusion label is synonymous with specialty sweaters. Some are novelties keyed to a particular season; others are just colorful patterns. All of the merchandise here is past season and discontinued, but the staff makes no bones about it; if you want the current line, head for the nearest mall. We saw sweaters that retail at $118 marked down here to $70. Private dressing rooms. —*PL*

IONA

South Bay: Pacific West Outlet Center,
8155 Arroyo Circle (Leavesley Rd at Hwy 101), Gilroy (408) 847-6460.
Mon–Fri 10 am–9 pm, Sat 9 am–9 pm, Sun 10 am–6 pm.
Major credit cards

Parking: Lot on premises

If you're looking for more of a sense of style than you find in most department stores and other outlets, Iona is the place to come. The clothes here range from casual to dressy separates—jackets, tops, skirts, pants, and dresses. There are a few exquisite sweaters and an excellent selection of original jewelry as well. A jacket that retailed at $129 was $65 here, and a pullover top that retailed at $89 was $45 here. Private dressing rooms. —*PL*

ISDA & COMPANY OUTLET

San Francisco: 29 South Park, SF
(415) 512-1610.
Mon–Sat 10 am–5:30 pm.
MasterCard, Visa
Parking: Street

Isda's gone up-market—the outlet store is now in fashionable South Park, where a whitewashed, minimalist space showcases the hip sportswear featured in specialty stores across the country. You'll find 40 percent

ALPHABETICAL STORE LISTING

discounts on separates made of sand-washed Fuji silk, wool, or a silky rayon-poly blend. Isda's prices aren't bargain-basement, but neither is the merchandise, which dates only one or two seasons back. It's hard to go wrong with wool blazers in colors like sage, indigo, or earth that have been marked down to $142 from $178. Fine-gauge cotton-knit crewneck and polo sweaters run $45 to $69 —the colors vary depending on the season.

IZOD

South Bay: The Outlets at Gilroy, 8300 Arroyo Circle (Leavesley Rd at Hwy 101), Gilroy (408) 847-1448.
Mon–Fri 10 am–9 pm, Sat 9 am–9 pm, Sun 10 am–6 pm.
Major credit cards
Other Stores: Factory Stores at the Nut Tree, Vacaville (707) 453-1074.
Parking: Lot on premises

This factory outlet carries first-quality over-runs with no seconds. Designed primarily as golf and tennis wear, all Izod clothing is slightly oversized with freedom of movement in mind. Both men's and women's shorts, pants, shirts, and jackets sell for from 20 to 50 percent off retail prices. Seasonal clearance prices are 40 to 50 percent off. You might find a $45 Izod windbreaker selling for $35. —*PL*

JEANNE MARC DOWNS

San Francisco: 508 Third St, SF
(415) 243-4396.
Mon–Sat 11 am–5 pm.
MasterCard, Visa
Parking: Metered street

San Francisco's own design team has a uniquely colorful and sophisticated signature—and for aficionados, this outlet is the place for bargains. Most of the merchandise is at least one season behind, with discounts of up to 50 percent; some less-current items are marked down 80 percent. Look for popular Fortuny-style pleating on jackets that were originally $420, later marked down to $199. A shimmery organza blouse in luscious colors, marked down from $398 to $119, could get you through any formal occasion. For those who sew at home, Jeanne Marc even sells bolts of its signature fabrics.

J.H. COLLECTIBLES

South Bay: Pacific West Outlet Center, 8155 Arroyo Circle (Leavesley Rd at Hwy 101), Gilroy (408) 847-4420.
Mon–Fri 10 am–9pm, Sat 9 am–9 pm, Sun 10 am–6 pm.
American Express, MasterCard, Visa
Parking: Lot on premises

The J.H. Collectibles line is a combination of career and casual sportswear that's by now imprinted on many women's minds thanks to the long-running advertising campaign featuring model Cindy Crawford. We found a plaid blazer that retailed at $220 priced at $146, and past-season sweaters that had been $90 retail here for $60. The selection includes some petite sizes. Private dressing rooms. —*PL*

JOANIE CHAR

**San Francisco: 285-A Sutter St, SF
(415) 399-9867.
Mon–Sat 10 am–6 pm.
MasterCard, Visa
Parking: Nearby garage**

Joanie Char used to have a loyal Bay Area following for her silk dresses and separates, but then for a while, the name virtually disappeared. The faithful will be pleased to find out that a new Joanie Char boutique opened recently with prices that are only 20 percent above or at wholesale. The merchandise is current season but won't be found in stores in the Bay Area—mostly Atlanta and Dallas. Typical prices are around $40 to $158, and selections are limited. Not everything is silk—there's also wool, rayon, and polyester. For just about $100, you could combine fluid rayon black-and-white awning-striped pants

with a long black tunic. —*DG*

JOCKEY

**South Bay: The Outlets at Gilroy, 8300
Arroyo Circle (Leavesley Rd at Hwy 101),
Gilroy (408) 847-5666.
Mon–Fri 10 am–9 pm, Sat 9 am–9 pm, Sun
10 am–6 pm.
Major credit cards
Other Stores: Factory Stores at the Nut
Tree, Vacaville (707) 451-8119.
Parking: Lot on premises**

One of only three Jockey factory outlets in California, this store sells at least 30 percent below retail with clearance items marked down as much as 70 percent. The store also carries fleecewear, turtlenecks, and pantyhose, but the biggest sellers are Jockey's full range of underwear, from sizes for boys and girls to big and tall for men and queen sizes for women. —*PL*

JOHN HENRY & FRIENDS FOR MEN

**South Bay: American Tin Cannery, 125
Ocean View Blvd #310, Pacific Grove
(408) 655-5622.
Sun–Thur 10 am–6 pm, Fri–Sat 10 am–8 pm.
Discover, MasterCard, Visa
Other Stores: Pacific West Outlet Center in
Gilroy (408) 848-1777.
Parking: Lot on premises**

This small, friendly store is the place to stock up on men's basic workday wear. We found great prices on department-store designer dress shirts—Liberty of London for $23, Perry Ellis Portfolio for $30, and, of course, John Henry for $20—with all the variations, such as stripes, button-down collars, and French cuffs. Add a pair of $30 John Henry trousers, pick out a $16 silk tie from Liberty of London or a $14 one from John Henry, grab some socks (plain and patterned, under $4 a pair), and it's off to work you go! When you get home, unwind in a $35 lush

ALPHABETICAL STORE LISTING

cotton terry robe in rich blue, burgundy, or green. —*SE*

JONES NEW YORK FACTORY STORE

South Bay: Pacific West Outlet Center, 8155 Arroyo Circle (Leavesley Rd at Hwy 101), Gilroy (408) 848-1411.
Mon–Fri 10 am–9 pm, Sat 9 am–9 pm, Sun. 10 am–6 pm
American Express, MasterCard, Visa
Parking: Lot on premises

The Jones New York label has been the mainstay of many a working woman's wardrobe for several years now. The clothes are conservative but stylish, and you know the blazer you buy now will serve you well for at least the next couple of years. We saw a blazer that retails at $200 selling for $150 here, and a wrap skirt that retails at $110 here for $83. Private dressing rooms. —*PL*

JORDACHE

South Bay: Pacific West Outlet Center, 8155 Arroyo Circle (Leavesley Rd at Hwy 101), Gilroy (408) 842-1037.
Mon–Fri 10 am–9 pm, Sat 9 am–9 pm, Sun 10 am–6 pm.
Major credit cards
Parking: Lot on premises

This place is a sea of denim for toddlers, juniors, men, and women. Jeans that retail at $25 are $18 here. There are other casual clothing styles, but denim dominates. Private dressing rooms. —*PL*

JOSEF ROBES

San Francisco: 510 Third St, SF (415) 546-5722.
Mon–Sat 10 am–4 pm.
Discover, MasterCard, Visa
Parking: Street

Savings at this attractive showroom aren't substantial, but you will find some of the most attractive terry-velour robes around. These are designer robes at designer prices minus 20 percent for first-quality merchandise and 50 percent for seconds. Available in all the colors Martex makes, the robes come with hand-braided belts and double-welted seams. Prices range from $116 to $150, which is a lot, but it's still less than you would pay at the gift shops of some of California's posh resorts—Inn at Spanish Bay, Ventana, Post Ranch, and the Claremont Spa—where you might also see these robes. —*DG*

KM WEAR OUTLET

San Francisco: 625 Second St, SF (415) 546-7331.
Mon–Sat 10 am–5 pm.
MasterCard, Visa
Parking: Street

KM, code name for a San Francisco designer, makes luxurious cotton-knit clothes with an upscale look and feel. The jackets, tops,

ALPHABETICAL STORE LISTING

pants, and leggings are designed locally and made in Turkey. The designer is about to open a boutique on Union Street, but the KM Wear Outlet will continue to carry her clothes at 50 percent off retail prices. The store's clean, architectural feeling is echoed in the clothes. These are better-quality cotton knits with construction that stands up to washing. A flax-colored jacket with a drawstring waist and zippered front was $55. Sizes range from 4 to 14 with separates generally ranging in price from $15 to $55. —*CB*

KORET OF CALIFORNIA

South Bay: Outlets at Gilroy, 8300 Arroyo Circle (Leavesley Rd at Hwy 101), Gilroy (408) 842-3900.
Mon–Fri 10 am–9 pm, Sat 9 am–9 pm, Sun 10 am–6 pm.
Discover, MasterCard, Visa
Parking: Lot on premises

This is a direct outlet for San Francisco-based Koret, which specializes in classic separates, including blazers, blouses, pants, skirts, and sweaters. On our recent visit, blazers that retail at $80 were $52 here, while pants were discounted from $42 to $27, and beaded T-shirts from $39 to $25. Most of the merchandise is first quality, lagging about one month behind the stores. The few irregulars are clearly marked and on a special rack. The selection includes petite and large sizes. Private dressing rooms. —*PL*

KUTLER BROTHERS

San Francisco: 625 Howard St (at New Montgomery), SF (415) 543-7770.
Mon–Fri 9 am–5:30 pm, Sat 9 am–4 pm.
Major credit cards
Parking: Street and validated parking around corner at 55 Hawthorne

They say that Kutler Brothers is not open to the public, and to enter you must provide a referral at the door. That's a clever gimmick that makes your shopping experience seem special. All merchandise was current and selling for 25 to 30 percent lower than retail, though men's styles change so subtly that it's often hard to tell what's new. We found some good-looking single—and double-breasted suits ranging from $350 for an olive worsted-wool single-breasted model by Oliver, to a stunning slate-gray worsted-wool suit by Caraceni, complete with topstitching on the lapels for $830. There was a good selection of handsome double-knit wool polo shirts by Proximo in charcoal, cognac, and black for $97. Kutler's own brand of placket-front sportshirts went for $80 to $90. We found names such as Burberrys, Aquascutum, Lanvin, and Halston mixed in among a lot of unfamiliar, mostly Italian names.

A gorgeous 100 percent black wool cashmere topcoat made in Canada was $870. Hand-rolled silk pocket squares were $6 and came in an assortment of colors. We even spied alligator and crocodile belts. Shoes are from Bally, Cole Haan, Allen Edwards, and Bostonian with discounts of 25 percent off retail. —*DG*

 ALPHABETICAL STORE LISTING

LEATHER MODE

South Bay: Outlets at Gilroy, 8300 Arroyo Circle (Leavesley Rd at Hwy 101), Gilroy (408) 848-4114.
Mon–Fri 10 am–9 pm, Sat 10 am–9 pm, Sun 10 am–6 pm.
American Express, MasterCard, Visa
Parking: Lot on premises

As the name implies, this is an outlet for leather. In addition to coats and jackets, there are a few dresses and lots of accessories such as wallets and purses. A men's trench coat that is $300 retail was $200 here, and there was also a selection of team jackets, including both 49ers and Raiders marked at $249. Private dressing rooms. —*PL*

LEATHER TO GO

San Francisco: 200 Potrero, SF (415) 863-6171.
Mon–Fri 9 am–4 pm, Sat 10 am–2pm.

MasterCard, Visa
Parking: Street

If you've been searching for that perfect leather jacket, chances are you'll find it here. The Leather to Go factory showroom features quality men's and women's leather jackets priced from $99 to $395 in aviator, motorcycle, western, blazers, varsity, and field jacket styles. The inventory, including some suede and shearling, is made up primarily of overruns, samples, and very few imperfects. The manufacturer, Golden Bear, makes lines for department stores, well-known clothing chains, and major catalog companies throughout the country. All merchandise is 40 percent off retail or more. Sizes range from men's 36 to 46 and women's 6 to 16, with many styles unisex. On a recent visit, we saw a heavy black leather motorcycle jacket for $199 that reminded us of James Dean and a $99 bomber jacket that would keep our friend, the pilot, both stylish and warm. —*SB*

LESLIE FAY

South Bay: Pacific West Outlet Center, 8155 Arroyo Circle (Leavesley Rd at Hwy 101), Gilroy (408) 848-4373.
Mon–Fri 10 am–9 pm, Sat 9 am–9 pm, Sun 10 am–6 pm.
American Express, MasterCard, Visa
Other Stores: Factory Stores at the Nut Tree, Vacaville (707) 447-7118.
Parking: Lot on premises

Labels found here include Leslie Fay, Kasper, and Outlander—all instantly recognizable to working women as reliable resources. The mix includes casual, career, and some dressy clothes. A black tuxedo coat dress that retails for $240 was $180 here, while a coatdress that retails at $199 was $149. There's also a good selection of petite and large sizes. Private dressing rooms. —*PL*

LEVI'S

South Bay: Pacific West Outlet Center, 8155 Arroyo Circle (Leavesley Rd at Hwy 101), Gilroy (408) 848-4533.
Mon–Fri 10 am–9 pm, Sat 9 am–9 pm, Sun 10 am–6 pm.
Major credit cards
Other Stores: Factory Stores at the Nut Tree, Vacaville (707) 451-0155.
Parking: Lot on premises

This huge store sells only Britannia, Docker, and Levi labels. All merchandise is irregular, which means that some imperfection was discovered during inspection (sometimes as minor as an incorrect color tint). Because the goods are not first quality, Levi's reduces the prices about 25 to 30 percent. Everything Levi's makes for men, women, and children are carried here in popular sizes and styles. —*PL*

LILLI ANN/L. ROTHSCHILD FACTORY OUTLET

San Francisco: 2701 Sixteenth St (enter around the corner on Treat Ave), SF (415) 863-2720.
Sat 9 am–2:00 pm.
MasterCard, Visa
Parking: Street

This factory store for Lilli Ann and related lines carries an abundance of pull-on pants and polyester tops for women. Irregulars, seconds, and discontinued styles from the Lilli Ann and L. Rothschild lines are discounted. There are dresses, suits, and sportswear. We saw some gold jackets for evening that were loose fitting enough for a larger woman. Sizes range from 4 to 20. Do not expect helpful salespeople. —*CB*

LONDON FOG OUTLET

North Bay: Village Outlets of Napa Valley,
3111 North St. Helena Hwy, St. Helena (707) 963-4650.
Mon–Fri 10 am–6 pm, Sat 10 am–7 pm, Sun 11 am–6 pm.
Major credit cards
Other stores: Factory Stores at the Nut Tree, Vacaville (707) 447-1124.
Parking: Lot on premises

To the extent that Fabio has muscles on top of muscles, the London Fog Outlet has markdowns on top of markdowns. The company's top-quality merchandise is remarkably inexpensive. The proprietors won't say blip about why or how their extensive selection of raincoats, parkas, umbrellas, and other inclement-weather accessories are so vastly marked down. Just take our word for it—they are. We saw children's ski jackets (12 months to size 14) originally priced at $90, marked down first to $68, and finally to $55. Raincoats, stocked in dozens of colors and styles, cost as little as $120 (most were originally $200). We homed in on a gorgeous green Mackintosh, originally $400, priced at $190. —*LC*

 ALPHABETICAL STORE LISTING

LUCIA

**South Bay: The Outlets at Gilroy, 8300
Arroyo Circle (Leavesley Rd at Hwy 101),
Gilroy (408) 848-3877.
Mon–Fri 10 am–9 pm, Sat 9 am–9 pm, Sun
10 am 6 pm.
MasterCard, Visa
Other Stores: Factory Stores at the Nut
Tree, Vacaville (707) 451-2676.
Parking: Lot on premises**

This outlet sells seconds under the Lucia and
Tambridge labels from the manufacturer for
Land's End women's sportswear, but that
label does not appear on any of the clothing
sold here. First-quality Land's End overruns
sell with the labels cut out. Sizes range from
petite 4 to 16, juniors 3/4 to 15/16, and misses 6 to 18. Discounts run from 40 to 60 percent off. *—PL*

MARAOLO

**San Francisco: 404 Sutter St (at Stockton),
SF (415) 781-0895.
Mon–Sat 10 am–6 pm.
American Express, MasterCard, Visa
Parking: Nearby garages**

Run, don't walk, to the only Maraolo outlet
on the West Coast. Maraolo carries its own
brand of exquisite Italian-made leather shoes,
along with a selection of Donna Karan,
DKNY, and Giorgio and Emporio Armani
for women. Men will find classic leather and
suede shoes from Maraolo and Cesare
Paciotti. Some of these are current styles at a
savings of 30 percent; others are only a season behind and are half price. Italian styling
is so forward that even shoes that are two seasons behind manage to look current.
Shipments arrive every two weeks, and the
spring lines begin to trickle in at the end of
January. A typical Maraolo selling for $240
will be $120 at the outlet. We stocked up on
pant boots in brown and black leather the day
we discovered the outlet. These classic styles
made of the finest leather were $110 and
$120 each. *—DG*

MAX STUDIO OUTLET

**South Bay: Pacific West Outlet Center,
8155 Arroyo Circle (Leavesley Rd at Hwy
101), Gilroy (408) 842-3636.
Mon–Fri 10 am–9 pm, Sat 9 am–9 pm, Sun
10 am–6 pm.
American Express, MasterCard, Visa
Parking: Lot on premises**

This is a factory outlet for Leon Max, a talented designer not easily found in Bay Area
stores. He is known for casual and dress
sportswear in his spare, clean lines. A black
blazer that retailed for $138 was $69 here,
and a white blouse that was $98 retail was $68
here. Clothes arrive shortly after being
shipped to boutiques that carry the Max lines,
so they're usually very much in season. Past-
season markdowns are found at the back of
the outlet. Private dressing rooms. *—PL*

MEN'S WEARHOUSE

San Francisco: 27 Drumm St, SF
(415) 788-6363.
Mon–Fri 9:30 am–7:30 pm, Sat 9:30 am–
6 pm, Sun noon–5 pm.
Major credit cards
Other stores: See telephone directory for
nearest store.
Parking: Street

Okay, maybe you hate the TV ads, but with 170 stores nationwide, the Men's Wearhouse has a lot of buying power when it comes to off-season merchandise.

We visited one of the chain's smallest outlets, where the friendly manager showed us around. All men's suits are graded from 1 to 6+, with 6+ being of highest quality and workmanship. There were plenty of suits by Halston, which are made by Hart Schaffner and Marx (known for 6+ suits).

We saw a handsome Halston Prince of Wales plaid, a beautiful double-breasted Givenchy suit in bird's-eye wool, and a sin-gle-breasted olive worsted wool by Yves Saint Laurent. All sold for $395 (regularly $615 to $645).

For the budget conscious, Pierre Balmain suits were only $199; the jackets are fully lined, but the double-pleated trousers are not. Why rent a tuxedo when you can own one for $199 by Giorgio Fellini (the house label); for $395 you could have a tux from Givenchy. Wool and cashmere topcoats in black and gray were only $199, while a luscious vicuña-colored wool and cashmere topcoat from Italy was $259. Florsheim and Rockport were among the available shoes, with prices ranging from $69 to $145. —DG

MIKI

East Bay: 5902 College Ave, Oakland
(510) 601-6272.
Mon–Wed 10 am–6 pm, Thur–Sat 10 am–7
pm, Sun 11 am–6 pm.
American Express, MasterCard, Visa
Parking: Street

Miki clothing has always been prized for comfortable, bright cotton women's and girls' fashions. We were thrilled to come across a new acquisition: Walker bags—those sturdy, stylish black purses and shoulder bags—for men and women at 40 percent off. A $58 shoulder book bag was marked down to $35.

A perennially popular hot seller is the women's cotton jumpsuit selling for 40 percent off its $54 price tag. In fact, as the large sign in the window announces, most everything is marked 40 percent off the price tag, including women's and girls' dresses, skirts, leggings, and tops.

Miki is able to offer such great savings because it's a manufacturers' outlet. Another recent winner: women's hand-knit cotton sweaters by Debby Mitchell, originally $250, going for $120. —LC

MODA ITALIA

South Bay: Vasona Station, 14107
Winchester Blvd, Los Gatos (408) 370-3780.

 ALPHABETICAL STORE LISTING

Mon–Fri 9 am–9 pm, Sat 9 am–6 pm, Sun
11 am–5 pm.
Major credit cards
Parking: Lot on premises

This store has some the wackiest radio com-
mercials in the South Bay. But don't let that
fool you—Moda Italia is serious about
menswear, and they carry suits by top Italian
makers, including Beroni, Luca Falconi,
Bugatti, Lineaesse, Enzo Tovareh,
Martinelli, Canali, and their own private
label in sizes 34 short to 60 long. If you buy
one suit you get three suits free and two
round-trip airfares to Hawaii (certain restrictions apply). No kidding. —*PL*

MONDIELLA

**San Francisco: 393 Sutter St (at Stockton),
SF (415) 788-7918.**
Mon–Sat 11 am–6 pm, Sun noon–5 pm.
American Express, MasterCard, Visa
Parking: Nearby garages

Most people in search of bargains would
walk right past this upscale-looking
European boutique, but the cognoscenti
know that the owners buy fashionable clothes
directly from factories in Italy and France
and pass enormous savings of 40 to 60 percent on to their customers. Here are some
examples that we saw: A black suit from
Genny was $480, originally $900; a white
silk cocktail suit with rhinestone buttons
(also from Genny) was $650, originally
$1456. Other familiar designer names are
Versus by Gianni Versace, Complice,
Erreuno, Rocco Barocco, Gattinoni, and
Alma Cauture. In spring, look for some
French designers among the mix. If you are
on the store's VIP mailing list you'll get an
extra 15 percent discount on sale merchandise. From time to time, Mondiella gets
beautiful leather luggage and handbags from
C. Bartolomei, a company that also supplies
a famous French jeweler. —*DG*

MOSHER'S

**South Bay: 315 S First St, San Jose
(408) 286-7065.**
Mon–Fri 11 am–6 pm, Sat 11 am–5 pm.
MasterCard, Visa
**Parking: Metered parking on street and a
pay lot (enter from San Carlos Street) on
South Second Street**

There is an Ivy League look that has with-
stood the winds of change in men's fashion.
The button-down collar shirt with a rep tie,
and a natural shouldered suit coat are part of
its signature. The enduring Ed Mosher's
store in downtown San Jose (near Ed's alma
mater, San Jose State) specializes in this traditional style. Dozens of clothing stores may
have deserted downtown San Jose, but
Mosher's remains, attracting college students
and graduates alike. Like any small, specialty
store, Mosher's capitalizes on personal attention and service. —*PL*

NEW WEST DESIGN

East Bay: 2967 College Ave, Berkeley
(510) 849-0701.
Mon–Sat 11 am–6 pm, Sun 11 am–5 pm.
American Express, MasterCard, Visa
Other stores: 426 Brannan St, SF
(415) 882-4929.
Parking: Street

The tie rack in New West's men section features designer silk ties for half of their retail price, such as the Bill Robinson we saw for $28. Even more so than the San Francisco outlet, the College Avenue location could pass for a chic retail boutique. The shop is divided into two rooms—women's clothes in one, men's in the other—and the entire store hosts a selection of hip designers' discounted merchandise neatly displayed. Men aspiring to an upscale, pulled-together *Details* look would do well to check out New West's wool blazers and 100 percent cotton dress shirts. For women, the markdowns generally run from 25 to 50 percent off, with even bigger savings on flawed or discontinued items. The Basco lines for both sexes are particularly up-to-date and stylish, featuring items such as women's palazzo pants that were marked down from $98 to $49. Recently, you could also pick up a pair of Girbaud jeans for around $40, along with assorted pieces from Celia Tejada's collection. —*LC*

OUTBACK

East Bay: 2517 Sacramento, Berkeley
(510) 548-4183.
Mon–Fri 11 am–7 pm, Sat 10 am–6 pm, Sun noon–5 pm.
Discover, MasterCard, Visa
Parking: Lot on premises

An only-in-Berzerkly phenomenon, Outback dares to offer politically correct "Clothing for Everysomebody," with lines named, for example, "Menopause A Go-Go," for older women. Signs in the dressing room advise shoppers to refrain from shoplifting, lest it bring bad karma. Outback is well stocked with free-spirited women's fashions ranging from comfortable and functional to racy and fancy.

Because this is a manufacturer's outlet (from fabric design to tailoring, factory production is done at this location), you'll find some first-quality merchandise drastically reduced. Cotton, silk, and rayon clothing come in sizes 4 to 14, and there's an impressive collection of equally fun and funky clothing for "abundant" sizes. With some sample items, you may not find what you covet in your size. There's an ample stock of Outback seasonal overruns and slightly damaged goods, as well as items from other lines. The savings range from 20 to 60 percent off. Racks of clearly marked retail-priced goods are scattered among the outlet racks. Outback holds occasional buy one–get one free sales. We saw some great solid-color Lycra tops marked down from $48 to $24. —*LC*

OUTERWEAR CO.

San Francisco: Six Sixty Center, 660 Third St, #114, SF (415) 777-4220.
Mon–Sat 10 am–5:30 pm, Sun noon–5 pm.
Major credit cards
Parking: Lot on premises

Bursting with bargains, this store may well draw shoppers to the Six Sixty Center, a collection of bargain outlets. The crowded racks hold men's and women's leather jackets and coats—in natural tones, colors, suede—from $89 to $300. If you're looking for wool coats, you'll find bargains here, too. On our visit, a clearance rack featured women's wool blazers for $59 and full-length wool coats for $99. Or stay dry—and solvent—with a trench coat, complete with a warm detachable lining and a leather collar for $99. —*CB*

PATRICK JAMES

South Bay: Pruneyard, 1875 South Bascom Ave, Campbell (408) 371-7474.
Mon–Wed and Sat 10 am–6 pm, Thur–Fri 10 am–9 pm, Sun noon–5 pm.
Major credit cards
Other Stores: Burlingame (415) 375-0179; Capitola (408) 476-0765; Palo Alto (415) 328-3071; Danville (510) 736-0787; Mill Valley (415) 383-2174; SF (415) 986-1043; Santa Rosa (707) 523-2346.
Parking: Lot on premises

"Purveyor to Gentlemen" of traditional styles from Burberrys, Southwick, H. Freeman, and their own private label, the chain emphasizes tailored clothing sold in a friendly atmosphere; customer relations and services are their highlights. They admit that while the same goods may be found for the same price at a department store, their level of personal attention brings customers back. An exceptional value here is the high-quality American-made Allen Edmond shoe line (so good, it's one of the few actually exported from the States), priced from $115 to $330. —*PL*

PRESIDENT TUXEDO

South Bay: Westgate Mall, 1600 Saratoga Ave, San Jose (408) 374-3957.
Mon–Fri 10 am–9 pm, Sat 10 am–7 pm, Sun 11 am–6 pm.
American Express, MasterCard, Visa
Other Stores: Westgate Shopping Center, San Leandro (510) 562-9551.
Parking: Lot on premises

Twenty-nine other stores of this chain are located in the greater Bay Area, but only this location features previously worn (but not worn-out) tuxedoes, accessories, and used rental formal attire. Recently, a $375 Pierre Cardin, 100 percent wool tuxedo being removed from rental use could be purchased for $199. Used accessories sell for 25 percent off. For men who need a tuxedo just once or twice a year, a purchase like this makes good sense. Formalwear styles change very slowly, so there isn't really such a thing as an out-of-date tuxedo. Besides Pierre Cardin, designers include Michael Jordan, Christian Dior, and Yves St. Laurent. President Tuxedo carries more than one hundred styles and colors. —*PL*

RAFFIA

East Bay: 2175 N California Blvd, #205-A, Tishman Ctr, Walnut Creek (510) 937-0232.
Mon–Fri 9 am–5 pm.
MasterCard, Visa
Parking: Lot on premises

Located off the plaza of a busy office building in Walnut Creek, Raffia may not be a destination for San Francisco shoppers. But if you're in the neighborhood, drop by and you'll see why this store has such a loyal following. Raffia is a boutique offering discount prices on well-known brands of men's and women's casualwear, sportswear, and footwear. Men will appreciate the selection of sweaters, jackets, shirts, and tennis wear by makers such as Alexander Julian, Santana, Bugle Boy, and Le Coq Sportif at savings of 20 percent or more off retail. Raffia can offer

good prices because its owner is a clothing wholesaler.

The selection is always changing, so if something catches your eye during a visit, you're better off purchasing it because it might not be available again. Look for racks marked "special" for incredible deals. When we last visited, Raffia was having a "Buy Two for the Price of One" sale on $154 Columbia ski jackets, and for that price we thought about outfitting the whole family. —*SB*

RAINCOAT OUTLET

South of Market: 543 Howard, second floor, SF (415) 362-2626.
Mon–Fri 7:30 am–3:30 pm, Sat 7 am–11:30 am.
Checks accepted
Parking: Street

The coats and jackets are nice, but the real treasure in this outlet is the owner. Marguerite Rubel is a true San Franciscan with forty-five years of experience in the "rag trade." She sell samples and overruns of her

jackets and raincoats in sizes 4–14. These jackets and coats are sold under private labels to national catalog companies and to specialty stores. Check out the large selection of patchwork jackets. You can even buy the same "Map of the World" jacket that President George Bush was seen wearing on CNN (and in the photo on Rubel's wall). It retails for $200, but you can buy it for $95. —*CB*

ROBERT SCOTT & DAVID BROOKS

South Bay: Outlets at Gilroy, 8300 Arroyo Circle (Leavesley Rd at Hwy 101), Gilroy (408) 847-3434.
Mon–Fri 10 am–9 pm, Sat 9 am–9 pm, Sun 10 am–6 pm.
MasterCard, Visa
Parking: Lot on premises

Conservative, classic separates are the specialty here—items you'd expect to see at Talbots and in Nordstrom's career-clothing section. Merchandise arrives here about two

 ALPHABETICAL STORE LISTING

or three months after it hits the retail stores. A silk print vest retailing at $72 was $47 here; a tailored blazer that retailed at $180 was marked down to $117. Selection includes petite and large sizes. Private dressing rooms. —PL

ROBERT TALBOTT FACTORY OUTLET

South Bay: Carmel Valley Village (eleven miles off Hwy 1 off Carmel Valley Rd on Chambers Ln), Carmel Valley (408) 659-4540.
Mon–Sat 10 am–5 pm, Sun noon–4:30 pm.
MasterCard, Visa
Parking: Lot on premises

The Robert Talbott label is synonymous with quality neckties. Here you'll find store returns, overruns, and seconds marked at least 50 percent off regular retail. A Talbott tie that retails at $75 may be as low as $25 here. This outlet has a wide variety of prices, with the least expensive ties found on the $5 rack, where you'll occasionally find special-order ties with unusual company or organization logos. Along with neckties, you'll find a few bow ties, matching cummerbund-and-bow tie sets, silk pocket squares, and some dress shirts. If you sew, you might find the bolts of silk priced at $8 a yard for 39-inch widths irresistible. The staff is very helpful. —PL

ROCK EXPRESS

San Francisco: 350 Spear St (between Folsom and Harrison), SF (415) 597-9799.
Wed–Fri noon–6 pm, Sat 10 am–4 pm.
American Express, MasterCard, Visa
Parking: Street

Dress warmly—this cavernous warehouse of rock 'n' roll memorabilia can be chilly. Rock Express is part of Winterland Productions, rock impresario Bill Graham's empire. With thousands of T-shirts to choose from ($8 for adults, $4 for kids) and sweatshirts marked $10, you'll be tempted to scoop up armloads for your favorite friends. For a dollar or less, you can coordinate your clothing buys with memorabilia such as rock-concert programs ($1), buttons, posters, bandannas, and headbands. It's a teen's paradise. You'll also find T-shirts from major corporations such as Apple Computer, Greenpeace, and the San Francisco Giants. —DG

ROYAL ROBBINS FACTORY OUTLET

East Bay: 841-A Gilman, Berkeley (510) 527-1961.
Mon–Sat 10–5 pm, Sun 11 am–5 pm (longer hours in spring and summer).
Discover, MasterCard, Visa
Parking: Lot on premises

If you like the look of casual and outdoor clothing made from natural fibers, then you'll appreciate the Royal Robbins clothing line, sold nationally through large retailers and small specialty shops. The well-organized outlet features overruns from previous seasons and some seconds. Although the colors are seasonal, Royal Robbins' well-made styles are classic. The majority of items, such as 100 percent cotton canvas tops and pants, can be worn throughout the year. Pants, shirts, jackets, sweaters, and shorts for men and women—most made from 100 percent cotton or wool—are 20 to 50 percent off retail. The outlet always has something on special for an additional 25 percent off, and clearance bins where you might find "older" stuff priced from $5 to $15. On a recent visit, we saw Royal Robbins' popular canvas pants with a double seat and double knees marked down from $58 to $41. A handsome canvas duffel coat marked down from $196 to $98 seemed the ideal gift for the friend who likes to stroll on cool evenings. —SB

SAN FRANCISCO MERCANTILE STORE (EILEEN WEST OUTLET)

San Francisco: 2915 Sacramento St, SF (415) 563-0113.

Mon–Sat 10 am–6 pm, Sun noon–5 pm.
MasterCard, Visa
Parking: Street

This so-called outlet will pull the wool (and flannel) over your eyes, fooling you into believing this is a retail boutique. Found on a quiet Pacific Heights street, this charming country French–style boutique has handsome hardwood floors, large-paned glass windows with lovely floral curtains, and bowls of fragrant potpourri. Yet amid this cozy ambience are outlet prices on a collection of Eileen West sleepwear, bed coverings, and fancy dresses.

Thanks to San Francisco's mercurial weather, the large stock of flannel pajamas, robes, and nightgowns, though past season (often up to one year behind) are rarely out-of-season. There are also plenty of cotton knits for warm nights. Most stock is 30 to 70 percent off the retail price. Many of the items are seconds, but in near-perfect condition.

Elegant 100 percent cotton white-and-periwinkle sheets were on sale for $5 when we were there. Duvets and fitted sheets are also in stock. The majority of the store's stock is late-night wear, but fancy rayon sample dresses for evening and daytime are now carried, too. We found a slightly flawed blue floral dress that would be perfect for weddings or garden parties; originally priced at $180, it was on sale for $65. —LC

SARATOGA SPORT OUTLET

San Francisco: Six Sixty Center, 660 Third St, second floor, SF (415) 974-6180.
Mon–Sat 10 am–5:30 pm, Sun noon–5 pm.
MasterCard, Visa
Parking: Lot on premises

This huge second-floor space is filled with moderately priced sportswear ready to pack for a great vacation or for relaxing weekends at home. Lycra stirrup pants that retail for $28 were selling for $10; $25 turtleneck tops were selling for $8; and shorts and shell tops that retail for $12 were selling for $6. Check out the sale tables, where everything is specially priced. The best bargain offered on the

ALPHABETICAL STORE LISTING

day we visited was a polyester-and-cotton–blend tank top for $2. These prices are like those found in the special discount markets in Hong Kong. —*CB*

SIERRA DESIGNS

**South Bay: Pacific West Outlet Center,
8155 Arroyo Circle (Leavesley Rd at Hwy
101), Gilroy (408) 842-6544.
Mon–Fri 10 am–9 pm, Sat 9 am–9 pm, Sun
10 am–6 pm.
Major credit cards
Parking: Lot on premises**

Rugged outdoorwear sells here for 30 percent off, but because the items are samples, sizes are limited. Jackets usually sold for $85 are $70, and $65 pants are $40. Sierra Designs also makes outdoor equipment and some of these items sell at the outlet, such as a $54 backpack we saw for $13. —*PL*

SIMPLY COTTON

**San Francisco: 610 Third St, SF
(415) 543-2058.
Mon–Sat 10 am–5 pm, Sun noon–5 pm.
MasterCard, Visa
Parking: Street**

This outlet is neatly arranged with the dozens and dozens of casual, 100 percent cotton-knit and woven-cotton weekend wear available for $6 to $30. In addition to the Simply Cotton label, you will find some items with the label Sabu. Most of the tops and bottoms are solid colors (check the dye lots if you are trying to match items), though there were a few separates in patterned fabric and the salesperson expected more. Sizes range from extra-small to extra-large, which fit women sizes 4 to 14. When you buy separates, the salespeople will give you a brochure showing you how to tie their cotton ties as a belt in a variety of styles. —*CB*

SMITH & HAWKEN OUTLET

**East Bay: 1330 Tenth St at Gilman,
Berkeley (510) 527-1184.
Mon–Sun 10 am–6 pm.
American Express, MasterCard, Visa
Parking: Lot on premises**

Smith & Hawken is an upscale purveyor of furnishings for the home and garden and natural fiber clothing sold through its stores and mail-order catalog business. Since closing its clothing outlet in Marin County last year, Smith & Hawken's discount clothing business has operated out of the company's Berkeley-based outlet, located adjacent to its retail store behind REI. The outlet opened in summer 1993 and the clothing department is still growing. But we've included it because you can find good savings here on natural fiber casualwear for the whole family. The outlet carries overstocks and some seconds. The outlet constantly receives clothing from the retail stores, and, at any given time, you might see sweaters, pants, shirts, pajamas, and gardening clogs. By the time merchandise arrives here, it has already taken two markdowns. Savings range from 20 to 50 percent off retail, and more on seconds. On a recent visit, we saw a man's courdoroy shirt marked down from $62 to $39, an ideal gift for the gardener who likes to work in brisk temperatures. Make sure to browse the rest of the outlet for good savings on garden furniture, housewares, and more. —SB

SPACCIO

San Francisco: 645 Howard St (at New Montgomery), SF (415) 777-9797.
Mon–Sat 9 am–6 pm.
American Express, MasterCard, Visa
Other Stores: 1840 Union St, SF (415) 923-0131.
Parking: Validated parking at garage around corner on Hawthorne

Not to be outdone by Kutler Brothers, new kid on the block Spaccio has pulled out all the stops. This is a stunning shop done up in contemporary Milanese decor. Wholesale and retail merchandise both bring savings of 30 to 40 percent.

Spaccio suits come in both single- and double-breasted styles, with a choice of from one to six buttons and four different cuts. Suit pants come double- and triple-pleated, and all jackets (in true Italian style) are ventless. Spaccio manufactures for the well-known Baldessari label, and some suits here bear that label.

We saw a beautiful wool gabardine selling for $589 that would be from $1200 to $1500 elsewhere. Most suits were $399 to $589. You'll find some lookalikes of the very expensive and colorful line of Coggi sweaters, knocked off by Gianni Sgarbi, for $109 and $114. Dress shirts were $49 to $65, and faux-alligator belts were $40. —DG

SPARE CHANGES

San Francisco: 695 Third St, SF (415) 896-0577.

Mon–Fri 9:30 am–5:30 pm, Sat 9:30 am–5 pm.
American Express, MasterCard, Visa
Parking: Street

This large, well-organized outlet is stocked with a selection of Karen Alexander dresses that would make most department stores envious. A red knit Karen Alexander dress that could take you through the day from the office and out to dinner was $80 instead of the retail $150. Shoppers will find women's and junior dresses, blouses, and some separates. The La Chine Classic blouses that look like silk but are really polyester were priced at around $40. There's also a selection of children's clothes. Ask about the special sales that trim an additional 30 percent off items. Also check out the discount rack against the wall for those items that are marked down below wholesale, including Karen Alexander dresses. —CB

TALBOTS

East Bay: Marina Square Shopping Center,

1235 Marina Blvd, San Leandro
(510) 614-1090.
Mon–Fri 10 am–9 pm, Sat 10 am–7 pm, Sun
11 am–6 pm.
American Express, MasterCard, Visa
Parking: Lot on premises

This is the only Talbots outlet on the West Coast, and it carries merchandise from the whole Western region at bargain-basement prices. Of the three hundred Talbots stores nationwide, thirty-two send unsold merchandise that is three months behind current season to San Leandro.

Customers reap savings of 35 to 75 percent below regular retail prices. Since it's company policy not to allow any store to sell imperfect merchandise (not even with a button missing), quality is high and deals are great. Recently, woven and knit cotton shirts in bright colors were only $5. In kidswear, colorful cotton knits were a terrific buy at $5 and $7.

U.S.O. (ULTRA SUEDE OUTPOST)

East Bay: 4125 Piedmont Ave, Oakland
(510) 652-1384.
Tues–Sat 11 am–5 pm.
MasterCard, Visa
Parking: Street

Don't confuse "outpost" with "outlet." You won't find discount prices on the tags at this Oakland women's fashion retail store. To snag U.S.O.'s truly impressive bargains on Ultrasuede fashions, ask owner Maria Cerqueira about her made-to-order clothing. She'll pull out a swatch book for you to pick out the color and style of Ultrasuede pants, jackets, skirts, or suits to fit your taste. The savings are significant. For example, a straight skirt in Ultrasuede that would normally go for $200 sells here for $155 to $185—and that's for a custom fit. Cerqueira will help you coordinate your suede outfits with blouses and accessories (all sold at retail prices). —*LC*

VAN HEUSEN FACTORY STORE

San Francisco: 601 Mission, SF
(415) 243-0750.
Mon–Thur 9 am–7 pm, Fri until 8 pm, Sat 9 am–6 pm, Sun 11 am–5 pm.
Major credit cards
Other Stores: Pacific West Outlet Center, 8155 Arroyo Circle (Leavesley Rd at Hwy 101), Gilroy (408) 842-5008; The American Tin Cannery in Pacific Grove (408) 372-4595; Factory Stores at the Nut Tree in Vacaville (707) 446-2836; 1300 Folsom, Lathrop (916) 985-0628.
Parking: Street

At Van Heusen Factory Stores, you'll find the same Van Heusen merchandise currently sold in retail stores throughout the country. The main difference is that you can expect to save 20 to 30 percent below retail through factory-direct pricing, and even more on selected clearance merchandise. Popular men's dress shirts come in a variety of colors and styles and are located upstairs in the cheery San Francisco store. Pinpoint oxford cloth shirts made of 100 percent cotton sell for $25; other dress shirts in cotton/poly blends are $16 to $18. Both regular and slim fits come in sizes 15½ to 19. Wool and 100 percent silk ties are priced at $9 to $19. Downstairs, men and women can find a good selection of casualwear such as pants, sweaters, short-sleeved tops and more. On a recent visit, we saw many items on promotion, including a soft 100 percent cotton gray polo shirt marked down to $13 from $22, a reduction of nearly 50 percent. —SB

VOGUE ALLEY

San Francisco: 432 Sutter St, SF
(415) 362-7200.
Mon–Sat 9:30 am–6:30 pm.
Major credit cards
Other stores: San Rafael (415) 492-1988;
Cupertino (408) 253-9680; Menlo Park
(415) 328-8838.
Parking: Nearby garages

It looks as if Sutter Street is becoming a discount shopper's paradise. At Vogue Alley, you'll find the JBH label, which is made by the manufacturer in Hong Kong and owner of the Vogue Alley stores in the United States, Hong Kong, and England. Best buys are the knits, which can be found in all-wool, cashmere, and silk bodysuits, pullovers, cardigans, skirts, and pants. You'll find some of these very same styles in the current collections of a famous American designer known for her sportswear, except that at Vogue Alley they will be 50 to 80 percent less. A black scoopneck cashmere bodysuit was selling for $57. Wool knits started at $28. You can expect to find silk separates for spring in sherbet colors. New groups arrive every couple of weeks. —DG

WE BE BOP/WE BE BOP FOR KIDS

East Bay: 1380 Tenth St, Berkeley

(510) 528-0761.
Mon–Sat 10 am–5 pm, Sun noon–5 pm.
American Express, MasterCard, Visa
Other Stores: 1903 Fillmore St, SF (415)
771-7294.
Parking: Street

We Be Bop aims at the extroverted dresser, believing in fashion with flair. Imaginative designs with bold, bright colors in batik and silk-screened prints adorn this collection of women's and children's clothing. We Be Bop's designers travel to Bali, where they work with Indonesian designers and bring back unique fabric and accessories. The result is comfortable, bold styles, marked 25 to 50 percent off retail. Handsome rayon dresses priced originally at $70 were marked $51. On the $10 and $15 racks we found a sumptuous, brightly colored rayon jacket for only $15. Frequent sales throughout the year offer even greater markdowns. In the store's adjoining room is We Be Bop for kids, offering a nice diversity of jackets, jumpers, shorts, and shirts in sizes from toddler through preteen. —LC

WEAVER WORLD

**East Bay: 2570 Bancroft Way, Berkeley
(510) 540-5901.**
Mon–Sat 10 am–7 pm, Sun 10 am–6 pm.
American Express, MasterCard, Visa
**Other Stores: 587 Castro St, SF (415)
487-9050.**
Parking: Lot on premises

If you've never heard of a Weaver's sweatshirt, you're in for a treat. Whether at this Australian-based manufacturer's outlet in Berkeley or its brand-new San Francisco location, both offer the same 100 percent cotton, garment-dyed sweatshirt that sells at Fred Segal for $48 for about $18. After a change of ownership and name (formerly Weavers' Factory Outlet), Weaver World has broadened its range to also include manufacturers such as Esprit and BUM, all at closeout prices. The merchandise consists of cotton basics such as leggings, tube skirts, and T-shirts—nothing fancy. Recently, it has begun to include all-organic cotton as well.

In Berkeley the clientele is primarily college aged; no wonder—Weaver World is a block from the UC Berkeley campus. The San Francisco store attracts a more diverse urban crowd. All the merchandise is clearance, closeout, or manufacturer's seconds, and the prices are truly rock-bottom. Irregular T-shirts go for around $4, or $2 for $5, depending on the flaw. When we visited, irregular sweatshirts sold for $15 to $18, $19 to $25 in perfect condition. The store's biggest drawback is that to find the good stuff, you may have to work your way through some truly flawed items. —*LC*

WESTON WEAR

**San Francisco: 900 Alabama, SF
(415) 550-8869.**
Fri 12:30 pm–5 pm, Sat 11 am–3 pm.
MasterCard, Visa
Parking: Street

San Francisco designer Julie Weston finally decided to use her own name for the outlet that sells her stretch, cotton-Lycra knit designs. Many designs feature body-hugging silhouettes and particularly suit younger women. Some customers have their clothes made-to-order in their choice of color and style for 30 percent above the wholesale price. Made-to-order Lycra separates are priced at $49 for a top or pants. This is still below the retail price charged by the specialty and department stores. Be sure to check out the $5 rack for hidden treasures. —*CB*

WOOLRICH

**South Bay: American Tin Cannery, 125
Ocean View Blvd #302, Pacific Grove
(408) 644-9218.**
Sun–Thur 10 am–6 pm, Fri–Sat 10 am–8 pm.
Discover, MasterCard, Visa
Parking: Lot on premises

You might get the urge to go mountain climbing or cross-country skiing if you shop here. This company originally specialized in outdoor hunting wear and blankets when it

ALPHABETICAL STORE LISTING

was founded in the early nineteenth century. The legacy continues in its high-quality, natural-fiber men's and women's clothing—and at these prices, who needs a better reason for a trip to the only Woolrich outlet in California?

When we were there, we wanted to touch all the beautiful, soft flannel chamois men's shirts ($16), but ended up buying a forest-green cotton-ramie sweater, knit with a muted pattern in purple and red for $34. There were also good deals on new outdoor gear. A light-loft Thinsulate jacket at $87 was a great buy, as were rich plaid wool blankets ($24 to $60). —*SE*

INSIDER TIP: MENSWEAR RESOURCES

These stores specialize in merchandise for men (see alphabetical listings for details):
AHC Outlet
Ballerini Italian Clothing
Bert Schroeder
Boston Trader
Brooks Brothers Outlet Store
Bugle Boy
Burlington Coat Factory
California Big and Tall
Cape Isle Knitters
Colours by Alexander Julian
Columbia Sportswear
Designer's Co-Op
Eddie Bauer Outlet
Emporium Capwell Clearance Store
Fila
Guess Outlet
Headsail
The Heat
Izod
Jordache
John Henry and Friends for Men
Josef Robes
Kutler Brothers
Leather to Go
Leather Mode
Levi's
London Fog Outlet
Men's Warehouse
Moda Italia
Mondiella
Mosher's
New West Design
Nordstrom Rack
Patrick James
President Tuxedo
Raffia
Robert Talbott Factory Outlet
Rock Express
Royal Robbins Factory Outlet
Smith and Hawken Outlet
Spaccio
The Outerwear Company
Van Heusen Factory Store
Woolrich ▥

INSIDER TIP

FABRIC

BRITEX FABRICS

San Francisco: 146 Geary St, SF
(415) 392-2910.
Mon–Sat 9:30 am–6 pm, Thur 9:30 am–8 pm.
American Express, MasterCard, Visa
Parking: Nearby garages

Britex sales are a good bet for fabric favorites you've been hoping would get discounted. The store holds two sales a year (Washington's Birthday and Columbus Day) when you can expect maximum savings of $50 per person (excluding linings, notions, and already reduced merchandise). There's also a 50-percent-off-remnants sale three times a year, with no per person limit. For more information about sales, call to be put on their mailing list.

JEWELRY

Fine jewelry bargains do exist in the Bay Area. You don't need to venture to Union Square or upscale malls to find great quality.

Whether you're shopping for estate pieces or a diamond engagement ring, you'll want to do your research. Our list includes stores where you can get significant savings. Retail prices often reflect a markup of three times or more the wholesale price of an item. For those unfamiliar with buying fine jewelry (gold, diamonds, semiprecious, and precious stones) and watches, we've included lots of details—tips you'll need to make you savvy jewelry shoppers.

ALLEY CAT JEWELS

San Francisco: 1547 Church St, SF
(415) 285-3668.
Mon–Fri, 1 pm–6 pm, Sun 10 am–5 pm.
MasterCard, Visa, checks accepted

Parking: Street

If Mexican painter Frida Kahlo were alive today, she would shop for antique Mexican silver cuffs, necklaces, and earrings at colorful Alley Cat Jewels. Christie Sekino and Jan Helman, the store's owners, don't sell gold, but they do have three large cases filled with a fine collection of Mexican silver jewelry from the twenties to the forties, copper jewelry, Art Deco pieces, vintage rhinestone jewelry, and Victorian cameos.

Although the pieces in the silver collection come and go, the prices are pretty stable. Nothing in the store is much over $100, and most items are considerably less. Sekino and Helman manage to keep their prices no more than two or three steps above flea-market prices due to the low rent for the store, located on a quiet block of Church Street in the outer reaches of Noe Valley. When we last visited, a heavy silver cuff with a floral design, priced at $68, was enticing. —SB

CRESALIA JEWELERS

**San Francisco: 278 Post St, second floor, SF
(415) 781-7371.**
**Mon–Sat 9:30 am–5 pm (Thur until 7 pm),
Sun noon–5 pm.**
American Express, MasterCard, Visa
Parking: Nearby garages

A family-owned business since 1912, Cresalia Jewelers offers a huge selection of diamond rings, pearls, gold chains, other fine jewelry, and watches in a spacious, five-thousand-square-foot showroom. Brand-name watches by such makers as Movado, Concord, Lassale, and Seiko are always discounted 20 to 25 percent; and quality fine jewelry—whether brand-name or custom designed and manufactured—is guaranteed to be 25 to 50 percent below regular retail prices at neighboring department stores. Cresalia provides full repair on the premises, along with appraisal services by graduate gemologists from the prestigious Gemological Institute of America in Santa Monica. The store also offers substantial savings on silverware, crystal, china, and other dining accessories. Joe Cresalia, son of the store's founder, says he is able to offer low prices because of the store's off–Union Square location and because he deals directly with gem dealers. When we last visited, a 14K gold channel band set with eighty-five points of diamonds and priced at $1500 sparkled prettily in a display case. —*SB*

DIAMONDS OF PALO ALTO

**Peninsula: 261 Hamilton Ave, Ste 320, Palo
Alto (800) 444-9912; (415) 322-1200.**
**Mon–Fri 9 am–6 pm, Sat 10 am–5 pm;
appointments available.**
MasterCard, Visa, checks accepted
Parking: Street

Owner Israel Zehavi's primary business is selling diamonds and colored stones to dealers all across the United States, but he also does a brisk business with the public, offering them watches, loose stones, gold chains, bracelets, earrings, and custom-designed pieces at a substantial savings. He also sells diamonds at up to 20 percent off recommended wholesale prices. Zehavi provides low prices because he buys direct from diamond cutters and has low overhead costs for his peaceful, third-floor office on Hamilton Avenue.

Zehavi, a graduate of the Gemological Institute of America, likes to educate every customer buying a diamond, and he asks them to compare his prices against others to assure customer satisfaction. "Every customer is an ambassador," he says. When we last inquired about 1.50-carat diamonds, Zehavi said he had recently sold a 1.42-carat, round brilliant-cut G, SI1 for $5538 that would sell for about twice his price in a retail store. —*SB*

EVANTON NIEDERHOLZER FINE JEWELERY AND GIFTS

North Bay: 503 Magnolia, Larkspur

ALPHABETICAL STORE LISTING

(415) 924-7885.
Tue, Wed, Sat 10 am–5 pm, Thur–Fri 10 am–6 pm, Sun 11 am–4 pm.
MasterCard, Visa, checks accepted
Parking: Lot on premises

Located on charming Magnolia Avenue, Larkspur's Evanton Niederholzer offers a 25 percent discount on suggested retail prices for fine jewelry and watches by the same manufacturers that sell to such stores as Tiffany's and Shreve's. "A lot of the time, our suggested retail is a lot less than other stores," says JoMarie Evans, the store's manager. Jewelry cases here are filled with 14K and 18K gold jewelry, men's signet rings and cuff links, pearls, diamonds, rings with precious and semiprecious stones, and ideally proportioned Lazare Kaplan diamonds. The store, which also carries famous-maker sterling-silver flatware, crystal, and china, moved to its current location from San Francisco's Union Square two years ago. Low prices reflect the lower rent, reduced overhead, direct resources, and a high sales volume. The store handles custom designs in plat-inum or gold as well as repairs and appraisals. A certified gemologist works on the premises. A pair of large lapis lazuli cuff links set in 14-karat gold for $488 at our last visit seemed ideal for the men in our life, but we secretly coveted a pair of periwinkle-colored tanzanite earrings priced at $600. —SB

THE FENTON COMPANY

San Francisco: 210 Post St, Ste 502, SF (415) 563-0258.
By appointment only.
Checks accepted
Parking: Downtown garages

San Francisco native Joan Fenton offers personal shopping services for fine jewelery and sells the jewelry at prices 25 to 40 percent above wholesale—a significant savings when you consider that retail prices can be more than three times wholesale. Fenton keeps no inventory on hand in her simple offices; instead, after you call her for an appointment and discuss your interests with her, she uses her broad resources to locate diamonds, colored stones, pearls, tennis bracelets, or cuff links, or have an item custom designed.

Fenton, who has an extensive background in the fashion business, attended the prestigious Gemological Institute of America. Since starting her business in 1982, she has employed expertise and a sense of style to help her customers. She is able to offer low prices because she doesn't advertise and shares office space with a friend. "What I do is very personalized, and there is a large return," Fenton says. "My customers, who are mostly professionals, are very happy to do repeat business." —SB

GOLD 'N' GOODY'S

East Bay: 3631 Mt. Diablo Blvd, Lafayette (510) 284-2233.
Mon–Sat 10 am–5 pm.
Major credit cards, checks accepted
Parking: Lot on premises

Tucked away in a small shopping center in

Lafayette, Gold 'N' Goody's is a small treasure trove of jewelry and gifts offered at 60 to 75 percent below retail prices of the major department stores. The store is often busy with moms (with children in tow) who have come to look over the wide selection of diamond rings, earrings, tennis bracelets, 14K gold jewelry, and sterling-silver necklaces. Loose diamonds are sold at below suggested wholesale prices, and the store also handles custom orders.

A good reputation with customers helps the store do a high sales volume and, in turn, offer bargain prices, says Penny Howard, the store's manager and a certified gemologist. "'Trust before Money' has always been the motto of our store," she says. Gold 'N' Goody's has a per-gram sale on gold four times a year, and when we last visited, 14-karat gold was selling for $15 per gram. During that same visit, we saw a lapis lazuli bracelet for $105, 75 percent below its suggested retail value of $420. —SB

HIGGINS JEWELRY CENTER

**East Bay: 22439 Foothill Blvd, Hayward
(510) 538-6660.
Tue–Fri 10 am–6 pm, Sat 10 am–5 pm.
Major credit cards, checks accepted
Other Stores: 1809 Holmes Street,
Livermore, (510) 606-7279.
Parking: Street**

A family-run business for forty-five years, Higgins Jewelry Center is where East Bay people in the know have been coming for years to get low prices on quality diamonds, colored stones, pearls, and wedding bands. The firm sells diamonds to the trade and is the only replacement jeweler in the East Bay for State Farm Insurance Company. Prices stay low because the company does its own casting, manufacturing, goldsmithing, and repair on the premises. Direct dealing with diamond cutters in Europe assures substantial savings.

"Everybody gets the same price and the same service," points out Dann Higgins, a graduate of the Gemological Institute of America and son of founder Richard Higgins, who still oversees the business. The Higginses are happy to educate any novices about buying diamonds. During our visit, we thought that a pair of floral motif ruby-and-diamond earrings priced at $450 were an excellent gift for Mother's Day. —SB

JEWELRY EXCHANGE

**Peninsula: 1301 Broadway, Burlingame
(415) 579-4700.
Mon–Sat 10 am–5:30 pm, Sun 11 am–5 pm.
Major credit cards, checks accepted
Parking: Street**

Since opening its doors in September 1993, the Jewelry Exchange has been doing a brisk business in its spacious showroom on Broadway. The Burlingame store is a branch of the Santa Ana–based jewelry manufacturer which sells merchandise at prices below wholesale. The store also sells all 14K gold jewelry according to gram weight based on the current price of gold. "Based on the way we buy our finished merchandise and loose stones, we guarantee that our items will appraise for double what we sell it for," says Pat Rowenhorst, the store's manager. Pat's son, Bill Doddridge, owns the company. If you're in a hurry to give your loved one a gift, you can choose a diamond and setting and walk out with the stone set in thirty minutes. On a recent visit, we couldn't resist trying on a bracelet set with three carats of emeralds and one carat of diamonds for $1333. —SB

OLD & NEW ESTATES

San Francisco: 2181 Union St, SF (415) 346-7525.
Tue–Sun 11:30 am–6 pm (Fri until 7 pm).
American Express, MasterCard, Visa, Diner's Club, checks accepted
Parking: Street

Walk into Old & New Estates on bustling Union Street, and you'll think you've entered a genial, tweedy English club that sells fine estate jewelry that even the Queen mum would love. Charles and Dianne Jacobs have an impressive collection of fully restored vintage Gruen Curvex and Hamilton watches, as well as wedding bands and wedding sets, earrings, pins, necklaces, and bracelets. The selection is strong on, but not limited to, the Art Deco era.

Charles Jacobs says that the age of estate pieces, and the fact that jewelers frequently buy them as part of large lots, means that they can generally be purchased well below sale prices of new jewelry in department stores. If you're searching for an Art Deco platinum engagement ring with a central diamond, this is the place to go.

The Jacobses don't sell loose precious or semiprecious stones, but bring in your own and they'll set it one of their many elegant settings. One elegant vision that called out to us on our recent visit was a thirties-era 1.40-carat diamond, I color, VS2, priced at $5500, a substantial savings—the same quality diamond has a suggested wholesale price of $4600 per carat, according to the *Rapaport Diamond Report*. —SB

PEARL OF ORIENT

San Francisco: Ghirardelli Square, 900 North Point, SF (415) 441-2288.
Mon–Thur, Sun 10 am–6 pm, Fri–Sat 10 am–9 pm.
Major credit cards, checks accepted
Parking: Ghirardelli Square Garage, street

Experts judge pearls for their luster, surface, shape, color, and size and then grade them from A (low quality) to AAA (highest quality). Pearl of Orient only sells AA and AAA white, pink, blue, gray, and black pearls. They offer a stunning collection of pearl earrings, bracelets, pendants, necklaces, rings, and loose pearls at prices usually below sale prices of major department stores.

The store, which has been in the same location since 1971, offers high quality for less money because the owners, Mr. and Mrs. Yoshinobu Akashi, buy their pearls direct from Japan and manufacture on the premises. The atmosphere of Pearl of Orient is as serene as the jewels it sells. It's no wonder that repeat customers have come from all over the country and even Japan. Restringing a necklace while you wait is no problem, nor is designing a custom piece.

On our last visit, a stunning AAA quality sixteen-inch strand of six millimeter pinkish-pearls seemed fit for Princess Diana, yet its $665 price made it affordable for commoners like us. —*SB*

PETER JACOBS JEWELRY RESOURCES

North Bay: Montecito Plaza, 369-C Third St, San Rafael (415) 459-4300.
Mon–Sat 10 am–6 pm, or by appointment.
MasterCard, Visa, checks accepted
Parking: Lot on premises

Peter Jacobs used to be a distributor of fine jewelry to major department stores, but now he uses his extensive business network to offer customers fine jewelry for at least 30 to 70 percent off the retail sale prices seen at these same stores. Location, minimal advertising, and low overhead permit Jacobs to pass on great prices to his customers. In the pleasant ambience of his upstairs showroom, you'll find cases filled with items such as gold necklaces, sterling silver, earrings, pearls, charms, and ring settings, plus diamond and other gemstone jewelry. If you have a picture of what you want, bring it in and Jacobs will locate the same item for you or have it custom made.

Jacobs specializes in selling better-cut loose diamonds, and he is very willing to spend time to educate consumers on diamond particulars. During our visit, a pair of perfectly round, cream-colored 9-mm pearl earrings for $90 seemed like a great bargain compared to the 7-mm pearl earrings we had seen recently at Macy's for $240. —*SB*

PRICE COSTCO

Price Club and Costco Wholesale, the two biggest chain club stores, recently merged to form Price Costco. Requiring membership to shop in its huge warehouses, the giant chain offers some of the greatest bargains anywhere—including fine jewelry at bargain prices—because it's a low-cost, no-frills operation that sells a high volume of goods.

If you can brave pushy shoppers and have the stamina to dodge carts loaded with the likes of bulk toilet paper and twenty-pound bags of cat food, the clubs are well worth a visit. The merchandise varies between the Price Club and Costco, and recent visits to the South San Francisco Price Club and San Francisco Costco demonstrated that the former had a significantly larger selection of items.

COSTCO

San Francisco: 450 Tenth Street, SF (415) 626-4288.
Mon–Fri, 11 am–8:30 pm, Sat 9:30 am–6

ALPHABETICAL STORE LISTING

pm, Sun 10 am–5 pm.
Discover, checks accepted
Other Stores: Check telephone directory for nearest store.
Parking: Lot on premises

As you walk into the busy store, you see a single, rectangular case containing a small selection of fine jewelry, including famous-maker watches, rings, and earrings with diamonds and precious stones, gold jewelry, men's rings, tennis bracelets, and more. Any item in the case can be purchased and taken home on the same day, and salespeople are on hand to help take orders or show you merchandise. Costco sells diamonds of VS2 clarity and I color or better and guarantees that their diamond rings will appraise by outside experts at twice the value. On our last visit, a 1.0-carat diamond set in a plain 14K gold band was priced at $3700. An 18-inch, 3.98-gram mirror box 14K gold chain for $49.99 was a steal compared to the same chain we saw recently at Macy's for $160. —*SB*

PRICE CLUB

San Francisco: 451 S Airport Blvd, South San Francisco (415) 872-2021.
Mon–Fri 10 am–9 pm, Sat 9:30 am–7 pm, Sun 10 am–6 pm, for non–business members.
Other Stores: Check telephone directory for nearest store.
Discover, checks accepted
Parking: Lot on premises

Crowds of people were looking in the cases of Price Club's jewelry section when we last visited the San Francisco warehouse. The store has a great selection of high-end, brand-name watches such as Cartier and Tag Heuer, as well as gold jewelry, pearls, diamonds and jewelery with precious and semi-precious stones. Orders must be taken for most of the merchandise, which is mailed to you with a shipping and handling charge added on to the price tag. If you don't see what you want in the case, chances are you can find it in Quest, the store's database of fine jewelry. Eye-catching items on our last visit included Chanel-style 16-mm mabe pearl earrings set in 14K gold for $254 and a 7-inch, multicolored bracelet set with semi-precious stones for $434. —*LC*

SHADOWS

North Bay: 429 San Anselmo Ave, San Anselmo (415) 459-0574.
Mon–Sat 11:15 am–6 pm, Sun noon–5 pm.
American Express, MasterCard, Visa
Other stores: Third Hand Store, 1839 Divisadero, SF (415) 567-7332.
Parking: Street

Known primarily as a mecca of quality vintage wedding and formal eveningwear, Shadows offers the lover of things past an exquisite selection of antique jewelry, reminiscent of the style Michelle Pfeiffer showed off in *The Age of Innocence*. The jewelry is elegantly fashionable, not the dowdy kitsch found so often in secondhand stores.

Many of the facets and pearl drops are designed by co-owner Jean Steward, and go for as little as $30—a great price for first-class vintage settings with pearls and semi-precious stones. Devote some time in the clothing racks for one-of-a-kind dresses and gowns. These items are consistently beautiful but not inexpensive; for genuine clothing bargains, go to Steward's other secondhand store, the Third Hand Store, San Francisco. —*SB*

TAYLOR & JACOBSON

East Bay: 1475 North Broadway, Ste 490, Walnut Creek (510) 937-9570.
Mon–Fri 11:30 am–5:30 pm by appointment only.
MasterCard, Visa, checks accepted
Parking: Garage across street

In the upstairs offices of Taylor & Jacobson, visitors can see expert goldsmiths, diamond setters, and jewelry designers at work for the firm's national jewelry-manufacturing business. Because Taylor & Jacobson offers a full-service shop, the firm passes on a significant savings for its high-quality work. The company has thousands of plastic molds of ring settings as well as portfolio of custom designs done for clients.

Taylor and Jacobson also sells loose stones, including diamonds, sapphires, pearls, lapis lazulis and others. Appointments are required. During our tour of the premises, we admired a sparkling 18-carat gold channel ring set with seventy-five points of sapphires and diamonds for $1100 that would make a wonderful birthday or anniversary present. —*SB*

ZWILLINGER & CO.

San Francisco: 760 Market (Phelan Bldg), Ste 800, SF (415) 392-4086.
Tue–Sat 9:30 am–5 pm.
Major credit cards, checks accepted
Parking: Downtown garages

The moment you walk into Zwillinger's, your eyes are dazzled by the elegant display of beautiful jewels and watches. For seventy-five years, Zwillinger's has had a reputation as a quality jeweler that offers substantial savings. Mel and Sheilah Wasserman, Zwillinger's friendly owners, say they are able to offer all the famous brand watches at a 20 to 35 percent discount and jewelry at 30 percent less than the average sale price at stores like Macy's because of the store's low overhead and off–Union Square location, and because they buy direct from manufacturers.

The store has particular expertise in quality loose diamonds and wedding sets, and you can have your own ring custom designed. You can also choose from gemstones and a large selection of pearls and gold chains. Well-known politicians shop at Zwillinger's, and the firm is the replacement jeweler for several insurance companies. One eye-catching item in the store recently was a pearl enhancer for $300, made of a large pear-shaped mabe pearl set in onyx and 14-carat gold with a diamond clip. "We are a fine-jewelry Price Club with professional guidance and full service," says Mel Wasserman. —*SB*

INSIDER TIP: BUYING A DIAMOND

By Sandra Braverman

In *Gentlemen Prefer Blondes*, Marilyn Monroe laid it right on the table when she sang, "Diamonds are a girl's best friend." But shopping for your best friend can be a headache, as diamond prices vary wildly and the industry is not regulated. *The Rapaport Diamond Report*, considered the blue book of the industry, is a New York–based trade publication listing "suggested" wholesale prices for diamonds, which some jewelers will show to customers for price comparison. Jewelers judge the value of diamonds by what is known as the "Four Cs"—cut, clarity, color, and carat. The best jewelers will educate potential customers about these magnificent stones, no two of which are alike.

CUT

Diamonds come in several shapes, including Round Brilliant-cut, Marquise, Emerald-cut (rectangular), Pear-shaped (shaped like a tear drop), oval, and the square Princess-cut. No matter what shape, the cut of a diamond determines the stone's brilliance and beauty. Although a painstaking process, a good cut is important because precision cutting on each of the stone's facets yields perfect proportions that reflect light and draw out the diamond's sparkle. On a classic Round Brilliant-cut diamond, the most popular shape that also maximizes the stone's natural sparkle, a whopping fifty-eight facets must be aligned.

CLARITY

Flawless diamonds are extremely rare—and extremely expensive. Most diamonds have inclusions, natural imperfections that can be seen under the standard ten-power magnification of a jeweler's loupe or, if the inclusions are larger, with the naked eye. Inclusions of the smaller type do not generally affect the stone's beauty, but each inclusion affects the stone's grade and price. Jewelers grade diamonds as FI (flawless), IF (internally flawless—minor surface blemishes), VVS1-VVS2 (very, very small inclusions), VS1-VS2 (very small inclusions), SI1-SI2 (small inclusions), and I1-I2-I3 (imperfect-eye-visible inclusions). Incidentally, Tiffany & Co, America's most upscale jeweler, sells diamonds only of VS2 clarity or better. So does Costco.

COLOR

The less color a diamond possesses, the greater its brilliance, rarity, and value. To the untrained eye, most diamonds appear colorless or white, although the majority contain very slight hints of yellow or brown, and they naturally occur in shades of pink, blue, green, red, and bright yellow. The clearer the diamond, the better light is able to pass through and ignite the stone's radiance. In addition to clarity, diamonds are graded according to color. A number of grades occur in each category, and the differences between grades are subtle.

Diamonds are graded as D-F (colorless), G-J (near colorless), K-M (faint yellow), N-R (very light yellow), and S-Z (light yellow). It is important to ask for an opportunity to compare the colors of several dia-

INSIDER TIP

monds so that you are able to recognize the differences.

CARAT WEIGHT

The weight of a diamond is measured in carats. Each carat is divided into a hundred "points," so that a stone weighing .80 carat may also be referred to as an eighty-point stone. Bigger is not necessarily better when it comes to diamonds because a diamond's value is based on its cut, clarity, and color as well as its size. Yet large stones are more rare than small ones, and size does increase the value of a good quality diamond.

Shop around and compare prices when you are ready to purchase a diamond and keep in mind that patience is a virtue, especially when it comes to buying diamonds. Be thorough and don't buy impulsively—it could cost you thousands of dollars. And don't be shy about asking a jeweler if you may look at stones through the standard jeweler's loupe. Keep in mind, too, that ring settings add to the cost of diamond rings. Costs for setting are based on the carat-weight of the gold (14K, 18K) or the weight of platinum.

Another note: Certification is important, especially for insurance purposes. Appraisals can never hurt but many experts advise that diamond appraisals be done from a certified gemologist unaffiliated with the store where your purchase was made, thereby avoiding any conflict of interest.

GOING FOR GOLD

To get the best bargains on gold chains, it is best to buy from a jeweler who will weigh items on an electronic scale to determine the weight in grams and price it according to the current price of gold. Most retailers will add slight to heavy mark-ups, but there are those who don't. Pure gold is 24 carats (24K), yet the majority of gold sold in the United States is 14K gold. ▥

 INSIDER TIP

KIDS' CLOTHES

Could there be any better place in the world to shop for kids' clothes? The Bay Area is brimming with manufacturers of whimsical childrenswear. A great resource for good prices are manufacturers' factory outlet stores. The styling is special, too, since Bay Area clothing designers take inspiration from European kidswear, making fun, colorful clothes mostly in durable natural fabrics. And, like their European counterparts, the designers follow seasonal color and style trends—comparable to grown-up fashions—so there's always something that looks new.

AMERICAN WIDGEON

San Francisco: 376 Brannan St, SF
(415) 974-6803.
Thur–Fri 10 am–5 pm.
MasterCard, Visa
Parking: Street

A leading producer of children's fleece jackets, rain gear, and skiwear, American Widgeon now has its own outlet, wedged into the front room of a second-story warehouse/office space. The collection includes discontinued styles, seconds, and samples in sizes from newborn to 14. Prices are discounted at least 40 percent from retail stores and catalogs. Some good deals we found included classic rain ponchos (in last season's color) for $20 and colorful parkas for $40. Parking nearby is difficult, but the outlet's prices merit the effort. Call to be placed on a mailing list for notices of special sale events. —JA

BABY BOOM

San Francisco: 1601 Irving St, SF
(415) 564-2666.
Mon–Sat 10 am–6 pm, Sun noon–5 pm.
American Express, MasterCard, Visa
Parking: Street

Baby Boom's floor space is crowded with an excellent selection of new and top-notch secondhand baby products and furniture. Used car seats and other equipment sell for 50 to 60 percent off retail price. The store also carries secondhand maternity and children's clothing in excellent condition. Infant and toddler clothes with designer labels are $15 and less. As an added bonus, Baby Boom buys back your used equipment and clothing in good condition. Grandparents and others with very young out-of-town visitors will love the store's weekly rental policy. From high chairs to baby joggers, everything is available for rent at reasonable prices. Maternity apparel is housed in a separate store two doors away. Ask owner for the key. —JA

BABY GUESS

South Bay: Outlets at Gilroy, 8300 Arroyo Circle (Leavesley Rd at Hwy 101), Gilroy
(408) 847-6333.
Mon–Fri 10 am–9 pm, Sat 9 am–9 pm, Sun 10 am–6 pm.

MasterCard, Visa
Parking: Lot on premises

This is the children's version of the Guess line, which means it's heavy on denim, sweatshirts, and T-shirts. There are some irregulars, which are clearly marked; the rest of the merchandise is past season. Items at the outlet, though, are still pricey. Sizes start at infants and go up to 14 boys' and girls'. Communal dressing rooms. —*PL*

BABY WORLD

East Bay: 5854 College Ave, Oakland
(510) 655-2950.
Mon–Fri 10 am–5 pm, Sat 10 am–5 pm, Sun noon–5 pm.
MasterCard, Visa
Parking: Street

Baby World, a next-to-new children's goods store, has it all, including infant to preteen clothing, toys, layette supplies, baby furniture, baby equipment, and an assortment other child-related knicknacks. The result is something of a hodgepodge, but if you know what you need, you could very well find it here. One of Baby World's discount specialties is their cribs, beginning around $139 new (they often are double that retail), and from $40 to $70 used. Infant car seats were priced recently at about $30 used and $70 new. At minimum, the owner knocks about 50 to 70 percent off original retail price, and if the goods are flawed, the owner will drop the price even more. Once in a while, you might stumble upon a real find. The day we stopped in, one shopper turned up a classic, custom-made rocking horse for $25. She bought it on the spot. —*LC*

BIOBOTTOMS

East Bay: 1253 Marina Blvd, San Leandro
(510) 352-9401.
Mon–Fri 10 am–9 pm, Sat 10 am–7 pm, Sun 11 am–6 pm.
Major credit cards
Other stores: 620 Petaluma Blvd North, Petaluma (707) 778-1948.
Parking: Lot on premises

Parents familiar with the Biobottoms catalog will delight in the new "fresh-air wear for kids" outlet in San Leandro. Twice the size of the Petaluma outlet, the San Leandro store contains a large selection of past-season merchandise and a smattering of seconds and samples marked from 30 to 70 percent below catalog price. Inventory includes children's leggings, tights, dresses, shoes, coveralls, outerwear, and accessories. All products are designed for comfort and durability. Biobottom diaper covers (the company's original product) are available at catalog prices, along with other helpful items for cloth-diapered babies. —*JA*

BOSTON TRADER KIDS

South Bay: Outlets at Gilroy, 8300 Arroyo Circle (Leavesley Rd at Hwy 101), Gilroy
(408) 848-3966.
Mon–Fri 10 am–9 pm, Sat 9 am–9 pm, Sun

10 am–6 pm.
Discover, MasterCard, Visa
Other Stores: Factory Stores at the Nut
Tree, Vacaville (707)453-0114.
Parking: Lot on premises

Here you'll find children's versions of preppy, classic clothes, noticeably tailored and conservative in comparison to places such as Esprit. Boston Trader Kids is a division of OshKosh B'Gosh, but it doesn't begin to compete in terms of color. Merchandise is first quality, with discounts of 30 to 40 percent off regular retail. We saw a boy's rugby shirt retailing at $39 for $26, and a girl's dress retailing at $35 here for $24. Best deals are in the back on the clearance racks where stock is discounted even more. Private dressing rooms. —*PL*

CALIFORNIA KIDS

East Bay: 621 Old County Rd, San Carlos
(415) 637-9054.
Mon–Sat 9 am–4 pm.

Discover, MasterCard, Visa
Parking: Street

Part outlet, part retail store, this factory outlet sells bedding designed and manufactured by California Kids, along with children's clothes and accessories. The best deals are on discontinued items such as crib sheets (starting at $5), crib quilts (starting at $15), and crib bumpers (starting at $13). Some crib sets (bumper, dust ruffle, and sheet) and bunk-bed comforters are manufactured specifically for sale at the outlet. The clothes are purchased end-of-season from outside manufacturers. Merchandise is generally discounted 35 to 65 percent below retail. —*JA*

CARTER'S CHILDRENSWEAR

South Bay: American Tin Cannery, 125
Ocean View Blvd #113, Pacific Grove
(408) 375-6498.
Sun–Thur 10 am–6 pm, Fri–Sat 10 am–8 pm.
Discover, MasterCard, Visa
Other Stores: Outlets at Gilroy (408) 847-

3553; Factory Stores at the Nut Tree in
Vacaville (707) 447-7440.
Parking: Lot on premises

Whether you're shopping for a baby's layette or a young child's back-to-school wardrobe, you'll find great prices at this factory-direct store. This venerable company, makers of children's clothing for more than a hundred years, offers lots of soft, comfy cotton attire for newborns to boys' size 10 and girls' size 14; both overruns and seconds are available at this outlet.

Most of the flawed infant apparel sells for under $10, and you can find comparable values on perfect merchandise. On a recent trip, we found an infant's one-piece coverall in 100 percent cotton, printed with bright balloons, clowns, or plaid, for only $9; a baby's striped overalls, in soft brushed cotton, with a baseball-mitt bib and a T-shirt was $16. You could stock up on thermal receiving blankets for $6, or bright polka-dot fitted crib sheets for $8.

Bigger girls prepared for summer with matching shorts and T-shirts for $7 each, while their brothers found neon two-tone swim trunks for $9. —*SE*

CARY CHILDREN'S CLOTHES

**East Bay: 2390 Fourth St, Berkeley
(510) 841-5700.**
Mon–Sat 10 am–4:30 pm, Sun 11 am–4:30 pm.
MasterCard, Visa
Parking: Lot on premises

Where to buy the perfect girl's party dress? First stop should be the Cary outlet, where samples, seconds, and overruns are snapped up almost as quickly as they are set out. Discounts start at 25 percent, and prices drop quickly during sales. Known for exquisite detailing, original fabrics, and European styling, Cary dresses start at around $60 at Nordstrom and other retailers. Long-sleeve, white-collared "heirloom" dresses in a variety of fabrics and styles were $37 at a recent outlet sale. And for boys, the outlet carries pants and dress shirts. Mailing-list regulars receive monthly notices about special events and the annual sales in October and June. Cary is also popular with home sewers who love the prices on overruns of fabric, trims, buttons, and collars. New this year is the company's swimwear line, Tinikini.

CHRISTINE FOLEY

**San Francisco: 430 Ninth St, SF
(415) 621-8126.**
Mon–Sat 10 am–4 pm.
MasterCard, Visa
Parking: Street

"Unbelievable mayhem" is how one employee describes the twice yearly sales of past-season Christine Foley sweaters for children and adults (samples and irregulars are also available). Patrons line the sidewalk, waiting to be let into the crowded factory warehouse a few at at time. An array of brightly colored, hand-loomed sweaters, priced 80 percent below retail prices of $108 to $148 in children's stores, get snapped up quickly. During regular business hours, discontinued styles are offered at wholesale prices (50 percent off retail); flawed current-season merchandise goes for 20 to 30 percent off. Call to be placed on the mailing list. —*JA*

COTTON ONES

**East Bay: Emeryville Public Market, 5800
Shellmound, Emeryville (510) 428-2974.**
**Mon–Thur 10 am–8 pm, Fri and Sat 10
am–9 pm, Sun 11 am–6 pm; hours subject
to change.**
MasterCard, Visa
**Other Stores: 8970 Northgate Mall, San
Rafael (415) 491-1676.**
Parking: Lot on premises

Straightforward low-priced, high-quality, 100 percent cotton active wear in primary colors is the Cotton Ones trademark. "Kids come shrieking into the store because they love the colors," says owner Susan Kramer, who began creating kids' clothing as a rebellion against the high cost of retail fashions.

This manufacturer's retail store is able to

offer great bargains because its overhead is so low. Prices typically range from $5 to $20. Bold-colored solids and patterns of stars, stripes, and squiggles adorn the assortment of T-shirts, dresses, shorts, pants, and jumpers (in sizes six months to ten years).

New this year for the hip teen girl: stretch cotton-velvet tops, sizes 2 to 10; and bike pants from $5 to $8. Be sure to check out the copiously stocked sales bin. After shopping, take the wee ones for a jump in the Emeryville Market's "ball room." —*LC*

CRACKERJACKS

East Bay: 14 Glen Ave (off Piedmont Ave), Oakland (510) 654-8844.
Mon–Fri 10 am–5:30 pm, Sat 10 am–5 pm.
MasterCard, Visa
Parking: Street

For the distinguished toddler, Crackerjacks takes the prize as one of the Bay Area's nicest consignment shops for children's clothes. On the day we stopped by, we found a boy's camel's hair coat in prime condition for $18. In addition, we found a near-new black tuxedo suit in a boy's size 2 for $25, and a good selection of patent-leather shoes for about $6 to $10.

Other frequently spotted labels: Ralph Lauren, Polo, Gunne Sax, Mousefeathers. Crackerjacks' stock is not only upscale; there's plenty of practical play clothing, skiwear, and school wear, sizes 0 to 14, all in excellent condition. Owners Mary Galvin and Elaine Unverferth accept only high-quality, undamaged clothing in exchange for store credit or cash. There is some new merchandise as well, such as shoes, hats, and pants. The shop is cozy and has toys and books for the kids while Mom and Dad shop. The shopkeepers are friendly and there's a Peet's Coffee right next door. —*LC*

ESSE PINK OUTLET

San Francisco: 2325 Third St, Ste 209, SF (415) 255-6855.
Fri 10 am–4 pm or by appointment.
Checks accepted, no credit cards
Parking: Street and city-owned lot (near Illinois and Twenty-Second)

Colorful children's clothes from last season, plus samples and overruns, are 50 percent off retail at the Esse Pink Outlet. This is the place to find sporty outfits for boys sizes six months to six years that they will actually wear. Esse Pink styles are boldly patterned and easy to mix and match. Many of the soft, 100 percent cotton clothes are fully reversible, and all are thoughtfully designed for comfort and convenience. The outlet also carries the Great Stuff line of infant and toddler flannel playwear at similar savings. Be sure to check the sale box for special deals. (Pia's Kids, another great children's design label, shares Esse Pink's space.) —*JA*

KID'S ZONE

South Bay: The Outlets at Gilroy, 8300 Arroyo Circle (Leavesley Rd at Hwy 101),

Gilroy (408) 847-3344.
Mon–Fri 10 am–9 pm, Sat 9 am–9 pm, Sun
10 am–6 pm.
MasterCard, Visa
Parking: Lot on premises

Lanz, Bryan, Hang Ten, A Star Is Born, and other manufacturers provide this outlet with overruns of current merchandise which then get marked down 20 to 30 percent. Out-of-season clearances reduce prices as much as 50 to 75 percent. Girls' sizes run infant to 14 and boys' infant to 7. For example, a $29 Lanz flannel nightie was $18. Keep an eye out for boy's playwear and sportswear and for little girls' better dresses. —PL

KIDS MART

South Bay: Westgate Mall, 1600 Saratoga
Ave, San Jose (408) 374-2213.
Mon–Fri 10 am–9 pm, Sat 10 am–7 pm, Sun
11 am–6 pm.
Major credit cards

Other stores: Check local phone directory
or call (800) Smart Kids to locate nearest
store. Hours may vary by location.
Parking: Lot on premises

This off-price chain discounts Rebecca's Kids, OshKosh, Hush Puppy, and other brands plus its own labels, U Bet for girls and Kid Terrific for boys, infant to size 16. Twice-yearly seasonal clearances are held in January and July. Although there is no longer a local clearance outlet, all stores offer "Green check" discounts of 25 to 50 percent on selected items daily and 70 percent discounts on promotional weekends.

An additional 10 percent discount is given every day for Preferred Customers. This designation costs $6 annually and is available at any Kids Mart location. For example, a $25 OshKosh dress with a 25 percent sale discount would be $19, with an additional "Preferred Customer" discount the final price is $17. —PL

KIDS 'R US

Peninsula: 19 Colma Blvd, Colma
(415) 756-2893.
Mon–Sat 10 am–9 pm, Sun 11 am–6 pm.
Major credit cards
Other stores: Newark (510) 796-2021;
Redwood City (415) 367-6005; Sunnyvale
(408) 730-5013.
Parking: Lot on premises

A full-scale department store for kids, Kids 'R Us offers at least a 20 percent discount on all merchandise including Bugle Boy, OshKosh B'Gosh, and Jordache. Special promotions reduce prices even further. For basic commodities—leggings, sweats, turtlenecks, and jeans—this is the place. There's also a selection of kids' accessories including underwear, socks, hats, and mittens. Don't expect super styling and detail, but like the parent company, Toys 'R Us, the prices and selection at Kids 'R Us are usually the best in town. —JA

ALPHABETICAL STORE LISTING

KIDSWEAR CENTER

San Francisco: Six Sixty Center, 660 Third St, SF (415) 543-4355.
Mon–Sat 10 am–5:30 pm, Sun noon–5 pm.
MasterCard, Visa
Parking: Lot on premises

Parents, grandparents, and honorary aunts and uncles can significantly improve the little ones' wardrobes with a visit to this spacious store. On our visit, classic OshKosh striped overalls in infant to toddler sizes went for $18; plaid and bright-colored versions were $23.

You may have a hard time outfitting boys who have outgrown the infant and toddler stage, but you will find a wide selection of girls' clothing. For young girls, pick from a multitude of multicolored stretchpants ($7), and choose matching cotton T-shirts ($6) and shorts set ($4). Frilly party dresses for sizes 4 to 16 were $20. Boys and girls of all ages may enjoy the $5 T-shirts, emblazoned with colorful fish and animals—and the name of a zoo or aquarium across the country, such as the Tennessee Aquarium. —*SE*

MAC

North Bay: 7049 Redwood Blvd, Novato (415) 898-1622.
Mon–Fri 10 am–6 pm, Sat 10 am–5 pm, Sun noon–5 pm.
Major credit cards and MAC credit card
Other Stores: 374 University Ave, Palo Alto (415) 323-0474; 281 Hartz Ave, Danville (510) 820-7757.
Parking: Lot on premises

On any given day, you're likely to find a piece that's beautifully tailored and impossibly discounted. We came across adorable red corduroy painter's-style kids' jackets in mint condition for $17, down from an original retail price of $66.

Tweeds has nothing on MAC in the color-naming department: Alligator, Tazmanian Red, Huckleberry, and Peanut are a few of the names assigned to describe the vibrant colors. It's easy to adhere to the "think globally, shop locally" principle here. Since 1978, all the classic, wearable styles have been made at this location (also the corporate headquarters) from fabric production to tailoring. Merchandise is discounted between 45 and 75 percent off retail, and there's always a rack with damaged items for $15 and $10, plus a sale every six to eight weeks.

To receive notices of sales, put your name on the mailing list. We recently saw cotton skirts that had been $42 sell for as little as $5, and cotton pants selling originally for $70 going for $10. Most discounts are based on freight damage, overruns, samples, and discontinued styles. —*LC*

MIMI THE SARDINE

San Francisco: 2325 Third St, Ste 209, SF (415) 241-0370.
Call for hours.
MasterCard, Visa
Parking: Street and city lot (near Illinois

and Twenty-Second)

Swedish designer Pia Andersson has created clothes for several top children's catalogs including Hanna Andersson and Bio-bottoms. Now she's producing her own catalog featuring an appealing line of colorful clothing for women and children. Bay Area customers will recognize past favorites such as plastic-coated cotton bibs, diaper bags, tote bags, and plush terry-cloth robes. Samples and overruns from the collection are reduced at least 30 percent. Having just moved into a new space at the end of 1993 (shared with Esse Pink), Pia's collection will be limited at first. Be sure to call ahead for hours and availability. —*JA*

MOUSEFEATHERS

East Bay: 1005 Camelia St, Berkeley (510) 526-0261.
Tues–Sat 10 am–5 pm.
MasterCard, Visa
Parking: Street

A girls-only line, Mousefeathers exemplifies the creative children's clothing made in the Bay Area. "Florals are our basic design—that's what we start with," says design assistant Molly Sorkin. "Then we do variations on that theme, like fruit prints. Our fabric designs vary with the seasons, but we do a lot of things with a black background." Mousefeathers' styles run the gamut from school clothes (featuring lots of jumpsuits) to dressy items. Sizes in the Mousefeathers line range from 12 months to size 14. The outlet sells most of its merchandise at slightly above wholesale prices. On our visit, garments on the sale rack ranged from $5 to $25—a steal for this well-made, unique clothing. —*GG*

MULTIPLE CHOICES

San Francisco: Yerba Buena Square, 899 Howard (at Fifth St), SF (415) 495-2628.
Mon–Sat 10 am–6 pm, Sun noon–5 pm.
MasterCard, Visa
Other stores: Andy's Dad's Place, Novato

(415) 892-2127.
Parking: Street and public lots

The biggest outlet of its kind, Multiple Choice has an inventory that makes the trek up to the third floor of the Yerba Buena building well worthwhile. The store is larger than the children's section of most major department stores, with racks and racks of apparel for boys, girls, and young adults.

Through a combination of direct buying and low overhead, the owner offers top brands at prices from 30 to 70 percent below retail. Some examples spotted on our recent visit: first-quality, irregular, and recycled (store-returns) Levi's jeans for just under $10 and last season's Spumoni and Esprit sportswear at over 50 percent off. These are but a few of the popular brands available (we were asked not to name others). Multiple Choices accepts exchanges for store credit. —*JA*

ALPHABETICAL STORE LISTING

OSHKOSH B'GOSH

South Bay: Outlets at Gilroy, 8300 Arroyo Circle (Leavesley Rd at Hwy 101), Gilroy (408) 842-3280.
Mon–Fri 10 am–9 pm, Sat 9 am–9 pm, Sun 10 am–6 pm.
American Express, MasterCard, Visa
Parking: Lot on premises

If you visualize your child in bright, cheery colors, this is the place to shop. You'll find everything from shoes to underwear to outerwear, all in OshKosh B'Gosh's trademark mix of colors in classic styles. Merchandise is first quality, past season, but only an expert could tell one season from the next. For extra savings, look to the sales racks, where you'll get an additional 40 percent off the already discounted savings of about 30 percent below regular retail. Sizes range from toddlers to boys' and girls' 7. There's an occasional rack of men's clothes, such as the jeans we saw at $17 a pair and the cotton plaid shirts at $17. Private dressing rooms. —*PL*

PETALS, INC

Peninsula: 969 Commercial Ave, Palo Alto (415) 494-2731.
Fri 10 am–4 pm.
MasterCard, Visa
Parking: Street

Petals, one of the Bay Area's newest and largest manufacturers of girl's clothing, sells fancy dresses that retail for between $60 and $100. Highest prices are on velvet and taffeta dresses. Overstocked items are discounted at least 50 percent and are housed in the Petals warehouse, which is open to the public every Friday and for periodic sales. There's a large selection of dresses and fabrics (from $2 to $7 per yard), buttons, trims, and accessories including baskets, hats, purses, and hair bows. Super bargains on styles from the previous year are found on the $20 sale rack. Call to be placed on the mailing list. —*JA*

REBECCA RAGGS

South Bay: 10200 Imperial Ave, Cupertino (408) 257-7884.
Mon–Fri 9 am–5:30 pm, call for Sat hours.
MasterCard, Visa
Parking: Street

A mother-daughter design team creates the Rebecca Raggs appliquéd velour dresses and jumpsuits that boutiques and pricey catalogs such as Storybook Heirlooms and Wooden Soldier carry. The small outlet, located in front of the factory (you can actually hear the sewing machines whirring in the background), sells whatever merchandise is left once orders have been shipped. The best (but unfortunately most crowded) time to shop is during annual winter and spring sales. Prices we saw of $34 to $42 for dresses and $32 to $39 for jogging suits represent a 30 percent markdown. Items with minor flaws are reduced even further. —*JA*

ALPHABETICAL STORE LISTING

SARA'S PRINTS

East Bay: 3018A Alvarado St, San Leandro
(510) 562-6666.
Mon–Fri 10 am–4 pm.
Checks accepted, no credit cards
Parking: Lot on premises

This well-organized outlet carries discontinued print clothes and seconds at prices at least 25 percent below retail. Shoppers will find the same popular styles carried by retail stores nationwide, but with last season's prints. The selection of cheerfully decorated long johns, coveralls, infant layette items, turtlenecks, underwear, and nightgowns is actually better than in most retail stores. Patrons willing to settle for less than perfection save the most. Long johns with seam rips, incorrect size tags, pattern irregularities, and other minor flaws sell for $10 to $13 compared to $23 to $32 retail if perfect. —*JA*

STORYBOOK HEIRLOOMS

South Bay: Outlets at Gilroy, 8300 Arroyo
Circle (Leavesley Rd at Hwy 101), Gilroy
(408) 842-3880.
Mon–Fri 10 am–9 pm, Sat 9 am–9 pm, Sun
10 am–6 pm.
American Express, MasterCard, Visa
Parking: Lot on premises

This is the outlet for overruns from the very successful Storybook Heirlooms mail-order catalog. Most of the clothing, from infants' to boys' and girls' size 14, is special-occasion and pricey. The appeal here is for grandparents wanting to indulge fantasies in velvet, lace, and ribbons. For example, a red velvet dress that is $210 in the catalog was $126 here. The majority of the merchandise is girls' clothing, but there is some for boys and a few items of women's clothing from the catalog's mother-daughter outfits. At the back of the store, we found terrific bargains on women's discontinued dresses and blouses— $13 each. Private dressing rooms. —*PL*

SWEET POTATOES OUTLET

East Bay: 1716 Fourth St, Berkeley
(510) 527-7633.
Mon–Sat 10 am–6 pm, Sun 11 am–6 pm.
MasterCard, Visa
Parking: Lot on premises

Sure to satisfy any splash-happy toddler is the discounted Marimekko swimwear at the Sweet Potatoes outlet. Discount-happy parents will be equally pleased with the ample stock of brightly colored Marimekko fabric—ideal for decorating a child's bedroom—marked down from $5 to $2.50 a yard. Along with Marimekko, Sweet Potatoes has three of its own children's lines.

Throughout the wide selection of high-quality cotton fashions for boys and girls, you find items that are equally practical and good-humored. The company is tuned into the younger set's tastes, so for young boys (infant to size 7), the SPUDZ line includes shirts, pants, shorts, and jackets decorated with glow-in-the-dark lizards and purple

ALPHABETICAL STORE LISTING

dinosaurs, as well as cars, airplanes, and automobiles. For girls, the Yazoo line (sizes 4 to preteen) includes leggings, dresses, pants, blouses, and T-shirts awash in polka dots, stripes, and flowers. And the Sweet Potatoes line (layette to size 14 for girls, layette to size 7 for boys) has everything for the truly younger set. Merchandise is neatly organized, and reductions are marked clearly on wall charts that list retail, flawed, and outlet prices.

For example, a Yazoo dress originally priced at $54 would sell for $27 if flawed, and $34 at the outlet price. Marimekko rompers may go through three markdowns: $21 to $13 to $11. The store is particularly child-friendly, with a small play corral filled with books and toys to entertain kids while parents shop. —*LC*

TIDDLY WINKS

East Bay: 1302 Gilman St, Berkeley (510) 527-5025.
Mon–Sat 10 am–5:30 pm (Fri until 6 pm), Sun noon–5 pm.
Discover, MasterCard, Visa
Parking: Street

"Our shoppers like to find expensive clothing at bargain prices," says Anne Raya de Schweinitz, one of the three Tiddly Winks owners. "We try to be selective so there won't have to be a lot of clothes you sort through to find what you're looking for," she adds. At this Berkeley bargain haven, parents can find high-quality used and new children's clothing, equipment, and furniture.

For example, we found a Jessica McClintock dress in prime condition for $6.50 and a High Sierra jean jacket for $9. Sizes here range from 0 through 12, although some preteen is available. Mousefeathers, Gap, and Esprit are frequently in stock. New Danskin leotards go for about $10 to $11; new underwear, socks, and tights are also available. —LC

WEE CLANCY

Peninsula: 2682-F Middlefield Rd, Redwood City (415) 366-5597.
Fri 10 am–4 pm, Sat 9 am–1 pm.
Checks accepted, no credit cards
Parking: Lot on premises

Lots of detail, but not at all fussy, Wee Clancy dresses are perfect for little girls who love beautiful dresses but also need to be able to climb a tree at a moment's notice. Fabrics are 100 percent cotton with colorful, vintage designs. This is a family-run operation; even Grandma gets into the act with handmade rugs braided with recycled trims. After orders are shipped out from the factory, what remains ends up at the small outlet. Prices are 50 percent below retail for newer items and up to 75 percent on past-season merchandise. Selection is strongest in sizes 4 to 6X. Call to be placed on the mailing list for special sale announcements. —*JA*

LEATHER GOODS & ACCESSORIES

You may think that discount means limited service. But this isn't true when you are shopping for luggage, briefcases, and handbags in the Bay Area. The stores we've listed are generally smaller-scale operations, run by people who know their bags. We found they're happy to help you decide which style and quality bags best suit your needs. Shoppers at these discount outlets are likely to get more attention than they would at larger stores, and more choices than they would at a specialty retail store.

AMERICAN TOURISTER

North Bay: Factory Stores at the Nut Tree, Vacaville (707) 446-1595.
Mon–Sat 10 am–8 pm, Sun 10 am–6 pm.
Major credit cards
Parking: Lot on premises

One of a proliferating breed of outlet mall stores, American Tourister packs molded and soft-sided luggage, garment bags, totes, cosmetic cases, duffel bags, attaché cases, book bags, wallets, purses, and travel accessories into a standard retail space lined with floor-to-ceiling shelves. Most items carried here are manufactured solely for the company's outlet stores, but overstock on current retail lines and deeply discounted factory seconds with cosmetic imperfections are also available. Discounts off suggested retail prices range from 40 to 75 percent. Lowest prices are in the clearance warehouse section at the back of the stores. On our latest foray, we found fabric-side pullmans for less than $30. —SS

CHOICE LUGGAGE

South Bay: 1742 El Camino Real, Mountain View (415) 968-3479.
Mon–Sat 10 am–6 pm.
MasterCard, Visa
Parking: Lot on premises

Choice Luggage sells an array of top brands, at discounts usually ranging from 10 to 50 percent. The stock is displayed in two separate bungalows. On the left lies a warren of the latest garment bags, pullmans, roll-aboards, and other styles plus upscale accessories laid out in glass cases. On the right sit the real deals—closeout items at remarkably reduced prices. Recent finds included duffel bags for $15; book bags for $19; giant Travelpro roll-aboards, originally $300, marked down to $179; a cordovan leather outing bag reduced from $705 to $352; and rows of Andiamo bags at good prices. —SS

THE COACH STORE

North Bay: Village Outlets of Napa Valley, 3111 North St. Helena Hwy, Suite 1B, St. Helena (707) 963-7272.
Mon–Fri 10 am–6 pm, Sat 10 am–7 pm, Sun 11 am–6 pm.

 ALPHABETICAL STORE LISTING

American Express, MasterCard, Visa
Parking: Lot on premises

Generally, discounts at the outlet range from 20 to 50 percent on Coach's line of classic handbags. Most items land here because of imperceptible visual flaws. But you can always count on Coach's trademark durability and quality.

New shipments of in-season and discontinued pieces, including briefcases, wallets, duffel bags, and purses, arrive weekly in a generous range of colors and styles. Monthly, selected pieces are singled out for an additional 20 to 30 percent markdown. Expect to see the same handsome decor and tony customers you see at Coach retail stores. Speical note: Particularly following the holidays, Coach retail stores send along many leather jackets to clear out for spring stock. As a result, a suede or leather jacket originally priced at $450 might go for $338. —LC

CONTINENTAL VOGUE LUGGAGE CO/AAA LUGGAGE REPAIR

San Francisco: 585 Howard St, SF
(415) 781-5007.
Mon–Fri 8 am–5 pm, Sat 9 am–3 pm.
American Express, MasterCard, Visa
Parking: Street or pay lot on same block

This is a vast warehouse where airline and other bags are repaired. But turn right after you walk in the door, and you'll find a small retail store offering 20 to 50 percent discounts on brand-new, brand-name luggage. Some items are closeouts, but most are current merchandise. According to manager Stephen Schnell, low overhead allows the company to come through with the nice prices.

In addition to selling at a discount, Schnell says, "We can fix anything." Stock includes Samsonite, Andiamo, Skyway, Delsey, Halliburton, and London Fog bags of all types. We recently spotted London Fog gar-

ment bags for $168, down from a suggested retail price of $210; Travelpro valet-style, roll-aboard garment bags for $220, marked down from $295; and a molded Delsey combination-lock bag for $80, down from $135. —SS

GOOD DEALS

East Bay: MacArthur Broadway Center,
3607 Piedmont Ave, Oakland
(510) 654-0779.
Mon–Fri 10 am–7:30 pm, Sat 10 am–6 pm,
Sun noon–5 pm.
Major credit cards
Parking: Lot on premises

If you have the patience to paw through a jumble of bags jammed into narrow aisles and piled onto ceiling-high racks, there are some good deals in this tiny store tucked into a corner off the parking garage. Generic brands abound, but top brands such as Travelpro roll-aboards, Eastpak duffel bags, and molded and soft-sided Samsonite luggage are thrown into the mix. Discounts range from 10 to 50 percent, with the biggest breaks on discontinued styles. This is the sort of place where a solid knowledge of the merchandise and standard retail prices is essential. For example, alongside many uninspiringly priced items we found a real deal: a Samsonite valet-style garment bag for just $170. —SS

GRIFFCO LEATHER FACTORY

East Bay: 204 Martin Luther King Jr. Way, Oakland (510) 444-3800.
Mon–Fri 9 am–5 pm, Sat 9 am–4:30 pm.
MasterCard, Visa
Parking: Street

Sturdy, basic leather book bags, briefcases, purses, and accessories are the stock in trade here. All bags are made on the premises from leather odd lots and overruns. The stitching is not the most delicate and the textures vary, but these bargain bags are built for use—the shop guarantees its work and will repair any-

thing that breaks. Book bags cost $54, large leather handbags cost $30, and briefcases cost $52 or $65.

In the unsolicited words of a Griffco customer, waiting at the counter with his dog for the completion of a custom order, "I bought a belt here eight years ago and I'm still wearing it. This is the second thing I've had made. Quality is excellent and the prices are good." —SS

THE HAND BAG FACTORY OUTLET

East Bay: 2100 Fifth St, Berkeley (510) 843-6022.
Mon–Fri 8 am–4:30 pm, Sat 10 am–4:30 pm.
Checks accepted
Parking: Street

Rich, substantial leather attaché cases, priced at about $150, along with capacious shoulder bags, priced at $103 when we visited, are the standout items here. Purses, wallets, belts, and accessories are also sold. In addition to

merchandise in the tiny up-front display area, there are shelves of bags behind the counter. When we visited, however, the store attendant didn't know if back-room stock was for sale, or how the store prices its items. When we tried calling another day for more information, we found that the Hand Bag Factory's phone line is picked up by an answering machine that doesn't take messages. The upshot is, you can find good bargains, but don't expect heaps of information about the goods. —SS

HARBAND'S LUGGAGE

North Bay: Gateway Plaza, 959 Lakeville St, Petaluma (707) 769-0610.
Mon–Fri 10 am–6 pm, Sat 10 am–2 pm.
Major credit cards
Parking: Lot on premises

A specialist in fine leather goods, particularly attaché and catalog cases, this small shop generally offers a 20 percent discount, carried over from its days as a wholesaler.

ALPHABETICAL STORE LISTING

Harband's carries only high-end cases, luggage, and travel accessories—"Cheap goods come back to haunt you," says owner Ted Wong. Samsonite, Briggs & Rily, and Florentine are among the lines stocked. The best deals are on pieces that have minor marks or were made by now-defunct manufacturers. These items, grouped on the right-hand side as you enter the store, are half-price. —*SS*

JANG GABANG

East Bay: 2556 Telegraph Ave, Berkeley
(510) 843-8767.
Mon–Fri 10 am–7 pm, Sat 11 am–6 pm.
American Express, MasterCard, Visa
Parking: Street

Although prices generally are only 10 to 15 percent off standard retail, some items are discounted 25 to 35 percent. Prices are held low because the store caters to students, and the best buys appear during the August back-to-school sale. We found high-quality

Jandd mountaineering packs (made in Santa Barbara by UC Berkeley alums) priced at $175, and giant Samsonite pullmans for $140. As you might expect, the store is particularly well-stocked with items to suit the student customer, such as book bags, backpacks, and large suitcases. —*SS*

THE LUGGAGE CENTER

San Francisco: 828 Mission St, SF
(415) 543-3771.
Mon–Fri 10 am–6 pm, Sat 10 am–5 pm, Sun noon–5 pm.
American Express, MasterCard, Visa
Other stores: twenty locations in Northern California, including 5741 Christie Ave, Emeryville (510) 653-1896; 2221 Shattuck Ave, Berkeley (510) 843-3385; 1200 Burlingame Ave, Burlingame (415) 579-0435; and 871 Fourth St, San Rafael (415) 459-0181. Check the telephone directory for additional stores.
Parking: Validated for one hour at Yerba

Buena Center garage.

Buying in bulk—thousands of pieces at a time—with a commitment to low prices means the Luggage Center sells major brands at discounts from 20 to 50 percent. The San Francisco store has an extra-large selection of roll-aboard bags, plus just about every other current style of leather attaché cases, packs, and travel accessories. Exceptional deals occur when the company makes special purchases. For example, we found blue Samsonite "piggyback" roll-aboards that double as luggage carts priced at $120—less than half the suggested retail price—because Luggage Center had bought an unsold lot from Montgomery Ward at a fire-sale price. The lowest prices are in the closeout section in the back left-hand corner, where we spied a twenty-nine-inch case for $52 and carryons from $19. Luggage Center bags come with three-year, five-year, or life-time guarantees, and the exceptionally helpful sales staff invites customers to take home a bag and work with it for up to thirty days before making a final purchase. —*SS*

ALPHABETICAL STORE LISTING

LUGGAGE TO GO

**North Bay: Marin Square, 75 Bellam Blvd,
San Rafael (415) 459-5167.
Mon–Sat 10 am–6 pm, Sun noon–5 pm.
American Express, MasterCard, Visa
Parking: Lot on premises**

The appealingly displayed, top-of-the-market luggage here—sold at a 15 to 35 percent discount—recalls the era of elegant ocean-liner travel, when fully loaded trunks and hat boxes were commonplace. Brands featured include French, Tumi, Hartmann, Lark, and Gralnick.

This is luggage that is made to last, priced below full retail. We fell in love with a beautifully finished, handmade Gralnick suit trunk tagged at $680, down from a suggested retail price of $895. A few lines, such as French, don't allow discounts, but co-owner Franca Detrick says, "We always do something special for our customers." Periodic manufacturer's specials offered through the store push prices a bit lower.

During our visit, customers who purchased a Tumi bag for $350 or more received a $100 discount on a second piece. In addition to luggage, the shop carries Italian leather purses, wallets, and travel accessories. —SS

THE OPTICAL OUTLET

**San Francisco: 951 Market St, SF
(415) 982-5106.
Mon–Sat 9 am–5:30 pm.
American Express, MasterCard, Visa
Parking: Nearby garages**

If you don't wear glasses, you'll wish you did after browsing through this amazing Market Street shop. Sales samples, overruns, and discontinued styles mean mega bargains for shoppers looking for trendy frames from the likes of Giorgio Armani, Alain Mikli, and Gianfranco Ferré. We're talking serious fashion frames here at prices close to wholesale—at least 40 percent below retail.

OWENS LEATHER AND MORE

**Peninsula: 201 E Fourth Ave, San Mateo
(415) 342-6276.
Mon–Fri 11:30 am–3:30 pm, occasional Sat
with appointment.
MasterCard, Visa
Parking: Street**

An outlet for Graffeo leather goods, which are sold in specialty shops and in department stores as private-label merchandise, Owens Leather and More boasts prices 60 to 80 percent lower than estimated retail value. The garment bags, totes, briefcases, handbags, and accessories sold here are either overstocked items, canceled orders, or samples from trade shows. Quality is high with soft, supple leather sewn into a variety of classic styles. Prices generally are $69 for backpacks and book bags, $29 for purses, $110 for garment bags, $99 for carryons, and $49 for totes. —SS

 ALPHABETICAL STORE LISTING

MATERNITY

DAX AND COE MATERNITY OUTLET

Peninsula: 935 El Camino Real, Menlo Park
(415) 327-4371.
Mon–Fri 10 am–6 pm, Sat–Sun noon–5 pm.
MasterCard, Visa
Parking: Street

The Dax and Coe outlet line of sophisticated sportswear is found in most better maternity stores, but at this outlet, the popular line goes for at least 40 percent below retail. Past-season clothes, samples, and excess inventory move rapidly from the warehouse out back to the outlet in front. Appliquéd cotton-ramie sweaters that can be worn before, during, and after pregnancy were $35 on a recent visit, and cotton skirts, leggings, lightweight jackets, and silk-screened T-shirts were $15 to $29. New at the outlet is a non-maternity line of women's sleepwear designed by Jane Tise, former Esprit designer. Call to be placed on the mailing list for seasonal warehouse sales.–JA

MATERNITY CENTER OF MARIN (MOM)

North Bay: 874 Fourth St, San Rafael
(415) 457-4955.
Mon–Sat 11:15 am–6 pm, Sun noon–5 pm.
American Express, MasterCard, Visa
Parking: Street

Sprinkled among new, in-season maternity apparel, MOM has superb discounted maternity wear. Best are the all-cotton, fashion-conscious Japanese Weekend wear, such as a $24 black-and-white ensemble that was originally $95; or a Pea in the Pod rayon romper marked down from $198 to $75. MOM carries a great assortment of reduced-priced party and formalwear, such as a blue beaded evening gown going for $145, down from $263; or a lovely black velvet piece on sale for $99, originally $340. Discounted merchandise tends to be a little past season or slightly flawed but of excellent quality. —LC

OFF-PRICE STORES

This section includes a range of stores where you'll find top brands at major markdowns—the very definition of "off-price." Most sell current or recent past-season merchandise at anywhere from one-third to two-thirds (or more) off the original retail price. Since merchandise changes often, what you find on any given day will vary. Occasional visits will usually yield bargains on good quality, name-brand garments. Most will be overruns (the manufacturer made too many), closeouts (fabric or style has been discontinued), or slow sellers that have been returned by retailers. Sometimes, too, these stores carry slightly irregular garments—at added markdowns.

ALPHABETICAL STORE LISTING

EMPORIUM CAPWELL CLEARANCE STORE

East Bay: Broadway at Twentieth St, Oakland (510) 891-5000.
Mon–Fri 10 am–8 pm, Sat 10 am–6 pm, Sun 11 am–6 pm.
American Express, Emporium Capwell charge, MasterCard, Visa
Parking: Pay lots

Located in the huge basement of Oakland's Emporium Capwell, the clearance center contains markdowns and sale items (some that have seen better days) that have trickled in from the retail stores. The center may lack atmosphere, but men can find good bargains on everything from shorts to suits by some well-known manufacturers, although the selection of goods is larger for women and children. Discounts range from 25 to 90 percent off the lowest ticketed price. On our last visit, we saw a pair of Chaps/Ralph Lauren 100 percent cotton khakis marked down from $30 to $24 and some $8 silk ties. —*SB*

I. MAGNIN FINALE

East Bay: Twentieth and Broadway, Oakland (510) 444-7722.
Mon–Sat 10 am–6 pm, Sun noon–5 pm.
American Express, MasterCard, Visa
Parking: Street

Some of the merchandise is a season or two old, but often European designers are so far ahead of stateside ones that you'll look like you're wearing this season's latest designs. There's YSL, Ferre, Lacroix, Chanel, and Valentino, to name a few. The evening clothes, often timeless in design, are a good bet. The shoe and jewelry selection is outstanding. There's even a small collection of menswear. Prices are at least 50 percent off the original price and can reach 70 percent off. There are no special-purchase buys here, just good old-fashioned markdowns. —*DG*

LOEHMANN'S

South Bay: 1651 Hollenbeck (at Homestead), Sunnyvale (408) 737-1900.
Mon–Fri 10 am–9 pm, Sat 10 am–7 pm, Sun noon–6 pm.
Discover, MasterCard, and Visa
Other stores: 75 Westlake Mall, Daly City (415) 755-2424; 222 Sutter St, SF (415) 982-3215; 3161 Crow Canyon, San Ramon (510) 866-9464.
Parking: Lot on premises

Loehmann's is where the whole off-price fashion game started, and it continues to be a key player. In Loehmann's early days, designers insisted that the labels be removed before their clothing was sold. Today you'll find plenty of labels, including Calvin Klein and Anne Klein. In instances where the labels are cut out, the salesclerk will often confidentially share the designer name with you. A Kenar blazer that retailed at $280 was $160 here; a silver Anne Klein II sweater that retailed for $377 was here for $170. The

ALPHABETICAL STORE LISTING

most expensive items and status labels are in the back room. The best deals are found on the clearance racks, where you'll find bargains such as a Jerri Sherman silk print skirt that retailed at $150 marked down to $30. Loehmann's has a free Insider Club; join it and you'll get occasional special mailings entitling you to additional discounts.

MARSHALL'S

South Bay: 5160 Stevens Creek Blvd at Lawrence Expressway, San Jose (408) 244-8962.
Mon–Sat 9:30 am–9 pm, Sun 11 am–6 pm.
Major credit cards
Other stores: Call (800) 627-7425 to locate the nearest store.
Parking: Lot on premises

Among the top five off-price stores in the United States, Marshall's is a no-frills department store with a mix of women's, men's, and children's clothes, as well as shoes, accessories, home furnishings, and gifts. It's a constantly changing mix of labels that even includes Liz & Co. and Esprit, which have their own outlet stores. You might find an Esprit print dress that retails for $68 marked at $25, or an Alexander Julian Colours men's sweater that retails at $85 marked down to $27. London Fog jackets that retail at $180 are $80 here.

From time to time, Marshall's will carry Perry Ellis sweaters, shirts, and pants for men, as well as Calvin Klein men's sweaters, pants, and shirts. Occasionally you can also find Ungaro neckties and Coogi sweaters (imported from Australia). It pays to shop at more than one Marshall's because they don't always carry the same merchandise. The clearance racks are where you'll find the very best prices. Private dressing rooms. —*PL*

NORDSTROM RACK

Peninsula: 280 Metro Center, 81 Colma Blvd, Colma (415) 755-1444.
Mon–Sat 10 am–9 pm, Sun 11 am–6 pm.
Major credit cards
Other stores: 1285 Marina Blvd, San Leandro (415) 614-1742.
Parking: Lot on premises

Nordstrom leftovers are tightly crammed together in this store, and you really have to search to find the good pieces. The shoe assortment, on the other hand, is excellent. And the men's area isn't as cluttered as the women's, so it's easier to find good styles. Prices vary from 30 to 70 percent off original retail.

ROSS DRESS FOR LESS

South Bay: Westgate Mall, 1600 Saratoga Ave, San Jose (408) 374-2444.
Mon–Sat 9:30 am–9 pm, Sun 11 am–7 pm.
Major credit cards
Other stores: Call (800) 945-7677 for location of nearest store.
Parking: Lot on premises

This is a great place to take skeptics, because even they can spy something immediately recognizable as a good deal. One of the top five off-price retailers in the country, Ross sells an ever-changing mix of labels and many sizes, including petites and large sizes.

On one trip you may find Calvin Klein; on the next, Ralph Lauren. There's clothing here to dress you from infancy through adulthood. Women may appreciate items like a Kasper check suit that retailed at $170 marked down to $80, or an Oleg Cassini silk print blouse that retailed for $36 marked at $19. We also saw a man's Robert Stack black silk blazer that was $70 retail, marked down to $30. Commonly available labels for men include Perry Ellis and Express; for women, Liz Claiborne and Young Edwardian. Best deals are found on the clearance racks where you might find items such as a $68 Jeanne Pierre black lambswool-and-cashmere blend sweater marked down to $21, or a Claiborne jacket that retails at $180 marked down to $20. Selection includes lingerie, shoes, and accessories. Private dressing rooms. —*PL*

T.J. MAXX

South Bay: 1825 Hillsdale, San Jose
(408) 266-1110.
Mon–Sat 9:30 am–9:30 pm, Sun 11 am–6 pm.
Major credit cards
Other stores: Call (800) 285-6299 to locate the nearest store.
Parking: Lot on premises

One of the largest off-price chains in the country, T.J. Maxx has a mix for the whole family. Many of the labels are familiar. You might find an Adrienne Vittadini sweater that retails for $80 marked at $40, or a Kenar top that retails at $88 here for $40. There's a nice mix of labels for men, including Liberty of London ties and even an occasional Nicole Miller tie. We saw Tommy Hilfiger shirts that retail at $60 here for $30. There's also a large selection of infant and children's clothing as well as women's accessories, shoes, and lingerie in both petite and large sizes. Clearance racks offer the best deals. Private dressing rooms. —*PL*

 ALPHABETICAL STORE LISTING

INSIDER TIP:
DEPARTMENT STORE SALES

By Diane Green

The Bay Area's two largest department-store chains, Macy's and Emporium, constantly engage in "sale wars" during the year. You can follow the papers, but wardrobe consultant Joan Hale suggests you spend your time inside the stores researching the merchandise.

"If you shop the majors often enough, you'll know when the merchandise will go on sale because of the length of time it's been there and the number of pieces the department has on hand," she explains. If enough pieces have been sold from a coordinate group and there's not enough left for a customer to mix-and-match, it's almost guaranteed the store will mark down the remaining pieces. Rest assured, certain styles of almost every label will eventually go on sale—even "better" brands such as Kikit and Liz Claiborne.

SHOPPING THE SPECIALTY STORES

By definition, specialty stores carry a limited assortment of merchandise, which is why chains like Neiman Marcus, Nordstrom, and I. Magnin cannot be relegated to the category of department store. One disadvantage to specialty shops is that by the time merchandise reaches markdown status, you'll probably find a lot of broken sizes and pieces of unrelated merchandise—jackets that don't have skirts or blouses from the same coordinate group. This doesn't mean you can't put a great outfit together, just that you no longer have the designer's expert eye to assemble it for you. You can trust in the expertise of the sales help or go it on your own.

NORDSTROM

Nordstrom carries moderate and better designer merchandise, with heavy emphasis on shoes, having started out as a shoe store in Seattle. The assortment is quite wide, but as in most large specialty stores, lines are not carried in great depth. Therefore, when sales do occur, you can't always find your size or color. Nordstrom has its Anniversary Sale July through August. It also holds Half-Yearly Sales for men in January and June, and for women in June and November.

I. MAGNIN

This store has a smaller selection of non-designer merchandise than does Nordstrom, but the savings can be terrific if you find your size. One trick is to cultivate a relationship with a salesperson. The salespeople keep a blue book on their customers and will put things aside for you or call you when, for instance, Donna Karan goes on sale.

Insider Tip: While most sales are advertised, some are by invitation only. On Designer Night Evening Sale, and during I. Magnin's Private Spring Sale, invited customers receive an extra discount on fine women's and men's apparel. Invitations go out to customers with I. Magnin credit cards and those in the know who call ahead.

INSIDER TIP

The store has been known to hold a charity shopping night in which customers pay to attend the event but receive a 10 percent discount on merchandise. Besides some great buys in ready-to-wear, there were savings to be had on designer accessories.

NEIMAN MARCUS

Neiman Marcus holds "Last Call" sales every January and July. If you're a gambler you'll hold out for these events, when you'll find designer merchandise at the lowest prices—50 to 75 percent off the original tag. There's ready-to-wear for men and women, and accessories. (If you're wondering about the Neiman Marcus Clearance Center that used to be in the basement of Emporium in Oakland, sorry; it moved to Texas and Philadelphia.)

WILKES BASHFORD

For those of us who wouldn't dream of spending $2000 on a suit, there is hope. Even this very upscale specialty store has sales, if only on "selected items storewide." Sale items consist of slow sellers and broken lots (you might find a women's jacket but not its matching skirt, for example). In menswear, markdowns can be found on suits, sportcoats, shirts, ties, trousers, and shoes. In women's departments, look for dresses, suits, sportswear, shoes, and some accessories.

MAC

MAC holds two sales a year (spring and fall) on men's and women's clothing. It's mostly end runs, which means that the designer can no longer make clothes from a given fabric because the fabric has been discontinued.

Super Find: Clothing from designers Hank Ford and Todd Oldham, at savings of 30 to 50 percent. ⅲ

INSIDER TIP

SECONDHAND BARGAINS

Secondhand doesn't mean cast-off anymore. There's a Bay Area boom in upscale consignment stores selling nearly new top-brand clothing in mint condition which means you can dress like a millionaire without breaking the bank. It makes sense to look for gently used kids' clothing and toys since they grow out of things so quickly.

You may be more surprised to learn that consignment stores are great resources for amazing markdowns on men's and women's clothing, including high-quality status brands such as Ralph Lauren, Anne Klein, Giorgio Armani, Hermes, and Christian Dior (the eveningwear—particularly tuxes and gowns—often looks like it's never been worn). You'll find upscale maternity and bridal wear, and reliables from the Gap, Guess, and Levi's, too.

AFTERWARDS

Peninsula: 1137 El Camino Real, Menlo Park (415) 324-2377.
Mon–Sat 10 am–6 pm, Thur 10 am–8 pm.
MasterCard, Visa
Other Stores: 1075 Curtis, Menlo Park (415) 324-3688.
Parking: Lot on premises

When Katie and Bob Hanson who used to manage Palo Alto's Polo store opened Afterwards, they converted their former Polo customers into consignors. One shopaholic brought in $250,000 worth of designer originals, and the good stuff keeps coming in from all over the country—from Texas, New York, Arizona, with not just Ralph Lauren labels but Escada, Chanel, Hermes, and the best European and American designers.

Afterwards replicates a posh antique-filled Polo store at a better price point. Top-quality used men's suits, sport coats, and neckwear go for a third of the original retail price. Try a cashmere Polo suit originally $2600 for $962.50 or a $700 Joseph Abboud sport coat for $245. You'll see a lot of new salesmen's samples—like $40, $50, and $85 Robert Talbott ties at half the price. The quality and selection of women's wear is equally impressive. For upscale maternity, bridal, and children's clothes (newborn to size 12) including Polo for boys, check out the new Afterwards just up the street. —*CA*

ALL THE MORE TO LOVE

East Bay: 2325 Alameda Ave, Alameda (510) 521-6206.
Mon–Sat 10 am–6 pm.
Checks accepted, no credit cards
Parking: Street

Finally a consignment boutique for Rubenesque women (size 14 to 32+) where the emphasis is on fun and glamour and the decor is straight out of a thirties musical. There's something for every full-figured gal from teenagers to grandmothers. Basic, everyday comfy clothes, conservative work suits—a three-piece Bleyle, originally $475, was $72—and dramatic dress up outfits can be found here. They carry most of the better known labels—Liz Sport, Elizabeth, Le Chois, Act III, Gemeni II—with prices set at about a third of new. You'll even find a few choice vintage garments—a fur-trimmed Lilli Ann coat was $60—and a great collection of vintage jewelry at prices you won't believe. You'd pay $200 in an antique store for the handsome three-piece Coro set we saw for $30. —CA

AMERICAN RAG

San Francisco: 1305 Van Ness, SF
(415) 474-5214.
Mon–Wed 10 am–9 pm, Thur–Sat 10 am–10:30 pm.
American Express, MasterCard, Visa
Parking: Street

This is not a discount store in the traditional sense. It features vintage men's and women's clothing plus a small collection of contempo-rary designs. Going the vintage route might be a clever and less expensive way of achiev-ing a couture look on a budget. Many of these garments have hand-bound buttonholes and wonderful detailing that would be too costly to reproduce in today's market. There's a good selection of round sunglasses, the current rage in some circles. —DG

BEST THREADS

North Bay: 866 Grant Ave, Novato
(415) 897–2201
Tues–Sat 10 am–5:30 pm.
MasterCard, Visa
Parking: Street

According to the mayor of Novato, "The city's best kept secret is the clothes at Best Threads." This handsome consignment bou-tique offers a selective array of casual, work, and dressy garments sizes 2 to extra-large with an added enticement: Store proceeds benefit the Novato Youth Center so you can have the satisfaction of doing good while you're doing well. Top-of-the-line labels start at 50 percent of new and go down. A two-piece Carole Little that sold for $225 new was down to $85 and a Lillie Rubin holiday dress originally $400 was selling for $45. The back room is devoted to sales merchandise. —CA

BIBBIDY BOBBIDY BO-TIQUE

Peninsula: 4222 Olympic Blvd, San Mateo
(415) 341-6577.
Mon–Fri 10:30 am–5 pm, Sat 11 am–4:30 pm.
Checks accepted, no credit cards
Parking: Lot on premises

The kids will amuse themselves in the play area while you shop. Good variety, great prices, and like-new condition are a few of the pluses in this clean, bright, well-orga-nized store. You'll find everything from sleepers to ski outfits (sizes 0 to 8), swings to strollers, all the popular brands—OshKosh, Gymboree, Health Tex, Carter's, Gerry,

Strolee, Graco, and Fisher Price. Prices start at a quarter of new and get better. Sleepers go for $1, bibs, rattles, and undershirts for 25 cents and breast pumps start at $4. —*CA*

BJ'S

East Bay: Delta Fair Shopping Center, 3030 Delta Fair Blvd, Antioch (510) 754-4310.
Mon–Fri 10 am–6 pm, Sat 10 am–5 pm.
Checks accepted, no credit cards
Parking: Lot on premises

This comfortable and cozy consignment shop doesn't skimp on the amenities such as kimonos in the dressing rooms and a shelf of books on tape for rent. Women of all ages and sizes (2–24) will find a full range of shopping options from playclothes to party-wear covering the retail spectrum from Mervyn's to I. Magnin. A blouse or sweater ($8–$15) is just as likely to have a Liz Claiborne label as a JC Penny one. A three-piece Paul Stanley suit originally priced at $500 was a steal at $99. —*CA*

THE BOTTOM LINE

Peninsula: 1236 Burlingame Ave, Burlingame (415) 340-9201.
Mon–Sat 10 am–6 pm, Sun noon–5 pm.
MasterCard, Visa
Parking: Street

The men's, women's, and children's apparel sold here is mostly on consignment from salespeople with out-of-season samples to unload. Sizes are limited and discounts vary. A real bonus is the Joie de Vivre clothing carried here at half price. This contemporary sportswear comes from Joy Elliot, an up-and-coming local designer. —*PL*

CHARLENE'S ON 2

San Francisco: 41 Sutter, Ste 215, SF (415) 989-0644.
Mon 11:30 am–6 pm, Tue–Fri 11 am–6 pm.
MasterCard, Visa
Parking: Take Bart or Muni

This hard-to-find second-floor consignment shop in the heart of the Financial District caters to professional women looking for sophisticated Monday through Friday clothes. Charlene's makes up for the no-frills utilitarian decor by having the lowest prices in town for tailored, high-quality go-to-work clothes. Skirts and silk blouses run $16 to $36, blazers $36 to $75, and suits $45 to $125. Charlene also has department store returns and the best selection of new fashion jewelry (designer knockoffs) at the best prices. The place is jumping at lunch-time and right after work, so take a late lunch, pick up a sandwich at one of the eateries in the lobby, and head for the second floor. —*CA*

CHILDREN'S EXCHANGE

East Bay: 2830 Pinole Valley Rd, Pinole (510) 758-1652.
Mon–Wed 10 am–5 pm, Thur–Sat 10 am–6 pm.
MasterCard, Visa

Parking: Lot on premises

Children's Exchange will not exchange your teenager for two toddlers, but they will sell you almost anything you need in the way of clothing or furnishings for the kids you are keeping if they're ten years old or under. Quality is so high and prices so low in this large, cheerful store that customers come from all over the Bay Area and beyond to outfit their youngsters. It's no wonder with bargains like the top-of-the-line Renolux car seat you'd pay at least $150 for new selling for $49.95, an English pram-style Carlton stroller for $99.95 instead of $200, Little Tike Cozy Car for $16.95 instead of $40. —*CA*

CIRCLES

Peninsula: 1113 Burlingame Ave,
Burlingame (415) 347-6162.
Mon–Sat 10 am–5:30 pm.
MasterCard, Visa
Parking: Street, city lot

Secondhand clothes on tony Burlingame Avenue? Better believe it. The upscale Circles consignment store just relocated in a former art gallery in Burlingame's high-rent district. They must have cut a deal on the rent because their prices are as good as ever, and the quality keeps getting higher. A third of the merchandise is genuine haute couture (we're talking real designer labels, not bridge lines) at a fraction of the original cost—a double-breasted black wool Yves Saint Laurent tuxedo suit was $275—originally $4000. The rest is high-quality, up-to-date fashions for ladies size 2–2X priced at a third of retail. —*CA*

COLLECTABLE DESIGNS

East Bay: 3344 Grand Ave, Oakland
(510) 444-2953.
Mon–Fri 11 am–6 pm, Sat 11 am–5 pm, Sun
11 am–4 pm.
MasterCard, Visa
Parking: Street

Loyal fans of Grand Avenue's most upscale consignment boutique have one thing in common—a passion for high fashion. The owner, a reformed shopaholic, believes resale shoppers deserve the same gracious setting and personalized service you'd expect from I. Magnin, Saks Fifth Avenue, and Neiman Marcus, where a lot of these clothes came from originally. The great strengths of this lovely shop are high-style business suits (a Kasper suit was $36 instead of $180), go-to-church outfits (we saw a $350 Anne Klein dress for $85), and an unbeatable selection of after-five dresses—a $1200 Victor Costa gown was priced at $150. —*CA*

CON MAN

East Bay: 1339 Park St, Alameda
(510) 769-7795.
Mon–Sat 10 am–6 pm, Sun noon–4 pm.
Checks accepted, no credit cards
Parking: Street, validation for pay lot on
Central

 ALPHABETICAL STORE LISTING

A Honda motorcycle in the window, the front end of a '53 Ford on the wall, and a resident Cockatiel named Odie set the stage here. Musicians and theater people go to Alameda's new men's consignment store for something unusual—a hot-pink *Miami Vice* sport coat previously owned by a well-known Bay Area jazz musician for $50, foreign army uniforms for $20 to $60, and very wide or very narrow ties for $3 to $5. Ordinary working stiffs can find classic suits—Botany 500, Majesty—in the $40 to $60 range, dress shirts—Ralph Lauren, Nordstrom and Arrow from $8–18 and casual clothes at a third the original price. We saw a $600 Aquascutum rain coat for $200—but that's probably been sold. —*CA*

DISCOVERY SHOP

**San Francisco: 1827 Union St, SF
(415) 929-8053.
Mon–Sat 11 am–6 pm.
MasterCard, Visa**

**Other Stores: 1410 Broadway, Burlingame (415) 343-9100; 10313 San Pablo Ave, El Cerrito (510) 527-1469; 746 Santa Cruz Ave, Menlo Park (415) 325-8939; 773 East Blithedale, Mill Valley (415) 389-1164; 928 Grant, Novato (415) 898-1149; 127 Forty-First St, Oakland (510) 601-0100; 1987D Santa Rita Rd, Pleasanton (510) 462-7374; 1451A Foxworthy Ave, San Jose (408) 265-5535; 266 Northgate One, San Rafael (415) 507-0157; 1538 Locust, Walnut Creek (510) 944-1991.
Parking: Street**

The Cancer Society, the I. Magnin of thrift stores, recently opened a new boutique in the former Laura Ashley store on fashionable Union Street. Louise Renne cut the ribbon, and columnist Herb Caen donated a slew of suits and sport coats from Wilkes Bashford priced from $95 to $125. Herb won't say what they cost new but we'll bet at least a grand. Well-known society women contributed designer fashions such as a Herbert Grossman suit which sells for $95, a Michael Novarese dress $50. The ongoing generosity of benefactor Doris Fisher ensures a steady supply of new merchandise from the Gap, Gap Kids, and Banana Republic. Also for kids: New shirts from Gymboree just $2 instead of $25. —*CA*

ENCORE

**North Bay: 11 Mary St, San Rafael
(415) 456-7309.
Mon–Sat 10 am–5 pm, consignments accepted Tues–Sat 10 am–3 pm.
MasterCard, Visa
Parking: Lot on premises**

The modest store is nothing to look at—but the clothes are. Not only may you chance upon a Chanel suit for a third of its original price, but you could walk away with a black Evan Picone dress for $38, a Liz Claiborne suit for $48, or a smashing strapless velvet Victor Costa evening gown for $58. Encore primarily caters to professional women, as reflected in its upscale, albeit next-to-new, apparel. Affable owner Linda Hensley accepts quality consignment pieces in good condition only, originally bought no more than two years previously. While it takes some patience to sort through packed racks, with persistence you might find that Donna Karan, Escada, Armani, or Anne Klein you never dreamed you could afford. The typical markdown here is about one-third off the original price. —*LC*

THE FASHION GALLERY

East Bay: 43513 Mission Blvd, Fremont
(510) 651-2703.
Mon–Fri 10:30 am–5 pm, Sat 10 am–5 pm.
MasterCard, Visa
Parking: Lot on premises

A preference for department-store brand-names over designers makes affordability the key note in this cozy Victorian consignment store. The owner will help you put together a career outfit—suit, blouse, pumps, and purse—with a currently fashionable look for under $80. You'd pay $350 to $400 for the same ensemble at Macy's, Emporium, or Nordstrom. We saw dresses by Axiom, Patty O'Neil, Silk Studio, and Ellen Tracy all under $36, and Liz Claiborne, Jaeger, Saville, and Harve Benard suits at $40 or less. You'll also find lingerie, party dresses, and sportswear sized 2–22 selling for a third to a fourth of the original retail price. —*CA*

GOOD BYES

San Francisco: 3464 Sacramento St, SF
(415) 346-6388.
Mon–Sat 10 am–6 pm, Thur 10 am–8 pm,
Sun 11 am–5 pm.
MasterCard, Visa
Parking: Street

Decorated with antiques, props, and pine, this comfortably appointed consignment store caters to men who prefer the updated classic look—in between stuffy conservative and high-style Italian. Giorgio Armani suits priced at $175 to $300 originally cost from $900 to $1600, Polo dress shirts now $18 once fell in the $62 to $100 range. If you can forgo the fancy labels you can walk out with a shirt, tie, and quality suit for $150. Friendly service and long shopping hours make this store a favorite. —*CA*

HEATHER'S BOUTIQUE

San Francisco: 2249 Clement St, SF
(415) 751-5511.
Tues-Sat 11 am–5 pm.
MasterCard, Visa
Parking: Street

Five racks are devoted exclusively to designers—Adolfo, Givenchy, Valentino and such—and the rest feature better quality labels from stores like I. Magnin and Nordstrom. The fanatically loyal following of career women who rely on Heather's for their business wardrobe and evening clothes know a sound investment when they see one. We saw a $2400 Chanel suit for $356, a $1300 Burberrys suit for $220, and an exquisite Jacqueline de Ribes evening dress, originally

ALPHABETICAL STORE LISTING

$3000, worth money in the bank at $550. Prices start at a third to half the original cost and are reduced by 50 percent after approximately three months. —*CA*

THE HOSPICE SHOPPE

East Bay: 1550 Olympic Blvd, Walnut Creek
(510) 947-1064.
Mon–Sat 10 am–4 pm.
MasterCard, Visa
Parking: Lot on premises

This nonprofit thrift shoppe gives new meaning to the term upscale. About eighty volunteers screen the donations for top-of-the-line items. Rejects go to the Salvation Army, keepers include high-class antiques like a hand-painted Nippon lidded cream pitcher $35 and an antique English walnut desk $800. Clothing is steamed before it's put out on the floor so items like the woman's $25 winter white Villager ensemble and the man's $35 Christian Dior suit we saw on our last visit looked as good as they did when they

were selling new for well over $200. —*CA*

THE KID'S CLOTHESLINE

South Bay: 10191 S. De Anza, Cupertino
(408) 865-0292.
Mon–Sat 10 am–6 pm.
Discover, MasterCard, Visa
Parking: Lot on premises

Not only is Kid's Clothesline the Bay Area's best-looking children's resale store, complete with mauve carpet, rainbow graphics, two bathrooms, and a changing table, but it also boasts an on-site laundry where everything is rewashed, disinfected, mended, and ironed before you see it.

The owners are equally fastidious about quality and good value. The only way to tell these things are secondhand is by the price. OshKosh overalls are never more than $4.99. Little London Fog coats priced originally from $20 to $45 go for $7 to $23. Double Graco strollers start at $149 new; we saw a beauty for $78. Sizes start with newborn and

go up to those hard-to-find 14s. —CA

LUNDBERG HABERDASHERY

East Bay: 396 Colusa, Kensington
(510) 524-3003.
Wed–Sat noon–4 pm.
Checks accepted, no credit cards
Parking: Street

Ralph Lauren (who has been known to knock off a style or have a fabric reproduced in Italy for his Polo collection) and a lot of guys who just like to be snappy dressers have discovered Jon Lundberg's Haberdashery, located off the beaten track in the tiny residential community of Kensington. This gorgeous store, the only one in the world devoted exclusively to men's vintage wear, carries top-quality garments in perfect condition from the 1850's to the 1950's. On any given day you'll be able to choose from five hundred vintage ties, a hundred pairs of vintage shoes, sweaters, suits, sport coats, tuxedos and dressing robes. One recent visit turned up a double-breasted Macintosh of Hollywood suit just like Duke Ellington used to wear for $450, and an Oxford gray velvet collared top coat custom made in 1906 for $225. You'd pay $1200 to $1500 for a comparable garment today if quality like this were available—which it isn't. A forties classic Harris tweed sport coat was going for $55, and a never-worn fifties mackinaw with the contemporary Seattle look was priced at $50. —CA

MARINO'S SECOND TIME AROUND

East Bay: 17279 Hesperian Blvd, San Lorenzo (510) 276-8705.
Mon–Sat 10 am–5 pm.
MasterCard, Visa
Parking: Lot on premises

Pat Marino's boutique is so clean, organized, and cheerful you won't believe it's resale— and the prices are so ridiculously low you won't believe they're for real. You can find

almost everything a baby needs in the way of clothes for less than a dollar—sleepers 99 cents, undershirts 79 cents, rubber pants 39 cents, socks 39 cents, and so on. Moms-to-be check out the back room for equally fantastic prices on fresh, stylish maternity clothes. They have two-piece outfits to wear to the office from $8.99 to $18.99. A glamorous brocade Dan Howard evening dress was going for $34—the original price was $120. —CA

OUTGROWN

North Bay: 1714 Fourth St, San Rafael (415) 457-2219.
Mon–Sat 10 am–4 pm.
MasterCard, Visa
Parking: Lot on premises

Just about anything kiddy related is available at this seventeen-year-old consignment shop whose selection of merchandise is daunting. Owner Sydne Robinson brings in heaps of fresh arrivals daily. Whether it's maternity

clothing, baby furniture, toys, or children's sizes 0-preteen clothing, if you don't find what you need the first visit, try again; you probably will the second. For example, we uncovered an unblemished Gerry Pack for $25, a stylish boy's letter jacket for $6, kids' bikes for $25, a toddler's blue ski suit for $20, and a killer cow-patterned stroller for $28. Esprit, Mousefeathers, Petit Bateaux, Gap Kids, and many new OshKosh overalls ($6–$12) are abundant. —LC

PLAY IT AGAIN: A CHILDREN'S RESALE BOUTIQUE

North Bay: 967 Grand Ave (one block north of Montecito Center), San Rafael (415) 485-0304.
Mon–Sat 10 am–5 pm.
Checks accepted, no credit cards
Parking: Lot on premises

There must be plenty of partying among Marin's younger set, because fancy dresses abound at this cream-of-the-crop San Rafael

 ALPHABETICAL STORE LISTING

consignment store co-owned by Sally Korhauser and Stephanie Shekar. Modestly tucked in between a video rental shop and a nail salon, Play It Again is a tidy, small store with well-organized, clean apparel. Items look new or slightly worn, but never worn out. Because of the store's diminutive size, you're not compelled to sort through endless racks of used goods. Gunne Sax, Laura Ashley, Sweet Potatoes, Mousefeathers, YSL, and Petite Gamine are regularly available in sizes 0 to preteen, and priced between $8 and $30. Boys' formal wear is also available (we found a Ralph Lauren suit for $35), along with infant clothing, furniture, shoes, casual attire, and skiwear. —LC

SAX

North Bay: 629 San Anselmo Ave, San Anselmo (415) 456-7655.
Mon–Sat 10 am–6 pm, Sun 11 am–5 pm.
American Express, MasterCard, Visa
Parking: Street

If you're over forty or go for the tailored dress-for-success look, forget Sax. This tiny up-tempo consignment shop features jazzy, sporty clothes for the young and hip, sizes 4–14. Nonstop music and popular labels make budget-conscious trendsetters feel right at home. You'll find all your favorites from Gap to Adrienne Vittadini priced at a third off retail plus new hats, socks, tights, leggings, and tees to complete any outfit. One visit turned up a red suede Maxima suit for $150, a two-piece outfit from the Limited at $35, a Carol Horn silk vest at $16, and a Sue Wong pant suit originally $225 for $85. —CA

THE SECOND ACT

South Bay: 12882 S Saratoga-Sunnyvale Rd, Saratoga (408) 741-4995.
Mon–Sat 10:30 am–5 pm, Sun 1 pm–5 pm.
MasterCard, Visa
Parking: Lot on premises

With almost five thousand square feet devoted to high-quality resale here, a woman can outfit herself from head to toe for work, play, and the most formal occasion. Hats, shoes, dresses, suits, separates—this beautiful consignment store has it all with a fine selection of furniture and antiques thrown in. Prices start at a third of new with the best buys in high-end designer garments. A two-piece silk Gibson Palermo outfit that originally sold for $3000 was $450. For casual dress you could walk away with a pair of DKNY jeans for $25 instead of $125, or a Carole Little silk blouse for $16.60 instead of $60. —CA

SECOND IMPRESSIONS OF DANVILLE

East Bay: 411 Hartz Ave, Danville (510) 838-1040.
Tues–Sat 10 am–5 pm, Sun 11 am–4 pm.
MasterCard, Visa
Parking: Street

The historic landmark building may be vintage but the fashions are up-to-date in this tiny consignment shop in the Danville Hotel.

Severe space limitations necessitate a small but select inventory of designer garments selling for a third of the original retail price. Cocktail wear is your best bet with labels such as Victor Costa, Donna Karan, A.J. Bari, and Carlisle. Full racks yielded a $900 Louis Feraud dress for $240, a $300 Nina Ricci cocktail suit for $68.50, and a $379 Anne Klein dress for $159. Look for never-been-worn finds on consignment from out-of-business boutiques and once-worn wedding gowns such as a gorgeous beaded Demetrios originally $2600 for $800. —CA

THE SHOP

East Bay: 408 Fourteenth St, Oakland
(510) 451-2704.
Mon–Sat 10 am–4 pm.
Cash only
Other stores: Next-to-New Shop, 2226
Fillmore St, SF (415) 567-1627; The
Discovery Shop of the Junior League of Palo
Alto, 2432 Broadway, Redwood City (415)
363-2238.
Parking: Street

Junior League members are required to donate their best discards to the Shop, which accounts for the high quality of the merchandise. Only a special god of bargain hunters could be responsible for the unbelievably low prices. Would you believe a men's tweed suit from Bullock & Jones selling for $25 or a women's Calvin Klein jacket for $9? How about a Paul Stanley gabardine suit for $10, or OshKosh overalls for $3? Women's clothing makes up the bulk of the merchandise, but you can always find great buys on togs for men and kids as well as first-rate housewares, linens, knickknacks, and costume jewelry. The annual Christmas toy sale held the first Saturday in December has shoppers lined up around the block waiting to get at the bargains. An added bonus: Your shopping dollars help the leaguers support children at risk. —CA

SOMETHING OLD– SOMETHING NEW

East Bay: 442 Hartz Ave, Danville
(510) 838-4492.
Mon 10 am–6 pm, Tues–Sat 10 am–5 pm.
American Express, MasterCard, Visa ($50
minimum purchase)
Parking: Street

Some women spend a fortune on their clothes. Others just look that way. The latter, according to owner Sandra Jones, are the ones shopping at her spacious consignment store—three rooms full of fashions featuring everything for today's woman in sizes 2–22, from casual to career, North Beach Leather to Liz. Business executives know they've found a deal when they see a rack of $600, Jaeger suits selling for $185. The ladies who lunch can pick up a St. John knit for $135 that originally sold for $600 and the mother of the bride and the teen prom queen will find the perfect evening dresses. —CA

 ALPHABETICAL STORE LISTING

SOPHISTICATED LADY

East Bay: 4020 Piedmont Ave, Oakland
(510) 654-1718.
Mon–Sat 10 am–6 pm.
MasterCard, Visa
Parking: Street

The Nordstrom of consignment stores, Sophisticated Lady knows how to pamper customers—three-way mirrors and chairs in the dressing rooms, and a silky kimono to put on so you can go back to the selling floor without getting dressed. More than fifteen hundred consignors ensure a large cross-section of sizes, prices, and styles covering every occasion from work to play to wedding day. A beaded Bob Mackie gown $500 (originally $1500) could take you to the Academy Awards, the $600 Armani suit would be perfect for work or lunch (originally $1700), or you could stay home in a $15 Liz Claiborne sweater and $22 Evan Picone pants. —*CA*

TIMELESS

Peninsula: 532 Bryant St, Palo Alto
(415) 473-0201.
Mon–Sat 10:30 am–5:30 pm.
MasterCard, Visa
Parking: Street

Teenagers come for the used jeans and Gap shirts, and business women shop lunch hours for the suits, blazers, and blouses. This darling little consignment boutique is full of gently worn career and sports clothes sizes 2 petite to 14 with a great selection of sweaters—a lot of them cashmere—and vintage jackets for the gals who don't like to see themselves coming and going. An Anne Klein II cashmere and wool jacket sells for $79—at least $200 new—and an Ann Taylor suit at $49 (originally $195) are typical of the good buys. —*CA*

WORN OUT WEST

San Francisco: 582 Castro St, SF
(415) 431-6020.
Mon, Tues, Sat 11 am–6 pm, Wed–Fri 11 am–7 pm, Sun 11 am–5:30 pm.
MasterCard, Visa
Parking: Street

Who says bargain hunting has to be grim? Try shopping as theater in a magnificent restored Victorian where you can indulge your taste for fashion or fantasy. The first floor, sporting a trendy southwestern decor, features used Western wear, flannel shirts, jeans, suits, sport coats, dress shirts, and new overruns from major department stores. Pick up a pair of $150 Tony Lama cowboy boots for $55 or a $800 Ralph Lauren suit for $150. Used Levi's and Wranglers jeans go from $7 to $18. Upstairs, the decor is high-tech chrome and the merchandise geared to the "eccentric individual" who fancies leathers, uniforms, and "dress up" garments. —*CA*

ALPHABETICAL STORE LISTING

WORTH REPEATING

North Bay: 237 Shoreline Hwy, Mill Valley
(415) 389-1315.
Tues–Sat 10:30 am–5 pm, Thur 10:30
am–6 pm.
MasterCard, Visa
Parking: Lot on premises

Hankering for that inimitable lift you get from something new? Take note: You can get the same lift at a third the price from a previously enjoyed garment. It takes a little bit more work to find the perfect piece, but sport shoppers will enjoy the hunt at this bright, handsome consignment shop stocking everything from casual wear to black-tie ball gowns. Could a $500 Missoni dress at $98 perk you up? How about a black label Giorgio Armani originally $600 now $65, or a $600 Zoran silk skirt for $125? Max Mara, Albert Nipon, Diane Fres, St John, Victor Costa—look for your favorites or put your name on the wish list to be notified when they come in. Ongoing 50 percent off sales. —CA

SHOES

Who doesn't need another pair of shoes? They're the ultimate wardrobe pick-me-up. Don't be discouraged by soaring prices, though, since we've scoured the Bay Area for bargains on shoes and boots—as well as athletic shoes for every kind of sport—for men, women, and children. We looked for high quality at rock-bottom prices and discovered stores that offer major discounts on brand-names such as Pappagallo, Capezio, Paloma, Bass, Bally, LA Gear, and more—sometimes because they get inventory direct from the factory, more often because they carry overruns, closeouts, or have end-of-season sales that can bring prices down up to 70 percent off retail.

A STEP FORWARD (JOAN AND DAVID OUTLET)

East Bay: 2010 Mountain Blvd, Oakland
(510) 339-0500.

Mon–Sat 10 am–6 pm, Sun noon–5 pm.
MasterCard, Visa
Other stores: 3319 Lakeshore Ave, Oakland
(510) 835-4300.
Parking: Lot on premises

There are plenty of reasons to fall head-over-heels in love with this so-called outlet. For starters, the ambience is fiercely anti-discount; the handsome decor is in keeping with the elegant Joan and David footwear. For shoe lovers who never scrimp on quality, these shoes and boots are well-made classics. The discounts are remarkable given the high caliber of the footwear. Finally, if this outlet doesn't have the shoes you want, the salespeople will call the other store to try to find them. Merchandise is discounted systematically, rather than arbitrarily. For example: When a $200 pair of shoes first arrives, it's automatically marked at $109. After a period of time, the shoes will be discounted another 20 percent, to $87, then 30 percent to $76, then 40 percent at $65. Keep your eye out for seasonal closeout sales in January and July, when all footwear is marked 40 percent off

 ALPHABETICAL STORE LISTING

already marked-down merchandise. Most of the pumps, flats, and boots that arrive from the Joan and David boutiques are overruns and past season. Because Joan and David's look is so sophisticated and classic, the footwear remains in fashion. There's also a wide selection of discounted handsome leather satchels, backpacks, briefcases, and larger handbags—Italian-styled but American-made to keep the prices low. —*LC*

ATHLETE'S FOOT OUTLET

North Bay: Vintage Oaks, 132 Vintage Way, Novato (415) 892-7769.
Mon–Sat 10 am–9 pm, Sun 11 am–5 pm.
Major credit cards
Other stores: Marina Square, 1237 Marina Blvd, San Leandro (510) 895-9738.
Parking: Lot on premises

If you're disappointed by the high prices of athletic shoes, you'll be thrilled with the Athlete's Foot Outlet, which offers good prices and a huge selection of athletic shoes by the biggest names in the business. Unlike many outlets, the Athlete's Foot Outlet carries the most current models and discounts them a standard 10 percent off retail.

Overruns, discontinued stock, and closouts, more typical outlet items, are reduced 35 to 40 percent or more. You'll see shoes for basketball, running, tennis, aerobics, hiking, walking, racquetball, and cross training by manufacturers such as Nike, Avia, Asics, Reebok, Converse, Saucony, New Balance, and others. The outlet has shoes for the whole family, including a large size selection for infants, children, and youths. Women's sizes range from 5 to 10 and men's from 6½ to 14. If you can't find your size on the self-serve shelves, ask a salesperson to check the stockroom. The outlet also carries workout wear, including shorts, sweats, T-shirts, and jogging suits discounted 10 to 50 percent off retail. On a recent visit, we saw a well-built pair of Saucony women's running shoes marked down from $70 to $40, and men's Nike Ultra Trainers marked down from $90 to $70. Another plus: The outlet is conveniently located right off Highway 101. —*SB*

BROWN BROTHERS SHOES
ALAMEDA SHOE WAREHOUSE

East Bay: 848 Lincoln Ave, Alameda
(510) 865-3701.
Mon–Sat 9:30 am–6 pm.
Checks accepted, no credit cards
Parking: Street

This third-generation, family-run business has been selling shoes to the well-shod man since 1881. This has a real neighborhood feel: small, straightforward, and refreshingly nonfranchised. The personnel is personable; the Brown brothers, Greg and Brian, and their dad, Jim, wait on you hand, and yes, foot. The store sells Nike, Reebok, Sperry Top-Sider, Rockport, Florsheim, Nunn Bush, Dexter, Stacy Adams, Lake of the Woods, Wolverine, H.H. Browns, and ASICS at 20 to 30 percent off suggested retail prices. Athletic, casual, and dressy shoes are all first quality and in style. The Browns are able to maintain such consistently good discounts because of their low overhead; they not only run the business, they own the building. —LC

BURLINGTON COAT FACTORY

**San Francisco: 899 Howard St, SF
(415) 896-6721.**
Mon–Sat 9:30 am–8 pm, Sun 11 am–6 pm.
Major credit cards
**Other stores: Westgate Mall, 1600
Saratoga Ave, San Jose (408) 378-2628;
1000 La Playa, Hayward (510) 782-7073.**
Parking: Street

Yes, they have shoes, too! This sprawling bargain emporium carries footwear for the entire family, all discounted 20 to 70 percent off suggested retail. The shoes sell for less than at most other department stores because Burlington receives its inventory directly from the manufacturers. There's always a sale in progress, and merchandise often goes through two markdowns. When we visited, Dressports—listed at a suggested retail price of $125—were 20 percent off the sale price of $86. Ralph Lauren tennis shoes were discounted 30 percent off the sale price of $30. Here you're better off finding a pair of dependable work or play shoes than anything high style or flashy. Selection ranges from casual sandals, docksiders, and athletic shoes, to dressy boots and work shoes. Men will find a generous selection of reliable brand-names such as Adolfo, Nunn Bush, Bally, and Rockports, as well Eagle Mountain hiking boots. For women there are Evan Picone, Pappagallo, Liz Claiborne, Dressports, Capezio, and Bandalino. Kids' Sesame Street tennis shoes go for about $11, and children's OshKosh, Keds, Pappagallo, Reebok, and Nikes are also well-stocked. What you see is what you get; all available merchandise is displayed. No cash refunds. —LC

CARLIN'S SHOE RACK

**East Bay: 561 Contra Costa Blvd, Pleasant
Hill (510) 680-8121.**
Mon–Sat 10 am–6 pm, Sun noon–5 pm.
Discover, MasterCard, Visa
**Other stores: Carlin's Shoe World, 880 El
Portal, San Pablo (510) 236-8121.**
Parking: Lot on premises

Formerly the Shoe Factory Outlet, Carlin's specializes in Jumping Jacks shoes for children as well as women's hard-to-find wide and narrow sizes. There is a fair sampling of comfortable, casual shoes at this smallish location. Children's merchandise includes all the major names, going from size 0 on up. In addition to Jumping Jacks, there's Buster Brown, Sam & Libby, Nike, Soft Spots, Capezio, and LA Gear, as well as high-trend shoes with, for example, a toddler-pleasing Aladdin design. Women's shoes include sandals, low and high heels, boots, and athletic footwear by Penaljo, Rockport, Easy Spirit, Cobbie, Clarks, and Stride Rites. Carlin's

 ALPHABETICAL STORE LISTING

mall-based stores have slightly higher prices, but at this location the overhead is low and so are prices. A pair of Nike athletic shoes selling for $80 retail could be as little as $59. Special sales go on year-round, such as a "two pair" sale—buy one pair at full price and the second pair is half off.　*LC*

CAROLE'S SHOE WAREHOUSE

San Francisco: 665 Third St, SF
(415) 543-5151.
Mon–Sat 10 am–5:30 pm, Sun noon–5 pm.
Major credit cards
Parking: Street and validated parking
across the street

Shoe buffs who've made the South-of-Market outlet scene their stomping ground know about Shoe Heaven. This year, the newly renamed Carole's Shoe Warehouse moved from its second-floor location to a ground-level storefront across the street, but fortunately it did not change ownership. Carole Raphael has been in the shoe business for twenty-five years and knows where to find high-quality designer and retailer merchandise from closeouts, overruns, and end-of-season sales. The markdowns fall anywhere between 20 and 70 percent off retail prices. With an average stock of six thousand to eight thousand pairs of shoes, Carole's has a wealth of Italian, Spanish, and American high-fashion designer names to choose from: Scafora, Christina Perez, Paloma, Anne Klein, Jose Vera, Kenneth Cole, Eastland, Cole Haan, Bass, LA Gear, and Bally. You're not paying for display here; as in the New York garment district, merchandise is separated into cardboard cartons by length and width (sizes 7 narrow, 9 wide, for example). It's not glamorous, but this system makes it easy to find your specific size and style. Their semi-annual "blowout" sales are in January and June. —*LC*

FAMOUS FOOTWEAR

South Bay: Westgate Mall, 1600 Saratoga Ave, San Jose (408) 378-5064.
Mon–Fri 10 am–9 pm, Sat 10 am–7 pm, Sun 11 am–6 pm.
Discover, MasterCard, Visa
Other stores: Roseville (916) 781-3394; Fremont (510) 796-4660; San Jose (408) 267-4433.
Parking: Lot on premises

You'll recognize many of the medium-to high-end brand-names at Famous Footwear, but the prices will be unfamiliarly low. The chain carries shoes for the whole family in current styles by manufacturers such as Naturalizer, Connie, Esprit, Sam & Libby, Liz Claiborne, Kenneth Cole, Chilis, Impo, White Mountain Dexter, Levi's, Rockport, Vans, and Florsheim and reduces them 10 to 50 percent off retail. You'll find everything from pumps and tasseled loafers to moccasins and hiking boots. There's a good variety of athletic shoes by Reebok, Asics, Nike, Etonic, and others. Sizes include 0 to 6 for kids, 5 to 12 for women, and $6^{1}/_{2}$ to 14 for men, including wide widths. The store often has promotions, offering even better discounts. Choose a pair of shoes from the clearance section and buy a second clearance pair at half price. Expect self-service, assisted by a friendly, knowledgeable staff. On a recent visit, we saw a comfortable-looking pair of women's thick-soled, black loafers by Perry Ellis Portfolio marked down from $65 to $40. —SB

FOOTWEAR FIRST WAREHOUSE OUTLET

East Bay: 2301 Fourth St, Berkeley (510) 848-8585.
Wed–Sun 11 am–6 pm.
MasterCard, Visa
Parking: Street

For Footwear First fans, shopping in this unglamorous, concrete-and-fluorescent-bulb warehouse in Berkeley's outlet district can be a disappointment. While markdowns on closeout items average between 30 and 70 percent off, the pickings can be disappointingly slim. You might chance upon a rare pair of upscale designer shoes in your size—marked down drastically—but Footwear First's usual selection of interesting designer footwear isn't represented at the outlet. However, the real prize here is cowboy boots, with an impressive selection of Texas-made Nocona boots, for real or wannabe cowpokes. The Noconas are seconds and come in an inventive myriad of designs and skins: ostrich, calf, bull-hide, and lizard. They're still an investment, but the reduction is substantial. A pair of $345 boots will typically sell here for $219. The rest of the stock—women's designer shoes and boots—are a mixed bag of past season, overruns, irregulars, and some creative knockoffs of more expensive designer names. The look here will appeal to the fad- and fashion-conscious younger shopper. There are more platforms than not, and some stunning, knee-high suede boots. For the more practical minded, there's a fair sampling of stylish sandals. Be forewarned: This outlet is closed Mondays and Tuesdays, and all sales are final. —LC

MARK'S SHOES

East Bay: 805 Marina Village Pkwy, Alameda (510) 769-9240.
Mon–Fri 10:30 am–7 pm, Sat 10 am–6:30 pm, Sun 10 am–5:30 pm.
Major credit cards
Other stores: See telephone directory for nearest store.
Parking: Lot on premises

Discounted men's and women's footwear comes here from the other nine Mark's stores in the Bay Area. Along with the reduction bestowed on all shoes and boots sent here, there's always a sale—a discount on top of a discount. Some sales are particularly impressive, such as the "$19.90" sale. Finding your selection in your size and color can be a hit-or-miss proposition. But this is still prime snooping ground for the stalwart footwear gumshoe, with reductions falling between 30 and 70 percent on Bally, Ferragamo, Bostonian, Jasmin, LA Gear, Joan and David, and Sam & Libby. Much of the mer-

 ALPHABETICAL STORE LISTING

chandise is past season but tends not to look particularly dated as the company leans tend toward a more casual, classic look. For kids, the small selection is limited to athletic shoes by Nike and Reebok. —LC

NORDSTROM RACK

Peninsula: 280 Metro Center, 81 Colma Blvd, Colma (415) 755-1444.
Mon–Sat 10 am–9 pm, Sun 11 am–6 pm.
American Express, MasterCard, Nordstrom, Visa
Other stores: 1285 Marina Blvd, San Leandro (510) 614-1742.
Parking: Lot on premises

Nordstrom is a Washington state–based clothing retailer known for its outstanding shoe department. Nordstrom Rack, which sells the retail store's overruns and past-season leftovers at great savings, is no exception. In fact, once you've seen Nordstrom Rack's incredible shoe selection and prices, it'll be difficult to buy shoes anywhere else. Plenty of tall racks are piled high with shoes in every style and color, often discounted 50 percent or more from Nordstrom's original retail prices. You'll find women's casual and dress shoes from top-quality manufacturers such as Ferragamo, Stuart Weitzman, Bally, Vittorio Ricci, as well as popular styles by Guess, Sam & Libby, Nine West, Esprit, Nickels, Via Spiga, Aerosole, Jasmin, and more. Women's sizes range from 5½ to 12. The selection is equally large for men (sizes 6 through 15), including merchandise from Cole-Haan, Johnston & Murphy, Timberland, Kenneth Cole, Rockport, Nunn Bush, and Ferragamo. The store also carries athletic shoes for adults and a good selection of children's shoes (sizes 2 to 12½). Among the thousands of shoes on display, you'll find a few brightly colored summer shoes and some pairs that have seen better days, but you'll also locate true gems. On a recent visit, we almost purchased a regal pair of two-toned, purple and black suede Ferragamo pumps that were marked down from $235 to $110, a savings of more than 50 percent. We were also tempted to buy a pair of brown Ferragamo tasseled men's loafers marked down from $335 to $130. A definite plus: If you have second thoughts about a purchase, Nordstrom Rack accepts returns within thirty days, but you must bring in your receipt with the merchandise to receive full credit. —SB

PAYLESS SHOESOURCE

North Bay: Marin Square, 75 Bellam Blvd, San Rafael (415) 453-8942.
Mon–Sat 9 am–9 pm, Sun 11 am–6 pm.
Major credit cards
Other stores: Check telephone directory for nearest store.
Parking: Lot on premises

Shoe aficionados who love a good bargain have been buying shoes at Payless for years. What the Payless ShoeSource chain lacks in atmosphere, it makes up in its abundance of low-priced knockoffs of current styles and traditional shoes for the whole family. The

ALPHABETICAL STORE LISTING

store carries racks of synthetic and leather shoes in styles such as clogs, pumps, sandals, mules, loafers, boots, thick-soled shoes, work boots, and athletic shoes. Most of the merchandise is priced under $15, but don't expect high quality at these prices. Promotions, such as half-price sales on all leather shoes or "buy two for the price of one," are typical. On any given day, you'll see kids gleefully pulling on athletic shoes that display well-known Disney cartoon characters as their moms try on stylish pumps. Recently, we saw a pair of attractive black nubuck sandals with wedge heels priced at $13. Keds-style white canvas shoes normally $5.99 a pair were on special at $10 for two pairs. At that price, we were tempted to buy four. —SB

SHOE DEPOT

Peninsula: 280 Metro Center, 43 Colma Blvd, Colma (415) 755-0556.
Mon–Fri 9:30 am–9 pm, Sat 9:30 am–7 pm,
Sun 10 am–6 pm.
Discover, MasterCard, Visa
Parking: Lot on premises

Shoe Depot is a large shoe store that specializes in men's work boots, but it also has a good selection of top-quality casual, dress, and athletic shoes. Stock includes work boots from Wolverine, Georgia, and Gorilla; casuals from Dexter, Rockport, and Sperry; and dress shoes from manufacturers such as Stacy Adams, Nunn Bush, and Florsheim. Most of the merchandise is priced 15 to 20 percent off retail. The store holds frequent promotions where you'll find sale items discounted 20 to 50 percent, which can add up to big savings on expensive styles. Sizes range from 6 to 14, with wide widths available. An interesting note: Many women also buy work boots here. On a recent visit, we saw a pair of Wolverine insulated work boots marked down to $130 from $150 that would appeal to any man or woman who works in cold temperatures or loves the rough look of outdoor gear. —SB

THE SHOE LOFT

San Francisco: 225 Front St, second floor, SF, (415) 956-4648.
Mon–Fri 10 am–6 pm, Sat 11 am–5 pm.
American Express, MasterCard, Visa
Other stores: Shoe Palace, 123 Second Street, SF (415) 777-3140.
Parking: Street

Financial District businesswomen, other locals, and tourists have discovered this unassuming, second-floor shoe haven. Despite the tight quarters, the store's packed heel-to-toe with an appealing hodgepodge of women's styles, sizes, and colors. The Shoe Loft's designer roster is impressive: Ferragamo, Nine West, Ellen Tracy, Vittorio Ricci, Telina, Sasha, Esprit, DKNY, Kenneth Cole, and even Charles Jourdan. Some stock is in season, some past, but all gets discounted anywhere between 30 and 80 percent off. If it's your lucky day, you might chance upon a dream pair in just your size. We landed some stunning forest-green Charles Jourdan

ALPHABETICAL STORE LISTING

pumps for $60, 50 percent less the suggested retail price. A pair of Chanel ballet slippers were a steal at $90, more than a third off the original $150 price tag. Anne Klein pumps, originally marked at $138, were $65.

While the store specializes in conservative, businesslike sensible flats and handsome pumps, there's also a fairly good selection of sexy, low-cut cowboy boots and slinky pumps for after-work and weekend wear. The stock turns over frequently, with weekly shipments of fresh goods from overstocks, closeout sales, and floor samples. You might not find something to your liking on the first try, but the Shoe Loft bears repeated visits. —LC

SHOE PALACE

San Francisco: 123 Second St, SF (415) 777-3140.
Mon–Fri 10 am–6 pm, Sat 11 am–5 pm.
American Express, MasterCard, Visa
Other stores: The Shoe Loft, 225 Front St,
second floor, SF (415) 956-4648.
Parking: Street

Shoe Loft owner Raffi Soghomonian stocks for a younger, hipper customer at his sister store. The Palace has a more daring, fashionable look, including discounted Dr. Martens oxfords selling for as low as $80, Timberland boots for $114 (normally $130), and Rockports (normally $90) at $50. Unlike the Shoe Loft, the Shoe Palace doesn't bill itself as a discount store per se. Still, there are some reasonable deals to be had on additional names such as Dexter, Zodiac, Kenneth Cole, Jazz, and Nine West. Bass shoes sell here for around $10 to $15 less than in department stores. It can be a crap shoot to get your desired style and color. But if you don't see what you want on display, be sure to ask—it just might be in stock. For more dramatic markdowns, search through the racks in the back of the store to find resoled floor models as well as slightly damaged and past season stock. —LC

SHOE PAVILION

North Bay: 323 Corte Madera Town Center, Corte Madera (415) 924-9011.
Mon–Fri 10 am–8 pm, Sat 10 am–6 pm, Sun 11 am–6 pm.
Major credit cards
Other stores: 65 Westlake Shopping Center, Daly City (415) 994-9802; Emeryville Plaza Center, 5753 Christie Ave, Emeryville (510) 601-7719; Pacific West Outlet Center, 8155 Arroyo Circle, Gilroy (408) 842-3959; 631 Broadway, Millbrae (415) 697-8139; 340 Sansome St, San Francisco (415) 397-8024; 899 Howard St, San Francisco (415) 974-1821; Lakeshore Plaza, 1543 Sloat Blvd, San Francisco (415) 753-2769; San Ramon Crow Canyon Commons, 3151 East Crow Canyon Plaza, San Ramon (510) 866-1772; Loehmann's Plaza, 1649 Hollenbeck Rd, Sunnyvale (408) 739-9325; Sunrise Plaza, 638 Blossom Hill Rd, San Jose (408) 972-4580; Vacaville Commons 2031-A Harbison Dr, Vacaville (707) 446-8717.

Parking: Lot on premises

The quantity of shoes in this large store may take your breath away, but the prices will certainly leave you speechless. Shoe Pavilion offers an excellent selection of moderate- to top-quality shoes at 30 to 80 percent off retail. The Shoe Pavilion chain buys new styles (usually overruns) factory-direct, which translates to great prices on casual and dress shoes by manufacturers such as Bally, Joan and David, Van Eli, Amalfi, Naturalizer, Bandolino, Aerosole, Jasmin, Chilis, Unisa, and more in women's sizes 4½ to 12 (extra-narrow and extra-wide widths are available). The impressive men's selection includes Clarks, French Shriner, Johnston & Murphy, Bass, Florsheim, Dexter, and Bally in sizes ranging from 6 to 12, with many wide widths.

The store also carries some athletic shoes. Displays feature the latest arrivals, but don't stop there. The store has literally thousands of shoes in a multitude of styles. If you can't find your size in a particular style on the self-serve racks, one of the knowledgeable sales-people can probably locate it in the stock-room. On a recent visit, we couldn't decide what we liked better: short black Joan and David boots marked down from $366 to an astounding $60, or the brown mock-croco-dile Bandolino sandals that reminded us of romantic walks on summer nights, marked down from $70 to $40. We also thought about buying a male friend a pair of brown leather French Shriner slip-ons marked down from $100 to $30.

True bargain hunters should visit Shoe Pavilion's Clearance Center in Millbrae, where all shoes (mostly past-season styles) sell for $18 and less. —*SB*

SHOE TOWN

Peninsula: 33 Westlake Mall, Daly City (415) 756-4151.
Mon–Fri 10 am–9 pm, Sat 10 am–6 pm, Sun 11:30 am–5:30 pm.
Major credit cards
Other stores: 700 El Camino, Menlo Park (415) 324-1948; 5104 Broadway, Oakland (510) 654-9964; 2915 San Ramon Valley Blvd, San Ramon (510) 838-3104.
Parking: Lot on premises

Once you walk into Shoe Town, you'll find it hard to leave. A national chain with more than two hundred stores, Shoe Town offers current-season shoes by some of the best names in the business at a savings of 20 to 45 percent off retail. The racks and racks of shoes may seem daunting, but they're necessary; the store likes to keep its selection current, and new merchandise comes in every ten days. Casual, dress, and athletic shoes are all here and arranged according to style and color, so it's easy to search for something specific. You'll recognize brands of women's shoes such as Talbots, Via Spiga, Unisa, Van Eli, Bandolino, Harve Benard, and Aerosole in sizes 4½ to 12 (wide widths available). Men can choose from Nunn Bush, Street Cars, Stacy Adams, Cedar Creek, Bostonian, and others in sizes 7 to 13. Some stores do carry children's shoes, making this a one-stop shop for the entire family (the Daly City

ALPHABETICAL STORE LISTING

Shoe Town plans to introduce children's shoes in 1994). The store also carries a nice selection of hosiery and handbags. Look in the clearance section for great buys on shoes from the past season. On a recent visit, we saw an elegant pair of women's black Unisa flats marked down from $54 to $40 as well as a pair of stylish Harve Benard brown suede wedge-soled sandals for $15, down from an original price of $55. Every three months, the store advertises sales in which shoppers can buy one pair of shoes and buy a second pair at half price. Bargain hunters may especially want to visit the San Ramon Center where shoes are typically priced at $11. Another plus—Shoe Town's frequent shopper club offers shoppers a $24 gift certificate when they buy $200 worth of merchandise. —*SB*

THE SHOE WORKS

Peninsula: 280 Metro Center, 51 Colma Blvd, Colma (415) 756-3413.

Mon–Fri 10 am–9 pm, Sat 9:30 am–8 pm, Sun 11 am–6 pm.
Major credit cards
Other stores: Berkeley (510) 845-9329; Los Gatos (408) 358-2161; Milpitas (408) 942-4808.
Parking: Lot on premises

The Shoe Works offers the latest styles at great prices. The store carries brands such as Candies, Jasmin, Mia, Keds, and LA Gear, as well as its own lines of quality reproductions of popular styles in leather and synthetic materials. When we visited, boots were priced from $20 to $78, and some of the athletic shoes ranged from $20 to $60, but all other shoes went for less than $20. The store often has promotions, and we saw many shoes priced between $5 and $13. There are plenty of trendy styles for teens and those young at heart, and women who prefer more traditional shoes won't be disappointed with the selection of flats and pumps in sizes 5 to 11 (some wide widths available). —*SB*

WHOLE EARTH ACCESS

East Bay: 2990 Seventh St (at Ashby), Berkeley (510) 845-3000.
Sat–Wed 10 am–6 pm, Thur–Fri 10 am–8 pm, Sun 10 am–6 pm.
Discover, MasterCard, Visa
Other stores: Willows Shopping Center, Concord (510) 686-2270; 3530 Stevens Creek Blvd, San Jose (408) 554-1500; 863 East Francisco Blvd, San Rafael (415) 459-3533; 3130 Arden Way, Sacramento (916) 489-1000; 401 Bayshore Blvd, SF (415) 285-5244.
Parking: Lot on premises

Put yourself in this politically correct, ecologically correct department store's shoes, and you'll probably be hiking, jogging, running, or sprinting in no time. Whole Earth Access leans more toward the actively functional than the flashy, with an emphasis on well-made quality brand-names such as Nike, Rockport, Reebok, Aerosole, and Avia at reasonable if not greatly reduced prices.

ALPHABETICAL STORE LISTING

You'll usually find merchandise for at least a few dollars less than in most other department stores.

For example, on our visit, Rockports for men ranged around $75 to $80, $5 to $10 less than at most other retail stores. For the rugged-minded wayfarer, there's a great selection of Timberland boots, priced at $119, down from $144.95. If you're in step with the Dr. Martens clodhopper crowd, you'll be happy to find the classic eight-eyelet boot priced at $105. (Some of the more fashionable Doc boutiques sell them for as much as $160.)

There's always a good sale taking place. Look for the specially marked sale racks, which feature a chosen brand at about 30 to 50 percent off. We found Aerosoles on sale for $25, down from $40, Esprits at $11 from $23, Nine Wests for $28 from $59, and Zodiacs at $98 from $149. Whole Earth Access also holds January and September closeout sales for fall and spring merchandise. —*LC*

INSIDER TIP:
TAILOR-MADE KNOCKOFFS

By Diane Green

The mystique of haute couture—an industry strictly controlled by the Chambre Syndicale de la Couture Parisienne in France—is available only to the 2500 couture customers worldwide who can afford to spend $8000 to $100,000 for a single garment. But the talent required for producing high-fashion clothing is not limited to the twenty-three couture houses of Paris.

If you crave the allure and glamour of Parisian fashion, consider hiring a gifted local designer who can produce a good knockoff. Starting with an idea, a photograph, or a sketch, these creative stitchers can concoct the dress of your dreams at substantial savings. To produce your garment from scratch, a designer may charge anywhere from $180 to $700, depending on the complexity of the design. Fabric and notions may range in cost from less than $100 to almost $400, depending on the garment's detailing.

Where to begin? A good place is Britex Fabrics, at 146 Geary St, SF (415) 392-2910. It is the largest fabric and notions shop on the West Coast. With fabric cramming every square inch of its four floors, the forty-two-year-old Britex is famous for its extensive inventory, from the finest double-faced silk satins and imported French laces to the simplest cotton knits. And Britex prices its stock competitively. Services

 INSIDER TIP

include a list of more than fifty dressmakers, organized geographically, and a "couture book" filled with photographs of the Paris collections.

"With custom dressmaking, you get quality fabric in a color flattering to your complexion," explains Beverly Spector, co-manager of Britex Fabrics. "You get a tailored fit and a garment that is individualistic." Spector suggests customers interview several dressmakers and look at their finished products. Ask if they know how to make their own patterns. If they do, then a photo of your desired garment will suffice. If not, Spector says, "there are wonderful *Vogue* patterns available that may not be exact duplicates of the Paris original but will be close enough."

With Spector's help, we found three experts from Britex's custom sewing and tailoring list. We brought photographs of couture garments, supplied fabrics and trim from Britex, and each one re-created what we had seen on the Paris runways.

THE DESIGNERS

Mercedes Kritsky (415/668-6532), who duplicated a pink Dior suit, says she had no difficulty with the complex garment. "I've been doing this for thirty years," she said, having acquired her skills in her native Chile. Though she sometimes does design a garment, she says she is not a designer but a dressmaker. About half of her customers bring her only a picture to copy, and Kritsky creates a pattern herself. Based in San Francisco, she specializes in suits, dresses, and coats.

Shermane B. Fouche (415/550-7349) says she has always "loved breaking things down and figuring out how they work." She specializes in reproducing high-end tailored sportswear and evening gowns, in collaboration with her clients—mostly businesswomen who want to present a professional yet feminine image. Of a Lacroix evening outfit she made, she says, "It's elegant—classic in shape." Trained in European sewing techniques and pattern making, Fouche works from her studio in San Francisco, by appointment only.

Sharifa Raouf (510/825-3947) studied fashion in Frankfurt, Germany, and is a graduate of the school of design at Diablo Valley College. Raouf has been designing for more than a decade. It was not difficult for her to copy the intricate piping of an Ungaro brocade cocktail suit. "I like to do tailoring," she says. She works out her designs with her clients after making a preliminary drawing. Then she usually makes a pattern after draping the garment in muslin. Based in Concord, Raouf specializes in wedding gowns and eveningwear.

The best testimonial for copying couture, relates Beverly Spector, came from one of her customers who attended a luncheon for a famous French designer. A makeup artist for the designer, seated next to her, leaned over to whisper, "The suit you have on is my favorite from the whole collection." The customer smiled and thanked him, knowing that her dressmaker had just finished putting the finishing touches on her copy the night before. ▪

INSIDER TIP

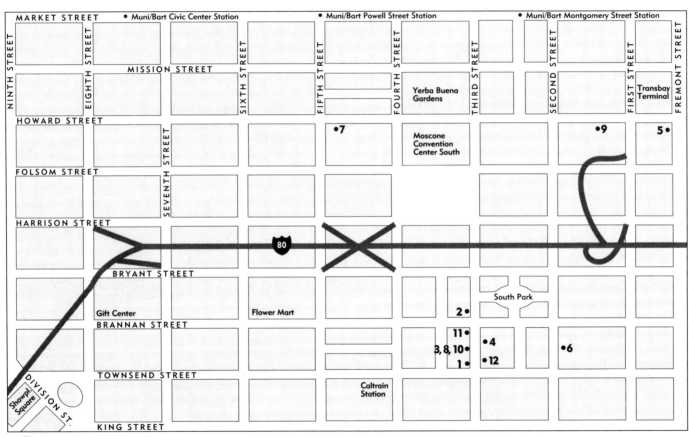

MARKET STREET   • Muni/Bart Civic Center Station   • Muni/Bart Powell Street Station   • Muni/Bart Montgomery Street Station

NINTH STREET

EIGHTH STREET

MISSION STREET

SIXTH STREET

FIFTH STREET

FOURTH STREET   Yerba Buena Gardens

THIRD STREET

SECOND STREET

FIRST STREET   Transbay Terminal

FREMONT STREET

HOWARD STREET

SEVENTH STREET

•7

Moscone Convention Center South

•9

5•

FOLSOM STREET

HARRISON STREET

80

BRYANT STREET

Gift Center

Flower Mart

South Park

2•

BRANNAN STREET

11•
3, 8, 10•
1•

•4

•12

•6

TOWNSEND STREET

Caltrain Station

DIVISION ST.

Showpl. Square

KING STREET

MAP

KEY TO SOUTH OF MARKET MAP

● **1** Cut Loose Factory
690 Third St
(415) 495 1581

● **2** Deja Vu A Paris
400 Brannan St
(415) 541-9177

● **3** Dress Market
660 Third St (Six Sixty Center)*
(415) 495-6768

● **4** Fashion Bin
615 Third St
(415) 495-2264

● **5** Fritzi Factory Outlet
218 Fremont St
(415) 979-1399

● **6** KM Wear Outlet
625 Second St
(415) 546-7331

● **7** Multiple Choices
899 Howard St
(415) 495-2628

● **8** Outerwear Co
660 Third St (Six Sixty Center)*
(415) 777-4220

● **9** Raincoat Outlet
543 Howard, second floor
(415) 362-2626

● **10** Saratoga Sport Outlet
660 Third St (Six Sixty Center)*
(415) 974-6180

● **11** Simply Cotton
610 Third St
(415) 543-2058

● **12** Spare Changes
695 Third St
(415) 896-0577

*no. 3, no. 8, and no. 10 are all
at the same address*

KEY

CHAPTER

FACTORY OUTLET CENTERS

2

FACTORY OUTLET CENTERS

The concept behind "factory-direct" malls is simple: By cutting out the middleman—the retailer—manufacturers can sell their goods directly to the consumer at significantly lower prices. What began as a venue for getting rid of inferior merchandise, however, has become a way for companies to sell overstocked items, past-season merchandise, and department-store returns.

So, though the savings you'll find are typically 20 to 70 percent off full retail prices, it's still the smart shoppers who get the deals. As outlet malls become more numerous and popular, however, there is the danger of manufacturers trying to fool consumers into believing they're getting a deal when in fact they're paying full price.

Still, factory-outlet malls mostly offer good discounts, which is why they're so hot. In fact, these centers—usually located off major highways between fifteen and sixty miles from competing retail stores—are growing twice as fast as retail malls.

---

280 METRO CENTER

Peninsula: Off Interstate 280 at the Serramonte exit, Colma (415) 388-4460.
Hours vary with stores.
Parking: Lot on premises

The 280 Metro Center is anchored by desirable discount giants such as Nordstrom Rack, Marshall's, Home Depot, and Kids 'R Us. While it may not be the most glamorous location, it's definitely central: 280 Metro Center is one of the most convenient places in the Bay Area to grab a bargain. Easily and quickly accessible from either San Francisco or the South Bay, the center is great because you don't have to go out of your way to find terrific buys on all kinds of merchandise from clothing to housewares to kids' stuff.

What you'll find: Beauty Store & More, Clothestime, Diamond Center, Discovery Zone, Fashion 'N' Save Petites, The Futon Shop, The Gap, Home Depot, Kids 'R Us, Lenscrafters, Marshall's, Men's Wearhouse, New York Fabrics, Nordstrom Rack, Ortho Mattress, Paper Image, Petco, Pier 1 Imports, Pierra Accessories, Shoe Depot, Shoe Works, Studio 5 Clothing, 39 Minute Photo, Videot's, Welcome Home, The Wherehouse.

---

660 CENTER

San Francisco: 660 Third St, SF
(415) 227-0464.
Mon–Sat 10 am–5:30 pm, Sun noon–5pm.
Parking: Lot on premises

This large, red-brick building has hosted both an MJB Coffee roasting plant and Butterfield & Butterfield, which used to hold auctions here. In its current incarnation, remnants of the building's past lives linger: Shoppers can both look for great bargains and sip coffee bought from the atrium café while strolling the 660 Center's two floors of

 ALPHABETICAL STORE LISTING

spacious outlet shops.

What you'll find: BC Jewelry, C.A.P.tive, Cotton Candy, Dress Market, Elena and Elise, Fifth Avenue, Heat, Kidswear Center, Kris Alyssa Michele, Kyda Trading, Laurel Burch, Madelle's, The Outerwear Company, Saratoga Sport Outlet, Sister Sister, Western Fragrances.

AMERICAN TIN CANNERY

South Bay: 125 Ocean View Blvd (two blocks from the Monterey Bay Aquarium), Pacific Grove (408) 372-1442. Sun–Thur 10 am–6 pm, Fri–Sat 10 am–8 pm. Parking: Two lots on premises

As you turn west toward the ocean and the Monterey Bay Aquarium in Pacific Grove, you can't miss a tall, white smokestack emblazoned with the words "American Tin Cannery." This beacon marks the bustling outlet mall, which is worth a special visit whether you're visiting nearby Carmel or the aquarium down the street. The mall occupies prime oceanfront real estate just a few blocks from the Cannery Row immortalized by John Steinbeck. Indeed, this rambling building dates back to the heyday of sardine fishing— it was originally the factory that produced the tin cans. In recent years, it has been home to many commercial ventures, but it really found its stride when the outlets started moving in. Today, the two floors of stores offer the savvy shopper bargains on brand-name clothing, household goods, and shoes. When you've exhausted those resources, you can replenish your own at several restaurants, dining either alfresco or with a view of the Bay.

What you'll find: Clothing: Anne Klein Factory Store, Bass Clothing, Cape Isle Knitters, Carole Little, Champion Hanes Activewear, Colours by Alexander Julian, Danskin Factory Outlet, Geoffrey Beene, John Henry & Friends for Men, Jonathan Martin, London Fog, Reebok Factory Direct Store, Van Heusen Direct, Westport Ltd. Outlet, Westport Woman, Woolrich.

Shoes: Banister Shoes, Bass Shoe Factory Outlet, Joan and David Designer Outlet, Reebok Factory Direct Store.

Accessories: Barbizon Lingerie; Designer Brands Accessories; L'eggs, Hanes, Bali Factory Outlet; Maidenform Outlet Stores; Sunglass World; Totes Factory Store.

For Children: Carter's Childrenswear, Danskin Factory Outlet, The Housewares Store.

China, crystal, and silver: Oneida Factory Stores, Royal Doulton.

Housewares: Home Again, The Housewares Store.

Luggage and Leather: Leather Loft Stores, MCM, Wallet Works.

Jewelry: Mr. Z Jewelers, Mrs. Z, Gemological Laboratory.

Gifts: Art Outlet, The Back Shop, Book Warehouse, Come Fly a Kite, Dynasty, Greetings 'N' More, Prestige Fragrance & Cosmetics, Ribbon Outlet, Royal House.

ALPHABETICAL STORE LISTING

FACTORY STORES AT NUT TREE

**North Bay: 321-2 Nut Tree Rd, Vacaville
(707) 447-5755.
Mon–Sat 10 am–8 pm, Sun 10 am–6 pm.
Parking: Lot on premises**

You can shop till the cows come home at this Vacaville-based discount-shopping oasis that rises above the horizon on a flat stretch of Interstate 80 between Sacramento and San Francisco. (We like to stop on the way to Tahoe.) With 130 outlets and counting, the Factory Stores at Nut Tree is an imposing shopping center, offering savings between 20 and 70 percent off retail prices. Plan ahead: Know the stores you'd like to visit, and budget at least a couple of hours. A free shuttle from eleven in the morning to six in the evening can transport you between buildings. Wheelchairs may be borrowed free of charge from the center office. When you're ready to drop, the Nut Tree Restaurant provides a nice respite.

What you will find: Aileen, American Laundry, American Tourister, Applause, Arrow Shirt, Ashworth, Barbizon Lingerie, Bass Shoes & Clothing, Benetton, Big Dog Sportswear, Black & Decker, Black Hills Gold, Bon Worth, Book Market, Book Warehouse, Boot Factory, Boston Traders, Brands Factory Outlet, Brass Factory, Brown Shoe Factory, Bugle Boy, BUM Equipment, Cape Isle Knitters, Capezio, Carter's Childrenswear, Champion Hanes, Chico's, Colours by Alexander Julian, Converse, Corning/Revere, Country Clutter, Danskin, Designer Brands Accessories, Diamonds Direct, English Country, Etienne Aigner, Evan Picone/Gant, Factory Shoe Outlet, Famous Brands Housewares Factory Outlet I and II, Famous Footwear, Farberwear, Florsheim, Full Size Fashions, Geoffrey Beene, Georgiou, Gilchrist Gallery, Greetings 'N' More, Harry and David, Home Again I and II, Houseplant Headquarters, Izod, Jockey International, Johnston & Murphy, Kids Mart, Kid's Zone, Kitchen Collection, L'accessory, Le Creuset, Leather Loft I and II, L'eggs, Hanes, Bali, Leslie Fay, Levi's, Lise J/Lise J Woman, Loly's, London Fog Sportswear, Lucia, Maidenform, Marika, Mitchell's Candles, Mikasa, Napier, Naturalizer, Nine West, No Nonsense, Olga/Warner's, Oneida, Oneida Too, QP Kids, Outlet Marketplace, Papa Joe's, Paper Outlet, Perfumania, Prestige Fragrance & Cosmetics, Pfaltzgraff, Reebok, Remington, Ribbon Outlet, Rocky Mountain Chocolate Factory, Royal Doulton, Ruff Hewn, Sam & Libby, Sanrio Sampler, SBX, Sergio Tacchini, Silver & More, Smith Corona, Socks Galore, Sugar & Spice, Stained Glass Factory Outlet, Sweatshirt Company, Totes/Sunglass World, Toy Liquidators, Trader Kids, Trend Club, Van Heusen, Vans, Westport Ltd., Westport Woman, Windsor Shirt Company.

ALPHABETICAL STORE LISTING

MARINA SQUARE SHOPPING CENTER

East Bay: Corner of Marina Blvd and Teagarden (take Interstate 880 to the Marina Blvd East exit), San Leandro (510) 351-5600
Mon–Fri 10 am–9 pm, Sat 10 am–7 pm, Sun 11 am–6 pm.
Parking: Lot on premises

You'll think you're in outlet heaven—and you are. Marina Square doesn't feel like a budget center, in fact, it's a very upscale factory-outlet center, selling high-quality goods at good bargains, which makes it a worthwhile destination as well as a handy resource for those who live in nearby East Bay communities. The stores are beautifully merchandised (that is, they're just as attractively appointed as most retail stores). And you'll even get nice service from store staff. Highlights include outlet stores for Eddie Bauer, Talbots, Nine West, The Athlete's Foot, and more. There aren't many restaurants in the outlet, but we think pizza and frozen yogurt make great energy food for an afternoon's shopping.

What you'll find: Activewear Outlet, The Athlete's Foot Outlet, Basics, Biobottoms, BizMart/Office Max, Designer Brands Accessories, Eddie Bauer Outlet, Gap Warehouse, Glassware Outlet, Kinko's Copies, Marshall's, Mikasa Factory Store, Nine West & Company Outlet, Nordstrom Rack, Party America, Publishers Outlet, Studio 5 Clothing, Supervision, Talbots Outlet.

PACIFIC WEST OUTLETS AND THE OUTLETS AT GILROY

South Bay: Highway 101 in Gilroy at Leavesley Rd exit, Gilroy (408) 847-4155.
Mon–Fri 10 am–9 pm, Sat 9 am–9 pm, Sun 10 am–6 pm.
Parking: Lot on premises

Not long ago, Gilroy was best known for its garlic. But lately, two adjacent, sprawling outlet malls have sprung up on the rural landscape to offer shoppers great bargains on everything from kitchenware, clothing, and shoes to outdoor gear and toys. (En route to the malls, you'll still pass lots of fruit and vegetable stands, including the Garlic Outlet, recently named by a witty proprietor.) Technically, the malls are two separate entities across the street from each other, but as far as consumers are concerned, they offer one huge shopping bonanza. Both lend a new air of sleekness to outlet shopping; the U-shaped Pacific West Center houses all the stores in shiny new green-and-white tile buildings, while the Outlets at Gilroy exhibit a little more variation in the large, often elegant storefronts with huge windows. Both offer great brand-name shopping. Outdoor tables at the Gilroy Café and Erik's Café are great spots from which to contemplate the lovely agricultural setting, the rolling hills—and your purchases.

The Outlets at Gilroy: Baby Guess, Banister Shoes, Boot Factory, Boston Traders, Brooks Brothers, Bruce Alan bags etc, Bugle Boy, Carter's Childrenswear, Chicago Cutlery, Colours & Scents, Columbia Sportswear, Designer Brands Accessories, Esprit, Garlic Grocery, Geoffrey Beene Woman, The Gifted Line, Guess Outlet, Impo and Chilis, Izod, Jockey Factory Store, Kid's Zone, Kitchen Collection, Koret of California, LA Gear, Leather Mode, Lucia, Olga/Warner's, OshKosh B'Gosh, Paper Outlet, Publishers Outlet, Reed & Barton, Remington, Robert Scott and David Brooks Outlet Store, Silver & More, Springmaid/Wamsutta, Storybook Heirlooms, Traders Kids, Windsor Shirt.

Pacific West Outlet Center: Adolfo II, Aileen, American Tourister, Anne Klein, Barbizon Lingerie, Bass Shoes, Brands, BUM Equipment, Cape Isle Knitters, Capezio, Carole Little, Champion Hanes, Corning/Revere, Chaus, Eddie Bauer, Executive Suite, Famous Brands Housewares, Galt Sand, Ganson, Gant, Geoffrey Beene, Harry & David, Harve Benard, He-Ro Group, Home Again, I.B. Diffusion, Iona, J.H. Collectibles, Joan and David,

John Henry & Friends For Men, Jones NY/Jones Sport, Jordache, Leather Loft, L'eggs, Hanes, Bali, Max Studio, Leslie Fay, Levi's Outlet, Liz Claiborne, Maidenform, Mikasa, Nike, Nine West, Oneida, Perfumania, Pfaltzgraff, Ribbon Outlet, Sassafras, Sierra Designs, Shoe Pavilion, Socks Galore, The Sweatshirt Company, Toys Unlimited, Unisa, Van Heusen, Wallet Works.

VILLAGE OUTLETS OF NAPA VALLEY

North Bay: 3111 North St. Helena Hwy, St. Helena (707) 963-9296.
Mon–Fri 10 am–6 pm, Sat 10 am–7 pm, Sun 11 am–6 pm.
Parking: Lot on premises

Boasting a courtyard with lush, green lawns, ivy arbors, and bright white benches—not to mention great deals on high-quality merchandise at some of the most upscale factory stores we've ever seen—the Village Outlets

of Napa Valley is one of the most charming places to shop. Surely part of the pleasure is the location itself; it's hard not to feel luxuriously relaxed when you're in Napa. The Village Outlets is a great destination in itself, but you might discover that it's a nice side trip to round out a spa- or wine-country weekend.

What you'll find: Brooks Brothers, Coach Leather, Colours & Scents, Donna Karan, Go Silk, Joan and David, London Fog, Movado Watches, New Territory, Zimbabwe Sculpture.

VINTAGE OAKS

North Bay: 208 Vintage Way (take the Rowland exit off Highway 101), Novato (415) 897-9999.
Hours vary with stores.
Parking: Lot on premises

Unless you live in Marin County, you may find this bargain-oriented shopping center a bit of a jaunt. But for the avid bargain shop-

ALPHABETICAL STORE LISTING

per, it's a valuable destination. Just off Highway 101 in Novato (about a forty-five-minute drive north from San Francisco), the hodgepodge architecture of this vast suburban center hints at the variety within. The center is anchored by Macy's Home Store (electronics and furniture only), Costco, and Target (the garden center has particularly good buys). It holds some surprises, too, including a Sharper Image Outlet and the extensive Oshman's Supersports USA store. Plan to stay for lunch. Like any good suburban destination, Vintage Oaks boasts an array of mostly chain restaurants (Jennie Low's Chinese Cuisine is our favorite).

Apparel: Contempo Casuals Outlet, Kotton Clothing Outlet, Marshall's, Miller Stockman Western Wear.

Beauty: Marin Beauty Company, New York Cosmetics.

Footwear: Athlete's Foot, Novato Shoe Mart, Payless Shoe Source.

Home Furnishings: Bellach's Leather, Macy's Home Store, Mattress Discounters.

Entertainment: The Wherehouse.

Major Stores: Price Costco, Target.

Specialty Stores: Amen, Ben Franklin Crafts, Cellular World, Future Kids Learning Center/Kids World, General Nutrition Center, ITC Jewelry, Joanne's Collection, New York Fabrics, Oshman's Supersports USA, Panda Room, Parties Galore, Pet Project, Sew & Sew Alternatives, Sharper Image Outlet, Supercrown Books, Triple "S" Sports.

Service: The Copy Center, Frame 'N' Lens, United Airlines.

ALPHABETICAL STORE LISTING

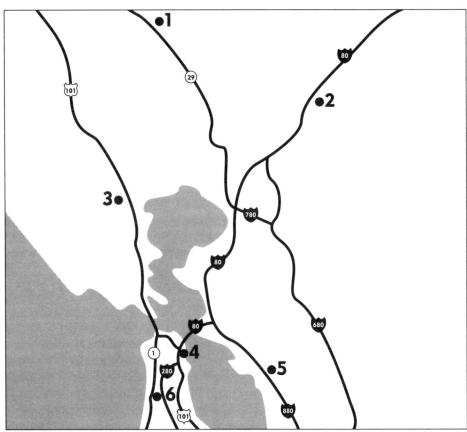

MAP AND KEY

FACTORY OUTLET CENTERS

● **1** Village Outlets of Napa Valley
Hwy 29 / Napa, north of the town
of St. Helena
(707) 963-9296

● **2** Factory Stores at the Nut Tree
Hwy 80 / Vacaville
(707) 447-5755

● **3** Vintage Oaks
Hwy 101 / Novato
(415) 897-9999

● **4** Six Sixty Center
South of Market / San Francisco
(415) 227-0464

● **5** Marina Square Shopping Center
Interstate 880 / San Leandro
(510) 351-5600

● **6** 280 Metro Center
off Interstate 280 / Colma
(415) 388-4460

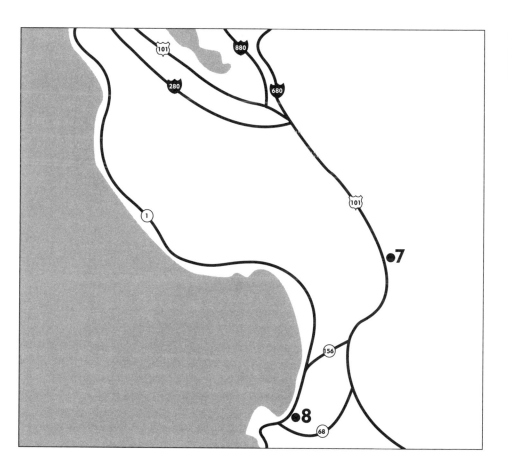

FACTORY OUTLET CENTERS

- **7** Pacific West Outlets & The Outlets at Gilroy
  Hwy 101 / Gilroy
  (408) 847-4155

- **8** American Tin Cannery
  Near Hwy 1 / Pacific Grove
  (408) 372-1442

MAP AND KEY

CHAPTER **3**

HOUSE &
GARDEN

HOUSE & GARDEN

According to pollsters, we're all "cocooning" like mad. So it's likely that you are feathering your current nest (especially if you've slashed your mortgage payments through smart refinancing) rather than buying a new home. You'll be glad to see that, in this chapter, we've gathered great money-saving tips for everything for your home, from garden equipment and plants to furnishings, floor coverings, and more.

FLOOR-COVERING OUTLETS

The following list of floor-covering businesses is not an endorsement and represents only a fraction of this huge industry. Salespeople at any flooring outlet you visit should be judged on their willingness to answer your questions. Comparison shopping is encouraged, but be sure you are actually comparing the same goods and services when comparing prices.

CARPETS OF NEW ZEALAND

East Bay: 1940-C Olivera Rd, Concord
(800) 289-9665.
Mon–Sat 10 am–6 pm.
American Express, MasterCard, Visa
Parking: Lot on premises

All-wool wall-to-wall custom carpets are available here for as little as $25 per yard, a price that compares favorably to the top synthetic carpet brands. Although no complete carpets are kept at this warehouse location, a full range of samples is on hand, and you can take samples home and return them by mail. Orders can be filled in three weeks for these carpets that feature New Zealand wool. You can order area rugs with any type of border. The carpets are rated by an independent lab for the quality of their pile content and resilience. Carpets of New Zealand offers full service, with measurement and installation of wall-to-wall carpeting done by the firm's subcontractors. Call before you visit to get full instructions on the store's exact location. —*PL*

CONKLIN BROTHERS FLOOR COVERINGS

Seven Bay Area locations; check local telephone directory, or call (800) 750-2250 for nearest store.
Open Mon–Fri 9 am–9 pm, Sat and Sun 10 am– 5 pm.
MasterCard, Visa

This is the granddaddy of retail floor-covering stores in the Bay Area, selling to both residential and commercial customers. The original Conklin brothers are long gone, but their philosophy of retail excellence continues. Carpets by Karastan, Bigelow, Lees, Salem, World, Galaxy, and Philadelphia are featured, with other brands available. Conklin Brothers also sells vinyl linoleum by Armstrong, Congoleum, Mannington, Tarket, and Kentile, along with hardwood by

 ALPHABETICAL STORE LISTING

Mannington-Bruce. Some ceramic-tile flooring is also available. Conklin is licensed to install floor coverings under California Contractor's license number 193068. —*PL*

LAWRENCE CONTRACT FURNISHERS INC.

South Bay: 470-B Vandell Way, Campbell (408) 374-7590.
Open Tues–Fri, 9 am–5:30 pm (8 pm Thur), Sat 9 am–3 pm.
MasterCard, Visa
Parking: Lot on premises

A small store compared to the multilocation outlets, Lawrence is packed with furniture, wallpapers, window coverings, as well as vinyl, wood flooring, and carpeting. Lawrence regularly carries carpeting by DuPont, Karastan, Bigelow, Mohawk, and it has the ability to draw from about a hundred other mills. The usual plethora of signs noting markdowns is nowhere to be seen; instead, there's a staff of three who will gladly answer questions and explain different carpet types. Lawrence's prices are kept low by not advertising and having a low-overhead industrial-park location. No towering sign marks the location, so call for directions. Lawrence is licensed to install floor coverings under California Contractor's license number 279695. —*PL*

MMM CARPETS

Six Bay Area locations; check local telephone directory, or call (800) 649-6662 for nearest store.
Mon–Fri, 10 am–9 pm, Sat and Sun 10 am–6 pm.
Discover, MasterCard, Visa
Parking: Lot on premises

Another longtime carpet seller, MMM opened in Santa Clara some thirty years ago and features DuPont, Karastan, Atlas, and Trevira plus many others. The MMM Carpetmobile makes house calls with carpet samples for home shoppers who can't visit the "World's Largest Showroom." Something is always on clearance at this huge business, and roll-end remnants are generally marked down as much as 50 percent. Other prices are consistently 50 to 60 percent below suggested retail. MMM Carpets also carries Congoleum vinyl linoleum. The company is licensed to install floor coverings under California Contractor's license number 346177. —*PL*

NISSAN TILE

San Francisco: 364 Bayshore Blvd, SF (415) 641-4500.
Open Mon–Fri 8 am–5 pm (Mon until 7 pm), Sat 8 am–2 pm.
American Express, MasterCard, Visa
Other stores (all retail): San Francisco (415) 931-3811; Redwood City (415)364-6547; Fremont (510) 623-6866; San Jose (408) 298-9766.
Parking: Lot on premises

With large inventories on hand, Nissan carries both domestic and imported tile, including many factory closeouts at discount prices. In addition to quarry and paving tiles, Nissan also features bathroom, kitchen, Mexican terra cotta, marble, granite, and slate tiles for counters and walls. Nissan sells tools and adhesives, and offers free instruction to do-it-yourselfers. —*PL*

OMID ORIENTAL RUGS

San Francisco: Ninth and Brannan, SF (415) 626-3466.
Mon–Sat 10 am–6 pm, Sun noon–5 pm, and evenings by appointment.
American Express, MasterCard, Visa
Other stores: 1245 South Main St, Walnut Creek (510) 937-4560; 3939 Stevens Creek Blvd (at Saratoga Ave), Santa Clara (408) 247-6151.
Parking: Lot on premises

Omid Oriental Rugs features an astonishing selection of rugs from Turkey, Pakistan, China, India, Nepal, Afghanistan, and a few from pre-embargo Iran. Founder, owner, and buyer Saïd Karkouti believes in selling at the marked price without haggling, bazaar-style, with potential buyers. Price tags usually indicate that a price reduction has already been made, and because Karkouti does his own buying, additional costs are saved. As a result, Omid's does not feature special sales. Old as well as new rugs are sold, trades are accepted, and washing and repair services are available. Salespeople will patiently explain to the novice how to judge the quality of hand-made carpets, an interesting experience in itself. —*PL*

STONELIGHT TILE

South Bay: 1651 Pomona Ave, San Jose (408) 292-7424.
Mon–Fri 8 am–5 pm, Sat 9 am–2 pm.
Checks accepted
Parking: Street

Stonelight Tile is a high-end tile manufacturer, selling tiles for upscale residences of Henry Kissinger and Barbra Streisand, as well as the guest palace of Saudi Arabia's King Fahd. Remnants from these impressive projects are available at Stonelight's "boneyard" at considerable savings: seconds ranged from 50 cents to $2.50 per square foot, while leftover tiles cost $3 to $4 per square foot—a substantial reduction from the usual prices of up to $10.00 per square foot. —*PL*

ALPHABETICAL STORE LISTING

INSIDER TIP: FLOOR COVERINGS

By Paul Lukes

When it comes to choosing floor coverings, your primary concern should be not the initial cost, but in what ways and how heavily your floor is to be used. The old adage "You get what you pay for" is particularly true when it comes to the four basic floor coverings: linoleum, hardwood, carpets, and ceramic tile. By paying more up front, you may be paying less in the long run.

Look honestly at your floor-covering investment and consider these tips from industry experts on finding the best value for your dollar.

LINOLEUM

Available since the nineteenth century in rolls, sheets, or tiles, linoleum has some inherent softness. Within the flooring industry it's commonly called resilient flooring. True, original linoleum was a mixture of linseed oil, cork, and rosins on burlap backing, but today, plastics and resins in the form of vinyl (like phonograph records) are most common. Solid vinyl is brighter, tougher, longer lasting, and easier to clean than printed vinyl, which is prone to scratching and the pattern wearing off. Embossed vinyl offers the look of wood grain or ceramic tile, but the raised areas are subject to greater wear, and dirt can collect in the lower surfaces.

Cushioned backings help make resilient floors even more comfortable to walk and stand on, but be sure to consider how tables, chairs, and other stationary objects will dent them. Also note that some backings rot when wet; take care when choosing cushioned linoleum for kitchens or bathrooms. Some resilient floorings have coatings designed to eliminate the need to wax, but these finishes can deteriorate with hard use.

HARDWOODS

Oak is the hardwood of choice, but other varieties include maple, beech, pecan, hickory, walnut, ash, cherry, and even black locust. (Pine and fir are softwoods usually used as subfloors below other floorings, but are occasionally used as floorings, too. The very soft redwood is popular for decking.) Hardwood flooring, milled with a tongue on one side and a groove on the other, is usually 3/4-inch thick by 2 1/4-inches wide and sold in lengths ranging from 9 inches to 8 1/2 feet; other widths and thickness are available by special order. These floorboards lock together when they are nailed to the subfloor. Wood can be prefinished, sealed and varnished, or left unfinished, depending on your preference.

Woodblock flooring, usually in one-foot-square tiles, is also tongue-and-groove but is glued with special mastic because it is only 5/16-inch thick; these tiles are not designed for high-traffic areas. The National Oak Flooring Manufacturers' Association will, for a small charge for the material and shipping, send you a listing of literature and videos on all aspects of oak flooring if you call (901) 526-5016 or fax (901) 526-7022.

INSIDER TIP

CARPETS

Carpets fall into two categories—synthetic and natural, of which wool is the dominant fiber. Wool, which is noted for its long life, durability, and appearance, is the benchmark for the carpet industry. All comparisons in synthetics are made to wool.

Today, most wool carpets are machine-made. Quality wool carpets are dense, with the fibers very close to each other so that they wear longer. The best wool has sheen, strength, and a wiry elasticity. Because of their durability, wool carpets compare favorably to synthetics despite their higher cost.

Most carpets are made from four synthetic fibers: nylon, olefin, polyester, and acrylic. Brand-names are not the same as generic fibers.

— Nylon represents about 66 percent of all synthetic carpet fiber produced in the United States. Highly elastic and very strong, it is resistant to abrasion and water-soluble stains, is easily dyed, and can be readily cleaned. Nylon brands include Anso, Antron, Ultron, and Zeftron.

— Olefin is not dyed; it is colored before it is made into fiber. Extremely resistant to moisture and mildew, olefin is a good choice for kitchens, bathrooms, and outdoor applications. It is naturally resistant to static electricity and is easily cleaned. Olefin brands include Herculon and Marquesa.

— Polyester is noted for retaining its excellent color clarity and luster. In thick, cut pile, it is very soft, yet resists water-soluble stains and is easy to clean. Polyester brands include Permalon and Trevira.

— Acrylic fibers are the most like wool in feel and appearance. They have low static levels and resist moisture and mildew. Acrylic brands include Acrilan.

When shopping for carpets, you first need to understand the common industry vocabulary used to describe what you're interested in:

— Density. The amount of yarn in a carpet determines its density—the greater the density, the better the overall quality. The height or length of the fibers is secondary to how close they are to each other. Bend the carpet to examine how dense it is.

— Weight. This is the amount of basic fiber per square yard. For example, nylon carpet varies from 18 ounces to 100 ounces per square yard, and as with the other factors, more is better. If you're unsure of the weight, ask for the specific percentage.

— Level loop pile. In this type of carpet, both ends of the yarn are anchored into the carpet back and are uncut. This makes for a smooth, level surface that wears well.

— Sculptured or carved. Multi-level loop pile often forms a pattern.

— Cut pile. Loop tops are cut in several variations including plush or velvet, which gives a very level and formal-looking finish. With saxonies, the cut tuft ends are distinctive and do not blend together as they do in plush. Friezes (pronounced free-zays) have dense and low pile, making them a good choice for high-traffic areas.

The Carpet and Rug Institute publishes several booklets on choosing, buying, and caring for new carpets or rugs. Call (800) 882-8846 or (706) 278-3176.

 INSIDER TIP

CERAMIC TILE

Ceramic tile is a sheet of clay that has been hardened by kiln firing. Unglazed tile has a solid color and texture from top to bottom. Unglazed tile, also called quarry tile, has stonelike qualities that make it virtually impervious to foot traffic for hundreds of years, so it's highly suitable for flooring. Glazed tile is covered with a thin, porcelainlike layer of glass that gives it a slick surface that rapidly wears off. Unsuitable for flooring, glazed tiles are used primarily on counters and walls.

INSTALLATION

Finding the right floor covering is only half the battle; getting it installed to your satisfaction is equally important. Use the following questions as a check list:
- Who will install your floor covering?
- Who will move your furniture, valuable items, and replace them?
- Who will remove and dispose of your existing floor covering?
- If you're not tackling the job yourself, is the subcontractor doing the work, licensed, bonded, and insured? Check with the Contractor State Licensing Board's toll-free automated service to learn if your installer is qualified. With the contractor's license number in hand, call (800) 321-CSLB.
- What is covered in your written guarantee?

If you plan to install the floor covering yourself, read every word written by the manufacturer regarding installation safety and procedures before you begin—and follow those instructions. Check on the cost of renting or purchasing any special tools the flooring manufacturer recommends to ensure proper installation. These can add costs to the job that may in fact make it more economical to use a professional installer. ▪

ALPHABETICAL STORE LISTING

FURNITURE

There's no reason to buy furniture from large department stores once you've seen the savings you'll find through the stores listed here. Traditional or contemporary styles, furnishings for the home or office—we found it all at prices you can't pass up.

Many of these businesses can offer such good savings because they sell furnishings mostly from manufacturers' catalogs rather than off the floor, take small markups, and rarely advertise. Their success is largely based on referrals by satisfied customers. While some stores have well-stocked showrooms, others have little or no furniture to show. Many offer furnishings such as draperies, wallpaper, and floor coverings, making them a one-stop design center for the home. When looking to buy furniture, keep in mind that you'll pay additional costs of freight and delivery, which can be incorporated into price quotes or billed separately.

We've also included information on Bay Area auctions, where you can find excellent bargains on furniture and decorative arts, and information about The Galleria and Showplace Square Design Centers, which have recently opened the doors of their exclusive showrooms to the public.

Since furniture can be expensive, you want to make sure it looks good and feels right before you buy. Remember that Goldilocks had to sit in two other chairs before she found the one that she liked the best.

ALIOTO & ASSOCIATES

**North Bay: 644 Third St West, Sonoma
(707) 996-4546.
Mon–Thur 9:30 am–5 pm, Fri and Sat by appointment.
Checks accepted
Parking: Lot on premises**

Alioto & Associates' charming showroom is located just a few blocks from the town square. Inside you'll find vignettes (the trade name for furniture arrangements) featuring traditional furnishings and accessories by manufacturers such as Century, Lexington, Ficks Reed (fine rattan), Stiffel, Barcalounger, Habersham, and Karastan (carpets). A back room holds hundreds of catalogs for office and residential furnishings, plus samples of fabric, carpet, and vinyl flooring. Friendly owners Tony and Gail Alioto can also help you with wallpaper, draperies, and all types of window treatments. Low overhead costs and the fact that Alioto doesn't advertise its many services allow them to offer discounts of 25 percent or more off factory-suggested retail prices.

The firm has a lot of experience working with architects and remodelers and offers interior-design services in the home at a rate of $35 per hour. For $75, they will take you to see furnishings at the manufacturer warehouses at the Showplace Square Design Center and Furniture Mart in San Francisco. A plus: Delivery is free. —*SB*

 ALPHABETICAL STORE LISTING

AMERICAN BLINDS AND DRAPERIES

**East Bay: 1168 San Luis Obispo Ave,
Hayward (510) 487-3500. Toll Free (800)
972-0660 (outside 510 area code).
Usually first Sat of May and last Sat of
October, 8:30 am–4:30 pm.
MasterCard, Visa
Parking: Lot on premises**

A wholesale manufacturer of blinds and draperies for homes, residential buildings, and offices, American opens its doors to the public twice a year for a huge factory sale to clear out more than 7000 new draperies and blinds. You'll find discontinued lines, close-outs, odd sizes, overruns, and specials at 50 to 70 percent off retail prices. An additional 20 percent discount is given on all draperies after 2:30 pm. Expect three-pronged, French-pleated, lined and unlined draperies, custom fabrics, cloth-lined draperies, and sheers in different colors, pre-pinned and ready to hang. A variety of mini-blinds, vertical blinds, and valances are also offered in standard sizes. Off-white mini-blinds are sold in the twenty most-requested sizes and come with a lifetime guarantee. Most items are priced from $20 to $60.

According to Paul Russo, American's co-owner, you can drape an entire house with sale merchandise for below $300. Come prepared with measurements and a yardstick. Sales are advertised, but call and put yourself on the mailing list so you won't miss the announcements. During the year, American Blinds and Draperies will also work by mail or phone with customers on individual orders at varying prices. —SB

ASID SALES

**San Francisco: The Galleria, 101 Henry
Adams St and The Showplace Design
Center, 2 Henry Adams St, SF
(415) 626-2743.
Admission to sales $5; MasterCard, Visa
Parking: Street**

Normally, you have to purchase furnishings at these design centers through a professional interior designer or buying service, but the ASID sales are the exception. The ASID (American Society of Interior Designers) sponsors two annual sales, usually in June and November. This year, the sale takes place June 11–12, 10 am–4 pm.

High-end furniture, accessories, and fabrics that are typically showroom samples, plus discontinued items and slightly damaged pieces, are featured for up to 70 percent off showroom list prices. Expect traditional and contemporary furniture, antiques, fine reproductions, "country pine" items, Japanese tansus, original art, rattan furniture, fabrics, lamps, Oriental carpets, and more.

Think of the sales as flea markets filled with luxury goods, and keep in mind that even at discount prices, some merchandise is out of the price range of the average furniture shopper. No returns, refunds, or exchanges. —SB

ALPHABETICAL STORE LISTING

BABIES UNLIMITED

North Bay: 5627 Paradise Dr, Corte Madera (415) 924-3764.
Mon–Sat 10 am–5 pm, Sun noon–4 pm.
Major credit cards; store also takes trade
Parking: Lot on premises

Parents come here to find a mix of competitively priced new and secondhand baby products, equipment, and furniture. The store offers frequent closeout and store sales. New, unfinished pine chests/changing tables—ready for a coat of paint or varnish—are a good value starting at $129.

There was also a large selection of quality used items including strollers ranging in price from $10 to $85. Several strollers looked as if they had never been used, with original tags still attached. Upstairs, secondhand backpacks started at $10, and battery-operated swings at $28. —*JA*

BUTTERFIELD WEST/COLLECTIONS

San Francisco: 164 Utah St, SF
(415) 861-7500, ext. 309.
Bimonthly weekends. Auction previews:
Butterfield West, Sat 10 am–5 pm, Sun 10
am–5 pm, Mon 9 am–1 pm; Collections, Sat
10 am–5 pm, Sun 10 am–5 pm, Mon 9
am–1 pm. Auctions: Butterfield West, Mon
10 am, Tues 10 am; Collections, Sun 1 pm.
Checks accepted
Parking: Lot on premises

The Butterfield West auction is an enormously popular thirty-thousand-square-foot extension of Butterfield & Butterfield, the largest and oldest auction house on the West Coast, and a terrific place to find bargains. As many as four thousand people attend Butterfield West's lively auction previews every two weeks to view almost three thousand moderately priced items on display. You'll rub elbows with antique dealers and bargain hunters armed with measuring sticks as you browse through cluttered aisles filled with contemporary and antique furniture, Oriental rugs and carpets, artwork, decorative arts, crystal, china, silver, jewelry, stamps, Asian art, and photographs. Books are also available under the aegis of the California Book Auction Galleries, and previously owned automobiles are sometimes auctioned. On recent visits, we saw everything from dilapidated futons to Baccarat crystal goblets, Chagall lithographs, and Japanese tansu chests.

On your right as you enter the huge facility, just around the corner from Butterfield & Butterfield's elegant main gallery, you'll notice attractive displays of collector-quality furnishings and decorative arts. These lots are part of Collections, a separate auction within the Butterfield West facility. Collections typically features period furniture and fine reproductions, decorative Asian and ethnographic art, estate jewelry, antique silver, and Oriental rugs. The catalog for Butterfield West and Collections includes descriptions of lots for both sales, but non-

ALPHABETICAL STORE LISTING

illustrated estimates are given for Collections' lots. Peter Scott, Butterfield West's codirector, says estimates for Collections generally range from $500 to $2500, but items have sold for under and over. An example: A William and Mary–style chair (c. 1900) recently sold for $800, well below the $2000 figure Scott thought it would reach in auction. At Butterfield West auctions, prices can range from $5 to $5000.

Collections also has "niche" auctions. In addition to the furnishings for sale at every auction, Asian furniture and decorative arts are featured approximately every six weeks. Niche auctions also focus on American country furniture (three times a year), silver (semi-annually), mid-century American and English furniture, decorative arts, and Italian glass.

Call to have your name put on the mailing list to receive a schedule and information about auction highlights. You can bid either on-site or absentee at Butterfield West and Collections auctions. Collections also accepts telephone bids. Sales tax and a buyer's premium (15 percent of the winning bid) will be added to each successful bid. Those who have a resale license are, of course, exempted from the tax. —*SB*

THE CONSIGNMENT COTTAGE

**East Bay: 228 Railroad, Danville
(510) 743-3906.
Daily 10 am–6 pm.
MasterCard, Visa
Parking: Lot on premises**

This new upscale consignment shop fills the niche between thrift store and antique shop. Corporate nomads unwilling to move a houseful of furniture cross-country and downsizing retirees who don't want strangers in their house eyeing the family treasures let Consignment Cottage sell their furniture and housewares for a quarter to a third of the original value. You could pay up to $5000 for sixty pieces of Royal Doulton china in a downtown department store; Consignment Cottage had service for twelve in Princess Di's Carlisle pattern for a mere $170 a place setting. A seven-piece almond dining set originally $3000 was selling for $825. If you don't see what you want on the main floor or in the upstairs bargain attic, check the catalog for deals such as an eight-piece Queen Ann bedroom set regularly $5535 for $1690, or submit your request to the computerized wish list. They'll let you know when it comes in. —*CA*

THE CONSIGNMENT SHOP

**North Bay: 818 Grant Ave, Old Town, Novato (415) 892-3496.
Tues–Fri 10:30 am–5:30 pm, Sat 11 am–5 pm
Checks accepted, no credit cards
Parking: Street**

The Consignment Shop specializes in home furnishings—antique, semi-antique, and contemporary pieces in traditional styles—no brass and glass here.

"It's not Butterfields but it's not the

Salvation Army either," said owner Sharon Hirte. Interesting and unusual describes a lot of the merchandise, and well priced describes it all. An antique English oak drop-leaf dining table with hand-turned barley twist legs and four matching chairs was $900. You couldn't duplicate it today for under $2000.

Hirte paid $1200 for a Drexel Heritage antique reproduction hall tree twenty years ago; today she is selling it for $425. Another Drexel Heritage piece, a Queen Ann walnut coffee table, which originally sold for $950, is now $250. —CA

CROW'S NEST INTERIORS

East Bay: 2100 San Ramon Valley Blvd, San Ramon (510) 837-9130.
Tues–Fri 10 am–4 pm, Sat 10 am–2 pm.
Checks accepted
Parking: Lot on premises

Crow's Nest Interiors specializes in discount prices on window treatments such as custom draperies, balloon valances, shades, pleated shades, mini-blinds, vertical blinds, and shutters. The small office location and low overhead translate to good savings for customers. Expect a 30 percent discount on fabrics by Robert Allen, Waverly, Norbar, Kravet, Davis, and others, and reasonable prices on custom jobs. Wallpaper is discounted 25 percent and coordinating fabrics 20 to 25 percent. Crow's Nest also discounts Ohline and Woodfold shutters 33 percent. Bring in your measurements or stop by to flip through manufacturers' catalogs. If you want in-depth advice, Crow's Nest's designers can work with you on a consulting basis for $45 per hour (the first hour is refunded when you place an order). In addition to window coverings, Crow's Nest offers upholstery services and can help coordinate fabric for bedroom ensembles. —SB

DAVID MORRIS CO.

San Francisco: 1378 Sutter St, SF
(415) 346-8333.
Mon–Fri 9 am–5 pm, Sat 10 am–2 pm.
MasterCard, Visa
Parking: Street

Located in a small, inconspicuous storefront close to Van Ness Avenue, this store is easy to miss but well worth a visit. With such low overhead, the company can offer 30 percent savings on most purchases, including freight and delivery.

The company specializes in custom orders from catalogs of major medium- to high-end furniture manufacturers such as Stanley, Highland House, and Leonetti. You'll also find savings on carpets by Shaw Industries and Karastan and on Persian and Oriental rugs. You can purchase draperies, window treatments, and vinyl floor coverings here, and receive free decorating assistance with any purchase. If you want to see a piece of furniture before you buy, the helpful staff can arrange for you to visit the manufacturers' showrooms. —SB

ALPHABETICAL STORE LISTING

DEOVELET & SONS

San Francisco: 1660 Pine St, SF
(415) 775-8014.
Mon–Sat 8 am–5:30 pm.
MasterCard, Visa
Parking: Street

The lighting may be dim, but you'll still see a good selection of medium-priced furnishings at Deovelet & Sons, plus kitchen and laundry appliances by major manufacturers. A family-run business since 1938, the store is managed today by the founder's friendly sons, Robert and Philip. They offer a 25 to 30 percent discount or better because of the store's low overhead. The main showrooms feature traditional furnishings such as lamps, curio cabinets, upholstered couches and chairs, rattan furniture, occasional pieces, even some Victorian reproductions. The second and third floors are packed with dining, breakfast, and bedroom sets, plus mattresses from Simmons, Serta, Sealy, and Restonic.

If you can't find what you like on the floor, you can browse through catalogs, choose fabric, and order merchandise from manufacturers such as Highland House, Kimball, Lexington, and Pulaski. Deovelet also carries carpeting lines such as Philadelphia, Columbus, Cabin Craft, Salem, and Evans & Black. On our last visit, we saw a lovely queen-sized pecan sleigh bed by Webb marked down from $795 to $500, a savings of nearly 40 percent. Another bonus: free delivery within a fifty-mile radius. —*SB*

DESIGN RESOURCE

Peninsula: 2024 Middlefield Rd, Redwood City (415) 369-3604 or (415) 851-2180.
Mon–Fri noon–5 pm, or by appointment.
MasterCard, Visa
Parking: Lot on premises

Design Resource looks like a simple home from the outside, but inside you'll discover a spacious showroom full of samples from such prestigious furniture manufacturers as Hickory, Harden, Pulaski, Fremarc, and Cavalier. High-quality alternatives to high-priced lines are another specialty. If you have a photo of a piece of furniture you like, bring it in and Design Resource will try to locate it—or something similar—in one of its many manufacturers' catalogs on hand. Prices, which include freight, are typically discounted 30 percent off suggested retail. Professional interior-design services are offered in the home for an initial consultation fee of $150, of which half will be reimbursed within sixty days with a purchase of $1000 or more. The staff can also arrange a visit to the wholesale showrooms in San Francisco for $50, refundable if you order merchandise within ten days. —*SB*

DICKER FURNITURE

East Bay: 37235 Fremont Blvd, Fremont
(510) 797-8884.
Tues–Fri 9 am–6 pm, Sat 9 am–5 pm, Sun noon–5 pm.
MasterCard, Visa

Parking: Lot on premises

Every inch of this store is packed with medium- to high-quality traditional furnishings and accessories, some Victorian reproductions and "country" style pieces. Dicker carries furniture by a wide range of European designers, plus gold-leaf mirrors, grandfather clocks, curios, Strass crystal chandeliers, accent sofas, formal dining sets, chairs, recliners, bedroom furniture, and more. What you don't find on the floor you can order from catalogs of well-known manufacturers including Lexington, Highland House, Bernhardt, Stiffel, Century, Pulaski, Waterford, and Kimball.

Low overhead and high sales volume mean that Dicker can offer 20 to 30 percent off retail, including freight (and a minimum 30 percent discount on Strass crystal). Buying pieces off the floor might save you another 10 percent. Delivery is free, and Dicker will Scotchgard your purchases at no extra charge. On a recent visit, we saw a beautiful cherry wood grandfather clock by Howard Miller marked from $4550 down to $3275. —SB

DON ERMANN ASSOCIATES

**San Francisco: 1717 Seventeenth St, SF
(415) 621-7117.
Mon–Sat 9 am–5:30 pm.
Discover, MasterCard, Visa
Parking: Lot on premises**

In Don Ermann's three showrooms, you'll find elegant vignettes representing many quality furniture lines. The friendly and knowledgeable staff can help you select home furnishings from catalogs as well as carpets, draperies, fabrics, floor coverings, and wallpapers. Ermann's carries manufacturers such as Century, Four Seasons, Glass Arts, Hekman, Hammary, Hickory Chair, La Barge, and Taylor Woodcraft. They also offer customers 40 percent off suggested manufacturers' retail, not including freight or delivery.

On our last visit, we saw a comfortable Leonetti Mission-style sofa for $896. They can also arrange trips to the nearby Galleria and Showplace Design Centers. Be sure to visit the second floor, where discontinued items and some floor samples are further reduced. If you want to purchase furniture for a home office or an office in a commercial building, browse through Ermann's vast selection of commercial-furniture catalogs and be sure to see the upstairs showroom full of office furnishings, sofas, and recliners. —SB

THE DRAPERY OUTLET

**Peninsula: 590 Taylor Way, Belmont
(800) 371-6100.
Mon–Fri 8 am–5 pm, Sat 9 am–1 pm,
appointments available.
MasterCard, Visa
Parking: Street**

A former subcontractor to department stores in the Bay Area, the Drapery Outlet is now a factory-direct outlet for custom-made draperies and window coverings. You can choose from the outlet's own fabrics offered at factory prices plus a slight markup. Or

ALPHABETICAL STORE LISTING

browse through manufacturers' catalogs to find the fabric you like at a savings of 25 to 30 percent off retail. You can even bring in your own fabric. Available styles include: balloon valances, clouds, swags, Roman and Austrian shades, traditional pinch-pleat drapes, and more. Matching bedspread and custom accessories can be made up to coordinate with your draperies. The factory has recently rounded out its home-decorating services and offers competitive prices on carpeting and reupholstery services. A big plus: The Drapery Outlet's design consultants will make free home visits to show you samples, give suggestions, and take measurements. —SB

ELEGANT CLUTTER

East Bay: 702 Sycamore Valley Rd West, Danville (510) 837-1001.
Mon–Sat 10 am–6 pm, Sun noon–5 pm.
American Express, MasterCard, Visa
Parking: Lot on premises

Elegant Clutter features tasteful giftware, home accessories, and furnishings sold at retail prices in a large, elegant setting. At the back of the store, you'll find Waverly and Kinney wallpapers and fabrics that are always discounted 25 percent off retail. The knowledgeable and friendly staff can help you pick out a wallpaper and then accessorize the rest of a room down to the rugs. Each year, during the first weekend in June, the store hosts its famous warehouse sale, when slightly damaged, discontinued, and seasonal merchandise are sold at rock-bottom prices. Contact the store to get on the mailing list so you can prepare for your arrival—people have been known to set up lawn chairs hours in advance to wait for the doors to open. —SB

FURNITURE EXPRESS OUTLET

San Francisco: 667 Folsom St, SF
(415) 495-2848.
Mon–Fri 11 am–7 pm, Sat 10 am–6 pm, Sun noon–6 pm.
American Express, MasterCard, Visa
Parking: Street

Save on basic furniture items such as tables, chairs, bookshelves, small armoires, desks, sideboards, and some small couches at the Furniture Express Outlet. Styles here are fairly basic, with Scandinavian and unpainted pine furniture predominating, but some contemporary styles can be found as well. The company's low overhead enables it to offer customers savings of 25 to 50 percent off such brand-names as Trend Lines, Inter Metro/Professional's Choice, and Sauder. Trendy storage towers were offered at $50, and a solid wood Windsor chair priced at Macy's for $50 sold here for $30. —SC

GALLERY WEST, SAN FRANCISCO FURNITURE MART

San Francisco: 1355 Market St (at Tenth

ALPHABETICAL STORE LISTING

St), Space 301, SF (415) 861-6812.
Tues–Fri 9:30 am–4 pm, Sat 10 am–4 pm.
MasterCard, Visa
Parking: Street

Because of Gallery West's low overhead, their friendly and knowledgeable staff offers a 40 percent discount (on average) on manufacturers including Highland House (fabrics and furniture), Hekman Designer Gallery Ltd. (upholstery), Howard Miller (clocks and curios), James Moder (crystal chandeliers), and Sumter Cabinet (solid wood furniture). To assure the best possible service, it's a good idea to make an appointment before you visit. Through Gallery West, you'll also have access to other wholesale showrooms in the San Francisco Merchandise Mart. If you can't find what you're looking for, the staff will show you an extensive collection of catalogs containing furniture, lamps, accessories, draperies, carpeting, and hardwood and vinyl flooring. On a recent visit, we saw a Highland House sofa covered in a pretty floral fabric that was marked down from $1230 to $738; a charming piece for our bedroom.

Note: The Furniture Mart is not open to the public so it's necessary to check in at the desk in the main lobby to receive a visitor's pass. —*SB*

HARRINGTON BROS. MOVING AND STORAGE

San Francisco: 599 Valencia St, SF (415) 861-7300.
Mon–Sat 8 am–6 pm.
American Express, MasterCard, Visa
Parking: Street

In the moving business since 1928, Harrington buys furniture from moving customers and estate sales and sells it to you for about half of what you'd pay elsewhere. If you keep coming back to this huge, two-story furniture emporium filled with an eclectic mix of periods and styles you're bound to find the item you need at the price you're willing to pay. A student we know picked up a simple box spring and mattress set for $125 and a twenties-era oak office chair for $75.

An innkeeper furnishing a new Bed-and-Breakfast opted for an ornate turn-of-the-century mahogany bed for $1400. —*CA*

HOME FURNITURE OUTLET

East Bay: 1099 Ashby Ave, Berkeley (510) 486-8000.
Mon–Wed 10 am–6:30 pm, Thur 10 am–8 pm, Fri and Sat 10 am–6 pm, Sun 11:30 am–5:30 pm.
Major credit cards; ATM
Parking: Lot on premises

While the Home Furniture Outlet offers some floor models, more than half of what fills this huge space is brand-new furniture. Everything here, which includes mattresses, sofas, chairs, bookshelves, tables, and dressers, runs 40 to 60 percent below retail. A queen sleeper available at department stores for $800 (marked down from $1450) sold here for $700. You can order items upholstered in different fabrics, but the best deals are on the many items in stock.

 ALPHABETICAL STORE LISTING

HOME WORKS

Peninsula: 1265 Veterans Blvd, Redwood City (415) 365-7800.
Mon–Wed 10 am–6 pm, Thur 10 am–8 pm, Fri and Sat 10 am–6 pm, Sun 11 am–5 pm.
MasterCard, Visa
Parking: Lot on premises

Contemporary furniture and home-office design are the specialties here. Prices are approximately 15 to 30 percent below manufacturers' list prices. Home Works features popular brand-names such as Furniture by Thurston and Techline for home offices, small businesses, and bedrooms. The staff will help you with space planning free of charge. Just bring your measurements.

HOUSE OF VALUES

Peninsula: 2565 South El Camino Real, San Mateo (415) 349-3414.
Tues–Sat 9:30 am–5:30 pm, Fri 7 pm–9 pm.

MasterCard, Visa
Parking: Lot on premises

It's not hard to find discounted furniture, but furniture that you'd actually be proud to own—now, that's another story. Unless you shop at House of Values, where three separate showrooms are closely packed with beautiful tables, chairs, sofas, dressers, armoires, bed frames, mattresses, and children's furniture made by Bassett, Lane, Bernhardt, Stanley, Century, Lexington, and Broyhill, among others. Due to low overhead, you'll find substantial savings on styles ranging from country to contemporary. While savings here usually run about 35 percent, one gorgeous Louis Philippe queen-sized sleigh bed sold for half the department-store price, a savings of about $1000. —*SC*

THE INTERIOR WAREHOUSE

East Bay: 7077 Village Parkway, Dublin (510) 829-7280.
Tues, Wed and Fri 10 am–5 pm, Thur 10
am–8 pm, Sat 11 am–4 pm.
Discover, MasterCard, Visa
Parking: Lot on premises

Walk into the Interior Warehouse and you'll find literally thousands of fabric, wallpaper, carpet, and floor samples displayed along its walls. Most of the business is done through catalog orders, and you can order furnishings by Bernhardt, Pulaski, Lexington, Stanley, Lane, Hekman, Hickory Tavern, Fremarc, Brown Jordan, and La Barge, to name a few. The Interior Warehouse bills itself as a discount design center and most items are discounted 25 to 50 percent off manufacturers' suggested retail. Depending on the company, the price sometimes includes freight. The Interior Warehouse can offer good savings because it represents manufacturers directly and works with many smaller specialty manufacturers not carried in larger stores. Wallpaper lines including Waverly, Imperial, Pierre Deux, and Ralph Lauren/Polo are discounted 25 to 30 percent. Carpets such as Philadelphia, Tufftex, Fabrica, and Masland are sold at cost plus 10 percent, and Ohline

ALPHABETICAL STORE LISTING

and Woodfold custom shutters are discounted 30 percent. Friendly staff design professionals, who work closely with the furniture showrooms in San Francisco, offer decorating services at home for $60 an hour. —SB

JUDITH A. FROST AND COMPANY

Peninsula: 81 Encina Ave, Palo Alto (415) 324-8791.
Tues, Wed, Sat 10 am–4 pm and by appointment.
Checks accepted, no credit cards
Parking: Street

A Quonset hut in Palo Alto seems an unlikely place to pick up on the latest decorating trends, but don't let the warehouse exterior fool you. The interior of this upscale consignment store is right out of the pages of *Architectural Digest.* You can deck your digs in the most current decorator chic such as Japanese obi sashes for table runners and Thai frog drum coffee tables for about half of what you imagined. Looking for dining furniture on a baronial scale? Frost had a French fruitwood table with ten matching chairs for $4000. She also has a lot of small-scale pieces perfect for apartments. Whether you spend $5 or $4000, you'll get good quality for your money. —CA

LAUREL HOUSE ANTIQUES

North Bay: Marin Art and Garden Center, Ross (415) 454-8472.
Mon 10 am–2 pm, Tues–Fri 11 am–4 pm, first Sat of the month 10 am–2 pm.
MasterCard, Visa
Parking: Lot on premises

Every Tuesday morning, when the new merchandise goes out on the floor, this venerable Marin institution is packed with antique dealers skimming off the cream to resell at twice the price.

Two buildings—one devoted to Asian arts and artifacts and the other to Western antiques and collectibles—are filled with treasures such as crystal, china, brassware, pottery, linens and laces, furniture, art, silver, and jewelry on consignment from some of Marin's best families.

Expect prices a notch or two above your typical thrift store but a lot lower than you'll see in antique stores for goods of comparable quality. Proceeds from the store support the Marin Art and Garden Center. —CA

LEON BLOOMBERG CO./ THE HOUSE OF KARLSON

San Francisco: 80 Carolina St (at Fifteenth St), SF (415) 863-3640.
Mon–Fri 9 am–5 pm, by appointment only.
Checks accepted
Parking: Street

Although he closed his well-known furniture showroom and catalog furniture business, The House of Karlson, several years ago, Leon Bloomberg continues to bring savings to shoppers with the help of his coworker, interior designer Jennifer Kelly. Bloomberg

and Kelly buy factory direct, and can save clients 35 percent or more off retail prices on furnishings by companies such as Lexington, Lane, Hancock & Moore, and Stiffel.

In a large showroom shared with others in the business, Kelly will sit down with you and help create an "environment for your taste and pocketbook" by showing you fine furniture catalogs and samples of carpets, rugs, window treatments, and floor coverings. If you see a chair you like, Kelly will take you at no extra charge to the wholesale showrooms in the Galleria and Showplace Square where you can examine the furniture directly. They also offer competitive prices on mattresses, TVs, and home theaters. Home visits for design services cost $50 an hour, of which two-thirds is refunded with a purchase. —*SB*

LIMN

**San Francisco: 290 Townsend St, SF
(415) 543-5466.
Mon–Fri 9:30 am–5:30 pm, Sat 11 am–5:30 pm.**

**American Express, MasterCard, Visa
Parking: Lot on premises**

If the steep prices of the gorgeous, high-style contemporary furniture in Limn make you want to turn around and walk out of this large, two-story store, the terrific bargains in Limn's cluttered storeroom will bring you back. Limn carries the kind of furniture seen in *Elle Decor* and *Metropolitan Home*—modern, whimsical, eclectic, and pricey pieces from leading designers in Italy, France, Scandinavia, and the United States.

In a smallish space among huge boxes in the storeroom, we recently saw light fixtures, couches, side tables, and chairs, all of which were heavily discounted because they were either floor samples, discontinued, or slightly damaged.

A comfortable black leather "Corian" armchair by Matteo Grassi that would add panache to any living room was marked down from $1879 to $800, while a small side-table with a mosaic tile top was marked down from $300 to $25.

Don't expect a huge selection, but new items are added all the time. A big secret: Floor samples currently on display in the store are also always available for sale for lower than the tagged price. —*SB*

LULLABY LANE CLEARANCE CENTER

**Peninsula: 570 San Mateo Ave, San Bruno
(415) 588-4878.
Mon–Fri 10 am–6 pm (Wed until 9 pm), Sat 9:30 am–5:30 pm, Sun 11 am–5 pm.
MasterCard, Visa
Parking: Lot on premises**

Located a few doors down from the retail store, Lullaby Lane's no-frills clearance center has over twenty-five styles of cribs on display with prices reduced from 30 to 50 percent. The outlet also carries closeout, floor-model, and discontinued strollers, car seats, dressers, and bedding. Employees point customers to best buys, such as cribs with minor nicks, and strollers in last season's less-popular colors. Due to limited space, furniture for older children is not displayed at the outlet. Shoppers should check Lullaby Lane's separate juvenile furniture store, Kids Furniture, for special deals. —*JA*

MACY'S CLEARANCE CENTER

San Francisco: 1556 El Camino Real, SF (415) 878-0802.
Wed–Sun 11 am–6 pm.
Macy's, MasterCard, Visa
Parking: Lot on premises

The Macy's Clearance Center offers good prices on furniture, electronics, rugs, mattresses, and vacuum cleaners. Items tend to be discontinued, damaged, or soiled, so look carefully before you purchase. All sales are final, and there are no returns. You'll find reductions on famous maker sofas and chairs, dining room and bedrooms sets, and coffee tables. If you want a good buy on a leather sofa, this is the place for you. On a recent visit to the vast, chilly center, we saw a high-grade black leather loveseat marked down to

$2000 from $3700. A slightly soiled club chair by Frederick Edwards was a great deal at $400, a reduction of more than 60 percent off its original $1200 price tag. Merchandise is sold right off the floor and cannot be put on hold. Delivery is available for $50. —*SB*

MILLBRAE FURNITURE COMPANY

Peninsula: 1781 El Camino Real, Millbrae (415) 761-2444.
Tues and Thur 10 am–6 pm, Wed and Fri 10 am–9 pm, Sat 9 am–5 pm.
MasterCard, Visa
Parking: Nearby lot

Millbrae Furniture may have a weary facade, but its large interior showroom is full of new, middle-to-upper-end lines of furniture, mattresses, appliances, carpets, electronics, and more at great prices. A high sales volume and the fact that the company has been in the same location for more than thirty-four years translates to good savings. Expect a 30 to 40

percent discount off suggested retail on traditional furnishings by manufacturers such as Stanley, Lexington, and Highland House. Window coverings, including shutters, are discounted 50 percent or more, and appliances are sold at 10 percent over cost. If you don't find what you like on the floor, browse through Millbrae's large selection of manufacturers' catalogs. During our last visit, we saw a beautiful overstuffed white couch marked down to $1050 from $1650. —*SB*

NEXT EXPRESS

San Francisco: 1315 Howard St (at Ninth St), SF (415) 255-1311.
Mon–Sat 10 am–6 pm, Sun 11 am–6 pm.
Discover, MasterCard, Visa
Parking: Street

Next Express carries lower-priced lines by the same contemporary furniture manufacturers featured in Next Interiors stores in San Francisco and Palo Alto. You'll find stylish upholstered chairs and sofas by American

West and Elite, as well as wrought-iron tables and chairs, and halogen floor lamps in fun designs. Check in the back room for floor samples and end-of-season stock, which can include merchandise from their main retail shops, at savings of 30 to 60 percent. On a recent visit, we saw a five-piece wrought-iron dining room set by Catwalk marked down to $960 from $1930. And a full-size sofa, available in ten different fabrics, looked like a real steal at $300. —SB

NORIEGA FURNITURE

San Francisco: 1455 Taraval St (at Twenty-Fifth Ave), SF (415) 564-4110.
Tues, Wed, Fri 10 am–5:30 pm, Thur
1 pm–9 pm, Sat 10 am–5 pm.
MasterCard, Visa
Parking: Street

Walking into the beautiful showroom of Noriega Furniture is like stepping into the pages of *Architectural Digest*. Noriega specializes in expensive, high-quality furniture.

Gorgeous, tasteful displays show off traditional furnishings by companies including Karges, Kindel, Widdicomb, Hendredon, Marge Carson, La Barge, plus Stickley reproductions and Oriental furnishings. Their manufacturers' catalogs feature furniture, draperies, carpets, artwork, and accessories discounted 20 to 30 percent or more.

You'll also find original antique Japanese block prints and English botanical drawings, and discounts on Lladro and Hummel porcelain and Lenox and Waterford lamps. The store's experienced decorators can work with customers in the store at no charge, or in the home for no charge with purchase.

Noriega operates on a lower profit margin than other retailers who sell similar merchandise, says Michael Vorperian, whose father, Jerry, founded the business in 1948.

If you love the Arts and Crafts period, visit the downstairs showroom featuring cherry and oak Mission-style furniture made by the Stickley Company, pottery in the Arts and Crafts style, and Mica lamps. Noriega offers an impressive 25 percent savings on Stickley.

On our last visit, we saw a classic Morris chair with a leather cushion marked down to $1980 from $2621. And we would have been happy to make room in our den for the Hancock & Moore cranberry-colored leather wing chair we noticed, marked down to $2235 from $2980.

There's no additional charge for delivery within a fifty-mile radius. Don't miss the semiannual sales every February and September when everything (except for the Stickley pieces) is discounted from 30 and 40 percent, depending on the manufacturer. —SB

R & R FRENCH BROTHERS

San Francisco: 333 Alabama (at Sixteenth St), SF (415) 621-6627.
Mon–Fri 9:30 am–6 pm, Sat 10 am–3 pm.
MasterCard, Visa
Parking: Street

This spacious twelve-thousand-square-foot warehouse is essentially a floor-covering showroom containing displays of hardwood and vinyl floor coverings and carpeting. But the company, which has been in San Francisco for thirty-eight years, offers furniture, too, at discounts of 30 to 40 percent off retail.

Manager and designer Suzi Levesque can show you catalogs of manufacturers including Stanley, Bernhardt, Pulaski, National Mt. Airy, Lane, Hendredon, and Highland House, to help you choose furnishings. She can also bring you by appointment to see the merchandise in wholesale showrooms. French Brothers is also a factory distributor for mattress giants such as Sealy, Serta, and Simmons.

The company offers window coverings such as draperies and custom treatments, mini-blinds, vertical blinds, pleated shades, and shutters. Expect an excellent selection of carpeting for residential and commercial buildings at varying prices. Some of the carpet lines represented: Shaw, Lees, Tuftex, Stevens, Gullistan, Royalty, and Fabrica.

French Brothers also carries Hartco hardwood, and vinyl floor coverings by Armstrong, Mannington, and Tarkett. —SB

RAFAEL HOMES

**San Francisco: 145 Rhode Island, SF
(415) 621-5080.
Mon–Fri 9 am–5 pm, Sat 10 am–5 pm.
American Express, MasterCard, Visa
Parking: Street**

Should one happen to purchase the Palace of Versailles, one could easily furnish the entire mansion here and still save a bundle for the mortgage payment. Furniture here tends toward the almost ridiculously ornate, but almost all styles are represented here—wicker, contemporary, Southwest, and country French, among others. A gorgeous, burl-finish oval dining table suitable for a party of ten of the most discriminating guests was selling for $2889—down from $9889, savings of more than 70 percent. This kind of markdown is common at Rafael Homes, proving that one need not actually be a dowa-

ger duchess to live like one. —SC

RUCKER FULLER OFFICES TODAY

**San Francisco: 601 Brannan St, SF
(415) 495-6895.
Mon–Fri 8 am–5 pm.
MasterCard, Visa
Parking: Spaces on premises**

Rucker Fuller specializes in business interiors, and their 42,000-square-foot warehouse outlet South of Market carries medium- to high-end office furniture from leading manufacturers, such as Steelcase, at great prices. The stock—including ergonomic seating, desks, computer workstations, file cabinets, and conference tables—is marked 20 to 30 percent off list, and there is even greater savings on used furniture, which is priced according to condition.

Savings on samples and close-out items can be up to 75 percent off list prices. Wear and tear on used or damaged items are point-

ALPHABETICAL STORE LISTING

ed out by the friendly staff before you make your purchase. On a recent visit, we saw many chairs priced under $150, as well as a used natural-oak desk, credenza, and hutch by Steelcase in nice condition that was marked down from $5300 to $2400, a savings of nearly $3000. —*SB*

deals to be had on everything from budget to luxury furnishings. The mart contains more than 350 showrooms, many of which are open for the sale; a directory available on sale days lists the participants. Look for sale announcements in local newspapers or call to be put on the mailing list. —*SB*

appliances are featured, and standard thirty-day warranties and maintenance agreements are available. On a recent visit, we were tempted by a country-style three-piece set that included a natural-wood table with a tile top and a two-piece hutch marked down from $800 to a clearance price of $320. —*SB*

SAN FRANCISCO FURNITURE MART SAMPLE SALES

San Francisco: 1355 Market (at Tenth St),
SF Information: (415) 552-2311, ext. 3300.
One-day sales in May and November, Sat 9 am–5 pm.
Admission to sales $5; MasterCard, Visa
Parking: Garage on premises

The sales in the two buildings making up the San Francisco Furniture Mart are similar to the ASID (American Society of Interior Designers) Clearance Sales. The only difference is that the merchandise in the Furniture Mart's showrooms is more extensive, ranging from low to high quality. There are good

SEARS FURNITURE & APPLIANCE OUTLET

East Bay: 1982 West Ave (at 140th), San
Leandro (510) 895-0546.
Mon–Fri 10 am–7 pm, Sat 9 am–6 pm, Sun 11 am–5 pm.
Major credit cards, Sears charge
Parking: Lot on premises

You'll see rows and rows of furniture and appliances at reduced prices in Sears' giant outlet. Floor samples, clearance items, slightly damaged pieces, and returns make up the merchandise, which includes mattresses, bureaus, couches, overstuffed chairs, and dining sets. Sears and other brand-name

SLATER/MARINOFF

East Bay: 1823 Fourth St, Berkeley
(510) 548-2001.
Mon–Sat 10 am–6 pm, Sun 11 am–5:30 pm.
MasterCard, Visa
Parking: Street, nearby lots

If you're looking for a designer upholstered chair at a fraction of the designer price, this is the place. For example, a good copy of a Donghia Madison club chair, upholstered in wonderful fabric, will cost between $338 and $750, depending on the fabric; the real McCoy would cost $1700—without fabric. The store also has terrific values on solid cherry, Shaker-style furniture, including

ALPHABETICAL STORE LISTING

handmade dining-room tables in various sizes, and a good selection of wool Indian dhurrie rugs at reasonable prices. Slater/Marinoff also carries lighting fixtures, desks, bed frames, coffee tables, and so on.

Although Slater/Marinoff has been in business for almost sixteen years, the owners have stuck to one store, "so that we can control what comes in and what goes out," says co-owner Patsy Slater. "We're about quality as well as bargains."

ST. VINCENT DE PAUL

South Bay: 2040 South Seventh, San Jose (408) 993-9500.
Daily 10 am–6 pm.
MasterCard, Visa
Other stores: 2315 Lincoln, Alameda (510) 865-1109; 3777 DeCoto Rd, Fremont (510) 792-3711; 22331 Mission Blvd, Hayward (510) 582-0204; 2009 San Pablo Ave, Berkeley (510) 841-1504; 2272 San Pablo Ave, Oakland (510) 834-4647; 9235 San Leandro, Oakland (510) 639-4712; 3325 North Main, Pleasant Hill (510) 934-5063; 1025 Thirteenth St, Richmond (510) 236-5521; 206 Parker, Rodeo (510) 799-6608; 1519 Haight St, San Francisco (415) 431-1830; 831 Main St, Redwood City (415) 369-5898; 113 South B St, San Mateo (415) 347-5101; 344 Grand Ave, South San Francisco (415) 589-8445.
Parking: Lot on premises

The oldest of the big-four thrift-store chains, St. Vincent de Paul has been selling second-hand goods in the United States since 1845. Their fourteen Bay Area stores range from downright dingy to neat as a pin and sell everything from low-priced, run-of-the-mill clothing and lackluster housewares to valuable antiques.

Furniture is usually the best buy. Diehard thrift shoppers routinely trek to San Jose's St. Vincent housed in an enormous corrugated steel warehouse, park the kids in the striped tent in the middle where they can play Atari games and watch cartoons, and head for the furniture section.

Genuine antiques and almost antiques are displayed in charming vignettes on raised platforms; more contemporary pieces are lined up on the floor. If you don't like the prices, talk to the manager. "We're willing to work with you," she said. Appliances are well priced and guaranteed to work. —*CA*

TWICE IS NICE

North Bay: 1015 Second St, San Rafael (415) 453-0690.
Mon–Sat 10 am–6 pm, Sun noon–4 pm.
MasterCard, Visa
Parking: Lot on premises

Twice is Nice rarely advertises. They don't have to. Satisfied customers tell their friends about this lovely consignment shop where they can find great buys on period furniture, fine antiques, quality twentieth-century pieces, and unusual collectibles. A cache of genuine Louis XV dining room chairs were a real steal at $100 each. French furniture not your cup of tea? Not to worry—there is

ALPHABETICAL STORE LISTING

something for every budget and style. An English pine drop-leaf table with six chairs was only $150, and china dinner plates start at $2 each. For $1000 you could pick up a Victorian chaise lounge in antique gold velvet. If gold doesn't suit your decor, have it reupholstered on the premises—at a price guaranteed to be the lowest around —*CA*

THE WALLPAPER CONNECTION

East Bay: Crow Canyon Commons, San Ramon (510) 275-8055.
Mon–Wed and Sat 10 am–6 pm, Thur–Fri 10 am–7 pm, Sun noon–5 pm.
MasterCard, Visa
Parking: Lot on premises

If you want to add a quick border to liven up your bathroom or coordinate wallpaper and fabrics in your bedroom, this is the place to go. The Wallpaper Connection is a charming store that has something for everyone at a wide range of prices. At the front of the store, you might find bins filled with borders and rolls marked to clear at up to 75 percent off retail. All wallpaper in stock is sold at 25 to 35 percent off, and there is always a clearance wall filled with rotating stock marked 25 to 75 percent off retail.

The store has an extensive selection of wallpaper books from well-known companies, and book orders are generally discounted 25 to 35 percent. Companion fabrics are discounted 15 to 25 percent off list, depending on the manufacturer. You can even order window treatments and comforters to match your Waverly wallpaper, for instance, at 20 percent savings. —*SB*

WALLSTREET FACTORY OUTLET

San Francisco: 2690 Harrison (near 23rd St), SF (415) 285-0870.
Mon–Fri 10 am–6 pm, Sat 9 am–5 pm.
American Express, MasterCard, Visa
Parking: Street

This is where interior decorators and set designers go looking for great selection and great prices. At Wallstreet, which began as an outlet for a San Francisco wallcoverings manufacturer, you'll find a huge inventory plus things like companion fabrics and borders to coordinate any room.

The store stocks well over a thousand wallpapers at 40 to 50 percent off retail. At any given time, they carry from fifty to a hundred companion fabrics priced at $4.95 to $11.95 per yard.

The store offers a 20 percent discount on all book orders from wallpaper catalogs by manufacturers such as Waverly, Laura Ashley Home, and Eileen West.

Eye-catching vignettes offer ideas for decorating everything from living areas to children's rooms, with an emphasis on French, country, floral, English, and teddy bear wallpaper designs. Owners of Victorian-style homes can choose among a dozen patterns of Anaglypta, a paintable, embossed wallpaper ranging in price from $9.95 to $14.95 per yard.

Service is another specialty, and the staff is happy to lend samples to help customers make decisions. Bring room measurements, and be sure to check the remnant bins for incredible deals. When we last visited, we were tempted by hand-painted silk murals from China, priced at $20 per panel, to be hung on a wall or mounted on a screen. —SB

GARDEN BARGAINS

By Mia Amato

It is rare to find real bargains in garden plants at nurseries and garden centers; the typical 20 percent off or half-price specials on root-bound, dried-out, or late-season plants are rarely bargains as they usually fail to grow as well as a premium plant sold at the proper time for planting.

However, there are reliable sources for rare and unusual plants at bargain prices. Well-established horticultural societies often hold annual plant sales, open to the public. This is where to find the latest hybrids, rarities, and exotic species at surprisingly low prices. Most offerings are divisions or rooted cuttings from plants grown by society members. Arrive early for best selection and bring a cardboard box or two to take your treasures home.

Here is a sampling of rare plant sales for 1994; admission is free unless noted.

ANNUAL PLANT SALES

African Violets: San Francisco County Fair Building, every May and September. Ninth Ave (at Lincoln Way), SF (415) 664-9308.

Bamboo: American Bamboo Society, annual sale in March or April. San Francisco County Fair Building, Ninth Ave at Lincoln Way, SF (707) 745-4091.

Bonsai: Golden State Bonsai Collection North Bazaar, annual sale every February. Sale also includes pots, wire, and bonsai tools, new and used. Lakeside Park Garden Center, 666 Bellevue Ave, Oakland (510) 525-4837.

Cactus: SF Cactus & Succulent Society, June 11–12, 10 am at San Francisco County Fair Building, Ninth Ave at Lincoln Way, SF. Northern California Regional Cactus and Succulent Society Show and Sale, July 23–24, 9 am, at San Francisco County Fair Building, Ninth Ave at Lincoln Way, SF (415) 665-8101.

California Natives: California Native Plant Society, East Bay Chapter, October 1–2, 10 am, at Merritt College Horticultural Department, Campus Drive, Oakland (510) 376-4095.

Dahlias: East Bay Dahlia Society tuber sale, every April, Lakeside Park Garden Center (shed behind the center). 666 Bellevue Ave, Oakland (510) 339-8657.

Ferns: Strybing Arboretum, September 10, 10 am, at Arboretum Nursery, entrance Martin Luther King Jr. Way (near Ninth Ave). Golden Gate Park, SF (415) 661-0668.

Irises: Sydney B. Mitchell Iris Society bearded rhizome sale, July 22, 7:30 pm, at Lakeside Park Garden Center, 666 Bellevue

Ave, Oakland. Also July 23, 10 am, at Rockridge Shopping Center, Broadway and Upper Happy Valley Rd, Oakland. Beardless sale on fourth Friday of October at Lakeside Park (510) 482-5252.

Orchids: San Francisco Orchid Society Pacific Orchid Exposition, every February. Fort Mason Center, SF, admission charged (415) 546-9608.

Proteas: UC Santa Cruz Arboretum Fall Sale, October 8, noon, in Eucalyptus Grove at the Arboretum. UC Santa Cruz Campus, Santa Cruz (408) 427-1305.

Rhododendrons: American Rhododendron Society, DeAnza Chapter, annual sale every April or May. Town & Country Shopping Center, El Camino and Embarcadero, Palo Alto (415) 325-3266.

Roses: Heritage Rose Group sale of heirloom and modern roses, every year on the Sunday after Mother's Day. El Cerrito Community Center, Moser Lane, El Cerrito (510) 526-6960.

ACTION RENTALS

San Francisco: 565 South Van Ness Ave, SF (415) 826-1830.
Mon–Fri 7 am–5 pm, Sat. 8 am–4 pm, Sun 9 am–4 pm.
American Express, MasterCard, Visa
Parking: Lot on premises

Action Rentals is a big hangar full of the tools you only need once a year. Mechanical tools, such as post hole diggers for building fences and lawn rollers for laying new sod, cost about $10 a day.

Gas-powered tillers, industrial-strength sod cutters, and chipper/ shredders run around $50 per day, with half-day rates available. All equipment is serviced regularly; a computerized setup allows clerks to give price and availability information over the phone. Delivery and pickup on larger items (for an additional fee). —*MA*

AMERICAN SOIL PRODUCTS

East Bay: 2222 Third St (end of Bancroft Way), Berkeley (510) 540-8011.
Mon–Sat 7:30 am–4 pm, Sun 9 am–3 pm.
Checks accepted
Other Stores: 565-A Jacoby St, San Rafael (415) 456-1381.
Parking: Lot on premises

A paradise of premium ingredients for your custom soil mix is available here by the truckload (shipping to curbside about $50 extra) and also by the bag. You'll never again pay $2 for a measly pound of red lava rock or fir bark when you can get three cubic feet, already bagged, here for under $3. Custom soil mixes include Chicken n' Rice (manure and hulls) and Walt Whitman blend, an all-organic mulch. Sample jars of all the wares are in the trailer office. A dollar tip to the guys who haul the bags to your car is not expected but suggested. —*MA*

ALPHABETICAL STORE LISTING

AW POTTERY

East Bay: 2908 Adeline St, Berkeley
(510) 549-3900.
Mon–Sat 9 am–5 pm.
American Express, MasterCard, Visa
Parking: Street

Aw (pronounced "ahw") imports and whole-sales to Bay Area garden centers but also sells retail at rock-bottom prices. Amid the junk-yard atmosphere you'll find terra-cotta cherub pots, $16 and up; large ceramic plant-ing bowls, glazed deep red, green, and blue, from $40 and big oil jars for around $120. Step carefully; piles of shards and shipments waiting to be unpacked clog the aisles. Don't overlook the "as-is" shelves, where a chip or a scratch gets you a very nice flower pot for a dollar or two. —*MA*

BAYLANDS NURSERY

Peninsula: 1165 Weeks St, East Palo Alto

(415) 323-1645.
Tues–Sat 8 am–4 pm, also open by appoint-ment.
Checks accepted
Parking: Lot on premises

A wholesale nursery, Baylands specializes in grasses, native shrubs, and trees. Pad around the muddy stock areas to find lusty ornamen-tal grasses in gallon sizes for around $5. Call ahead for directions, and try to arrive early in the morning, before the neighborhood awakes. —*MA*

BENEDETTI MILL

North Bay: Santa Rosa (707) 938-9357.
By appointment only; ask for Rock Koch.
Checks accepted
Parking: Lot on premises

Composted turkey manure, the preferred mulch of many landscapers, is available inter-mittently from the folks who raise free-range Willie Bird fowl for the table. Cost: a mere $15 per small truckload, $50 per dump

truck-load.

No deliveries: Bring your own truck to the farm, and they will fill it for you in a matter of minutes. Arrangements *must* be made in advance: Call Mr. Rock Koch for availabili-ty, the address, and directions. —*MA*

BERKELEY EQUIPMENT RENTALS

East Bay: 2747 San Pablo Ave, Berkeley
(510) 845-6797.
Mon–Fri 7:30 am–5:30 pm, Sat and Sun 8 am–5 pm.
Discover, MasterCard, Visa
Parking: Lot on premises

A friendly, funky garage rental shop, geared to the small-time gardener, offers tool rental by the hour (with a four-hour minimum on most items) or by the day. Gas lawnmowers can be rented here for $25 a day; power rototillers are $39 per day or $10 an hour. Sod rollers and nonelectric tools run $7 to $10 per day. Delivery and pickup are avail-

able for an extra charge. —*MA*

BLACK OAK BOOKS

East Bay: 1491 Shattuck Ave, Berkeley
(510) 486-0698.
Daily 10 am–10 pm.
American Express, MasterCard, Visa
Parking: Street

Black Oak has big shelves full of garden books, many of them pristine review copies or recent releases. It's also a good source for out-of-print books. Computerized inventory allows clerks to tell you over the phone if a new book is in stock, and they will sometimes check the stacks on used books. They also buy secondhand garden books. —*MA*

BUTTERFIELD & BUTTERFIELD

San Francicso: 164 Utah Ave, SF
(415) 861-7500.
Daily 8:30 am–5 pm; exhibition hours daily
10 am–5 pm.
Call for credit arrangements and preview
dates
Parking: Nearby lots and street

Genuine Victorian stone garden ornaments and classy real garden art sell here at auction for the price of a reproduction, if not less. Their annual special springtime auction of garden antiques is held every May. Piero Mackenzie, vice-president and resident expert in garden antiquities, says the 1994 auction "will be the largest one we've ever had." Last year's bargains included a set of seventeenth-century stone capitals from the estate of interior designer Michael Taylor, which sold for $8000. —*MA*

COLLEGE OF SAN MATEO

Peninsula: 1700 West Hillsdale Blvd, San
Mateo (415) 574-6161.
December holiday season only; call for sale
dates.
Cash only

Parking: Lot on premises

Horticultural students under the direction of Matthew Leddy tend poinsettias and houseplant gifts for this annual sale; proceeds go toward student scholarship programs. A holiday spirit prevails in the greenhouses, where the sale is held for two days each year. —*MA*

CONNECTICUT STREET PLANT SUPPLY

San Francisco: 306 Connecticut St, SF
(415) 821-4773.
Winter hours: Wed and Thur 10:30
am–5:30 pm, Fri and Sat 9:30 am–5 pm.
Beginning in April: Also open Tues 9:30
am–5 pm.
American Express, MasterCard, Visa
Parking: Street

This store handles special orders of live ladybugs (when in season), trichogramma wasps, green lacewing eggs, and other beneficials, in garden-sized amounts, about $10 and up.

Notice by Friday noon is required. The shop

also carries organic garden supplies. —*MA*

COOPERATIVE EXTENSION

Peninsula: 300 Piedmont Ave, Bldg C, Room 305-A, San Bruno (415) 871-7559.
Mon–Fri 8 am–noon, 1 pm–4:30 pm.
Other Stores: 224 West Winton Ave, Room 174, Hayward (510) 670-5200; 1700 Oak Park Blvd, Room A-2, Pleasant Hill (510) 646-6540; 1682 Novato Blvd, Ste 150-B, Novato (415) 899-8620; 2175 The Alameda, Ste 200, San Jose (408) 299-2635; 2604 Ventura Ave, Room 100, Santa Rosa (707) 527-2621.

The Cooperative Extension program is a joint operation by federal, state, and county departments of agriculture, designed to provide free advice to farmers.

In recent years, in urban counties, the old "Farm Agent" now handles questions from backyard gardeners about ornamental plants as well. In California, the Cooperative Extension is linked with the University of California, with Master Gardener volunteers trained to diagnose and prescribe your pest or disease problems over the telephone.

A leafy stem of a sick plant can also be brought to the Cooperative Extension office for diagnosis. Whether you have a question about which tree to plant in your area, or how to get rid of whitefly on your carnations, you'll get free and knowledgeable advice for the price of a local phone call from Cooperative Extension. —*MA*

COST PLUS NURSERY

San Francisco: 2633 Taylor St, SF (415) 885-5100.
Mon–Sat 9 am–8 pm, Sun 10 am–6 pm.
MasterCard, Visa
Other Stores: 2040 Redwood Hwy, Greenbrae (415) 924-8410; 1910 El Camino Real West, Mountain View (415) 965-1551; 101 Clay St, Oakland (510) 465-6384; 2685 Santa Rosa Ave, Santa Rosa (707) 523-1138.

Parking: Indoor garage and meters

Seasonal bargains on fresh-cut flowers and greens, including Christmas garlands and wreaths, are always nearest the door. Year-round, there is an assortment of potted flowers, budget-priced orchids with blooming spikes, cactus, packaged bulbs, and other gift plants. Good prices on dried and silk flowers and containers as well. —*MA*

DIRT CHEAP ORGANICS

North Bay: 5645 Paradise Dr, Corte Madera (415) 924-0369.
Mon–Sat 8 am–4 pm.
American Express, MasterCard, Visa
Parking: Lot on premises

You'll find Dirt Cheap, a down-home hippie garden center, tucked away in a garage behind a haircutter's in a mini-mall. The site is muddy, the red earthworms are fresh daily, and deals vary. Best bets include "Mango Mulch," a custom mix of local farm grape or peach pomace and different manures.

Amendments run about $3 per large bag; some, like Clodbuster, for clay soils, are available in five 5-, 10-, and 50-pound parcels. — *MA*

GOODMAN'S LUMBER

San Francisco: 445 Bayshore, SF
(415) 285-2800.
Mon 8 am–8 pm, Tues–Fri 8 am–5:30 pm,
Sat 8:30 am–5 pm, Sun 9 am–5 pm.
Major credit cards; ATM
Parking: Lot on premises

Goodman's offers weekly sales specials and everyday low prices on construction material, tools, bagged fertilizers, garden furniture, outdoor lighting, and seasonal plants. Everyday savings include square or oblong stepping stones, in granite-gray or brick-red, 65 to 99 cents apiece; picket fencing is just $2.49 per 42-inch section. Biggest sales precede Memorial Day and Labor Day holidays. —*MA*

HORTICA

San Francisco: 566 Castro St, SF
(415) 863-4697.
Wed–Sun 10 am–6 pm.
American Express, MasterCard, Visa
Parking: Street

An oasis in the heart of the Castro, Hortica specializes in water gardens. Wall fountains start at about $80, with many freestanding fountains in a garden setting at the rear of the store. Staffers are real experts in aquatic plants, and there is a better-than-ordinary selection, $2 and up. Consultations are free; browsers are welcome. —*MA*

HYDROFARM OUTLET

North Bay: 3135 Kerner Blvd, San Rafael
(415) 459-7898.
Mon–Fri 9 am–6 pm, Sat 10 am–3 pm.
MasterCard, Visa
Parking: Nearby lot

This is the outlet of a national mail-order firm catering to hydroponic, greenhouse, and indoor gardeners. You'll find good deals and monthly specials on full-spectrum, halide and sodium plant lights, liquid fertilizers, and—for those who grow who-knows-what in their basement—CO_2 injectors and climate controllers. Hydroponic garden setups, with lights, start at $235. *MA*

JIM GREMEL STUDIO

East Bay: 1625 Kains Ave, Berkeley
(510) 524-4726.
By appointment only.
MasterCard, Visa
Parking: Street

Handmade, traditional bonsai pots in delightful glazes, including pale-blue, crackle-white, and textured browns, are offered here. Prices start at $12 for small containers; large oval trays with several drainage holes are $65 to $174. The artist also makes rakku and ikebana vases; seconds

ALPHABETICAL STORE LISTING

cost $10 and up. Special sales are held during the December holiday season, otherwise open by appointment only. —*MA*

JIVANO'S

San Francisco: 3674 Eighteenth St (near Dolores), SF (415) 552-7997.
Call for hours.
Checks accepted
Parking: Street

Jivano's provides repair and sharpening services for your garden tools. —*MA*

LYNGSO GARDEN MATERIALS INC.

Peninsula: 19 Seaport Blvd, Redwood City (415) 364-1730.
Mon–Sat 7 am–5 pm, Sun 8 am–4 pm.
MasterCard, Visa
Parking: Lot on premises

This is a drive-in service where you provide the labor and they provide the bags and shovels. Lyngso carries hard-to-find rock and stone items such as crushed pumice and pink gravel in bulk. These, plus organic mulches such as fir bark, run about $2. Tools, paving stones, and some plant supplies also available. —*MA*

MACCON MASONRY MATERIALS

San Francisco: 367 Bayshore Blvd, SF (415) 285-5025.
Mon–Fri 7 am–5 pm, Sat 8 am–5 pm.
MasterCard, Visa
Parking: Lot on premises

Buy your rock and stone here by the pound or by the piece. Everyday prices for clean, used bricks are 50 cents each (five hundred or more, 45 cents). New bricks are 40 cents each.

Occasional finds include boulders for Japanese gardens, already encrusted with lichens and moss, at 8 cents per pound. Gray-slate, peachy-beige, or reddish Arizona flagstones are 12 cents a pound; weigh it yourself on the outdoor scale, and they'll help you carry it to your car. Delivery on large orders can be arranged. If you are looking for a single piece of slate or unique stepping stones, this is the place. —*MA*

MCALLISTER WATER GARDENS

North Bay: 7420 St. Helena Highway (Hwy 29), Yountville (707) 944-0921.
Open March through October only, Fri–Sun 9 am–4 pm.
Discover, MasterCard, Visa
Parking: Lot on premises

McAllister's is a family-run nursery wholesaling water lilies and other aquatic plants to Bay Area nurseries. Prices here are usually 30 percent off (except water lilies) and the selection is comprehensive. It is definitely worth a trip. —*MA*

 ALPHABETICAL STORE LISTING

MOMIJI NURSERY

North Bay: 2765 Stony Point Rd, Santa Rosa (707) 528-2917.
Open by appointment only.
Checks accepted
Parking: Lot on premises

The Umehara family specialize in grafted Japanese maples for landscapes. Nursery prices here ($10 to $350) may seem steep, but are often 30 to 50 percent less than similar trees at your local garden center. —*MA*

NATURAL GARDENING COMPANY

North Bay: 217 San Anselmo Ave, San Anselmo (415) 456-5060.
Mon–Sat 9:30 am–5:30 pm, Sun 10 am–5 pm.
MasterCard, Visa
Parking: Street

The Marin alternative to Smith & Hawken offers 10 percent savings to professional gardeners on English-made garden tools and organic fertilizers. Alfalfa meal, the preferred fertilizer for rose growers, was $11.50 per 50-pound bag on our visit. Bins of bulk wildflower seeds and by-the-pound prices on exotic seed potatoes allow you to buy as much (or as little) as you need. —*MA*

OVERNIGHT SERVICE

San Francisco: 3488 Mission, SF (415) 824-9464.
Call for hours.
Checks accepted
Parking: Street

Even garden tools require upkeep, and Overnight Service is an excellent place to have your garden tools repaired and sharpened. —*MA*

POTTERY & FLORAL WORLD

San Francisco: 685 Brannan St, SF
(415) 543-5455.
Mon–Sat 8:30 am–5 pm, Sun 11 am–4 pm.
American Express, MasterCard, Visa
Parking: Lot in rear, access via Bluxome St

In the outside lot near the parking area you'll find reasonable garden art at about $50 a pop, plus everyday discounts of 20 to 50 percent off cement, cast stone, and terra-cotta statues, birdbaths, troughs, and pots. Tacky seasonal decor, baskets, vases, and silk flowers indoors are similarly discounted, with many priced 50 percent off for clearance. All sales are final. —*MA*

RESTORATION HARDWARE

East Bay: 1733 Fourth St, Berkeley (510) 526-6424.
Mon–Sat 10 am–6 pm, Sun 11 am–6 pm.
American Express, MasterCard, Visa
Other Stores: Blackhawk Plaza, Danville (510) 736-0255; Old Town, Eureka, (707) 443-3152.
Parking: Nearby lots

ALPHABETICAL STORE LISTING

Restoration Hardware carries American-made outdoor furniture, weather vanes, mailboxes, birdhouses, Mission-style outdoor lighting fixtures, and fountains—all about 15 percent off other local retailers' prices. On our visit we spotted a solid maple folding rocker, in outdoor clear or white urethane finish, for just $95. Advertised sales are especially good around the holidays. —*MA*

SAMMY'S PET WORLD

San Francisco: 2404 Sixteenth St, SF (415) 863-1840.
Mon–Fri 10 am–7 pm, Sat 9:30 am–6:30 pm, Sun 11 am–5:30 pm.
MasterCard, Visa; ATM
Parking: Street and nearby lot

This is a discount source for alfalfa pellets, a rose fertilizer which is sold here as rabbit food for 45 cents a pound or $15 for a 50-pound bag. Sammy's also sells compressed pure alfalfa blocks, 10 ounces for $2.49, enough to feed four rosebushes. Aisles are crowded and the place has that hamsterish smell of a pet store, but clerks are helpful and patient. They also sell bulk seeds for outdoor bird feeders (millet swags for 45 cents, sunflowers $1 per pound) and carry glass hummingbird feeders for under $10. —*MA*

SAN FRANCISCO HERB CO. OUTLET

San Francisco: 250 Fourteenth St (between Van Ness and Mission), SF (415) 861-7174 and (800) 227-4530.
Mon–Fri 10 am–4 pm.
MasterCard, Visa; mail orders may be sent COD
Parking: Street

Because this wholesale outlet does not import directly from overseas, some of the florals are too dried and faded to offer much fragrance but can still be used for wreaths or dried-flower crafts. The best deals here are spices and fixatives such as hard-to-find myrrh gum and cut orris root ($12.25 per pound), synthetic oils (about $3.29 per ounce), and the brighter flowers such as marigold used as potpourri filler ($2.60 per pound). A bargain corner offers 15 percent or better off seasonal items and pre-made potpourris. —*MA*

SAN FRANCISCO LEAGUE OF URBAN GARDENERS (SLUG)

San Francisco: 2088 Oakdale Ave, SF (415) 285-7585 or (415) 285-7584.
Mon–Fri 9 am–5 pm.
Checks and money orders accepted
Parking: Street

For San Francisco residents only, SLUG has teamed up with San Francisco Recycling Program to offer heavy-duty plastic "Earth Machine" backyard compost bins for $32.50. That's 66 percent off the retail price of similar composters advertised at $100 or more. Price includes delivery to your home address. Worm compost boxes are sometimes available for $25. Contact the office for an application form and for information on free composting classes held throughout the year. —*MA*

 ALPHABETICAL STORE LISTING

SARATOGA HORTICULTURAL RESEARCH FOUNDATION

South Bay: 15185 Murphy Ave, San Martin (408) 779-3303.
Sales office open Fri only, 8 am–4:30 pm.
Checks accepted
Parking: Lot on premises

Tree and shrub introductions from this non-profit horticultural research group focus on drought-tolerant, hardy plants that are grown and wholesaled to landscapers and retail and wholesale nurseries. In 1994, the headquarters opened up for public sales on Fridays only. Prices are near retail but foundation members get an additional discount, and anyone who comes on Fridays will be encouraged to become a member. The foundation recently celebrated its fortieth year. —*MA*

SMITH & HAWKEN OUTLET

East Bay: 1330 Tenth St, Berkeley
(510) 527-1184.
Daily 10 am–6 pm.
American Express, MasterCard, Visa
Other Stores (retail): 35 Corte Madera Ave, Mill Valley (415) 381-1800; Stanford Shopping Center, Palo Alto (415) 321-0403.
Parking: Lot on premises

Everyday discounts of about 25 percent or more on discontinued designs and returned items, with the best selection and prices during winter months. Recently spotted: Star-and-Dolphin metal garden armchairs, $175, originally $275; French metal bistro chairs, $75, originally $130; slatted garden chairs $10 off. Summer sales on S & H's famous teak garden benches are usually advertised in local newspapers. Choose carefully; all outlet sales are final. —*MA*

SOKO HARDWARE

San Francisco: 1698 Post St, SF (415) 931-5510.
Mon–Sat 9 am–5:30 pm.
MasterCard, Visa
Parking: Street

This Japantown hardware store has a fine selection of flower vases, in sleek, modern ceramic shapes, from $10 to $30. You can also buy florist wire, pin frogs and foam blocks for flower arranging, Ikebana shears, and bonsai tools at reasonable prices on the back counter. On the lower level you'll find an entire aisle crammed full of bonsai pots, $1.60 and up, and bargains in lacquered bamboo baskets, from $3.60. Soko also carries Asian vegetable seeds (pak choi, mizuna, daikon) year-round. —*MA*

SONOMA ANTIQUE APPLE NURSERY

North Bay: 4395 Westside Rd, Healdsburg (707) 433-6420.
Open bare root season: Jan 15–March 31, Tues–Sat 9 am–4:30 pm.
Mail order available, free catalog
MasterCard, Visa

Parking: Lot on premises

Any time you can get a full-sized fruit tree for under $25, you're getting a bargain. Owners Carolyn and Terry Harrison specialize in "antique" apples, plus hard to find pears, peaches, plums, and nut trees sold bare root at planting time. Multiple graft trees, custom orders, and UPS shipping are just a few dollars more. Trees are healthy and well suited to Bay Area climates. You can order by phone from the comprehensive and informative catalog. —*MA*

URBAN FARMER STORE

San Francisco: 2833 Vicente, SF
(415) 661-2204.
Mon–Fri 7:30 am–6 pm, Sat 9:30 am–5 pm.
Winter hours: Mon–Fri 7:30 am–5:30 pm.
MasterCard, Visa
Parking: Street

A specialty hardware store, Urban Farmers has wares arrayed in numbered bins and shelves. Co-owners Tom Bressan and John Stokes enjoy a national reputation for water-saving irrigation systems they design and install, and their consulting business is run out of the back of the store. If it's not too busy, they will offer advice on your own design plan. Free classes on drip irrigation are given throughout the year. —*MA*

U-SAVE RENTAL

San Francisco: 1800 Third St, SF
(415) 864-2811.
Mon–Fri 7 am–6 pm, Sat 7 am–5 pm.
American Express, MasterCard, Visa
Parking: Lot on premises

Here are dirt-cheap rentals for the weekend gardener: gas lawn mowers, $20 per day; rototillers, $35 per day; small cement mixers, $20 per day. Power chipper/shredders are $65 per day; most manual tools are $10 and under for a twenty-four-hour period. Ask for the "Weekend Special"—pick up your tools on Saturday, bring them back Monday but pay only for one day. Fee for delivery. —*MA*

WISNOM HARDWARE

Peninsula: Corner of First and Delaware
Sts, San Mateo (415) 348-1082.
Mon–Sat 8 am–5:30 pm.
MasterCard, Visa
Parking: Street

The granddaughter of the original owner runs the store, which stocks tools for older or movement-impaired gardeners. Frequent specials on American-made tools, fertilizers, and other supplies, plus a caring staff, make this one of the most pleasant places to shop for garden gear. —*MA*

KITCHEN, BED, AND BATH

Sure you've got great taste—and your home reflects that. There's still no reason to pay full price—even for top designer lines of kitchenware, dinnerware, crystal, or linens. With this

ALPHABETICAL STORE LISTING

list of great bargain resources, you can outfit your whole house in fine style without going broke.

AIRPORT APPLIANCE

East Bay: 20286 Hesperian Blvd, Hayward
(510) 783-3494.
Mon–Fri 10 am–9 pm, Sat 10 am–6 pm, Sun 11 am–6 pm.
Major credit cards
Parking: Lot on premises

It cannot be said that Airport Appliance is much to look at. A small parking lot fronting an inauspicious building scrawled with advertisements for products within, Airport Appliance is nonetheless a great place to shop for a bargain. Nowhere did I find a friendlier sales staff, and the list of perks for shoppers, prominently displayed over the sales counter, goes on and on. While this store carries mostly low- to mid-price stoves, refrigerators, dishwashers, washers, and dryers, some of the top names can also be found here, includ-

ing Traulsen, Wolf, Creda, and Sterling. Some items are manufacturer floor models or come with minor scratches or dents, and prices are accordingly lower. No price, however, is firm, and you can always negotiate a better bargain. —SC

ANGELUS FURNITURE WAREHOUSE

East Bay: 55 Fourth St, Oakland
(510) 268-0265.
Wed–Sun 10 am–5:30 pm.
Discover, MasterCard, Visa
Parking: Lot on premises

This enormous warehouse is stocked with a huge range of styles by respectable makers such as Bassett, Stanley, Kincaid, Elite, Bernhardt, Lexington, Highland House, and Taylor Woodcraft. While all of the items can be ordered through catalogs, the impatient need not despair—almost anything can be purchased directly off the floor. Angelus' challenging location and a low markup are

the key to savings that run up to 50 percent off full retail. Selected finds included a Stanley "cottage treasures" armoire selling for $1000, down from $1800 elsewhere. Additional special samples can offer savings of as much as 75 percent. —SC

BED AND BATH SUPERSTORE

San Francisco: 555 Ninth St, SF
(415) 252-0490.
Mon–Fri 9:30 am–9 pm, Sat 9:30 am–6 pm, Sun 10 am–6 pm.
Major credit cards
Other Stores: 590 Second St, Oakland
(510) 834-9484.
Parking: Lot on premises

The enormous building South of Market is indeed a superstore, but by no means are the products within limited to the bed and bath. Here you'll find a wide array of articles suitable for virtually every room in the house—china, silver, frames, small furniture items, potpourri, candles, toys, kids' books, curtains, rugs, small appliances—and all at very good prices made possible by this large chain's buying power. One such bargain is the Copco vegetable tea kettle, which sold for $29.99, more than $10 off Macy's price. The Oakland store is smaller and therefore has a more limited selection of items, but you'll still find the same great prices, such as Laura Ashley bramble towels selling for $9.99—45 percent off the $18 price at the Laura Ashley shop in San Francisco. —*SC*

BEDSPREAD IMAGE

East Bay: 39201 Farwell Dr, Fremont (510) 795-0539.
Mon–Fri 11 am–7 pm, Sat 11 am–6 pm, Sun 12:30 pm–5 pm.
American Express, MasterCard, Visa
Parking: Lot on premises

Crammed full of one-of-a-kind bedspreads ranging in price from $40 to $700, this cavernous store has bargain-basement prices. In fact, it has a thirty-day lowest price guarantee. They will reimburse you the difference plus 10 percent if you find the same bedspread elsewhere for less. When we visited, a white cotton king spread cost $109. —*MM*

BLACK & DECKER

North Bay: Factory Stores at Nut Tree, 321-2 Nut Tree Rd, Vacaville (707) 453-1256.
Mon–Sat 10 am–8 pm, Sun 10 am–6 pm.
Major credit cards
Other Stores: 1500 Monument Blvd, Concord, (510) 682-4880; 15206 East Fourteenth St, San Leandro (510) 276-1610.
Parking: Lot on premises

This is a store at which both the cook and the handyman can shop happily. Half the space is taken up by small kitchen appliances, while the other is occupied by workbenches, power tools, and other workshop accoutrements. Food processors, mixers, toasters, can openers, irons, coffee makers, and dustbusters are a few of the appliances sold here, and you'll also find a very small selection of nonmotorized kitchen tools. Many of the items come in blemished cartons, which, though the item inside is still in top condition, means savings for the consumer of 35 to 70 percent. For example, a food steamer in a slightly dented box sold here for $26, while Emporium Capwell sought $50 for the same item. Service products, which have been reconditioned, are also for sale. —*SC*

CASH AND CARRY WAREHOUSE

North Bay: 452 Dubois, San Rafael (415) 457-1040.
Mon–Fri 8:30 am–5pm, Sat 8:30 am–3 pm.
Checks accepted
Parking: Lot on premises

Located in an industrial area of San Rafael next door to the Marin airporter bus yard, this spotlessly maintained and uncrowded warehouse is perfect for caterers, party givers,

ALPHABETICAL STORE LISTING

and small restaurants. Stacked on one side is a handsome array of paper and plastic party wares, the kind you might find in a fancy party store. Restaurant supply items such as big sheet pans, colanders, serving platters, aprons, and storage equipment are openly displayed between wide aisles. You will find name brand frozen foods and dry goods along with all kinds of paper and industrial-strength janitorial supplies. To give you an idea, they have a wide variety of paper napkins including recycled small white napkins. They offer 250 for $1.69 and better quality napkins at $4.39 for a hundred. —*PK*

CENTRAL CASH & CARRY

South Bay: 190 Keyes, San Jose
(408) 287-7780.
Mon–Fri 7:30 am–6 pm, Sat 9 am–5 pm,
Sun 11 am–5 pm.
Discover, MasterCard, Visa
Other Stores: 1131 Elko Dr, Sunnyvale
(408) 745-0770.

Parking: Lot on premises, delivery service

Central Cash & Carry, not far from San Jose State, is a warehouse for party givers, churches, schools, and nonprofit organizations. (Ask about discounts for nonprofit organizations.)

You'll find paper goods and favors for birthday parties, weddings, baby showers, anniversaries, and Mexican fiestas (piñatas are $5, with new shipments biweekly). There is no minimum, no membership, and it is not necessary to buy in large quantities.

The management is proud of great service and is willing to work with "self-caterers." On hand are plenty of snack foods, sauces, condiments, and industrial supplies. —*PK*

CHEF'S CORDON BLEU

Peninsula: 28 Westlake Mall, Daly City
(415) 756-0200.
Mon–Fri 10 am–6 pm, Sat 10 am–5 pm, Sun
noon–5 pm.
MasterCard, Visa

Other Stores: 1135 Industrial Rd, San Carlos (415) 637-8405.
Parking: Lot on premises

"We sell anything and everything for the kitchen," says Gerald James, general manager. He's not exaggerating. This is a wonderland for the chef in the family: pots, pans, and bakeware from such makers as Calphalon, Le Creuset, Vollrath, and Pyrex; small appliances from Cuisinart, Krups, and KitchenAid; and cutlery from J.A. Henckels, specialty foods, candles, tables, and chairs. All are at 20 percent off manufacturers' list price.

We recently saw a Le Creuset cast-iron Dutch oven for $192, marked down from $240, and a Maverick juice extractor, marked $90, down from $178. A third of the store is filled with charming, wholesale-priced Cordon Bleu porcelain kitchenware.

Items are usually half the regular price: A quiche pan goes for $12, a six-cup teapot for $15. Plus, look out for weekly specials. When we visited, a serving tray had gone from $25 to $10, and prices on stools and chairs had been slashed. A Bannister chair that was originally priced $325 had gone from $253 to a final markdown of $166. —*MM*

CHERIN'S

San Francisco: 727 Valencia St, SF
(415) 864-2111.
Mon–Fri 9:30 am–5:30 pm, Sat 10 am–5 pm.
Checks accepted
Parking: Lot on premises

The secret to Cherin's low prices on appliances is their location (which the wise would care if venturing after dark). But by day you'll find top-of-the-line names such as Viking, Wolf, Thermador, Five Star, Dynasty, Gaggenau, Traulsen, Sub Zero, Asko—the list goes on and on. Cherin's specializes in top brands, which appeal to today's remodelers, and offers one low "contractor's price" to all comers, be they of the trade or of the general public. "There's more to a trans-

action than just price," says owner Marty Cherin. "We want our customers to have confidence in what they're buying and who they're buying it from." —*SC*

CHICAGO CUTLERY ETC.

South Bay: The Outlets at Gilroy, 8300
Arroyo Circle (Leavesley Rd at Highway
101), Gilroy (408) 842-3810.
Mon–Fri 10 am–9 pm, Sat 9 am–9 pm, Sun
10 am–6 pm.
Discover, MasterCard, Visa
Parking: Lot on premises

You can buy all the knives any budding Julia Child could ever need at Chicago Cutlery. Cookware and other kitchen accessories are also available, including some blemished pieces that sell for 60 percent below department-store prices, which is where the real bargains are. An irregular Magnalite classic six-piece cookware set sells for $60—more than 75 percent off full retail for a top-quality equivalent. For unblemished items, pay

department-store sale prices—a walnut six-piece knife set and block from Chicago Cutlery sells for $90, $10 less than Macy's price, and an eight-piece set of Magnalite professional cookware costs $115, a savings of $15. —*SC*

CORNING/REVERE

North Bay: Factory Stores at Nut Tree, 321-
2 Nut Tree Rd, Vacaville (707) 446-2981.
Mon–Sat 10 am–8 pm, Sun 10 am–6 pm.
Major credit cards
Other stores: Pacific West Outlet Center,
Gilroy (408) 848-3484.
Parking: Lot on premises

You never knew Revere's pots and pans came in so many shapes and sizes. But that's not all you'll find here—glassware, bakeware, serving dishes, and cooking accessories by Corelle, Crown Corning, Visions, and Pyrex.

Buy Revere pots and pans or Corning casserole dishes in bulk—read: no boxes—and save an additional 20 percent off marked

 ALPHABETICAL STORE LISTING

prices. A ten-piece set of casserole dishes sells here for $50, while a fourteen-piece copper-clad set of Revere cookware went on sale for $100, $60 less than what Macy's charges. —*SC*

CRATE & BARREL OUTLET

East Bay: 1785 Fourth Street, Berkeley
(510) 528-5500.
Mon–Sat 10 am–6 pm, Sun 11 am–6 pm.
Major credit cards
Parking: Lot on premises

Seconds and discontinued items as well as items purchased specifically for the outlet make up the merchandise here, but you'll still be hard-pressed to distinguish it from the full price stores. Selection here is just as bountiful, including rugs, small furniture items, dishware, glassware, pillows, cooking and serving dishes, kitchenware, flatware, candles, kitchen linens, sheets, comforters, throw pillows, and other home and kitchen accessories. The big difference is in the prices,

which can run as much as 20 to 80 percent off the original cost. A Mission-style coffee table, once sold for $120, here sported a price tag of $80; a ten-piece set of aluminum cookware went for $150, less than half its full price of $380. —*SC*

CYCLAMEN STUDIO

East Bay: 1825 Eastshore Hwy, Berkeley
(510) 843-4691.
Mon–Sat 9 am–5 pm.
Checks accepted
Parking: Lot on premises

Julie Sanders' handcrafted ceramic dinnerware has been featured in *Metropolitan Home* and sold at posh department stores and gift shops around the country, including Bendel's and Barneys in New York. It's all slab-constructed at her Berkeley studio, which includes a shop in front where she sells seconds and discontinued items at 50 percent off. Most of the flaws are minor—a speck of iron, an embedded piece of grit, or a streak in

the glaze. The stock includes her satiny-glazed ceramics in lush solid colors. Dinner plates were $15, salad plates $11, and mugs around the same, depending on how serious the flaw; big oval and round serving platters went for $30 and up. A former fashion designer, Sanders' greens, plums, soft yellows, and melons enhance rather than distract from the food. Her quirky forms look intriguing in white and metallic black, too. This is a place to go back to again and again to pick up a couple of extra mugs, or another serving platter. —*SIV*

DAISY BEDSPREADS

North Bay: 820 Piner St, Santa Rosa
(707) 571-1867.
Mon–Sat 9:30 am–6 pm, Sun noon–5 pm.
Major credit cards
Parking: Lot on premises

In the age of comforters, a wide assortment of bedspreads is hard to come by, but you will find it here. A handsome store filled with

ALPHABETICAL STORE LISTING

prettily made-up beds (some with matching window treatments and wallpaper for sale, too), this family-owned business offers brands such as Bates, Croscill, Dakota, Fabricuts, and Pacific Designs at considerably lower prices than department stores. When we visited, a woven-cotton chenille spread that would sell at department stores for $189 was only $110. Prices range from $30 to $400 for custom-made items. Special note: You can take home a spread on approval to make sure it works with your decor. The bed frames—mostly daybeds of painted iron and brass—are also for sale at 20 percent off: the "Sabrina" daybed floor sample cost just $159. Once a year, there's a summer (dates vary) storewide sale of 20 percent off everything on the premises. —*MM*

DANSK FACTORY OUTLET

North Bay: Dansk Square, 801A Main St, St. Helena (707) 963-4273.
Daily 10 am–6 pm.

MasterCard, Visa
Parking: Lot on premises

If you're visiting the Napa Valley, it's only a small detour to this downtown St. Helena Dansk outlet. The large, attractive shop is stocked with discontinued patterns, seconds, and limited editions of dinnerware, flatware, crystal, cookware, and gift items. Everything is discounted from 20 percent up to 50 percent and more. Most items are seconds with minor visual flaws, but there are also department-store returns. Best buys are the sales on top of the normal discount. One month selected dinnerware patterns were marked $5 to $10 off each place setting, beyond their normally discounted price, and flatware got an extra 10 percent off. Everything is clearly marked with retail price, discounted price, and percentage of savings. —*SIV*

DINNERWARE OUTLET

South Bay: 4155 Stevens Creek Blvd, Santa Clara (408) 244-4464.

Mon–Wed, Fri and Sat 10 am-6 pm, Thur 10 am–8 pm, Sun 10 am–5 pm.
Major credit cards
Other stores: 570 Work St, Salinas (408) 422-4962.
Parking: Lot on premises

This company imports high-end porcelain ware—French Pillivuyt, mostly—which it sells to fancy restaurants and then discounts to the public in two venues: a Santa Clara store and a factory outlet in Salinas, both well worth the trip. The former is a large, bright space off Stevens Creek, and, while there are a lot of seconds on sale, we dare you to find their flaws.

During our latest visit, a five-piece white Spirito place setting was selling for $17, while an ornate Pillivuyt "Manaos" five-piece setting cost $42. You'll find lots of fun European things: café au lait bowls, escargot plates, and café filtre pots. In the four-thousand-square-foot Salinas warehouse, you can have your own plates custom-decorated on the premises in the only fast-fire kiln in the US. —*MM*

 ALPHABETICAL STORE LISTING

DISCOUNT DEPOT

East Bay: 2020 San Pablo Ave, Berkeley
(510) 549-1478.
Mon–Fri 11 am–7 pm, Sat–Sun 10
am–6 pm.
Major credit cards
Parking: Lot on premises

While this shop offers a selection of bed linens and throw pillows, come here for small furniture items—chairs and tables, small bookshelves, screens, bed frames, and futons. While selection is not great, savings are—a five-piece tray table set sold for $59, 40 percent less than what it goes for at Emporium Capwell.

A maple Windsor chair sells for $39, less than half EC's $80 price, and a four-panel shoji screen can be had for $89. Also featured here: a shelf of inexplicable items including a wok, a Crockpot, and four *101 Dalmations* desk sets. —*SC*

FAMOUS BRANDS HOUSE-WARES OUTLET

North Bay: Factory Stores at Nut Tree, 321-2 Nut Tree Rd, Vacaville (707) 451-8546.
Mon–Sat 10 am–8 pm, Sun 10 am–6 pm.
Major credit cards
Other Stores: Pacific West Outlet Center, Gilroy.
Parking: Lot on premises

Two stores at the Vacaville outlets feature an abundance of kitchen accessories and other items, including knives, bakeware, utensils, baking dishes, flatware, stemware, some linens, candles, and picture frames. Huge blue signs and giant orange exclamation points direct customers to exceptional deals and clearance items. Brand-names, including Farberware, Revere, Ecko, Cordon Bleu, and Copco, sell for 20 to 70 percent off regular retail prices. The Farberware twenty-one-piece cutlery and kitchen tools set sold for $40, less than half Macy's price, and a special on Crystal D'Arques glassware offered a set of four for $15. While there is a second location at the outlets in Gilroy, the selection did not seem quite as good as the Vacaville store. —*SC*

FARBERWARE

North Bay: Factory Stores at Nut Tree, 321-2 Nut Tree Rd, Vacaville (707) 452 0533.
Mon–Sat 10 am–8 pm, Sun 10 am–6 pm.
MasterCard, Visa
Parking: Lot on premises

This shop is a cook's dream. Overflowing with small appliances, cooking tools, glassware, pots and pans, serving dishes and stemware, the store offers savings of up to 60 percent on blemished, overstock, and discontinued items. A chic stainless-steel tea kettle that sells elsewhere for $47 here went for $21, and a two- to four-cup coffee maker sold at $28, more than $30 off regular department-store prices. —*SC*

ALPHABETICAL STORE LISTING

FIELDCREST CANNON

Sacramento: 1300 Folsom Blvd, Ste 101, Folsom (916) 351-0849.
Sun–Tues 10 am–6 pm, Wed–Sat 10 am–8 pm.
MasterCard, Visa
Parking: Lot on premises

A good two-thirds of this outlet store is devoted to Fieldcrest Cannon irregulars at 40 to 60 percent off—bedding, towels, kitchen accessories—and the rest to first-quality merchandise. Irregular bath towels ($5) and hand towels ($1.50) are best-sellers, while sheets are in the medium price range: king-size sheets start at $19. —*MM*

FOOD SERVICE EQUIPMENT

East Bay: 710 East Fourteenth St, San Leandro
(510) 568-2922.
Mon–Fri 8 am–5 pm, Sat 9 am–2 pm.
Discover, MasterCard, Visa
Parking: Lot on premises

Visiting this store, which usually caters to the restaurant trade, is like flashing back to every small-town diner you've ever visited. The thick china with kitschy patterns, the clear brown glass ashtrays, the plastic burger baskets, even the vinyl seats—they're all here, and at yard-sale prices.

The big secret here is an attic-like room on the second floor that resembles, well, your grandmother's attic. Piles of mismatched dishes, glassware, restaurant equipment, and even a dusty set of antlers or two fill the room, and you can pick and choose to your heart's content.

Downstairs you'll find newer kitchen equipment—cookware, utensils, flatware, dishes, glassware, and chefs' knives—at savings of 20 to 30 percent off full retail (the actual discount is determined by how much you buy). A dozen butter knives sell for $14, while odd-sized glasses go for 40 cents each. —*SC*

FRIEDMAN'S

East Bay: 1923 San Pablo Ave, Oakland
(510) 444-0544.
Mon–Sat 9 am–5 pm.
Discover, MasterCard, Visa
Parking: Lot on premises

Friedman's has an unusual goal for an appliance store—to attract the repeat customer. "We've been around since 1922," says sales manager Chuck Anderson. "We want our satisfied customers to come back." Come back they should, and in droves. With names such as Creda, Kitchen Aid, GE, Maytag, Jenn-Air, Amana, Whirlpool, and Magic Chef to choose from, there's plenty of selection, and savings can add up quickly. While Friedman's low overhead makes for noticeable discounts, consumers can also find slightly nicked appliances that run an additional 30 percent less. One GE Monogram refrigerator fit for the most discriminating yuppie's kitchen, which was returned to the factory unused by a contractor, sold here for

ALPHABETICAL STORE LISTING

$520—savings of more than 80 percent off the full retail price of $2800. —*SC*

GLASSWARE OUTLET

East Bay: 1265 Marina Blvd, Marina Square, San Leandro (510) 351-2666.
Mon–Fri 10 am–9 pm, Sat 10 am–7 pm, Sun 11 am–6 pm.
MasterCard, Visa
Parking: Lot on premises

While you won't find many dishes here, if you're looking for glassware to complement your fine china, this is the place to stock up. Everything is inexpensive, and savings run about 25 to 75 percent off full retail prices. Serving platters and bowls, vases, serving dishes of all kinds, and stemware at great prices abound. Don't miss the salt and pepper grinders and all the candles your dinner party could ever need. Farberware stemware sold here for $1.79 each, while a pair of Mikasa Jamestown candle holders went for $20. —*SC*

GORHAM

North Bay: 801 Main St, Ste B, St. Helena (707) 963-7532.
Daily 10 am–6 pm.
MasterCard, Visa
Parking: Lot on premises

Browsing in this shop makes you wish you knew more newlyweds. The wondrous selection of fine china, vases, glassware, candlesticks, silver serving dishes and utensils, flatware, brassware, and decorative items all cry out "wedding gifts!"—but that's no reason why you should deny yourself a special treat or two, especially when savings can add up to more than 60 percent off department store prices.

Seconds and discontinued items mean the greatest discounts, and even the well-stocked will be sorely tempted by shelves of discontinued full lead crystal glasses, normally tagged at upwards of $30, clearance priced at $8 each. A five-piece set of fine lead china in the Masterpiece gold style went on sale at $40, a healthy savings off the full retail price of $90. —*SC*

HEATH

North Bay: 400 Gate Five Rd, Sausalito (415) 332-3732.
Daily 10 am–5 pm.
MasterCard, Visa
Parking: Lot on premises

Located in the thirty-year-old factory, this bright and airy store sells stoneware seconds—hard-to-spot glaze defects, usually—at a 40 percent discount: $11 for a dinner place that retails for $18; $78 for an enormous casserole dish with a retail price of $130 (restaurateurs come in droves). Great seconds on tiles and overruns, too. Look for wicker baskets and shelves stacked with even greater bargains: $4 for a chipped plate. And for something really out of the ordinary: birdbaths ($200 to $400) made out of broken crockery. —*MM*

ALPHABETICAL STORE LISTING

HERITAGE HOUSE

San Francisco: 2190 Palou Ave, SF
(415) 285-1331.
Mon–Sat 10 am–6 pm, after 6 pm by
appointment.
Discover, MasterCard, Visa
Parking: Lot on premises

Heritage House has an immense showroom, where you can find one of the largest selections in Northern California of top-of-the-line china, crystal, silver, and flatware at up to 40 percent below retail. Some of the brand-names that are sold here include Lenox, Royal Doulton, Fitz & Floyd, Sasaki, Orrefors, Waterford, and Wedgewood. A Fitz & Floyd china pattern called Starburst, available at department stores for $220 per five-piece setting, was $150 here. The Heritage House warranty promises that any item, broken for whatever reason, can be replaced at 50 percent off.

HOME EXPRESS

East Bay: Bayfair Mall, San Leandro
(510) 278-7003.
Mon–Sat 9 am–9 pm, Sun 10 am–7 pm.
Major credit cards
Other Stores: 39125 Fremont Hub, Fremont
(510) 795-7111; 1600 Saratoga Rd, San
Jose (408) 374-2266; 2020 El Camino Real,
Santa Clara (408) 261-9884.
Parking: Lot on premises

Practically every item your house could possibly use can be found at Home Express, and at savings of 20 to 50 percent off full retail. You'll run across bedding, bath accessories, rugs, clocks, art, frames, lamps, small furniture items, small kitchen appliances and accessories, glassware, dishware, and kitchen linens by such makers as Springmaid, Croscill, Proctor Silex, Crown Corning, Krups, Revere, Black & Decker, Kitchen Aid, Oneida, Reed & Barton, and Farberware. A twin comforter in the Kabuki pattern by Atelier Martex costs $90, compared with $115 elsewhere. A six-piece chef set of "just white" Corningware casserole dishes that cost $43 at Macy's was priced at $30, while a J.A. Henckels 4-Star eight-inch chef knife, $85 at Macy's, went on sale here for $68. —SC

KITCHEN COLLECTION

North Bay: Factory Stores at Nut Tree, 321-2 Nut Tree Rd, Vacaville (707) 446-7823.
Mon–Sat 10 am–8 pm, Sun 10 am–6 pm.
Discover, MasterCard, Visa
Other Stores: The Outlets at Gilroy, Gilroy
(408) 847-3747.
Parking: Lot on premises

Here you'll find a plethora of small kitchen appliances from makers such as Proctor Silex, Hamilton Beach, and Kitchen Aid at prices that are hard to beat. Kitchen accessories, glassware, and bakeware also make an appearance, and if the birthday of someone special is approaching, be sure to check out the largest selection of cake-baking tools

ALPHABETICAL STORE LISTING

we've ever run across. A Hamilton Beach juicer, normally retailing for $60, was on sale at Kitchen Collection for $25, and the top-of-the-line Kitchen Aid heavy-duty mixer sold for $270, more than 40 percent less than Williams-Sonoma's price of $455. —*SC*

LE CREUSET

North Bay: Factory Stores at Nut Tree, 321-2 Nut Tree Rd, Vacaville (707) 453-0620.
Mon–Sat 10 am–8 pm, Sun 10 am–6 pm.
Major credit cards
Parking: Lot on premises

The enameled, cast-iron cookware sold at this outlet shop is so classically stylish you may want to send your dinner straight to the table without benefit of serving dishes. While the store concentrates on every conceivable assortment and color of its bakeware, you'll also find a small array of kitchen supplies. Savings here can be substantial—35 to 60 percent, with the biggest discounts on overstock and discontinued items. A twelve-piece set of Le Creuset bakeware sold for $290, less than half the $625 price demanded elsewhere. Occasionally, unusual items such as a Japanese table grill also pop up, as does the largest collection of fondue pots we've ever seen. Well, after all, it is a French company. —*SC*

LINEN FACTORY OUTLET

San Francisco: 475 Ninth St, SF (415) 861-1511.
Fri and Sat noon–4 pm, hours subject to change.
Discover, MasterCard, Visa
Parking: Street

This factory store doesn't exert itself over decor; it's not always open, and the selection is very limited. But once you do get inside, the savings are tremendous. Rugs, pot holders, towels, blankets, pillows, shower curtains, tablecloths, sheets, and aprons are among some of the miscellaneous kitchen and dining room linens you'll encounter piled high in this tiny shop. Most items are overruns, with some seconds also available, and savings amount to 40 to 60 percent off full retail.

While most items are generic, some well-known brand-names here include Palms & Pomegranates, Wamsutta, Martex, and Early's of Witney. Dish towels sell five for $6.25, four place mats cost $8, and an Early's of Witney blanket normally retailing for $228 went on sale for $100. —*SC*

LINENS UNLIMITED

East Bay: 3566 Mt. Diablo Blvd, Lafayette (510) 284-7415.
Mon–Sat 10 am–5:45 pm.
MasterCard, Visa
Other Stores: 5400 Ignacio Valley Rd, Concord (510) 672-8484.
Parking: Lot on premises

You won't find many recognizable brand-names or a very wide selection here, but what you will find are savings, which generally run about 25 percent off full retail. While the store carries mostly first-quality items, some irregulars and closeouts make for discounts on towels, rugs, throws, comforters, pillows, blankets, kitchen linens, and bath accessories. The few names you will find are Springmaid, Dan River, Dundee, Cannon, and Lady Pepperell, among others. First-quality shower curtains by Creative Bath, which sell elsewhere for $50, here go for half that price. —SC

MARJORIE LUMM'S WINE GLASSES

North Bay: 112 Pine St, PO Box 1544, San Anselmo (415) 454-0660; fax (415) 454-4486.
Mon–Fri 10 am–4 pm, weekends by appointment.
American Express, MasterCard, Visa
Other Stores: Mail-order catalog
Parking: Nearby lot

For more than twenty-seven years now,

Marjorie Lumm has been selling well-designed, well-priced, crystal-clear wine glasses, mostly by mail-order, but also from her San Anselmo shop. One of her best-sellers is an all-purpose glass from Germany. "They are perfectly clear, and perfectly colorless—both assets when judging wine very critically," Lumm explains. And at $4 each for either the eight-ounce or the larger twelve-ounce glass, these are eminently affordable. She also carries the renowned Riedel glasses of Austria in the so-called "restaurant quality," that is, seconds with minuscule visual flaws at 50 percent off the retail price perfect. Prices recently ranged from $10.50 each for port glass or champagne flutes, $11.50 for the Chardonnay glass, to $13.50 for the popular Bordeaux and Pinot Noir glasses. All of her glasses are unconditionally guaranteed. —SIV

MARSHALL'S

South Bay: 5160 Stevens Creek Blvd, San Jose (408) 244-8962.
Mon–Sat 9:30 am–9 pm, Sun 11 am–6 pm.
Major credit cards
Other Stores: Call (800) 627-7425 to locate the Marshall's nearest you.
Parking: Lot on premises

Don't forget this discount chain when you're shopping for items for the home. Sheets, pillows, blankets, china, dishes, flatware, and other home accessories can be found here, and at substantial savings over the department stores.

Marshall's regularly features top names such as Oneida, Mikasa, Gorham, Laura Ashley, Ralph Lauren, and Springmaid. Prices here are generally lower than those at other discount stores, but what you gain in savings you lose in selection, which is limited and very irregular.

Recently spotted in the Colma store: Waterford crystal goblets at $35, as opposed to $50 for a comparable item at Macy's. Twin sheets by Laura Ashley and Ralph Lauren were clearance priced at $10, and Spode's popular Christmas Tree china line,

ALPHABETICAL STORE LISTING

which returns annually, also went for bargain prices: the fourteen-inch platter sold for $60, and the buffet set went for $20—$140 and $43, respectively, at department stores. —*SC*

MIKASA

North Bay: Factory Stores at Nut Tree, 321-2 Nut Tree Rd, Vacaville (707) 446-8485.
Mon–Sat 10 am–8 pm, Sun 10 am–6 pm.
Major credit cards
Other Stores: Pacific West Outlet Center, Gilroy (408) 842-4641.
Parking: Lot on premises

You can't help but feel like a bull in this china shop. Table after table is filled with elegant crystal stemware and beautiful glassware, all at savings of up to 70 percent off full retail. And if you search out the shelves of closeouts and factory seconds, savings can run even higher. An irregular fifteen-inch oval platter that sells for $55 when top-quality was selling for $14 here. First-rate china patterns are also sold here at substantial sav-

ings. A twenty-piece set of Biltmore Platinum fine china runs at $140, compared to as much as $300 elsewhere. Don't forget to look over the pitchers, candlesticks, ashtrays, perfume bottles, frames, and serving dishes and trays also available. The Vacaville store seems to be a bit better stocked, and carries additional items such as flatware, silverplate, crystal objets d'art, and a small selection of dining linens. —*SC*

ONEIDA

North Bay: Factory Stores at Nut Tree, 321-2 Nut Tree Rd, Vacaville (707) 448-5803.
Mon–Sat 10 am–8 pm, Sun 10 am–6 pm.
MasterCard, Visa
Other Stores: Pacific West Outlet Center, Gilroy (408) 847-5254.
Parking: Lot on premises

There's more to Oneida than just silver and flatware. Stemware, frames, desk sets, and perfume bottles mingle with impressive tea services fit for the queen, and all sell for less

than half of full retail. Single pieces of flatware in assorted styles are selling for as little as 49 cents at the Vacaville store; prices in Gilroy for open stock are a little higher. —*SC*

PACIFIC LINEN

East Bay: Emery Bay Public Market, 5800 Shellmound, Emeryville (510) 652-4895.
Mon–Fri 10 am–8 pm, Sat 10 am–6 pm, Sun 11 am–5 pm.
Major credit cards
Parking: Lot on premises

Selection is the operative word for this large store, which devotes almost all of its 22,000 square feet to towels, linens, comforters, pillows, and sheets. A smaller selection of kitchen items, beds, wallpaper, and lamp shades is also available.

With forty-one stores in this linens chain, the company is able to buy items in bulk, which means routine savings for the customer on such brand-names as Croscill,

ALPHABETICAL STORE LISTING

Collier Campbell, Atelier Martex, Springmaid, Joe Boxer, Eileen West, and Laura Ashley, whose bramble twin sheets sold for $15—45 percent off the designer shop's price of $27.50 for exactly the same item. To top it off, Pacific Linen will beat any competitor's price by 5 percent. —*SC*

PAPER WHITE LTD.

North Bay: 769 Center Blvd, Fairfax (415) 457-7673.
Open only during special sales.
MasterCard, Visa
Parking: Lot on premises

The sale, which occurs four times a year—early March, mid-May, mid-September, and early December—is worth waiting for if you crave luxury linens. Paper White, whose fine merchandise is sold in stores such as Scandia Down and Wilkes Bashford, makes its overstocks, discontinued lines, samples, and slightly damaged linens (also, children's special-occasion clothing) available at significant discounts: a $250 sheet can go for $95. The best way to be informed of the sale is to call and ask to get your name on the mailing list. —*MM*

REED & BARTON

South Bay: The Outlets at Gilroy, 8300 Arroyo Circle (Leavesley Rd at Highway 101), Gilroy (408) 847-5454.
Mon–Fri 10 am–9 pm, Sat 9 am–9 pm, Sun 10 am–6 pm.
MasterCard, Visa
Parking: Lot on premises

While you might think that silverware, candlesticks, and serving items are the only things you'll encounter at this famous silver manufacturer's outlet, you will find fine china, barware, crystal stemware, and glassware here as well.

Don't look for much giftware, though—items tend toward fine dining staples, although they can be discounted as much as 35 percent off full retail prices for first-quality items. Savings are the highest on their limited selection of overruns, discontinued, and slightly irregular items. Silver-plated flatware in assorted styles sells singly for 50 cents to $3 for larger serving utensils, and a sixteen-inch rectangular serving tray in the Plymouth style runs at $35—more than $50 less than department-store prices. —*SC*

RITCH STREET OUTLET

San Francisco: 688 Third St, SF (415) 546-1908.
Mon–Sat 10 am–5 pm, Sun call first.
MasterCard, Visa
Parking: Street

No longer on Ritch Street, the store has bargains galore on discontinued, overrun, limited-supply kitchen linens: 40 to 80 percent off department-store prices. The best-sellers are oven mitts ($2.75 for a long mitt) and pot holders (below $2), but there are also designer aprons ($10), place mats (a wide variety in popular prints at $3), tablecloths, napkins,

ALPHABETICAL STORE LISTING

cookware, and handmade fabric dolls of sundry ethnic background ($7 to $22). There's always a sale going on. When we visited, gardening aprons had gone from $6 to a low of $3, and at the after-Christmas extravaganza you could get pot holders and napkins at $1 each. We especially liked the chef hats ($5) and the brightly decorated bread keepers ($6.50). —*MM*

ROYAL DOULTON

North Bay: Factory Stores at Nut Tree, 321-2 Nut Tree Rd, Vacaville (707) 448-2793.
Mon–Sat 10 am–8 pm, Sun 10 am–6 pm.
Discover, MasterCard, Visa
Other Stores: American Tin Cannery,
Pacific Grove (408) 372-1793.
Parking: Lot on premises

With fine china from this prestigious company you'll impress your friends and family— but if you tell them what you paid for it at this outlet shop, they'll be completely bowled over. For first-quality five-piece china sets,

savings run 20 to 60 percent, but on the huge stacks of seconds in the back of the shop, you'll pay as little as 70 percent less than full retail prices.

A five-piece setting of the Pavanne style china cost $40—as opposed to $140 full retail—and the same set in the Harlow style went for $165, more than $100 less than department-store prices. Don't forget to check out the other items in the store, however, including glassware, stemware, crystal glasses, and an enormous collection of animal figurines representing more species than Noah invited onto the ark. —*SC*

SASSAFRAS

South Bay: Pacific West Outlet, 8155 Arroyo Circle (Leavesley Rd at Highway 101), Gilroy (408) 848-4500.
Mon–Fri 10 am–9 pm, Sat 9 am–9 pm, Sun 10 am–6 pm.
Discover, MasterCard, Visa
Parking: Lot on premises

Almost everything in this store—the bright colors, the selection of merchandise, even the signage—recalls Crate & Barrel, except the prices. Dishes, outdoor patio items, bakeware, dishes, linens, candles, and baskets sell at savings of up to 25 to 70 percent.

While most items are top-quality, there is a small selection of seconds at the back of the store. —*SC*

SILVER AND MORE

North Bay: Factory Stores at Nut Tree, 321-2 Nut Tree Rd, Vacaville (707) 451-2114.
Mon–Sat 10 am–8 pm, Sun 10 am–6 pm.
MasterCard, Visa
Other Stores: The Outlets at Gilroy (408) 842-3999.
Parking: Lot on premises

Anything you could ever want made of silver you will find at Silver & More. Tea sets, frames, letter openers, coasters, desk sets, flasks, wine caddies, jewelry boxes, lipstick cases, brush and comb sets, key chains, business-card holders, baby gifts—and that's not even considering the items that are not made of silver, including crystal figurines, vases, dishes, and stemware. This is definitely the place to come for special gifts that don't cost an arm and a leg—including candlesticks and bud vases for under $6. Savings on larger items run at better than 50 percent. We found sets of Towle flatware for $130 that sell for $280 at the department stores. —*SC*

SPRINGMAID/WAMSUTTA

South Bay: The Outlets at Gilroy, 8300 Arroyo Circle (Leavesley Rd at Highway 101), Gilroy (408) 847-3731.
Mon–Fri 10 am–9 pm, Sat 9 am–9 pm, Sun 10 am–6 pm.
Major credit cards
Parking: Lot on premises

If you do not care for designer patterns but insist on quality, this is one place you'll be able to fill your linen closet at big savings. Comforters, sheets, mattress covers, towels,

blankets, throws, throw pillows, and bath accessories come to the store direct from the factory, which enables them to sell for 40 to 70 percent below full retail. The middle of the store is a sea of tables packed with "manager's specials" and seconds, giving additional savings of up to 30 percent off their discount prices. Irregular Springmaid twin sheets start at $4; a regular twin sheet set runs at $15. —*SC*

STROUD'S

Peninsula: 700 El Camino Real #120, Menlo Park (415) 327-7680.
Mon–Fri 10 am–9 pm, Sat 10 am–6 pm, Sun noon–5 pm.
Major credit cards
Other Stores: 731 Market Street, SF (415) 979-0460; 75 Serramonte Center, Daly City (415) 991-9597; see telephone directory for east and south bay locations.
Parking: Lot on premises

You'll never shop department stores for

linens again after a quick pass through this linens chain. Top brand-names abound— look for Palms & Pomegranates, Perry Ellis, Adrienne Vittadini, Laura Ashley, Royal Sateen, Collier Campbell, and Eileen West alongside the usual Croscill, Wamsutta, Waverly, Dan River, and Springmaid. —*SC*

WARM THINGS

North Bay: 180 Paul Dr, San Rafael (415) 472-2154.
Mon–Fri 8:30 am–5 pm, Sat 10 am–5 pm.
MasterCard, Visa
Parking: Lot on premises

Shoppers at this factory store must first squeeze through an obstacle course of desks in the front office to get to the inauspicious door in the rear that leads to substantial savings over its three retail outlets. But once you've overcome that hurdle, you'll find yourself in a warehouse, a corner of which is appropriated by first-quality items selling at appreciable discounts. Flannel sheets, slippers, pillows, down quilts, throws, duvet covers, coats, and vests sell here at 30 to 70 percent savings. We found full-length goose-down robes selling for $89 instead of the $160 they go for elsewhere, and a body pillow with cover was marked down from $119 to $39. —SC

WELCOME HOME

Peninsula: 280 Metro Center, 31 Colma Blvd, Colma (415) 992-0311.
Mon–Fri 10 am–9 pm, Sat 10 am–7 pm, Sun 11 am–6 pm.
MasterCard, Visa
Parking: Lot on premises

This mid-sized shop carries lace-edged curtains, blankets, throws, pillows, rugs, towels, place mats, bath accessories, and all window treatments. While the brand-names are not always top-of-the-line, savings here can abound. Shelves of beautiful Atelier Martex sheets are priced at 30 percent off already low prices. We found a Laura Ashley twin comforter that retails at $148 priced at $70 at Welcome Home, while an Atelier Martex full comforter set in the Triomphe pattern that sells for $319 at Macy's was $218 here. —SC

MATTRESSES

Few items are more confusing to shop for than a new mattress. Without a corporate decoder of some sort, it's almost impossible to do comparison shopping because the major bedding companies, such as Sealy, Simmons, and Serta, all make specialized models for each of the stores they distribute to. The same model that goes by "Crown Comfort" at one store might go by the name "Presidential Plush" at another.

Rather than going out in search of a particular model name, you're better off going to a local store and finding one or two models that feel comfortable and fit your price range. While you're there, be sure to find out the basics of how the mattresses you've picked are constructed. Are they classified as firm, medium, or soft?

Do they have a continuous coil? How many layers of padding do they have? How long are they guaranteed? With these factors in mind, you'll have some kind of basis from which to compare prices at other stores. Granted, it's a little tedious. But you can easily save yourself $100 or more by asking some basic questions and taking a few notes.

In addition to their discount prices, the following stores were chosen on the basis of selection, service, and the availability of their merchandise. While every store has its strong and weak points, these establishments overall deliver what most people would consider a good bargain. All prices quoted refer to queen-size mattresses.

COMMUNITY MATTRESS COMPANY

East Bay: 1811 Broadway, Concord (510) 798-9785.
Mon–Sat 8 am–5:30 pm, Sun 10 am–4 pm.
Major credit cards

ALPHABETICAL STORE LISTING

Parking: Lot on premises

Established in 1959, Community Mattress Company specializes in custom-built mattresses for antique beds, boats, campers, and extra-tall people. All beds are designed and built on the premises to fit any and all specifications. Prices on standard queen-size mattresses range from $300 to $450. Free local delivery and setup is available, and all beds come with a ten-year unconditional guarantee. —*MS*

THE FUTON SHOP FACTORY OUTLET SHOWROOM

San Francisco: 1011 Twenty-Fifth St, SF
(415) 920-6801.
Mon–Sat 9:30 am–5:30 pm, Sun 11 am–5 pm.
Major credit cards
Other Stores: Fifteen Bay Area retail stores; check telephone directory for nearest location.
Parking: Street

It's hard to beat the Futon Shop for low prices on futons and frames, but you can save an additional 10 to 40 percent by visiting the factory-outlet store in San Francisco. True to its name, the outlet is located across the street from the company factory where all the futons are manufactured. Inside the showroom, you'll find the same merchandise and models that are offered at the company's fifteen retail stores, plus a wide selection of floor models and slightly nicked frames. Because they deal in huge volumes, you'll also find good bargains on futon covers, decorative pillows, and matching tables. —*MS*

HOME FURNITURE OUTLET

East Bay: 1099 Ashby Ave, Berkeley
(510) 486-8000.
Mon–Wed 10 am–6:30 pm, Thur 10 am–8 pm, Fri and Sat 10 am–6 pm, Sun 11:30 am–5:30 pm.
Major credit cards
Parking: Lot on premises

If you need to take delivery on a new mattress immediately, then Home Furniture Outlet is the place to go. Because they buy in large quantities, you'll get 20 to 30 percent savings on mattress sets that are available for delivery the same day (or the next day, depending on where you live). During our visit, we found their friendly, non-aggressive sales staff extremely helpful in selecting a mattress that was within our budget and promised years of comfortable nights to come. Unlike most mattress stores, Home Furniture Outlet will also sell mattresses individually without the box spring. —*MS*

MASTER MART

Peninsula: 32 East Twenty-Fifth Ave, San Mateo
(415) 345-5271.
Mon–Fri 8:30 am–5:30 pm, Sat 9 am–5 pm, Sun noon–5 pm (call first on Sundays).
American Express, MasterCard, Visa
Parking: Street

In addition to an average 20 to 30 percent

savings off department-store prices on Simmons and Serta mattresses, Master Mart offers free setup, haul away, and delivery to just about anywhere in the Bay Area. The store is able to discount prices by carrying only the most popular models and stocking them in large quantities so that delivery can be made immediately. The result is a minimal loss in selection, which is more than made up for by great prices and even better service. —*MS*

MATTRESS EXPO

East Bay: 2691 Monument Blvd, Concord (510) 798-8600.
Mon–Fri 9 am–9 pm, Sat 9 am–6 pm, Sun 10 am–6 pm.
Major credit cards
Other Stores: 2386 Buchanan Rd, Antioch (510) 778-9101; 6894 Village Pkwy, Dublin (510) 829-7747.
Parking: Lot on premises

A small California chain with three stores in

the Bay Area, Mattress Expo is able to discount mattresses by purchasing overstocked models from larger department-store chains. With their comfort guarantee, you can return your mattress within thirty days if it doesn't meet with your full satisfaction. Delivery, setup, and disposal of your old mattress are all free. Bargains during a recent visit included the Simmons "Harmony" Beautyrest, reduced from $1000 to $800 per set; the Stress-O-Pedic "Chiro-Cashmere," reduced from $1200 to $800 per set; and the Spring Air "Royal Caress," reduced from $1000 to $500 per set. —*MS*

MATTRESS FACTORY OUTLET

South Bay: 4910 Stevens Creek Blvd, San Jose (408) 984-8238.
Mon–Fri 10 am–8 pm, Sat 10 am–6 pm, Sun 11 am–5 pm.
Discover, MasterCard, Visa
Parking: Lot on premises

A factory-authorized outlet for Englander

mattresses, the Mattress Factory claims to have prices that are nearly half off what you'll find at Ethan Allen and other department stores. Delivery on most models will take three to four days and there's a nominal fee for delivery and haul away, but the overall savings are truly impressive. During a recent visit, for instance, the Englander "Renaissance" with luxury pillow was reduced from $900 to $700, while the top-of-the-line Lady Englander "Velvet Touch" was reduced from $1700 to $900. —*MS*

NATIONAL MATTRESS CLEARANCE CENTER

East Bay: 15430 Hesperian Blvd, San Leandro (510) 481-1623.
Mon–Sat 9 am–6 pm (open Thur until 8 pm), Sun noon–5 pm.
Discover, MasterCard, Visa
Parking: Lot on premises

A family-run business since 1939, the National Mattress Clearance Center offers three distinct levels of savings. The first category is on direct-from-the-factory mattresses such as the Simmons "Royalty" Beautyrest, which sells for about 30 percent less than other stores at $500 per set. The only drawback here is that you'll have to wait seven to ten days for delivery (or less depending on where you live), but most people find that another week on their old mattress is well worth the savings. The second level of savings is on new models that have mismatched mattresses and box springs. Under this category, the "Royalty" Beautyrest would go for approximately $400 per set. The final level of savings involves "as-is" models that may have small scuffs, tears, or misplaced seams. Under this category, the "Royalty" Beautyrest would sell for $275 per set. While the factory will not provide warranties on the "as-is" models, the store provides a one-year warranty. —*MS*

RENOVATION SOURCES

If you love to renovate—whether updating a kitchen or bath or just on the prowl for reproductions of Victorian hardware—you'll find many sources to choose from all over the Bay Area. Berkeley, in particular, became a salvage mecca in the late sixties, when a company called Sunrise Salvage obtained the salvage rights to buildings that were condemned to make way for the 580 freeway. Sunrise stored its bounty in a Berkeley warehouse, and before long was selling there, too. Other companies joined in, and—with the town's natural penchant for recycling, respect for history, and plain old thriftiness—a thriving industry was born.

APPLE ANTIQUE APPLIANCE

East Bay: 2973 Sacramento, Berkeley

(510) 841-8711.
Mon, Thur–Sat 11 am–6 pm, Tues–Wed by appointment.
Checks accepted
Parking: Street

This sixteen-year-old business in a snug storefront off Ashby Avenue repairs, reconditions, and sells gas stoves from the early 1900s to the 1960s—Magic Chef, Occidental, O'Keefe & Merritt, Roper, Spark, Tappan, Wedgewood, Windsor, Wolf—and caters mostly to homeowners, chefs, and contractors. Stoves range from $400 to $1000, and prices are generally negotiable. They also carry the occasional pot-belly stove, plus kerosene heaters and vintage refrigerators. —*MM*

BATAEFF SALVAGE

North Bay: 244 Mountain View, Santa Rosa
(707) 584-8401.
Mon–Sat 8:30 am–5:30 pm, Sun 10 am–4 pm.
MasterCard, Visa

ALPHABETICAL STORE LISTING

Parking: Lot on premises

A family operation since 1936, Bataeff sells both used and new steel, aluminum, hardware, tools, drums, buckets, and rope. Items are spread out, sometimes helter-skelter, over eleven acres of land plus a couple of converted barns, so equip yourself with sturdy shoes and a lot of energy.

New materials come from trade shows and liquidation sales, and is available at considerable discounts: steel, for instance, is 30 percent less than anywhere else, according to the owner. —*MM*

BERKELEY ARCHITECTURAL SALVAGE

East Bay: 722 Folger, Berkeley (510) 849-2025.
Mon–Sat 10 am–5 pm.
Checks are accepted
Parking: Lot on premises

The best way to shop this twelve-thousand-square-foot warehouse is to ask owner Alan Goodman for information. Call first, since the inventory changes according to Goodman's salvage projects. When we visited, he was dismantling parts of a historic building, the 1880s Dominican Convent in Marin County, and had a vast display of thick Eastlake doors available as well as oak cabinets ($50 to $3000)

From the wine country, he had huge wine barrels that are "big enough to live in," as he puts it. In the past, we've found wondrous things such as library ladders, industrial lighting fixtures perfect for loft living, exquisite carved oak mantles, and the sort of office doors we associate with the era of Sam Spade.

Always available are boxes of hardware and tools, rows of doors, bathroom fixtures, lumber, plus some new building materials sold at wholesale prices, but the great fun is in ferreting out the odd architectural remnant and the one-of-a-kind find. —*MM*

C&M DIVERSIFIED

South Bay: 330 North Montgomery, San Jose (408) 294-5185.
Mon–Fri noon–5 pm, Sat 11 am–3 pm.
MasterCard, Visa
Parking: Driveway

Customers have been frequenting this yard since 1945 for its bargain-basement prices. Doors, windows, and sinks are offered, but toilets are a specialty: a complete American Standard toilet can be had for $35.

According to manager Velda Mitchell, she has three kinds of steady customers: people who are refurbishing homes and are looking for vintage fixtures that are no longer being manufactured, renters who are replacing broken appliances (and don't want to buy new), and low-income folks.

Be aware that the recently inaugurated San Jose Arena, a stone's throw from the yard, has made street parking impossible, so you'll have to squeeze into the driveway. —*MM*

CALDWELL BUILDING WRECKERS

**San Francisco: 195 Bayshore, SF
(415) 550-6777.
Mon–Fri 8 am–4:30 pm (8:30 am–5 pm during summer months), Sat 9 am–4:30 pm.
MasterCard, Visa
Parking: Lot on premises**

Caldwell's is a family-run-business—and the only salvage yard of its kind in the city—with fantastic deals on both used and new products. Recycled building materials—lumber, roofing tiles, bricks, railroad ties, ornamental ironwork, marble, hard-to-find cobblestones—are a specialty. But this is also the place to shop for brand-new doors, windows, moldings, trims, stair parts, granite, and marble, which Caldwell's buys from companies that are going out of business, or at closeouts, and sells at a 70 percent discount. French doors start at $85, and a $1000 door with a slight imperfection can be yours for $350. Owner Rob Caldwell goes by this motto: "You can cut costs without cutting corners." —*MM*

MATHEWS & BARNARD

**San Francisco: 188 Hooper, SF
(415) 864-5666.
Wholesale: Mon–Fri 8:30 am–4:30 pm;
retail: by appointment.
Checks accepted
Parking: Street**

Although open to retail customers by appointment only, this company, which gets its damaged and distressed goods from insurance and steamship companies, is worth a look for the determined bargain hunter. Inventory changes constantly—canned goods, clothing, furniture, building products such as Sheetrock and roofing material, a load of French doors, artificial stone, and so on. Only for determined bargain hunters. —*MM*

OFF THE WALL ARCHITECTURAL ANTIQUES

**South Bay: Lincoln between Fifth and Sixth, Carmel (408) 624-6165.
Mon–Sat 11 am–5 pm.
Checks accepted
Parking: Street**

The focus of this shop in downtown Carmel is to "find new homes for what would otherwise have been trashed," says owner Anne Marie Ferguson—chiefly parts of buildings from the Victorian era and up to 1930. You'll find fireplace fronts, leaded glass, pedestal sinks, claw-foot tubs, period lighting, hardware, doors, and windows.

Tubs range from $200 to $1600, but do keep an eye out for the unique pieces, such as the 1870 eight-foot-wide cherry-wood Gothic fireplace and the two lifesize and lifelike church angels we saw at $3200 each. —*MM*

ALPHABETICAL STORE LISTING

OHMEGA SALVAGE

**East Bay: 2407 San Pablo Ave, Berkeley
(510) 843-7368.**
Mon–Sat 9 am–5 pm, Sun noon–5 pm.
MasterCard, Visa
**Other Stores: Ohmega Too, 2204 San Pablo
Ave, Berkeley (510) 843-3636.**
Parking: Street

Catering primarily to designers, homeowners, and architects, this fifteen-thousand-square-foot yard handpicks mostly older building materials, from toilets and tubs to marble mantels, columns, fancy wrought iron, lighting fixtures, doors, and windows. On our last visit, we saw a used but immaculate claw-foot tub for $450.

Expect the unexpected—ancient street lights, hand-carved pediments, transom pieces, odd garden statuary. Everything is negotiable, says owner Steve Drobinsky, and package deals are encouraged. To wit: a group of sixty-five leaded windows at half price. In business since 1975, Drobinsky believes that salvage and restoration are in vogue in Berkeley because the locals are "good conservators of the architecture they've inherited." —*MM*

OHMEGA TOO

**East Bay: 2204 San Pablo Ave, Berkeley
(510) 843-3636.**
Mon–Sat 9am–5pm, Sun noon–5 pm.
MasterCard, Visa
**Other Stores: Ohmega Salvage, 2407 San
Pablo Ave, Berkeley (510) 843-7368.**
Parking: Street

This storefront is the showcase for Ohmega Salvage's cream of the crop: antique lighting and plumbing fixtures, sparkling tubs and sinks, gleaming brass, stained-glass windows, and wrought-iron lawn and garden furniture. In addition, they sell brand-new reproductions of various items. A five-foot claw-foot tub repro, for instance, costs around $1400.

When shopping for a bargain, first take a look at the salvage yard, then move on down the street to the store. —*MM*

RELIANCE APPLIANCE

**East Bay: 830 Gilman, Berkeley
(510) 525-5921.**
Mon–Fri 9:30 am–5:30 pm, Sat 10 am–4 pm.
MasterCard, Visa
Parking: Street

A self-described mom-and-pop operation in a medium-sized bungalow located next to Urban Ore, Reliance combines two recycling businesses: They refurbish classic Wedgewood and O'Keefe & Merritt gas stoves for private customers or for sale on the premises, and they make furniture—tables, chairs, nightstands, hutches, spice cabinets—from imported, reclaimed antique European country pine. Stoves range from $500 to $2500, and a table made from re-milled century-old lumber starts around $500. —*MM*

RESTORATION HARDWARE

East Bay: 1733 Fourth St, Berkeley
(510) 526-6424.
Mon–Sat 10 am–6 pm, Sun 11 am–6 pm.
American Express, MasterCard, Visa
Other Stores: 1700 Redwood Highway,
Corte Madera Village (415) 924-8919;
Blackhawk Plaza, Danville (510) 736-0255;
417 Second St, Old Town, Eureka (707)
443-3152.
Parking: Lot on premises

Started by someone who wanted to renovate Victorians and couldn't find original hardware, this elegant store, located in the fashionable Fourth Street area, sells just that: Hardware in marble, chrome, porcelain, glass, and brass—mostly reproductions of the old knobs, hinges, handles, pulls, house numbers—plus gardening tools, statuary, and some furniture.

Don't miss the annual October sale on lighting fixtures—some of which, like Arroyo and Mica, are reproductions of Art Nouveau and Arts and Crafts originals. There's always something interesting to be discovered at Restoration Hardware: Iron towel bars from Arkansas; whimsical knobs ($2 to $15) in the shape of seashells, boughs, cherubs, and stars; or a one-time-only load of antique French bread trays and perfume bottles. —*MM*

SANGER SALES

South Bay: 1355 Felipe Ave, San Jose
(408) 288-5308.
Tues–Fri 10 am–4:30 pm, Sat 9 am–1 pm.
Checks accepted
Parking: Lot on premises

The biggest salvage yard in the Bay Area, Sanger Sales has three acres of mostly used building materials from bricks and lumber to windows, doors, bathroom fixtures, and plumbing supplies. Of special interest are brand-new factory closeout items such as hundreds of doors and windows at half their retail prices. Also, look for hardly used office furniture obtained from the local aerospace and electronic industries—an executive desk can go for as little as $40—though you may have to compete with school districts who buy truckloads. Everything is self-serve, but the yardman has a forklift to help transport materials to your car or truck. —*MM*

SINK FACTORY

East Bay: 2140 San Pablo Ave, Berkeley
(510) 540-8193.
Mon–Sat 9 am–5 pm.
American Express, MasterCard, Visa
Parking: Street

This fifteen-year-old storefront, which splintered off from the now-defunct Sunrise Salvage, has two distinct functions. They sell high-end, used, pre-WWII bathroom fixtures—sinks range from $100 to $1000, and marble sinks are a specialty. And they manufacture custom-built basins, tubs, toilets, and sinks. Nothing's inexpensive, but the quality is generally excellent, and they'll refurbish antique parts and hold your hand though any plumbing headache. As owner Ragnar Boresen puts it, "There isn't a problem that we can't solve. We're the only plumbing shop that's retail-oriented, and we know more about plumbing than anybody else." —*MM*

URBAN ORE

East Bay: 1333 Sixth St, Berkeley
(510) 559-4450.
Daily 8:30 am–5 pm.
MasterCard, Visa
Parking: Lot on premises

Urban Ore began some twelve years ago in a "mud hole," says assistant manager Peter Gillette, scavenging much of its wares from the dump, a practice it still keeps up. Today, they do a booming business with a two-acre yard and a twenty-thousand-square-foot warehouse in the Berkeley flats. Wear comfortable, sturdy shoes, and prepare to root through zillions of things—building materials of all kinds, cabinets, doors, windows, bathroom implements, appliances, housewares, as well as antique furniture, centuries-old books, old family photographs, clothing, and whatever else comes along. They'll sell anything and everything, and since it's up to the buyer to separate the wheat from the chaff, set aside several hours to rummage. Good deals can be had whenever there's a surplus: Mismatched drawers at $4 a piece can go for as little as 50 cents each. "We're cheaper than the Salvation Army," Gillette points out. The staff is good-humored and helpful, and the entire experience, between the easygoing banter and the scrounging around for old stuff, is suffused with that particular Berkeley spirit. And, true to that spirit, Urban Ore also offers "ecological disposal" of refrigerators ($25) and larger appliances ($5 for hot-water heater). —*MM*

INSIDER TIP: AUCTION ETIQUETTE

By Julie Carlson

Most people are intimidated by auctions: They envision suave collectors bidding on million-dollar van Goghs, or they fear they'll raise their paddle at the wrong moment and be stuck with a white elephant.

Auction houses have felt the squeeze recently, however, and prices have come down along with attitude. The majority of items sold at auction go for less than $2000, and occasionally you can pick up a real deal. Butterfield & Butterfield, California's largest auction house, recently auctioned off a Baker dining table for $70, a Biedermeier side chair for $300, and a collection of Sammy Davis Jr.'s Italian-made lizard shoes for $80.

Butterfield has two locations in San Francisco: the Main Gallery, at 220 San Bruno Avenue, which sells fine art, antiques, and jewelry; and Butterfield West, at 164 Utah Street, where biweekly auctions of inexpensive household goods and furniture are held. To find out auction schedules and to order catalogs, call (415) 861-7500.

Before each sale, a three-day auction preview gives you a chance to inspect the offerings. If something catches your eye and you decide to take the plunge, there are a few things to know.

You must fill out a registration form for a credit check in advance of the auction if you're a first-time bidder. Bids can be placed in person, by filling out an absentee form, or by phone. If you plan to bid in person, you'll need to determine when your item will be sold. Auctions take place over a three-day period; consult the directory at the cashier's window or a catalog for sale information.

You have the most control if you bid in person, but if you can't make the auction, placing an absentee bid is the best alternative. Indicate the maximum price you're willing to pay for each item on an absentee form and drop it in the slot marked "Absentee Bids" at the cashier's window. During the auction, a representative bids for you. You can also bid by phone at the Main Gallery; call customer service at ext. 550 for details.

If your bid is successful, Butterfield will contact you, or you can call the automated auction line at ext. 711 for quick results. You must pick up your item the following week or risk paying a $5 a day storage fee. A 15 percent buyer's premium is added to your winning bid, and an 8½ percent sales tax is computed on the total. This means that the $100 table you won will actually end up costing you about $125.

HELPFUL HINTS

— You have a better shot at picking up a bargain around holidays and in the summer, when dealers and decorators are on vacation.

— Improve your chances of winning by avoiding standard, rounded bids. For instance, bid $110 rather than $100.

— Moving is do-it-yourself. Butterfield provides no packing materials and minimal moving assistance. As one Butterfield staff member said recently to a buyer picking up a purchase, "It's you and me moving this stuff, and mostly you." ▥

 INSIDER TIP

INSIDER TIP: RENEWING OLD FURNITURE

By Robert M. Krughoff

Do you have a favorite piece of furniture that's getting old and worn? You may be able to prolong its life and save money in the process by reupholstering—rather than replacing—the item.

A key point to consider is how well the reupholstered piece will hold up. Furniture of reasonable quality, if in good condition, should hold up through at least one round of reupholstery.

You can easily check basic aspects of an item's condition. Be sure there are no cracks in exposed wood and that legs or castors are solid and firmly secured. Check what's beneath the surface. Take hold of the arms of a sofa or chair and push from side to side; the arms shouldn't wobble or creak. Also, lift one end of a sofa to be sure the frame doesn't sag.

A frame that doesn't seem solid may be easily repaired if the piece of furniture itself is of good quality. Check by turning the piece over: Look for solid hardwood rather than plywood or fiberboard in key structural components, and use of reinforcing blocks at the corners. Coil springs under the seat, with each spring tied by twine in eight directions, are almost always a sign that a piece of furniture was of high quality when first made.

Even if an item is good enough to last, that doesn't mean you will save money by reupholstering it. You do salvage the frame, the springs, and probably some padding and stuffing. But a high-production factory may be efficient enough to produce a comparable new piece of furniture for as little or less than it will cost you to restore an old piece.

Ask upholsterers for their opinions about a piece's potential, but keep in mind that they might be biased toward restoration rather than lose you to a retail store for purchase of something new. To assess cost, you'll need to compare price quotes from upholsterers with retail prices you find for comparable pieces of new furniture in the stores.

Be sure to ask exactly what is included in the price. Depending on the shop, the quoted price may or may not include regluing, retying springs, replacing the webbing beneath springs, touching up exposed wood, wrapping cushions in new polyester batting, supplying arm covers, and/or delivery.

These points—along with the price and a promised completion date—should all be covered in the contract or receipt you eventually sign after you select a shop.

The price quotes you get on reupholstery work and the advice you receive from high-quality shops will help you decide whether to fix the furniture or replace it with something new.

When your reupholstered item is finished, check it over, referring to the quality points previously discussed. If a piece doesn't meet the standards you and the shop have agreed upon, insist that the work be done again. ▪

INSIDER TIP

INSIDER TIP: TOP-RATED BAY AREA UPHOLSTERERS

By Robert M. Krughoff

Here are some of the upholsterers rated highest for service quality by the Center for the Study of Services, 52 Sylvan Way, Oakland, CA 94610; (415) 397-8305.

Alameda Upholstery, 859 W. San Carlos St, San Jose (408) 295-7885.

California Furniture Service, 152 Kennedy Ave, Campbell (408) 379-8330.

Delaney Brothers Upholstery, 2500D Old Middlefield Way, Mountain View (415) 328-4460.

Gallardo Interiors, 2642 Ashby Ave, Berkeley (510) 848-2066.

Kay Chesterfield Mfg, 6365 Coliseum Way, Oakland (510) 533-5565.

Michael's Upholstery, 1241 Andersen Dr, Suite G, San Rafael (415) 459-0208.

Robert Polak Upholstery, 104 Constitution Dr, Unit K, Menlo Park (415) 321-6400.

Sterling Interiors, 1250 Alma Court, San Jose (408) 293-1700. ▥

 INSIDER TIP

CHAPTER

FOOD 4

FOOD

Even if you don't dine out extravagantly or often, food eats up a good chunk of your paycheck. So in the spirit of discerning gourmands who want to keep a balanced budget, we've gathered some savvy ideas for saving money on food that are as fun as they are sensible.

DINING UNDER $20

Is there a way to dine out in San Francisco for less than $20 per person, without wine? Follow the lead of our seasoned expert, food writer Sharon Silva, and you'll be able to sample an exotic array of international cuisines and still have money for cab fare.

APPAM

San Francisco: 1261 Folsom St, SF

(415) 626-2798.
Lunch Mon–Fri, dinner daily.
Major credit cards
Parking: Street

This enchanting South of Market restaurant, with its exquisite murals and lovely garden, is the San Francisco beachhead of *dum pukht*, a north Indian style of steam cooking that was embraced by the Mogul rulers. Foods sealed in special clay pots cook slowly in the steam the containers create as they heat in a double-walled oven.

One taste of salmon *mouli*, a subtle curry of fish fillets, onion, tomatoes, and tamarind, will make you a convert to the beauties of *dum pukht*—and at considerably less than Mogul prices. Lamb shank baked with apricots and saffron, stuffed quail with tamarind, and chicken breast in a tomato masala are also recommended, as are the wild-mushroom masala and the *aloo tikki*, an herb-flecked potato patty that comes with tamarind and mint chutneys. —SS

BAKER ST BISTRO

San Francisco: 2953 Baker St, SF
(415) 931-1475.
Dinner Tues–Sat.
MasterCard, Visa
Parking: Street

In France, diners regularly cut costs by ordering a bistro's prix fixe menu. In San Francisco, you can do the same thing at the postage-stamp-size Baker St Bistro. Chef-owner Jacques Manuera assembles a new quartet of courses daily, attracting a steady stream of loyal patrons.

On one evening Manuera might entice diners with a simple purée of vegetable soup, flank steak in a light shallot sauce, vinagrette-dressed *mesclun* salad, and silky crème caramel surrounded with ladyfingers. Or the menu might open with a slice of pate, to be followed by *blanquette de veau*, salad, and a wedge of homemade *tarte au fruit*.

No matter what the lineup, the price on our recent visits was always a reasonable

ALPHABETICAL STORE LISTING

$14.50. Diners who opt for à la carte can still slide under the limit here and not leave the least bit hungry. This place has been discovered, though, so be sure to reserve one of the dozen tables. —*SS*

BARRIO FIESTA

San Francisco: 909 Antoinette Ln, South San Francisco (415) 871-8703.
Lunch and dinner daily.
MasterCard, Visa
Parking: Lot on premises

Inside an enclosed gazebo-style building that captures the tropical warmth of the Philippines, waiters clad in the native *barong tagalog* deliver the classic dishes of the islands to an almost always packed house. Barrio Fiesta's popularity is no surprise.

Its flagship restaurant in Manila is a Filipino tradition, a place where families flock for Sunday dinner. Offerings at Barrio Fiesta on both sides of the Pacific are reasonably priced—enormous helpings of *adobo*

(chicken and/or pork braised in vinegar, soy sauce, and garlic), crispy *pata* (seasoned pork hock), *pinakbet* (braised eggplant, okra, green beans, and pumpkin), *bangus* (milkfish), and *kare-kare* (oxtails, tripe, eggplant, and long beans in a rich peanut sauce). —*SS*

CAMBODIANA

East Bay: 2156 University Ave, Berkeley (510) 843-4630.
Lunch Mon–Fri, dinner daily.
Major credit cards
Parking: Street

Prewar Cambodia had virtually no Cambodian restaurants. The dining-out trade was historically divided between the families of Chinese immigrants and the French overlords.

For the most part, Khmer classics were found only in the royal palace. But in the restaurant-crazy Bay Area, Cambodian immigrants have found a market for their memorable plates. Sidney Ke and his chef

and wife, Carol Bopha Ke, offer an exquisite array of Khmer dishes with French influence just steps from the UC Berkeley campus gate.

Bopha, a master of sauces and marinades, prepares, among other culinary treasures, Cambodian-style garlicky escargots; crisply cooked marinated stuffed quail; tender, fragrant lamb rib chops; fish mousse steamed in a banana leaf; and wonderfully smoky eggplant topped with seasoned pork and shrimp. —*SS*

CITY OF PARIS

San Francisco: 101 Shannon Alley (at Geary), SF (415) 441-4442.
Breakfast, lunch, and dinner daily.
Major credit cards
Parking: Lot on premises

The partners behind City of Paris call the place a "people's bistro, where you don't have to break the bank to pay for dinner." And you'll believe them if you order their herb-coated roasted half-chicken accompanied with a mile-high mound of *pommes frites* that are almost good enough to make you forget your last trip to the City of Light. A good number of hearty main courses qualified for our budget. Indeed, there is even money left over for a simple mixed-greens salad or a more complex blend of celeriac, apples, and endive. Located in the heart of the Union Square theater district, the large, high-ceilinged dining room stays open late to welcome diners after the shows. —*SS*

DES ALPES

San Francisco: 732 Broadway St, SF
(415) 391-4249.
Dinner Tues–Sun.
MasterCard, Visa
Parking: Nearby garage

From the moment you walk into the *intime* bar that fronts Des Alpes and take your first stab at the thin and perfectly crisp *pommes frites*, you'll know you're in the presence of

restaurateurs who recognize that "French" means more than creamy sauces. Opened in 1908, this was for years the checkered-table-cloth retreat for folks who didn't believe in retreat—the anti-Fascist vets of the Spanish Civil War's Basque legion. The seven-course meal (the menu changes nightly) is hearty enough to satisfy the most ravenous soul and costs less than a pair of movie tickets.

There is a choice of two so-called appetizers—big enough to be dubbed entrees in any other place—and one of two main courses. Among the recent best dishes are leg of lamb, calf's sweetbreads, trout, panfried sand dabs, and a casserole of clams with rice. —*SS*

EL NUEVO FRUTILANDIA

San Francisco: 3077 Twenty-fourth St, SF
(415) 648-2958.
Lunch and dinner daily.
Master Card, Visa
Parking: Street

This bright, friendly Caribbean bistro along

busy, colorful Twenty-fourth Street in the Mission district serves real home cooking to a loyal clientele. Among other things, it offers Puerto Rican dumplings, a *campesino* favorite that wraps a dough of crushed plaintain and yuca around flavorful shreds of pork and olives. These are served with deliciously spiced black beans and rice. Those orbs that resemble oranges which many of the regulars order are actually *papas rellenas*, deep-fried balls of whipped potato enclosing meat, raisins, and peppers.

You'll also find Cuban-style roast pork, served with black beans and rice, and many other hearty plates. Nuevo Frutilandia also serves up a host of the refreshing tropical shakes for which the Caribbean is famous. —*SS*

EMPRESS COURT

Peninsula: 433 Airport Blvd, Fifth Floor,
Burlingame (415) 348-1122.
Lunch and dinner daily.
Major credit cards

ALPHABETICAL STORE LISTING

Parking: Lot on premises

The Bay Area's Chinese restaurant competition is always at a fever pitch, and any place that weathers the race deserves recognition.

That's the story with Empress Court, an upmarket Cantonese establishment with an excellent menu, a busy dining room, and a price list that won't empty your pocketbook. A small menu of special dishes and set dinners lists a number of intriguing items, and may include a dish composed of layers of egg white and soft bean curd strewn with shredded dried scallops, and diced roast duck and black mushroom.

You also won't go wrong with a plate of tender pea shoots stir-fried with garlic, one of the many interesting clay-pot dishes, the seafood *lo mein* that mixes young bok choy and bits of shellfish with delicate noodle ribbons, or the somewhat pricey black cod. If there is still room in your budget, cap off the meal with black sesame seed-filled dumplings or mango pudding. —SS

FINA ESTAMPA

**San Francisco: 2374 Mission St, SF
(415) 824-4437.
Lunch and dinner Tues–Sun.
MasterCard, Visa
Parking: Lot parking across the street**

This is a small, simply decorated storefront in the heart of the barrio. Chef-owner Gus Shinzato, a Peruvian of Japanese descent, cooks up the fare of his native country and its former ruler, Spain—in portions to appease a lumberjack. Peru's best-loved soup, *parihuela de mariscos*—white fish, squid, and clams in an aromatic tomato-based broth—is ladled up to the brim of an oversize bowl.

Equally huge, and equally good, is another seafood soup, this one with rice and a cilantro-laced broth. Accompanied with the bread and incendiary *aji* (chili) sauce that come with every dinner here, both soups are meals in themselves. A trio of classic Peruvian meat dishes also glide in under our monetary limit: *lomo saltado*, a sensational sauté of beef, onions, potatoes, and tomatoes doused in a vinegar; *bistec a la pobre*, grilled filet topped with onions, tomatoes and deep-fried bananas; and *carnero a la parrilla con yerba buena*, lamb ribs squired by a vibrant salsa of fresh mint. —SS

GINGER ISLAND

**East Bay: 1820 Fourth St, Berkeley
(510) 644-0444.
Lunch Mon–Fri, dinner daily.
Major credit cards
Parking: Lot on premises**

With the 1993 opening of Ginger Island, executive chef Bruce Cost, the Bay Area's undisputed maestro of the pan-Asian menu, has turned his estimable talents to melding Eastern and Western cuisines. This light-filled spot done up in tropical kitsch, sited in the heart of Berkeley's trendy Fourth St, embraces not only wontons and satay but also hamburgers with Southeast Asian salsa and tossed green salads. Partisans of Cost's tea-

ALPHABETICAL STORE LISTING

smoked duck of the past will want to check out his excellent ginger-marinated grilled duck served with tossed greens and steamed jasmine rice. Thai curry noodles, grilled fish with black bean sauce, and a variety of stir-fries also turn up on the regularly changing menu. A glass of the house-mixed fresh ginger ale suits every order. —SS

GIRA POLLI

San Francisco: 659 Union St, SF
(415) 434-4472.
Dinner daily.
American Express, MasterCard, Visa
Other stores: 590 E. Blithedale, Mill Valley
(415) 383-6040.
Parking: Metered street

The story of Gira Polli opens in the mid-eighties, when Michele and Norine Ferrante spotted the world's most spectacular rotisserie in Palermo, Michele's hometown. The rotisserie could roast 126 chickens simultaneously over a great aromatic wood fire. The Ferrantes couldn't resist that oven, so they brought one home and opened Gira Polli — which roughly translates as "rotating chickens." The small, handsome North Beach restaurant is a showcase for their exquisite machine. The Ferrantes prepare the plump birds in true Sicilian fashion, rubbed with garlic and herbs and basted with olive oil, and each serving comes with roasted potatoes and bread rolls. Start your meal with tomatoes and creamy fresh mozzarella. —SS

HELMAND

San Francisco: 430 Broadway St, SF
(415) 362-0641.
Lunch Mon–Fri, dinner Mon–Sat.
Major credit cards
Parking: Lot on premises

Named for the great Afghan river that winds northeast from the Iranian border, the elegantly appointed Helmand—a touch of true class on the Broadway strip—offers dishes that incorporate culinary elements from Central Asia, India, the Middle East, and sometimes beyond. Indeed, one of Helmand's best dishes, *aushak*, may well have been left behind by the Mongols when they marched through Afghanistan to the Middle East. The leek-filled wheat triangles topped with both a yogurt-mint sauce and a beef sauce unmistakably recall the dumplings of the Far East.

Another echo of the nomadic world resounds in *chowpan seekh*, a grilled rack of lamb on paper-thin flat bread (a cousin of Iranian *nane lavash*) that is an upscale takeoff on the Afghan shepherd's campfire meal. Still other kitchen glories include *kaddo borawni*, pumpkin atop a garlic-flavored yogurt sauce, and *bowlawni*, leek-and-potato-filled pastries. —SS

HONG KONG VILLA

San Francisco: 2332 Clement St, SF
(415) 752-8833.
Lunch and dinner daily.

ALPHABETICAL STORE LISTING

MasterCard, Visa
Parking: Street

It's no secret that Chinese restaurants can be fertile hunting grounds for penny-pinching diners. But many of the most intriguing bargains, designed with the kitchen's strengths and the season in mind are, are often hidden from non-Chinese speakers, announced only on ideogram-rendered menu inserts. Sometimes waiters are willing translators, but not always. So kudos to the smartly appointed Hong Kong Villa, with its bilingual menus that offer first-rate meals—no clichéd sweet-and-sour pork or cashew chicken— that fall within our budget.

On our recent visit, Hong Kong Villa was offering a meal for four within our budget that included seafood-filled bean curd rolls, soup, Peking duck, a hefty two-and-a-half-pound lobster, baby beef ribs, stir-fried vegetables, and dessert. Hong Kong Villa also has more than half a dozen different whole crab dishes—fresh—the crustaceans plucked fresh from the tank. —SS

LE SOLEIL

San Francisco: 133 Clement St, SF
(415) 668-4848.
Lunch and dinner daily.
MasterCard, Visa
Parking: Street

More than 130,000 former residents of Vietnam dwell in three major Little Saigons in the metropolitan Bay Area: the Larkin Street area of the Tenderloin in San Francisco, near downtown Oakland, and in the heart of San Jose. With them have traveled the glories of Vietnamese food. One of the premier outposts for this distinctive fare is the bright and handsomely appointed Le Soleil, a temple of authentic Vietnamese specialties in the Richmond District.

The kitchen adroitly handles the preparation of everything from the commonplace *cha gio* (imperial roll) to the more esoteric *banh cong* (crisp, savory pastry shells filled with shrimp and green beans) and *bo nhung dam* (beef fondue in a vinegary broth). Don't miss the clay pot of jumbo prawns in the shell in a sauce that begs to be eaten with a spoon. —SS

LITTLE CAFE

San Francisco: 914 Clement St, SF
(415) 668-3829.
Dinner daily.
American Express, MasterCard, Visa
Parking: Street

When Frank Chow opened the Little Cafe in the late eighties, he wasn't interested in serving anything even vaguely suggestive of his native Shanghai. A veteran of two decades in the kitchens of pricey Italian restaurants in the Bay Area, Chow knows *la cucina italiana* and that is what he offers in his intimate Richmond District tablecloth trattoria, one of the best values in town.

He's a stickler for quality, personally selecting every ingredient and personally preparing every dish, which you can watch him do in the modern open kitchen that stands at the rear of the dining room. Try the pasta sauced with a blend of saffron, artichoke hearts, prosciutto, and cream, or with a simple mix of seafood and a smattering of tomato. Simple meat courses and modestly priced appetizers round out the appealing menu. —SS

STRAITS CAFE

San Francisco: 3300 Geary Blvd, SF
(415) 668-1783.
Lunch and dinner daily.
Major credit cards
Parking: Street

The coastal cities of Malacca, Penang, and Singapore, which lie along the Strait of Malacca, harbor one of the world's most fascinating melting pots: a blend of influences from India, south China, Europe, and the Malay archipelago. The culinary results are just as complex, and Chris Yeo has made his Straits Cafe the top spot in the Bay Area to explore them. In his coolly understated din-

ing room (one wall recreates the laundry-draped shophouse fronts of old Singapore), you may find *kway pai ti* (pastry shells with slivered vegetables and chili), *otak-otak* (ground fish steamed in banana leaves, resembling a paté), *Hai nan* chicken rice, and *laksa* (tamarind-scented broth containing fish, chilies, and rice noodles). —SS

SUPPENKÜCHE

San Francisco: 525 Laguna St, SF
(415) 252-9289.
Lunch Tues–Sat, dinner Tues–Sun.
American Express, MasterCard, Visa
Parking: Street

The dining room at Suppenküche, on the edge of the Civic Center, recalls a hip Berlin *gasthaus*—bleached wood tables, bundles of dried flowers pinned to the wall, waiters in stylishly well-worn fedoras, the din of gregarious chatter. The food is classic German, with delicious bratwurst, long-marinated sauerbraten, and schnitzels galore on the reg-

ular menu; on any given day, specials might include a casserole of *spaetzle* and cheese or slabs of smoked pork loin. Big scoops of old-fashioned mashed potatoes and vinegary red cabbage or sauerkraut flank most of the main courses. And, of course, everyone is bending elbows to lift steins of the best German beers. —SS

THEP PHANOM

San Francisco: 400 Waller St, SF
(415) 431-2526.
Dinner daily.
Major credit cards
Parking: Street

From the day it opened in the mid-eighties, Thep Phanom has been a sensational success, despite the city's astounding proliferation of Thai restaurants. Part of the reason is the eye to aesthetics which is evident in everything from the decor and the outfits of the staff to the presentation of the food. But you can't credit style alone for Thep Phenom's success.

 ALPHABETICAL STORE LISTING

It is the food that really matters, and the food here captures all the tastes that traditionally define the best Thai fare—hot, tart, salty, sweet. Indeed, a biteful of the roast duck curry, quail with chili-garlic dipping sauce, squid salad, or lemongrass-infused catfish will have you dreaming of sunny Thailand in no time. —*SS*

TIMO'S

San Francisco: 842 Valencia St, SF
(415) 647-0558.
Dinner daily.
Visa, MasterCard
Parking: Street

Timo's (the lone survivor of the Zanzibar) is Carlos Corredor's tiny kitchen, an oasis of top-drawer Spanish tapas with a strong Catalan accent. Bread arrives with a bowl of northeastern Spain's *alioli* (garlic mayonnaise) for dipping. The same irresistible *alioli* garnishes crusty new potatoes and a plate of homemade pork sausage with white beans.

Potatoes also star in *bunyol de bacallà*, where they are mixed with salt cod in a crisply finished cake resting atop cilantro-mint salsa. And don't overlook the spinach sautéed with pine nuts and dried apricots. —*SS*

TON KIANG

San Francisco: 3148 Geary Blvd, SF
(415) 752-4440.
Lunch and dinner daily.
MasterCard, Visa
Other Stores: 5821 Geary St, SF
(415) 386–8530.
Parking: Lot behind building

Due to immigrants arriving from every part of China, Taiwan, and Hong Kong, Chinese food in the Bay Area has evolved recently into a complex of regional Chinese cuisines. One of the least known of these is Hakka, the food of a southern Chinese subculture whose origins not even Chinese scholars can agree upon. In San Francisco, the place to explore Hakka cuisine is Ton Kiang, where

the amiable Chine Wong oversees the delivery of the classic dishes of her Hakka forebears: salt-cooked chicken, stuffed bean curd, fresh bacon braised with dried mustard greens, fish ball soup, and a host of fermented wine-flavored dishes. A second Ton Kiang restaurant, at 5821 Geary, serves the same distinctive fare in slightly more upscale surroundings. —*SS*

UZEN

East Bay: 5415 College Ave, Oakland
(510) 654-7753.
Lunch Mon–Fri, dinner Mon–Sat.
MasterCard, Visa
Parking: Street

Kazuo Shimizu opened his stark yet congenial Uzen in food-savvy Rockridge in late 1991 with an eye to innovation. Knowing that he would be catering to a largely non-Japanese clientele, he decided to incorporate some of the Bay Area's own epicurean traditions with those of his birthplace, and the culinary compromise works. One of Uzen's best dishes is a salad of seaweed, raw scallops, and salmon tossed with a basketful of organic greens that would make a Chez Panisse regular smile. An order of "Rocky the Range" chicken teriyaki delivers a substantial serving of Sonoma County's famous free-range bird, accompanied by a mound of sautéed zucchini that is pure East Bay. The tempura selection includes shrimp and the best seasonal vegetables, and if you take a seat at the sushi bar, you can chat with Simizu while he assembles the full range of *nigiri-zushi*. —SS

YA YA CUISINE

San Francisco: 1220 Ninth Ave, SF
(415) 566-6966.
Lunch Mon–Fri, dinner Mon–Sat.
MasterCard, Visa, American Express
Parking: Street

Yayah Salih has brought the historic kitchen legacy of Mesopotomia to an utterly charming restaurant in the Inner Sunset. A lovely mural depicting the ancient city of Babylon sets the tone for diners to feast on Salih's visually stunning dishes, which marry Near Eastern culinary traditions with a Californian-Mediterranean twist. A first course of date and spice–filled raviolis with a sauce of olive oil, walnuts, and Parmesan cheese vividly illustrates just such a blend. Don't miss Salih's many inventive sauces, such as saffron and sumac. It's a sublime mix that will keep you coming back. —SS

FOOD BARGAINS

This is an internationally renowned food town. Naturally, our food writers know about more terrific, money-saving tips on fine gourmet items than just about anybody. We've asked S. Irene Virbila and Peggy Knickerbocker to secure the latest information on food buys that make it fun and affordable to keep a well-stocked pantry.

AUNTIE PASTA

San Francisco: 1501 Waller St, SF
(415) 681-4242.
Mon–Fri 11 am–9 pm, Sat–Sun 11 am–8 pm.
Discover, MasterCard, Visa
Other Stores: 741 Diamond St, SF (415) 282-0738; 3101 Fillmore, SF (415) 921-7576; 2139 Polk St, SF (415) 776-9420; 4043 Piedmont Ave, Oakland (510) 428-2909; 6311 College Ave, Oakland (510) 655-4094.
Parking: Street

Auntie Pasta has long featured mix-and-match fresh pasta and sauces, but the stores also carry a range of breads from local bakeries, including Fran Gage Pâtisserie Française, Acme Baking, Semi-Freddi's, Grace Baking Co., The Bread Workshop, and Metropolis.

The last hour of the day, the stores discount these handmade breads 50 percent, depending on how many loaves are still unsold. Every day, there's a special price on

dinner for two: that's pasta, sauce, and a green salad for about $7.99. It's ready to eat in the time it takes you to cook the pasta. —*SIV*

BOBBY LEE'S COUNTRY SMOKE HOUSE

East Bay: 850 Sycamore at Mission,
Hayward (510) 889-1133.
Daily 9 am–6 pm.
MasterCard, Visa; ATM
Parking: Lot on premises

This refrigerated retail factory outlet smoke house catches the eye with big red and black letters advertising the specials of the day. The signs say, "We accept Food Stamps!" and "All products are vacuum packed for freshness."

Bobby Lee offers fifty-four different wholesale priced products including a variety of sausages such as Cajun hot and Chorizo for $1.99 per pound, Linguica all pork for $2.99 per pound or $2.49 in three pound bulk. The Marina Safeway in San Francisco sells Chorizo for $5.99 per pound. and smoked turkey breast for $6.99 per pound while Bobby Lee offers it for $3.69 per pound.

He never uses liquid smoke—only hickory chips. Bobby Lee is proud of his cold smoke process where he filters his smoke through cold water for a twenty-four hour period to get unparalleled smoked hams. Customers can bring in meat to smoke for a minimum charge of $45. —*PK*

BUFFALO WHOLE FOODS

San Francisco: 1058 Hyde St, SF
(415) 474-3053.
Mon–Sat 9 am–9 pm, Sun 10 am–8 pm.
MasterCard, Visa
Other Stores: Nineteenth and Castro, SF
(415) 626-7038.
Parking: Street

Forget those puny sacks of flour you can pick up at the supermarket. Real bakers and cooks on a budget know that buying in bulk is the way to go. Not only is the flour fresher, the price is generally lower—plus you can buy organic.

Over sixty bins at Buffalo Whole Foods are stocked with flours, grains, and dried beans. Most of the flours and grains are milled at Giusto's in South San Francisco, a renowned producer of organic, stone-ground flours. *SIV*

C & M MEATS

East Bay: 2843 San Pablo Ave, Berkeley
(510) 848-3460.
Mon–Fri 7 am–3 pm.
Checks accepted; no credit cards
Parking: Lot on premises

Instead of buying packaged pork chops or steaks from the grocery store, you can save a lot by ordering a whole pork loin or sirloin strip from the same whole meat supplier that supplies local restaurants with primarily choice meats.

Place your order in the morning (before

one in the afternoon), pick up before three. No price sheet—the prices change every week. For example, prices for prime rib and leg of lamb are highest just before the Christmas holidays and fall off abruptly at the first of the year. Ask for the prime rib "export" cut, which is the rib eye; it costs a bit more per pound than the regular cut, but there's no heavy fat on the back.

Top sirloin strip might typically sell for $2.25 per pound and weigh in at anywhere from twelve to fifteen pounds. Cut it into twenty steaks, or use half as a roast and cut the rest into two-inch-thick London broil. The cross-rib roast we saw was another good buy at $2.10 per pound—all meat, all hand tied, and a particularly tasty cut.

C & M is also proud of the hand-tied legs of lamb for under $2.25 per pound. Pick up pork shoulder, fatback, and hog casings for home sausage-making. —*SIV*

THE CHEESE BOARD COLLECTIVE

**East Bay: 1504 Shattuck Ave, Berkeley
(510) 549-3183.
Tues–Sat 7 am–10 am for coffee and pastries, Tues–Fri 10 am–6 pm and Sat 10 am–5 pm for cheese and bread.
Checks accepted; no credit cards
Parking: Street**

This twenty-six-year-old workers' collective directly across from Chez Panisse was one of the first shops in the Bay Area to specialize in cheese. Despite declining cheese sales, it still offers more than two hundred imported and domestic cheeses. And, to the amazement of Italian friends we've brought there, the sales staff will actually take the time to give tastes of cheeses under consideration.

Prices are generally about 20 to 25 percent lower than grocery stores. The Cheese Board manages that because of high volume, but also because the delicious handmade breads subsidize the cheeses. Plus, there's very little waste, because cheese ends are used in the savory cheese bread. The Bay Area's best baguette costs $1 (all the breads are weighed out by the pound and range from $1.50 to $2.50 per pound for the cheese breads).

Seniors discounts are based on a sliding scale. Those aged sixty to sixty-nine get a 10 percent break; seventy to seventy-nine, 15 percent; eighty to eighty-nine, 20 percent; and ninety and over, 25 percent.

A blackboard lists each day's half a dozen cheeses to note, either because they're exceptionally good, a particularly great buy, or perfectly *à point*—to be eaten that day. Best bets: their aged Parmigiano Reggiano at $10 per pound, the raw-milk Camemberts, fine Cheddars, *chèvres*, and any of the French cheeses from the distinguished Parisian fromagerie Chantal Plasse. —*SIV*

COUNTRY CHEESE

**East Bay: 2101 San Pablo Ave, Berkeley
(510) 841-0752.**

Mon–Sat 9 am–6 pm; Sun 9 am–5 pm.
MasterCard, Visa
Other Stores: 415 Divisadero, SF
(415) 621-8130.
Parking: Street

If buying cheese in one- or two-pound increments is no problem, you can find extremely good prices on over two hundred kinds of domestic and imported cheeses at this modest storefront shop. Most are from commercial producers rather than small artisans, so don't expect to find many specialty or raw-milk cheeses. However, prices are often 30 percent below other cheese merchants.

"We're really a wholesaler, selling to the public and to people in the trade," explains the Berkeley store's owner, Phithak Raxakoul. "We give 10 percent off to caterers, even more to restaurants. And you don't have to buy a whole wheel of cheese (though you can if you want to)." Country Cheese has the best price on Parmigiano Reggiano around ($7.99 when we last looked) and Monterey jack and mild cheddar were just $2.29 per pound.

Every month, up to ten cheeses are on sale, along with several selections of dried fruits, nuts, and organic flours. We found smoked Gouda and English Cheshire for $2.99 per pound, and Swiss Emmenthaler was $3.99— all $0.80 to $1 off their regularly discounted prices. —*SIV*

CREATIVE SPICES

East Bay: 33372 Transit Ave, Union City
(510) 471-4956 and (800) 471-4990.
Mon–Fri 8 am–4 pm.
Checks accepted; no credit cards
Parking: Lot on premises

Creative Spices sells to market distributors and custom-blends spices for meat packers, taco vendors, and crouton makers. They also sell good quality spices to the public from their office or by mail order (UPS). Either way, check out the price list and order one-pound plastic jars of black cracked pepper (18 ounces for $4.47), whole fennel seeds (14 ounces for $3.03) or ground cinnamon

(1 pound for $4.25).

All spices are subject to availability and prices might change without notice. Depending on the product, 16-ounce jars are considered small jars and these spices come twelve jars to a case, but they will split a case in half. They also offer 24-ounce jars of ranch style salad dressing mix for $5.73 that yields twelve gallons of liquid dressing when you add your own liquids. —*PK*

ENTENMANN'S-OROWEAT BAKERY OUTLETS

San Francisco: 1798 Bryant St, SF
(415) 863-4773.
Most stores are open daily from 9 am–5 pm, but call for hours. Some stores are closed on Sundays.
First party checks and food stamps accepted; no credit cards
Other Stores: 1033 Bascom Ave, San Jose (408) 998-4351; 325 Third St, Napa (707) 224-8422; 8039 Gravenstein Highway,

ALPHABETICAL STORE LISTING

Cotati (707) 795-6237; 2740 Soquel Ave, Santa Cruz (408) 476-5027; 456 West Maude, Sunnyvale (408) 732-0382; 264 South Spruce Ave, South San Francisco (415) 583-5828; 2631 Springs Rd, Vallejo (707) 649-1317; 2034 North Main St, Walnut Creek (510) 937-1491.
Parking: Lots adjacent to outlets

These bakery outlets offer supermarkets' returned goods on which the fresh code has expired at a 50 percent discount of retail price. In most cases, the goods are three to four days old. Oroweat, the number one premium bread company in the Bay Area, offers value pricing on a daily basis. Top selling items are Boboli, whole grain breads, fat-free cookies and cakes. —*PK*

FOODS CO

East Bay: 7000 Bancroft Ave, Oakland (510) 569-9884.
Open twenty-four hours a day.
Discover, MasterCard, Visa; ATM

Other Stores: 345 Williams Ave, SF (415) 330-1870; 1250 Macdonald Ave, Richmond (510) 412-4444; 1401 Broadway, Redwood City (415) 366-5547; 1800 Folsom St, SF (415) 558-9137.
Parking: Lot on premises

These huge cavernous discount food emporiums are owned by the Los Angeles–based Yucaipa Corporation, one of the largest food corporations in California, which also owns Cala, Bell Markets, Alpha Beta, and Market Basket. Foods Co claims to always be cheaper than Lucky or Safeway and their own sister stores.

Be sure to lock your car in the well-lit parking lots because most Foods Co are located in marginal neighborhoods. The checkout lines are long and shoppers pack their own bags. The best deal is their "wall of values" that display big truck buys of products that might include chips, toilet paper, cleaning products and juices. They also have ATMs and a full-service deli. It is not necessary to buy in large quantities and no membership is required. By the end of 1994 they

plan to have ten Foods Co stores in the Bay Area. —*PK*

THE FOOD MILL

East Bay: 3033 MacArthur Blvd, Oakland (510) 482-3848.
Mon–Sat 8:30 am–6 pm.
MasterCard, Visa; ATM
Parking: Lot on premises

Years ago my household used to receive a Friday night delivery from The Food Mill: flours, oils, peanut butter, dried fruits, nuts, bread, and whatever else we needed that week. (They still offer that service to their oldest customers.)

The crowded store, which is over sixty-one years old, is a great resource for more than thirty kinds of flour, most of which are stone-ground on the premises, plus fifty or more grains, all available in bulk. Recently, one pound of whole wheat flour was 33 cents; buy ten pounds, and it drops to 29 cents.

The Food Mill has dynamite prices on

spices and herbs bought in quantities from two ounces up. The peanut butter is fresh ground from a mix of Spanish and Virginia peanuts. It was $3.57 if you brought your own quart jar and $4.19 if you didn't.

The Food Mill's bakery offers astonishing prices on breads, burger buns, and cookies. Best bargain? Their regular whole wheat pound-and-a-half loaf for 95 cents and three dozen of their oatmeal or sunflower-sesame cookies for $2.39. —*SIV*

G. B. RATTO

East Bay: 821 Washington, Oakland
(510) 832-6503.
Mon–Fri 9:30 am–6 pm, Sat 9:30 am–5 pm.
MasterCard, Visa
Parking: Street

Savvy Bay Area cooks know the aisles of Ratto's International Grocery like the back of their hands. Founded in 1897 and housed in a ramshackle Victorian building in downtown Oakland, Ratto's is a treasurehouse of every-

day and esoteric ingredients for any cuisine you can name, including soul food, Italian, French, Middle Eastern, Caribbean, and African. Ratto's has great prices on olives (imported directly) and bulk flours and grains.

The house-brand California virgin olive oil was just $8.50 a quart last time we looked, and the oak-aged double strength wine vinegar was $2.25 a quart. Check Ratto's for large tins of anchovy filets in oil, and salt-packed capers weighed out by the ounce. Two-pound jars of capers were $9.49—compare that with those tiny supermarket jars.

Ratto's has one of the best selections of dried beans in the Bay Area. Occasionally you can find good buys on basmati rice; recently broken wild rice sold for $2.49 per pound or 5 pounds for $10. Over in the spice section, the whole peppercorns—Tellicherry, Lampong or Malabar—were just $6 per pound ($10 elsewhere); white peppercorns were $9 a pound. A fourteen-ounce Val Rhona Equatoriale couverture chocolate bar was $7.99 (over $10 elsewhere), and jagged

chunks of Callebaut Belgian chocolate were just $7 per pound. But best buys were the Guittard bittersweet and French vanilla chocolate at just $3.95 per pound. —*SIV*

GOLDEN GATE PRODUCE TERMINAL

San Francisco: 131 Terminal Court, South
San Francisco (415) 761-3360.
Mon–Fri 3 am–9 or 10 am.
Mostly cash; varies with vendor
Parking: Lot on premises

It's a real urban adventure to head out to South San Francisco to shop the wholesale produce terminal. And for me, the only reason to get out of bed before dawn is just to experience the buzz as buyers for restaurants and small groceries do their daily shopping.

For regular folks, this is a once a year excursion to be made either for a gigantic party that requires cases of avocadoes and tomatoes, or when you're planning to spend the week putting up a year's worth of jams,

ALPHABETICAL STORE LISTING

preserves, and chutneys. Or make out a list with a group of friends and take turns going to the market.

Most of the twenty-two businesses inside sell by the case or flat, but potatoes, onions, and some other items come in twenty-five or fifty-pound sacks. —*SIV*

THE GOODBUY STORE

**East Bay: 2919 Seventh St, Berkeley
(510) 849-1055.
Mon–Fri 10 am–5:30 pm, Sat 10 am –5 pm,
Sun 11 am –5 pm.
MasterCard, Visa
Parking: Street**

When San Francisco wholesaler Taylor & Ng says goodbye to ceramics, cookware, and so on, they place it in their Goodbuy Store, near Whole Earth Access in Berkeley.

The wares are always changing, but you can expect to find good buys on sturdy ceiling racks for hanging pots and pans. We saw $127.50 and $94.99 racks marked down from $170 and $140, for example.

There were great prices on aprons ($7.99), oven mitts ($3.99), and pot holders ($1.99), all in whimsical prints. One day stainless-steel fish poachers, regularly $40, sold for $24.99, and handsome bamboo utensils for your wok cooking were just $1.25 to $2.99, with basic two-handled carbon-steel woks going for $8.99. Check their store of spice racks, breadboards, and baking stones, too. Espresso cups recently sold for just $0.79. —*SIV*

THE GOOD LUCK SUPERMARKET

**East Bay: 259 Tenth (at Alice), Oakland
(510) 208-1944.
Daily 8:30 am–6:30 pm.
MasterCard, Visa
Parking: Lot on premises**

"Open every day except happy new year!" said the cheerful voice on the phone. This is a small, sparkling-clean Chinese-Vietnamese supermarket on the outskirts of Oakland's Chinatown.

This store has shopping carts and the whole deal. Aisles are neatly arranged with all sorts of sauces, condiments, canned goods, dried mushrooms, and so on. We saw gallon tins of Panther brand peanut oil for $5.29, and handsome ceramic "sand" pots with lids for just $11.99 (use them for cooking all sorts of casseroles on top the stove).

But the real draw here is the meat department. There's every cut of beef, including the shank and tendon, for making *pho*, a Vietnamese beef soup. On special one day, freshly killed stewing hens (head and feet on) went for $3.99 each.

Buy two pieces of good-looking pork loin, tie them together every inch or so, and voilà—a pork loin roast for $2.89 per pound rather than the more usual $4.99. Pork chops were $1.99 a pound, pork spareribs $1.69, and ground pork $1.29. There's plenty of lean cuts for stir-fry dishes. —*SIV*

GROCERY OUTLET

**San Francisco: 1717 Harrison St, SF
(415) 552-9680.
Mon–Sat 8 am–9 pm, Sun 9 am–7 pm.
ATM; checks accepted; no credit cards
Other Stores: 2001 Fourth St, Berkeley
(510) 845-1771; 1833 Broadway, Redwood
City (415) 364-7406; 187 Harder Rd,
Hayward (510) 537-4616; 2079 Twenty-
Third St, San Pablo (510) 232-7993; 80 E.
Washington St, Petaluma (707) 763-2700.
Parking: Lot on premises**

You'll always find a crowd shopping for bargains at any of the Canned Food Grocery Outlets. That's because there's no membership fee, and you can buy in small quantities if you want. Savings on most items are from 25 to 40 percent on closeouts, excess inventory, and seconds.

How do they do it? "We have long term relationships with major manufacters," one manager told me. "When they change their packaging or add a new ingredient to their product, we buy out their old inventory."

Shopping here demands the same skills as the flea market—the stock changes constantly and it's really a treasure hunt. This outlet is great for canned goods, but there's also a frozen-food section where you can scoop up Weight Watchers meals, day-old bakery goods; and packaged foods at or nearing their expiration date.

Notably, every product is 100 percent money-back guaranteed. Name brands include Yoplait, Dannon, Kraft, Armour, Oscar Mayer, Pepperidge Farm, Sara Lee, and Oroweat, among others.

Recently found great buys on Old El Paso thick and chunky salsa ($1.49 for 24-ounce jar) and Louisiana Pride hot sauce at three bottles for $1. Save up to 40 percent on day-old breads, hot dog and burger buns, even sourdough English muffins. —*SIV*

HALF-PRICE BAKED GOODS

San Francisco: Suzanne's Muffins, 87
**Fremont St, SF (415) 495-6064.
Mon–Fri 5:30 am–6:30 pm, hours vary at
other locations.
Checks accepted; no credit cards
Other Stores: Holey Bagel, 1206 Masonic
Ave, San Francisco (415) 626-9111; and
other locations in the Bay Area. Noah's
New York Bagels, 2075 Chestnut St, SF
(415) 775-2910; and other Bay Area locations.**

In seven Bay Area locations, Suzanne's Muffins bakes traditional (blueberry, corn, poppyseed, bran), savory (bacon/corn/cheddar), and dessert (chocolate cream cheese) muffins every day of the a year. Any remaining fresh-baked products are sold at half price during the last hour of the day (closing time differs at each location). Muffins retail for $1.45, so they're approximately 75 cents half price.

Stock up on the power food of the nineties: At Holey Bagel buy six bagels after five in the evening and get six bagels free. A variety of traditional bagels (poppyseed, sesame seed, plain, raisin) and unusual varieties like honey-corn go for 50 cents each. And at Noah's New York Bagels, purchase six or more bagels for half price between 6:30 pm and 7 pm Mon–Thurs. Bagels freeze well and defrost in seconds in a microwave.

HERMAN GOELITZ CANDY COMPANY FACTORY STORE

North Bay: 2400 North Watney Way, Fairfield (707) 428-2800.
Mon–Fri 9 am–5 pm, Sat 10 am–4 pm.
MasterCard, Visa
Parking: Lot in industrial park

President Reagan popularized this company's Jelly Belly Beans by becoming publicly addicted to them. The factory also makes candy corn, big gummi spiders and dinosaurs, thirty-inch pet snake candies, sour gummi products, and French peanuts which are all sold in bulk. But on Saturday Belly Flops are for sale.

Belly Flops are Jelly Belly Beans that are too small, too big, or are clustered together. Belly Flops are normally $3.75 per two-pound bag, but on Saturdays the first two-pound bag goes for $3.75 and the second bag goes for a penny. This is subject to availability—the more flops the better. —*PK*

HOG ISLAND OYSTERS

North Bay: On Hwy 1, midway on Tomales Bay, Marshall/Tomales Bay
(415) 663-9218.
Tues–Thur by appointment only, Fri–Sun 9 am–5 pm.
Local checks accepted
Parking: Lot on premises

Only four words need be said: Exquisite Tomales Bay oysters. Make the beautiful drive up to Marshall on Tomales Bay, and stop in at Hog Island Oysters to sample the Pacific sweetwater oysters and bélon produced here. Or bring an ice chest, make this the last stop of the day, and take home several dozen.

Extra-small sweetwaters were recently $5 a dozen; small were $6; medium were $7; and bélons were $6 a dozen. A bushel of oysters (that's ten dozen) is $40—about 33 cents each by our reckoning. Imagine getting to eat as many oysters as you want all at one sitting. The fact that you have to shuck them yourself does tend to slow down the pace a bit, however. If you want a large quantity of oysters, it's best to call ahead. —*SIV*

HOMESTEAD RAVIOLI

San Francisco: 120 Fourteenth St, SF
(415) 864-2992.
Mon–Fri 7 am–noon; 1 pm–3:30 pm.
Checks accepted; no credit cards
Parking: Lot on premises

Founded in 1917 by Emilio Lavezzoli as the Lavezzoli Ravioli Company, Homestead has some customers who have been buying its ravioli for more than forty years. At the factory, walk-in customers can buy ravioli by the one- or two-pound box at prices close to wholesale. Of their seven types of ravioli,

most are $2.50 a pound (about $4 retail), and a couple as low as $1.38.

Available frozen, they should be used within three months. They're great for kids—just pop a handful in boiling water to make an instant, immediately appealing meal. The easiest sauce for ravioli is the classic melted butter infused with fresh sage leaves.

All Homestead ravioli are made without preservatives or MSG. Try the new "primavera" made with spinach pasta stuffed with vegetables and dried mushrooms, or the "romato" with a stuffing of ricotta blended with dried tomatoes, olive oil, garlic, basil, and almonds. Homestead's "suprima" is a meat ravioli filled with extra-lean veal, pork, and turkey, seasoned with organic white wine. Of course you can also find the more traditional beef or cheese ravioli, too. —*SIV*

HOOPER'S CHOCOLATES

**East Bay: 4632 Telegraph Ave, Oakland
(510) 654-3373.**

**Mon–Fri 9:30 am–5 pm, Sat 10 am–5 pm.
MasterCard, Visa
Parking: Street**

This old-fashioned pink and white Victorian candy store offers mainly high-end chocolates and make no pretensions at being trendy—its clientele is elderly and the factory supplies to drug stores and florists. The most popular item is homemade rocky road (they make their own marshmallows) at $7.35 per pound.

If you don't find that a bargain, check out their blooper bags of chocolates for $4.59 per pound. "They are," according to owner Ben Masri, "whatever we blew it on that day"—items too big or too small to fit into the little wrappers.

In February, the store offers a 10 percent discount to anyone who places an order one week before Valentine's Day—but you have to mention this book. —*PK*

HOUSEWIVES' MARKET

East Bay: Eighth and Jefferson, Oakland

**(510) 444-4396.
Mon–Sat 9 am–6 pm.
Mostly cash, varies with vendor
Parking: Lot on premises**

According to the management, this covered market in the heart of downtown Oakland may be one of the oldest in the country. Founded in 1907, it is now run by the dozen vendors inside.

Taylor's Sausage at (510) 832-6448 makes all its own sausages, including New Orleans–style *boudin blanc*; "bull-dang," a mix of pork, chicken, and rice, spiked with hot pepper; Louisiana hot sausages for gumbo; spicy Cajun-style barbecue links; and "little pig" breakfast links. At $2.50 to $3.45 per pound, these links were a steal. Taylor's also sells sausage makings, including hard-to-find caul fat and natural casings.

Across the hall, Bean Bag at (510) 839-8988 features dozens of esoteric varieties of beans and legumes. Just recite the names: black valentine, New Mexico appalloosa, calico cowpea. The more you buy, the bigger the discount.

Prices on tiny French lentils are the best we've ever seen. Stock up on spices and herbs weighed out by the ounce from the big jars stacked at one end of the counter. And don't forget the Belly Bustin' bean seasoning or New Orleans red-bean mix we saw for $1.49 an ounce. Allan's Ham & Bacon at (510) 893-9479 sells smoked ham hocks, thick-cut hickory-smoked bacon ends, and slabs of salt pork, all at good prices.

And if you like to make your own head cheese, Jack's Meats at (510) 451-6795 can supply you with calf's heads (as well as suckling pigs and goats). Pigs' feet, pig tails, and all cuts of pork can be found here too. —*SIV*

JOSEPH SCHMIDT CONFECTIONS

San Francisco: 3489 Sixteenth St, SF
(415) 861-8682.
Mon–Sat 10 am–6:30 pm.
MasterCard, Visa
Parking: Some street parking

In this veritable museum of fine Belgian chocolates, surplus seasonal items are on sale after holidays (Christmas, Valentine's Day, Easter, Groundhog Day and St. Patrick's Day). These are for chocoholics and are not intended to be saved until the holiday rolls around next year. After Christmas, special batik gift boxes filled with Christmas wrapped truffles usually selling for $14.50 go for $8.50.

The chocolate theme at the store changes every few weeks and a variety of price points are always available. Joseph Schmidt candies are also available at Macy's, Neiman Marcus, Confetti and specialty stores throughout the country. —*PK*

LAZZARI FUEL COMPANY

Peninsula: 11 Industrial Way, Brisbane
(415) 467-2970.
Mon–Fri 8 am–4:30 pm.
Checks accepted; no credit cards

Parking: Drive into the warehouse to pick up charcoal

The name Lazzari writ large on rust-colored bags of mesquite is familiar to barbecue aficionados all over northern California. Founded in 1908, the firm started out selling coal to heat drafty Victorian-homes and got into mesquite about fifteen years ago. They still sell coal to blacksmiths, says general manager Richard Morgen, and every year, a handful of ladies in their nineties receive hundred-pound sacks of coal to heat their old San Francisco houses.

A stop at Lazzari's Brisbane warehouse to pick up mesquite imported directly from Mexico is worth a short detour. On my visit, one bag went for $10.45; three or more for $9.95 each (compared to the retail price of about $14.50 for the 40 pound bag). Mesquite or hickory wood chips for smoking were $2 for a two-pound bag, while alder, cherry, or apple wood chips were $2.50. —*SIV*

 ALPHABETICAL STORE LISTING

MISSION MARKET FISH AND POULTRY

**San Francisco: 2590 Mission St, SF
(415) 282-3331.
Mon–Sat 8:30 am–6 pm.
MasterCard, Visa
Parking: Nearby lot, meters**

Nestled in a corner of the Mission Street Mall at Twenty-second Street, Mission Market Fish and Poultry displays fish in a style reminiscent of Harrods in London. Grand quantities and varieties of impeccably fresh, glistening fish are displayed atop mounds of ice and sold for amazingly low prices. The amiable counter staff is happy to provide cooking tips. We found filets of king salmon for $6.99 per pound (usually $8.99 elsewhere) and ahi tuna for $8.45 per pound ($14.29 at supermarkets). The market also offers seasonal items such as shad roe and crab at very competitive prices.

NAPA VALLEY OLIVE OIL COMPANY

**North Bay: 1135 Charter Oak Ave, St. Helena (707) 963-4173.
Daily 8 am–5 pm.
Checks accepted; no credit cards
Parking: Lot on premises**

Just down the road from Tra Vigne, in the midst of Napa Valley glitz, is the white clapboard storefront which houses the venerable Napa Valley Olive Oil Company and a storehouse of reasonably priced ingredients for Italian cooking. Partners Osvaldo Particelli and Policarpo Lucchesi have been dispensing their dark golden green California olive oil by the quart bottle or half-gallon jug for over seventy years.

Pure olive oil recently went for $6 per quart, $11 per half gallon, but go ahead and spend a couple of dollars more for the real stuff, the fruity extra-virgin oil at $8 a quart, $13.50 a half gallon. That's compared with imported extra-virgin oils at up to $40 a liter.

Particelli and Lucchesi also grate Wisconsin Parmesan fresh every day. It was selling for $5 per pound, and Reggiano was selling for $10. —*SIV*

OAKLAND PRODUCE MARKET

**East Bay: Bounded by Second St and Fourth St, Franklin and Broadway, Oakland.
Daily, 3 am–11 am.
Mostly cash; varies with vendor
Parking: Street**

The East Bay equivalent of San Francisco's wholesale produce terminal is a bit more manageable in size, and since it's set among historic brick warehouses, more picturesque and accessible. Try to arrive before seven in the morning, buy your produce by the case, and load it into your car and then head over to Washington Street for breakfast. Cafe 817, at Washington and Eighth, opens at 7:30 am and serves the best espresso and cappucino in town. —*SIV*

PAK 'N $AVE

South Bay: 4950 Almaden Expressway, San Jose (408) 267-6243.
Most PAK 'n $AVEs are open twenty-four hours, but hours may vary, so call ahead.
ATM and checks accepted, no credit cards
Other Stores: 375 N. Capital Ave, San Jose (408) 258-1194; 762 Saratoga Rd, Sunnyvale (408) 720-0244; 6605 Dublin Blvd, Dublin (510) 829-2101; 2255 Gellert Blvd, South San Francisco (415) 588-9008; 555 Floresta Blvd, San Leandro (510) 483-2681; 4405 Century Blvd, Pittsburg, (510) 706-4060; 610 Hegenberger Rd, Oakland, (510) 636-7970.
Parking: Lot on premises

Pak 'n $ave, a division of Safeway, does two to three times the volume of its major competitors and thereby provides a 10 to 15 percent saving. Management goes to great lengths to keep costs down by finding existing buildings in order to avoid new construction costs.

The warehouse concept (cut-open boxes displayed on racks) keeps labor costs down. The decor leaves something to be desired; some stores have concrete floors and the customer bags his or her groceries. Most stores have produce, fish, meat, deli, and bakery departments, in addition to dried and canned goods. Make no mistake, this is no-frill shopping about as bare as it gets. —*PK*

PEERLESS COFFEE CO.

East Bay: 260 Oak St, Oakland (510) 763-1763.
Mon–Fri 8:30 am–5:30 pm, Sat 9:30 am–5 pm.
MasterCard, Visa
Parking: Lot on premises

Peerless Coffee started out on Washington Street in Oakland in 1924, and it's still run by the same family, now in its third generation. Owners George and Sonja Vukasin buy most of their beans direct and supervise the daily roasting. When the facility moved to Oak Street, the Vukasins brought the original counter and old-fashioned coffee-making and -roasting equipment along to create a small informal museum.

Peerless' Colombian Supremo recently won the *San Francisco Chronicle's* local taste test. Best bargains here are to be found in the bulk corner, where whole-bean coffees are sold in five-pound bags at 10 percent discount; buy five five-pound bags and get a Krups grinder. Coffees range from their least expensive, Central American and Brazilian beans that were $4.45 a pound, to $32 for Jamaican Blue Mountain.

Most medium-roast, middle-of-the-road coffees clustered around the $5.35 per pound. Two-pound packages of loose tea are also subject to the same 10 percent discount. Spices and herbs sell in one-pound plastic containers, but they also come in 2-ounce packs that you can mix and match to make a twenty-four unit case, ideal for gift baskets. Get on the mailing list to receive the quarterly newsletter. You'll receive a discount card each quarter, good for $1 off a pound every month. Great mail-order service, too. —*SIV*

PLUMP JACK WINES

San Francisco: 3201 Fillmore St, SF
(415) 346-9870.
Mon–Fri 11 am–8 pm, Sat–Sun 10 am–7 pm.
American Express, MasterCard, Visa
Parking: Validated garage

This stylish Pacific Heights wine store (owned in part by Getty offspring) offers surprisingly competitive prices considering its tony location and white-glove service. "We'll match any price on any bottle of wine as long as it's not below our cost," says manager Gavin Newsom. "We also have 130 wines for under $10." Newsom's picks? A 1990 Château Souverain Cabernet for $8.49 (at supermarkets it's $4 more) and a 1991 Edna Valley Chardonnay for $9.99 ($11.88 in supermarkets).

PRICE RITE CHEESE

East Bay: 1385 North Main, Walnut Creek

(510) 933-2983.
Mon–Sat 10 am–8 pm.
American Express, MasterCard, Visa
Parking: Lot on premises

Shop for over 150 domestic and imported cheeses at this cheese, wine, and liquor shop. If your heart's desire is not in the cheese case, Price Rite can special-order almost any variety, with store deliveries twice a week. French Roquefort was recently priced at $8.99 per pound. Among the best bargains here were Monterey jack and mild Cheddar, both at $1.99 per pound, and Swiss cheese went for $2.99. —SIV

R. IACOPI MEATS

San Francisco: 1462 Grant Ave, SF
(415) 421-0757.
Daily 9 am–6 pm.
MasterCard, Visa
Parking: Street

R. Iacopi Meats has supplied a discerning North Beach clientele since 1910. More

recently, its customers have included restaurants such as Il Fornaio, Piatti, Boulevard, and Fog City Diner. Not long ago, owner Leo Rossi offered cross rib roasts at $1.98 per pound (normally $3.98).

ROBERTS CORNED MEATS

San Francisco: 1030 Bryant St, SF
(415) 621-2624.
Mon–Fri 7 am–3 pm.
Checks accepted; no credit cards
Parking: Street

This family-owned business, now in its fourth and fifth generations, has specialized in corned beef since 1910. Employing a method introduced by his great-grandfather, G. H. Roberts, Jim Dixon cures the meat from the inside out by injecting the arteries of the beef brisket with spice-laden brine. The result is a more evenly cured brisket, a perfect centerpiece for an Irish-style boiled corned-beef dinner, surrounded with cabbage, potatoes, carrots, and onions.

Retail is a minuscule part of the firm's business, but stop in at the production facility (that is, if you can find a place to park) and pick up any size piece of corned beef brisket from about three pounds on up; it was just $1.90 per pound on our most recent visit. The bottom round was $2.40 per pound. Also available: New York pastrami, hams, pork hocks, and bacon.

Roberts' latest product is povi masima (salt beef), made from a piece of the brine-brisket ($1.50 per pound). This version of this Samoan delicacy is less salty than the old-fashioned variety. —*SIV*

ROBIN'S NEST

North Bay: 116 E. Napa, Sonoma
(707) 996-4169.
Mon–Sat 10 am–6 pm, Sun 11 am–5 pm.
MasterCard, Visa, American Express
Parking: Lot on premises

This could quickly become my favorite weekend excursion: lunch at Charles Saunders' Eastside Oyster Bar & Grill just off Sonoma's historic plaza, followed by a thorough browse through the eclectic wares at Robin's Nest.

Owner Debra Friedman spent years in the restaurant business and really knows her cookware. Her tactic is to buy up manufacturers' samples, overruns, closeouts, and seconds and offer them deeply discounted. Most items are 40 to 50 percent off normal retail. "I build my inventory around lines I have carried and worked with myself," she explains. That way she knows just how they will perform in the kitchen. She also happens to have very good taste in ceramics and often has lovely hand-painted platters, pitchers, and dinnerware.

You can expect to find the unusual and the high-end, too, such as a beautiful hand-turned wooden salad bowl marked down from $110 to $69. Some of the bakeware closeouts are irresistible: Individual oval bakers at $1.99? Classic lion's head soup bowls under $3? We're on our way. —*SIV*

ROSIER COFFEE

East Bay: 2824 Regatta Blvd, Richmond
(510) 233-5530.
Mon–Fri 8:30 am–5 pm, Sat–Sun 10 am–5 pm.
Checks accepted; no credit cards
Other Stores: 4100 Redwood Rd, Oakland
(510) 482-5282.
Parking: Lot on premises

This custom roaster and coffee wholesaler is strategically located just across from the entrance to the Richmond Price Club. The rich smell of coffee roasting wafts right out the door of this informal warehouse space decorated with coffee bags. Owner Mel Rosier mans the roaster and dispenses steaming cups of coffee to regulars seated on a few stools.

When we visited, he had over sixty coffees listed on the board, from Colombian Supreme, Costa Rica, or Panama at $5.95 per pound, to Moka Java and Sumatra each at $6.45, to Jamaican Blue Mountain at $19.95. Buy two pounds and get five percent

off; three to four pounds gets you 10 percent off; five to nine pounds gets you 15 percent off, and anything over ten pounds gets 25 percent off (which brings the house blend down to about $4.50 per pound, Italian roast slightly more). You can mix blends, and Rosier will grind it, too, if you like.

A second location in Oakland, open since December of '93, features live music on Friday and Saturday nights, starting at 8 pm and going until midnight or so. —*SIV*

SHEW WO MEAT CO. NO. 2

San Francisco: 1151 Stockton St, SF
(415) 982-7234.
Daily 8:30 am–6:30 pm.
Checks accepted; no credit cards
Parking: Street

For some of the best-looking pork in Chinatown, check this bustling meat market on Stockton Street. Turnover is high, and the pork is very fresh and of high quality. Prices are especially good for pork shoulder, pork chops, pigs' feet, and other common cuts of pork. You can find pork kidneys, tripe, snouts, ears, and other less common cuts, too, plus pork liver for charcuterie. Fresh Petaluma chickens and Hong Kong-style ducks are sold at good prices, too. —*SIV*

SMART & FINAL

Peninsula: 1185 Broadway, Redwood City
(415) 306-2450.
Mon–Sat 8 am–7 pm, Sun 9 am–5 pm.
Checks accepted, no credit cards
Other Stores: 1941 San Pablo Ave, Berkeley
(510) 649-2381; 701 South Van Ness, SF
(415) 864–8240; 141 East El Camino Real,
Mountain View (415) 962–1092.
Parking: Lot on premises

Primarily a resource for small businesses, markets and restaurants, Smart & Final gives retail customers the same prices on canned foods, groceries, paper goods, and cleaning supplies. House brands, Smart Buy, Iris, and Table Queen labels offer some of the best buys. You do generally have to buy in institutional-size quantities, but unlike Price Costco, there is no membership fee, and the warehouse-like stores are generally smaller, so you can get in and out faster.

Every few weeks Smart & Final runs ads in major newspapers showing special sales on selected items. You can also save on some items by the case. The stores are great sources for party supplies. You can also find good buys on basics such as plastic storage containers, kitchen twine, paper plates, napkins, food wrap, and aluminum foil.

Swanson beef and chicken broths in 48½-ounce cans, were recently $2.15. House brand chicken soup base was $5.99 for a four-pound jar. For a 25-pound bag, Jasmine rice was $8.19; 50-pound bags of pinto beans were $20.45. We liked the Harina de Trigo (wheat) flour from Mexico in paisley cloth bags (25 pounds for $5.99) and the 2-pound bags of Fleischmann's active dry yeast for $4.49. For your home theater, pick up a 50-pound bag of Jolly Time popcorn ($17.99), and while you're at it, pick up movie popcorn containers over in the paper supplies. —*SIV*

SOLANO CELLARS

**East Bay: 1580 Solano Ave, Albany
(510) 525-0379.
Mon and Tues 11 am–8 pm, Wed–Sat
11 am–9 pm, Sun noon–5 pm.
MasterCard, Visa
Parking: Street**

Owner Bill Easton stocks a fine selection of reasonably priced wines at bargain prices of between $4 and $10 in the red-tag section of his East Bay wine shop. Among the deals we found: a 1988 Montecillo Rioja from Spain for $5.99; and 1992 Anderson Valley Negociants Pinot Noir or Chardonnay for $5.99.

STELVIO DISTRIBUTORS, INC, IMPORT EXPORT

Peninsula: 1461 Old Bayshore Hwy,
**Burlingame (415) 343-6642.
Mon–Fri 9 am–5 pm, Sat 10 am–4 pm.
Checks accepted; no credit cards
Parking: Lot on premises**

This upgrade cash-and-carry store is filled with low-priced familiar Italian delicacies. The same wholesale items sold to restaurants and gourmet stores can be had by customers willing to drive a bit south of the Airport across from Alamo Car Rentals on the Old Bayshore Highway.

Look for Reggiano Parmigiano at $7.75 per pound, good olive oil at $8.98 per gallon, assorted one-pound bags of pasta for 80-85 cents, two cans of Italian coffee (Kimbo) for $7.90, Conforti special pastas for $4 a package (17 ounces) and various cookies, bread sticks, wines, and meats galore. —*PK*

SUGARIPE FARMS, COUNTRY STORE FACTORY OUTLET

**South Bay: 2070 South Seventh St, San Jose
(800) 628-3493 and (408) 280-2349**
**Mon–Fri 8:30 am–5 pm, Sat 10 am–3 pm
MasterCard, Visa
Parking: Lot on premises**

This is the country store outlet for plump, prime dried fruit, fresh shelled nuts, sweets, and handsomely packed jams and mustards. The Bleinheim apricot at $4.50 per pound is the most popular item in the catalog.

Drop by to pick up, or have delivered to your door, competitively priced dried cherries ($3.90 for eight ounces), dried blueberries ($4.50 for eight ounces), raw cashews at $3.30 per pound, premium biscotti for $5.25 for a nine-ounce bag, or raspberry jam for $3.20 a ten-ounce jar. Holiday gift packs are shipped for as little as $12.00 plus postage and handling. —*PK*

TRADER JOE'S

**North Bay: Montecito Plaza, 337 Third St,
San Rafael (415) 454-9530.
Daily 9 am–9 pm.
MasterCard, Visa**

Other Stores: Westlake Shopping Center, Daly City (415) 756–2192; Powell Street Plaza, 5700 Christie Ave, Emeryville (510) 658–8091; The Willows Shopping Center, Concord (510) 689–2990; 720 Menlo Ave, Menlo Park (415) 323–2134; 4040 Pimlico, Pleasanton (510) 734–3422; 99 Danville Square, Danville (510) 838–5757; stores also in Campbell, Capitola, San Jose, and Santa Rosa.

Parking: Lot on premises

Trader Joe's was founded in the early sixties by one Joe Coulombe, who recognized that the advent of jumbo jets and affordable world travel presented an opportunity to do good business selling imported and gourmet food-stuffs to increasingly well-traveled Americans. He started out by buying up special lots of imported cheeses, coffee beans, and such. Later the company developed its own house label for a number of products, including a wonderful marinara sauce made with extra-virgin olive oil, and vitamins.

Today the sixty-odd Trader Joe stores in California and Arizona feature a huge mix of in-house brand items and specially purchased limited lots of imported foodstuffs. When Ben & Jerry changed the flavor profiles on two of their flavors, Trader Joe's offered pints at $1.49 instead of $2.89 or more. The price-to-quality ratio is very high—and that's what keeps people coming back.

How do they keep prices so low? Because Trader Joe's invariably buys direct from suppliers in large volume, they get a very good price. For dried fruits and nuts, for example, Trader Joe's may even set the price before the crop is in.

Other best buys: $2.99 per pound frozen ahi-tuna steak, which, like all their seafood, is processed without sulfites and, in this case, "longline caught, frozen at sea"; just $2.39 per pound for bittersweet chocolate in 500-gram bars; and gourmet goodies like tree-ripened sour morello cherries at $1.99 for a twenty-four-ounce jar. The best way to keep up with the latest values at Trader Joe's is to get on the mailing list for the quarterly newsletter. —*SIV*

VALLEY CHEESE SHOP INTERNATIONAL GOURMET FOODS

East Bay: 20573 Santa Maria Ave, Castro Valley (510) 886-8627
Mon–Fri 9:30 am–6 pm, Sat 9:30 am–5 pm.
MasterCard, Visa
Parking: Available in front of store

This small family-run business (mom, pop, and son) looks and feels like the old country. It caters to traditional culinary needs of an international clientele (Greek, Austrian, Polish, Croatian, etc). Prices are competitive since overhead is small, and the payroll is limited to family members. Maurice Soulis, the son, speaks many languages and remembers customers by name and often by their car.

Look for pastas from nine countries (five pounds of Alita pasta made with 100 percent semolina goes for $3.79), Greek and Austrian preserves ($2.99 for a sixteen-ounce jar), and Robertson's Lemon curd ($2.99 for an 11¼-ounce jar). Look for fresh filo dough at $2.29 a pound—($2.50 at Haig's on Clement in San Francisco) or shredded filo at $2.59 per pound frozen. Danish Feta is $1.99 per pound. Special Eastern European baking ingredients are thoughtfully imported for the holiday baking needs of the clientele. —*PK*

VERONICA FOODS

East Bay: 7373 Village Parkway, Dublin (510) 829-1260.
Mon–Sat 9 am–8 pm, Sun 10 am–6 pm
Checks accepted with proper ID, no credit cards
Other Stores: VGO2, 1300 Bush St (northwest corner) (415) 921-2993.
Parking: Lot on premises

Veronica Foods, a family-run grocery business since 1927, owns a pair of grocery outlets that sell canned foods at 20 percent below Safeway prices and offer remarkably low prices on wine. The Dublin Store is spare,

displaying goods from stacked cases. The San Francisco store is a typical uncrowded supermarket with produce, meats, and fish. Here you can pick up Price-Club-size bags of string cheese, thirty-six ounces for $2.99, and five-pound bags of shredded jack and cheddar for $6.99.

In order to provide low prices, owners buy inventory from distressed and bankrupt stores and they work with the insurance industry to buy up the remains of transit accidents. They also buy over-productions from wineries like Silver Oak and Fetzer (look for R.H. Phillips wines—1991 Cabernet and 1992 Chardonnay at $3.99 a bottle). —*PK*

WHOLE EARTH ACCESS

East Bay: 2990 Seventh St (at Ashby), Berkeley (510) 845-3000.
Sat–Wed 10 am–6 pm, Thurs–Fri 10 am–8 pm.
MasterCard, Visa, Discover
Other Stores: 401 Bayshore Blvd, SF (415)

285-5244; Concord Willows Shopping Center, Concord (510) 686-2270; 863 East Francisco Blvd, San Rafael, (415) 459-3533. Also in San Jose and Sacramento.
Parking: Lot on premises

The original Whole Earth Access, inspired by visionary Stewart Brand's *Whole Earth Catalog*, operated from a storefront on Shattuck Avenue in Berkeley. That's where we first bought Wüstof Trident knives at a steep discount, huge ochre-colored bowls for bread making, and a small, hand-operated flour mill. Today's Whole Earth Access, an enormously successful chain of six stores, still offers some of the best prices on cookware and small kitchen appliances around. The store also has an enlightened return policy. Check Whole Earth for German and French baking pans, kitchen scales, high-quality knives, and cookware from Calphalon, All-Clad, and other manufacturers. Atlas pasta machines that retail elsewhere for $45 were just $29. And prices on Cuisinart food processors, along with reliable Kitchen Aid mixers and accessories, are very competitive.

ALPHABETICAL STORE LISTING

The classic chrome-and-glass Osterizer blender is just $75.

"One reason we can offer such good prices and work on a shorter profit margin," cookware buyer Mike Heflin explains, "is because we don't have the overhead and the peripheral staff." And rather than run special sales, Whole Earth's policy is to offer cookware at low prices every day. If you don't buy it today, don't worry, the price won't go up tomorrow. Chicago Cutlery is always 20 percent off, but every now and then Heflin can offer 40 percent off on the walnut-handled line. He cautions, however, that wood handle or not, no knife should go into the dishwasher. "The strong detergent damages the blade and bleaches out the wood. Clean the blades in warm soapy water, rinse well, and dry right away." —*SIV*

THE WINE CLUB

San Francisco: 953 Harrison St, SF
(415) 512-9086; (800) 966-7835.
Mon–Sat 9 am–7 pm, Sun noon–5 pm.
MasterCard, Visa
Parking: Parking: Lot on premises

Operating out of a small, bare-bones warehouse on Harrison near Fifth Street, The Wine Club offers some of the lowest prices in town on top-notch imported and domestic wines.

Last year the store also introduced fresh Russian caviar to its line-up. The caviar, packed in Russia by the Borisovich Company, is sold in one-, two-, and four-ounce jars under the name Black Pearl. The markup is just 10 percent, so that The Wine Club's prices come in at almost half those of the Pétrossian boutique at Neiman Marcus.

A four-ounce jar of Beluga for $99.99, osetra for $45.99, and sevruga for $42.99—these prices make turnover high, a requisite for fresh caviar. Even better, the price per ounce is almost the same whether you buy one ounce or four, so it's easy to put together a tasting of two or more types. (Though it does ship wine, The Wine Club does not currently ship caviar at this time.) Call for availability. "The rule-of-thumb for caviar," says manager Jim Smith, "is to get more than you want to pay for—there's never enough." —*SIV*

YUEN HOP

East Bay: 824 Webster St, Oakland
(510) 451-2698.
Mon–Sat 8 am–6 pm.
Cash only
Parking: Street

This Oakland Chinatown noodle factory mainly wholesales to East Bay Chinese restaurants, but passersby can also buy there. Everything is clearly labeled and priced. Fresh egg noodles, both the regular chow mein and wider Shanghai-style noodles go for about 70 cents a pound; buy five pounds for $2.75, and ten for $4.50. Pure egg noodles were $1.10 per pound ($4.75 for five pounds).

You can also pick up square and round skins for won ton, egg-roll skins, plus several kinds of tofu, and Yuen Hop's own bean sprouts. Twenty-five- and fifty-pound bags of fragrant Jasmine rice were $10.25 and $18.50, respectively. —*SIV*

FARMERS' MARKETS

The keys to a great bargain—price, quality, and selection—make farmers' markets the ideal spot to buy inexpensive produce. Costs are low since you buy directly from farmers. Quality is high because fruits and vegetables are picked ripe and sold within a day or two, and selection is incomparable. Where else can you choose from ten different kinds of potatoes, eight types of mushrooms, or fifteen varieties of apples?

You can shop at a farmers' market in some part of the Bay Area every day of the week, and it isn't necessary to be up at dawn to get the best selection. There are nearly two hundred farmers' markets in California today, and many run all year long. In spring and summer you can find peaches, cherries, tomatoes, melons, and berries that will surpass the taste and quality of those in the produce section. There is winter bounty, too, including root vegetables, greens, apples, nuts, beans, kiwis, citrus fruits, and avocados. Organic produce is often available, and some markets even specialize in certified organic goods. —By Clary Alward

BERKELEY FARMERS' MARKETS

East Bay: Derby St at Martin Luther King, Berkeley
Open Tues 2 pm–7 pm in summer and 1pm to dusk in winter.

Now in its eighth season, this is the oldest of Berkeley's three farmers' markets, which are all sponsored by The Ecology Center, a twenty-five-year-old organization. These markets specialize in produce from organic growers, and the majority of their vendors are local. —*CA*

BERKELEY FARMERS' MARKETS

East Bay: Center St at Martin Luther King Jr. Way, Berkeley
Open Saturday 10 am–2 pm, year-round.

This four-year-old market has a relaxed, Saturday atmosphere suitable for coffee-sipping and strolling as you shop. —*CA*

BERKELEY FARMERS' MARKETS

East Bay: Haste St at Telegraph Ave, Berkeley
Open Sunday 11 am–3 pm, May–November.

Berkeley's newest market has all the quality organic produce of the other two markets with the ambiance of the UC Berkeley campus and People's Park. —*CA*

 ALPHABETICAL STORE LISTING

DOWNTOWN SAN RAFAEL FARMERS' MARKET FESTIVAL

North Bay: On Fourth St between Cijos and B streets, San Rafael
Thurs 6–9 pm, April through October.

This is one of the largest markets in the Bay Area, with five blocks of over 135 vendors, food and craft booths, bakers, and live entertainment. Since it begins unusually late in the day, stop by after work with friends and family and spend a few hours perusing the vast selection. —*CA*

FERRY PLAZA FARMERS' MARKET

San Francisco: On Embarcadero in front of the Ferry Building, SF (415) 481-3004.
Sat 9 am–2 pm, year-round.

Launched just last year, the Ferry Plaza Farmers' Market has brought life—and green leafy vegetables—to the Ferry Building. It's already become a popular Saturday destination since it features great produce plus local talent. Bay Area chefs including Bradley Ogden of Lark Creek Inn and One Market and Alice Waters of Chez Panisse have participated in special events like Shop with the Chef, where they're on hand to give suggestions for choosing and preparing seasonal produce. In the works? A fun program to teach kids about agriculture, biology, and cooking.

Many vendors are open to bargaining, especially toward the end of the day. The market also has some of the best street food around, with items such as frozen fruit paletas from Latin Freeze at $1 each. In spring, look for culinary herbs and organic vegetable starter sets at good prices. —*CA*

HEART OF THE CITY FARMERS' MARKET

San Francisco: United Nations Plaza, off Market St, between Seventh and Eighth streets, SF.
Open Wed and Sat 7 am–5 pm, year-round.

Though this market takes the purist approach (no arts and crafts or food vendors) the variety reflects all that is available in the city. Fresh fish and seafood, cut flowers, and even ducks and chickens make the Heart of the City market appealing to neighborhood locals and the City Hall employees who shop during the week. —*CA*

MARIN FARMERS' MARKET

North Bay: Marin Civic Center, San Pedro Road exit off Highway 101, San Rafael.
Mailing address: 1114 Irwin St, San Rafael, 94901 (415) 456-3276 or (800) 897-3276.
Thur and Sun 8 am–1 pm.
Checks accepted
Parking: Civic Center parking lots

This state-certified organic foods marketplace includes vendors selling organically grown cut flowers and gift plants. All flowers are grown at nearby local family farms, so prices vary, according to season and availability. Generally, you'll find discounts from 10 to 15 percent on freshly cut bouquets. —*MA*

THE SAN FRANCISCO FARMERS' MARKET

San Francisco: 100 Alemany Blvd (off Hwy 280), SF (415) 647-9423.
Sat dawn to dusk.
Parking: Lot on premises.

The San Francisco Farmers' Market on Alemany Boulevard is a San Francisco institution—1994 marks its fifty-first year. More than 140 stalls (during the peak summer months) get set up each Saturday along an arcade.

This market is bustling. Trucks pull up in front, vendors set up their scales and display their goods. The market is mostly fruit and vegetables, many of them as diverse as the shoppers who crowd in front of stands that sell Chinese pea shoots, Indian ridge gourd, and long sweet European cucumbers.

You can find heavy garlic braids, strings of dried hot peppers, homemade herb vinegars, and home-cured olives. Most items sell by the pound, and in most cases, the more you buy, the better the price. By 3 pm, the prices start to go down. Farmers don't want to take their produce home again, so they're definitely open to bargaining. —*SIV*

SAN JOSE TOWN & COUNTRY

South Bay: Town & Country Center, 2980 Stevens Creek Blvd at Winchester, San Jose
Fri 10 am–2 pm, year-round.

This farmers' market is truly enormous, with as many as seventy to eighty vendors in the summer months. —*CA*

SANTA ROSA ORIGINAL FARMERS' MARKET

North Bay: Veterans' Memorial Building, 1351 Maple Ave, Santa Rosa

Wed and Sat 9 am–noon, year-round.

This is not only the largest farmers' market in Sonoma County, but—after seventeen years—one of the oldest markets in the state. The market focuses on Sonoma County growers, featuring specialties like "heirloom" vegetables (older breeds that have not been cross-bred for mass production). Local bakers and restaurants can also be found selling their wares. —*CA*

SONOMA FARMERS' MARKET

North Bay: On Sonoma Plaza in front of City Hall, Sonoma
Tuesdays 5:30–8:30 pm, June through October

Open on summer evenings, the Sonoma Farmers' Market is more than a place to buy fresh produce. You can browse the local stores (it's set in the middle of town), grab some barbecue from a street vendor, and settle in the park to enjoy live music and entertainment. —*CA*

ALPHABETICAL STORE LISTING

INSIDER TIP: FARM STANDS

Cardoza's Farm Stand and Pumpkin Farm, 5869 Lakeville Highway, Petaluma (707) 762-2207.
Sweet corn, melons, tomatoes, summer squash, and cucumbers. June or July–October, Thurs–Sun, 10 am–6 pm or by appointment. Petting zoo and picnic area, tours and hayrides (October only), too.

Keig Ranch, 3165 Silverado Trail, Napa (707) 257-3453.
Apples of distinction: Gravenstein, Golden and Red Delicious, Pippin, Jonathan. Mid-July through mid–November, Mon–Sat 8:30 am–5:30 pm.

Oak Hill Farm, 15101 Sonoma Highway, Glen Ellen (707) 996-6643.
Middle of June through end of October is a great time for fresh flowers, organic fruit, and vegetables. Sold at the barn. Thurs–Sat 10 am–4 pm.

von Uhlit Ranch, 3011 Soscol Avenue, Napa (707) 226-2844.
Daily noon–4 pm.
Pears, peaches, plums, prunes, dried apricots, and apples—sold "right here at the barn." ▥

INSIDER TIP: PICK YOUR OWN PRODUCE

The sun's hot. Bees are buzzing. Big, fat peaches are juicy and ripe. Especially after such a nice, rainy winter, the Bay Area has some of the lushest farm country anywhere. And summer is the time to grab the kids and get out on the farm and pick your own fruit. These are a few of the local farms and ranches that let you pick your own produce:

Coast Ways Ranch, Highway 1, near Año Nuevo State Park (30 miles south of Half Moon Bay) (415) 879-0414.
Through June and July, you can pick your own olallieberries (a clever cross between a boysenberry and a raspberry). Later in the season: pumpkins (October), kiwi (November through January), and Christmas trees (December). Call ahead for hours and exact picking dates.

Happy Haven Ranch, 1480 Sperring Road, Sonoma (707) 996-4260.
Pick your own strawberries. Jams and chutneys for sale.
Closed Christmas through April, Saturday 10 am–6 pm, Sun by appointment. Tours welcome. Call ahead.

Hoffman Farm, 2125 Silverado Trail, Napa (707) 226-8938.
You pick pears, imperial prunes, peaches, and sugar prune-plums. Later in the season: walnuts, persimmons. All grown without chemical sprays (except walnuts). August to November, 9 am–5 pm daily. ▥

INSIDER TIP

CHAPTER **5**

HOME ELECTRONICS

HOME ELECTRONICS

Whether you're in the market for a new refrigerator, laptop computer, or a top-of-the-line stereo system for your home, you'll want to do your research when you invest in electronics equipment. We recommend comparison shopping—and following the tips of our experts, reporters Michael Sharon and Suzanne Stefanac.

APPLIANCES

You should approach hunting for a bargain on appliances in the same manner as you would shop for any big-ticket item. Few situations can make one feel more vulnerable than having to depend solely on a salesperson for information about a major purchase. The better informed you are walking into a store, the more likely you are to walk out with a good deal on a model that fits your needs.

ABC APPLIANCE

**San Francisco: 2050 Taraval St, SF
(415) 564-8166.
Mon–Sat 9 am–4 pm, Sun 10 am–2 pm.
Discover, MasterCard, Visa
Parking: Street**

If you're shopping for a large appliance in San Francisco, be sure to check out ABC's crowded showroom. Not only are you likely to save $100 to $150 on all the major brands and models, but most of the appliances are hooked up "live" so that you can try them out before buying. On a recent visit, a Maytag sealed-burner gas range (advertised at Montgomery Ward for $700) was marked $645, while a General Electric 19.6-cubic-foot refrigerator (advertised at Sears for $900) went for $819. Discounts and free delivery are offered if you purchase more than one appliance, but you can save even more by picking up the merchandise yourself. *—MS*

APPLIANCE CONSIGNMENTS

**East Bay: 48 Monument Plaza, Pleasant Hill
(510) 676-3300.
Tues–Sat 9:30 am–5:30 pm.
MasterCard, Visa
Parking: Lot on premises**

Whether you're starting out on your first mortgage or just looking for a refrigerator for your summer home, this small shop has good deals on reconditioned appliances. Owners Audie and Rose Trantham will explain the history of each item and provide a thirty-day warranty on parts and service. In general, prices on washers begin around $99, ranges and refrigerators at $140. *—MS*

APPLIANCE SALES AND SERVICE COMPANY

**San Francisco: 655 Mission St, SF
(800) 424-6783.
Mon–Fri 8:30 am–5:30 pm, Sat 9 am–5 pm.**

 ALPHABETICAL STORE LISTING

Major credit cards
Parking: Street

For one of the largest selections of small appliances in the Bay Area, check out this crowded downtown shop. During a recent visit, for instance, we counted over twenty different clothes irons, each priced well below normal department-store prices. In addition to everyday household items, you'll also find professional mixers and grinders, hard-to-find items such as coffee percolators, and replacement parts for just about any small appliance. Extra savings can be found on a wide assortment of floor models, salesman's samples, and service units, which are sold for $20 to $40 less than their everyday low prices. By no means a Bay Area secret, the store conducts well over half its business by mail. —*MS*

C. G. ELECTRIC APPLIANCE

Peninsula: 6422 Mission St, Daly City
(415) 756-3931.
Mon–Fri 9 am–6 pm, Sat 10 am–5 pm.

Discover, MasterCard, Visa
Parking: Lot on premises

Thirty-five years in the same location, this family-run business scores high marks for its low prices and big selection, and for having in-house repair on the premises. "If a person wants something today, they get it today," boasts co-owner Sam Parisis, who claims his warehouse takes in five truckloads of merchandise per week. Good bargains during a recent visit included a Jenn-Air 15.3-cubic-foot, side-by-side refrigerator-freezer, which was reduced from $1399 to $999. —*MS*

CIRCUIT CITY

San Francisco: 1200 Van Ness Ave, SF
(415) 441-1300.
Mon–Sat 10 am–9 pm, Sun 10 am–6 pm.
Major credit cards
Other stores: Fifteen Bay Area stores; check telephone directory for nearest location.
Parking: Garage on Post St

Although all of the appliances here carry a

low-price guarantee, the best deals to be found at Circuit City are a large selection of floor models and returned items. For instance, during a recent visit to the Circuit City on Van Ness in San Francisco, a Magic Chef gas range was reduced from $220 to $100; a GE Profile refrigerator was reduced from $1490 to $1270; and a Panasonic Jet-Flow vacuum cleaner was reduced from $190 to $150.

Good deals on open items can be found throughout the year, but one of the best times is right after the holidays. —*MS*

DAVIES APPLIANCE

Peninsula: 1580 El Camino Real, Redwood City (415) 366-5728.
Mon–Wed 9 am–6 pm, Thur 9 am–9 pm, Fri–Sat 9 am–6 pm, Sun 10 am–5 pm.
Discover, MasterCard, Visa
Other stores: Strait Appliance, 2240 South El Camino, San Mateo (415) 349-2190.
Parking: Lot on premises

For nearly sixty years, Davies Appliance has offered a wide selection of discounted appliances and reliable, factory-authorized service. The salesmen are anything but pushy and they're more than willing to explain all the basics. With three warehouses in the immediate area, most products are in stock and available immediately. You can pick up extra savings on nicked and scratched models, so be sure to check out the clearance center on the main floor at the Redwood City store. —*MS*

FRIEDMAN'S MICROWAVE

East Bay: 2301 Broadway, Oakland (510) 444-1119.
Mon–Fri 10 am–5:30 pm, Sat 10 am–5 pm.
Major credit cards
Other Stores: 5509 Geary Blvd, San Francisco (415) 221-0888; 17 South B St, San Mateo (415) 347-6612; 60 Town and Country Village, Palo Alto (415) 324-1262; 22400 Foothill Blvd, Hayward, (510) 886-

0575; 7180 Amador Plaza Rd, Dublin (510) 829-2626; 2304 Monument Blvd, Pleasant Hill (510) 602-1360; 402 San Pablo Town Center, San Pablo (510) 233-7214; 216 North Gate #1, San Rafael (415) 479-9080.**
Parking: Street

If you're looking for a microwave oven, you need go no further than your nearest Friedman's. A national chain with nine stores in the Bay Area, Friedman's offers great prices and even better service. While beating most department store prices, Friedman's carries dozens more models than even the biggest super stores.

Most importantly, with the store's sixty-day exchange policy, you are assured of finding the right microwave to fit your needs. To help you on your way, be sure to take advantage of your life-time membership entitling you to the free cooking classes that take place weekly at each of the Friedman's outlets. —*MS*

HOOVER FACTORY OUTLET STORE

East Bay: 15099-B Hesperian Blvd, San Leandro (510) 278-9880.
Mon–Sat 9 am–5 pm.
MasterCard, Visa
Other stores: 860 South Winchester Blvd, San Jose (408) 243-7060; 3628 Geary Blvd, San Francisco (415) 668-5101.
Parking: Lot on premises

These outlet stores offer factory-direct prices on the complete Hoover line and discounted prices on select floor models. Recent bargains at the San Leandro store included the Power-Max Supreme variable-speed cleaner, reduced from $500 to $240; and the PowerMax self-propelled heavy-duty cleaner, reduced from $420 to $255. Meanwhile, a Hoover Spirit four-horsepower floor model was reduced from $500 to $140. Each store offers in-house service by factory-trained personnel. —*MS*

LZ PREMIUMS

**South Bay: 1162 Saratoga Ave, San Jose
(408) 985-9718.**
**Tues–Sat 10 am–6 pm, Fri 10 am–8 pm,
Sun 11 am–5 pm.**
MasterCard, Visa
Parking: Lot on premises

For almost seventeen years, LZ Premiums
has maintained the philosophy that low overhead can translate into low prices. Ordering
direct from the factory, the owners have literally jammed the store with all the popular
makes and models of dishwashers, ranges,
washers, and dryers.

Good deals during a recent visit included a
General Electric Potscrubber 2230, marked
down from $459 to $439, and a General
Electric gas range with 4.4-cubic-foot oven
capacity, marked down from $720 to $670.
—*MS*

REED SUPPLY COMPANY

**East Bay: 1328 Fruitvale Ave, Oakland
(510) 436-7171.**
Mon–Sat 9:30 am–5 pm.
Checks accepted
Parking: Lot on premises

The decor of this almost fifty-year-old business isn't as fancy as other stores, but it
doesn't need to be. Reed Supply has built a
loyal clientele of consumers and contractors
who know a fair price when they see one.

"We're survivors," one manager told me as
he reflected on the many failed businesses in
Oakland. "We buy right and we sell right."

In addition to close-out prices on standard
brands, you'll also find great deals on com-
mercial-style gas ranges by Garland and
Thermador. But remember to bring cash or a
personal check: Reed doesn't accept credit
cards. —*MS*

TELECENTER

**Peninsula: 1830 South Delaware St, San
Mateo (415) 341-5804.**
**Mon, Wed, Fri 9 am–6 pm; Tues, Thur 9 am–
8 pm; Sat 9 am–5 pm; Sun noon–5 pm.**
Discover, MasterCard, Visa
Parking: Lot on premises

By purchasing direct from the factory
through a national buying group, the
Telecenter is able to offer a large selection of
appliances at discounted prices. On a recent
visit, we found the prices on General Electric
products to be extremely good. A GE
Monogram sealed-gas range, for example,
was reduced from $749 to $700, while a GE
Potscrubber dishwasher was reduced from
$290 to $250.

If you're using a licensed contractor to
remodel your kitchen and can provide the
contractor's name and license number, you'll
receive a special discount. —*MS*

ALPHABETICAL STORE LISTING

WHOLE EARTH ACCESS

South Bay: 3530 Stevens Creek Blvd, San Jose (408) 554-1500.
Mon–Fri 10 am–9 pm, Sat–Sun 10 am–6 pm.
Discover, MasterCard, Visa
Other Stores: 1975 Diamond Blvd, Concord (510) 686-2270; 863 East Francisco Blvd, San Rafael (415) 459-3533; 2990 Seventh St, Berkeley (510) 845-3000; 401 Bayshore Blvd, SF (415) 285-5244.
Parking: Lot on premises

Whole Earth Access remains a good place to go if you're shopping for small appliances. During a recent visit, a 325-watt KitchenAid heavy-duty mixer with five-quart bowl was reduced from $400 to $299; a Cuisinart Custom II food processor was reduced from $250 to $199; and a Krups Cafe Bistro combination espresso/cappuccino/coffee maker was reduced from $250 to $189. —MS

COMPUTERS

Buying computer equipment or software is inevitably frustrating. Today's bleeding-edge technologies are constantly being superseded by tomorrow's newer, spiffier versions. Sorting the hype from the true bits and bytes requires a doctorate in bulldata detection. And prices seem to have half-lives—whatever you're pricing at the moment is likely to cost a lot less a few months down the line.

Here are a few tips for the best possible deal. Assess your needs and avoid buying more features than you really need. Take ads from the major computer magazines and free computer tabloids with you when shopping; many vendors will meet or beat a competitor's published price. While mail-order houses and large chain stores inevitably boast the cheapest prices, there is much to be said for the knowledgeable enthusiasm, personal attention, and post-purchase technical support that many smaller vendors routinely offer. —Suzanne Stefanac

BERKELEY SYSTEMS

East Bay: 2095 Rose St, Berkeley (510) 540-5535.
Mon–Fri 8 am–5 pm.
MasterCard, Visa
Parking: Street

No computer is a bargain if you can't use it. Berkeley Systems, a company usually associated with its nifty Star Trek and AfterDark screensavers—animated programs that appear on the monitor when the computer is left unattended—also offers two products that prove invaluable to many visually impaired individuals.

The first, inLARGE, is a $195 software program that allows a Macintosh user to enlarge any portion of the screen image from two to sixteen times. Simply use the cursor to identify the part of the screen you would like to see magnified.

The second, outSPOKEN, is a $495 software program that reads aloud any text that might appear on the screen, including menus and dialog boxes. A Windows version will be available soon. Although you can buy at the Rose Street office, most people order over the phone. —SS

BMUG

East Bay: 2055 Center St, Berkeley
(510) 549-2684.
(Mailing address: 1442-A Walnut St, #62,
Berkeley, CA 94709)
Mon–Fri 8:30 am–4:30 pm.
Membership fee: $28 for six months, $45
for one year
MasterCard, Visa; personal checks
Parking: Street

If you sometimes sit in front of your computer feeling stumped and wishing you could turn to someone for help, you might consider joining a computer user group. Thousands of Bay Area Macintosh users find BMUG an indispensable source of information when buying or installing new software or hardware. Regular meetings (every Thursday in Berkeley, as well as the last Monday of the month in San Francisco and the third Monday of the month in Santa Clara) include forums for general questions and sessions with vendors who demonstrate new products.

Members also have access to telephone help lines, SIGs (special interest groups), and a lively electronic bulletin board. As if all this weren't enough, BMUG sells useful books and software such as the 650 megabyte BMUG PD-ROM, a CD-ROM packed with hundreds of public domain fonts, system extensions, utilities, snippets of clip art, handy applications, and educational programs such as a vocabulary quiz, a Morse code tutor, and more than thirty math programs—all for $40. —SS

CJS SYSTEMS

East Bay: 2750 Adeline St, Berkeley
(510) 849-3730.
Mon–Fri 10 am–6 pm.
MasterCard, Visa
Parking: Street

The repairman says you have to replace the entire motherboard on your Mac. You have no choice. Right? Wrong, if you know about CJS Systems.

Started in 1985 by a trio of computer specialists, this business is unique in that the excellent technical staff will actually wield snippers and a welding iron to repair your Macintosh computer at the component level. Prices are more than fair—$35 for a half-hour diagnostic and $70 an hour for actual repairs on our recent trip.

Installing a new power supply runs about $70 plus parts; simple keyboard repairs can be as low as $25 plus $5 for replacement keys; and printers can generally be fixed in one or two hours. As an added bonus, CJS also offers excellent data-recovery services. —SS

COMPU DATA

San Francisco: 22 Third St, SF

(415) 495-3422.
Mon–Fri 9:30 am–6:30 pm, Sat 11 am–5 pm.
American Express, MasterCard, Visa
Parking: Street

Like many local computer stores, Compu Data may not always be able to promise the rock-bottom price, but service and sound advice are worth more than a little cash when investing in computers.

Known for savvy in setting up customized networks of IBM–compatible computers (a number of satisfied Bay Area law offices have availed themselves of this service), Compu Data also enjoys helping individuals interested in adding multimedia and MIDI capabilities to their system.

For less than $2000, a budding electronic musician might put together a MIDI system that includes a 486-33 computer, an Orchid SoundWave 32 sound card for excellent compatibility with many music file formats, stereo pre-amp speakers, and CakeWalk Professional, the industry standard for music-sequencing software. —SS

COMPUTERLAND OF SERRAMONTE

San Francisco: 409 South Spruce Ave,
South San Francisco (415) 615-9020.
Mon–Fri 9 am–6 pm, Sat 10 am–5 pm.
MasterCard, Visa
Other stores: Computerland of Hayward, 22540
Foothill Blvd, Hayward (510) 538-8080.
Parking: Lot on premises

Computerland franchises generally deal with larger businesses, buying excess product from Apple Computer, Hewlett-Packard, Toshiba, and NEC and selling it at a discount. Two outlets—the stores in Serramonte and Hayward—do sell directly to the public, however.

The storefronts are comparatively small, but the prices are definitely competitive. If you've already shopped around and tried out the hardware at a larger store, you might want to drop by Computerland and see if the sales staff won't match or beat your best price. —SS

DOMINO COMPUTER

San Francisco: 3400 Geary Blvd, SF
(415) 668-9311.
Mon–Fri 9:30 am–6:30 pm, Sat–Sun
10 am–4 pm.
Discover, MasterCard, Visa
Other Stores: 1552 Beach St, Ste B,
Berkeley/Emeryville (510) 653-6286; 486
Campbell Ave, Ste 102, Campbell (408)
374-7477; 1130-D Burnett Ave, Concord
(510) 682-8934; 26222 Industrial Blvd,
Hayward (510) 732-0377; 111 Plaza North,
Los Altos (415) 941-7778; 231 Millbrae
Ave, Ste 101, Millbrae (415) 259-8080; 976
Hanson Ct, Milpitas (408) 946-6991; 3019
Arden Way, Sacramento (916) 972-0311;
461 Blossom Hill Rd, Ste H-1, San Jose
(408) 363-1800; 757 Lincoln Ave, San
Rafael (415) 453-8525; 2217 San Ramon
Valley Blvd, Ste C, San Ramon (510) 820-
6022; 1740 Santa Rosa Ave, Santa Rosa
(707) 523-2055; 1214 Apollo Way, Ste
404.2, Sunnyvale (408) 749-0217; 480

ALPHABETICAL STORE LISTING

Redwood St, Ste 12, Vallejo/Napa (707) 644-5055.

The do-it-yourself set can save money (if not time) by shopping at one of the fifteen Bay Area Domino Computer outlets. The informed and friendly staff will help you select all the components you might need: microprocessor, motherboard, case, keyboard, floppy drive, hard drive, monitor, video card, modem, memory, even a CD-ROM drive, and soundcard, if you like. Then, under their watchful eye, you assemble the computer yourself. If you give up midway, the staff will complete the job gratis. Should you bring in your own components, you can pay $25 an hour for advice and access to tools. Best of all, Dominos offers a lifetime warranty on labor.

ELITE COMPUTERS & SOFTWARE, INC

South Bay: 10601 South De Anza Blvd, Ste 305, Cupertino (408) 725-1556.

By appointment only.
American Express, MasterCard, Visa
Parking: Adjacent lot

The rapidity with which computer models are superseded spawns a buyers' market in discontinued units. Elite Computers and Software in Cupertino sells some new and used computers, but the real deals lie in their ever-changing inventory of discontinued and refurbished Macintosh computers.

On a recent visit, for instance, a sleek PowerBook 170 laptop with a 25 MHz 68030 microprocessor and crisp black-and-white active-matrix screen, plus a SuperMac SuperView thirteen-inch color monitor, was just under $2000.

When the 170 first hit the streets back in early 1992, it retailed for $4600—without the spiffy color monitor. Superseded models come with the full Apple warranty, as do factory-tested refurbished models. Printers, CD-ROM players, hard drives, and other peripherals are also available. —*SS*

FRY'S ELECTRONICS

South Bay: 1177 Kern Ave, Sunnyvale (408) 733-1770.
Mon–Fri 8 am–9 pm, Sat 9 am–8 pm, Sun 9 am–7 pm.
MasterCard, Visa
Other Stores: 600 East Hamilton Ave, Campbell (408) 364-3700; 440 Mission Ct, Fremont (510) 770-3797; 340 Portage Ave, Palo Alto (415) 496-6000.
Parking: Lot on premises

Fry's Electronics is an example of a store run by computer enthusiasts that evolved into a home-grown super-store chain. The first store opened in Sunnyvale, and three more outlets—Palo Alto, Fremont, and Campbell—followed. Each is cavernous, and the many aisles bulge with computer bargains. Although Fry's Electronics is not a national chain, the sheer volume of computers and software sold in the stores allows the mini-chain to offer prices that are competitive with the giants. Plus, the staff is generally well informed and willing to help customers sort through the plethora of options. Plan to grab a big cart and stock up on floppies, screen cleaner, magazines, mouse pads, and other computer accoutrements while you're there. —SS

LOGITECH FACTORY OUTLET

East Bay: 6607 Kaiser Dr, Fremont (800) 231-7717, option 5.
Mon, Wed, Fri 9 am–6 pm; Tues, Thurs 10 am–7 pm; Sat 10 am–4 pm.
MasterCard, Visa
Parking: Street

Finally, an outlet store for the digital set. Fremont-based Logitech has been selling peripherals such as mice, scanners, and digital cameras for more than a decade. In late 1993, the company opened a discount outlet. Some products have a scratch or two, others are as good as new, but all have been tested and come with a sixty-day warranty. The deals are hard to beat. Recently, a mouse that would normally sell for about $30 was $9. The PhotoMan camera, which records photo images digitally in 256 shades of gray and then downloads them to your computer, was running a low $250 instead of the normal retail price of $649. 800K diskettes are a steal at five for a dollar. Plus, there are bargain T-shirts, sweatshirts, bags, mugs, and even calculators—all with the Logitech logo, of course. —SS

MACADAM

San Francisco: 1062 Folsom St, SF (415) 863-6222.
Mon–Fri 10 am–7 pm, Sat 10 am–5 pm, Sun 11 am–4 pm.
American Express, MasterCard, Visa
Parking: Lot on premises

A picture is worth a thousand megabytes. Any Macintosh user in search of the best deal in monitors need look no farther than San Francisco's MACadam. Although working within the constraints that any non-chain neighborhood store must face, MACadam scours the market to find the best bargains.

Also, as a cost-cutting measure, the store offers a 3 percent discount for those choosing not to pay with credit cards. Recent examples of prices reflecting this discount are the 8-bit Radius Color Pivot/LE with an adapter card for $599.

PowerBook users will need to add the PowerView SCSI box for an extra $50; the PowerView alone generally runs $250. For those who regularly traffic in 24-bit color, the Radius Rocket 25i accelerator with a Precision Color 24X card is a steal at $1250. —SS

PERSONAL COMPUTERS FOR LESS

San Francisco: 1309 Fillmore St, SF (415) 346-1692.
Mon–Fri 9 am–6 pm, Sat noon–5 pm.
Discover, MasterCard, Visa
Parking: Lot on premises

If personalized service is your wont, you can't do better than Personal Computers for Less. This storefront on San Francisco's Fillmore Street houses a few new computers and a selection of nicely priced used computers. The real bargains, however, begin when you explain to owner Don Marshall what, exactly, you would like your computer to do. For the past six years, Marshall has been building custom configurations that are 100 percent IBM–compatible and he includes a one-year warranty for parts and a full two-year warranty for labor. Repairs and training are also available. —SS

SATURN TECHNOLOGY, INC

South Bay: 3945 Freedom Circle, Ste 770, Santa Clara (800) 532-3903 or (408) 982-5910.
Mon–Fri 9 am–6 pm.
MasterCard, Visa
Parking: Lot on premises

Replacing the ink/ink-jet cartridge in any printer is a costly proposition, but owners of Hewlett-Packard DeskJet or DeskWriter printers are in luck. Santa Clara–based Saturn Technology, Inc. (STI) produces a refill kit that allows you to use the same cartridge up to ten times. Traditional cartridges for HP printers cost $17.95, and you throw them away when they run out of toner. The $17.95 HP 51608A kit includes enough toner for four refills; that's less than $4.50 per refill. The $28 HP 51626A kit fills cartridges that are twice as large. Owners of Hewlett-Packard plain-paper fax machines (HP Fax-200, Fax-300, or Fax-310) can use these refills for their ink-hungry machines as well. Available directly from the STI. —SS

SFSU MULTIMEDIA STUDIES PROGRAM

San Francisco: 425 Market St, SF, call (415) 904-7700 for information and a free catalog.
MasterCard, Visa
Parking: Street and garage (evenings)

With interactive media being touted as the next big job market in the Bay Area, hundreds of hopefuls are enrolling in extension courses at San Francisco State University's Multimedia Studies Program. The instructors are first rate, and the fees are truly reasonable. Hal Josephson, director of industry relations for 3DO, conducts a $125 day-long seminar on Careers in Multimedia, for instance.

Adding value is the fact that those enrolled in the extension courses are eligible for student discounts on computer hardware and software at the university bookstore, which can result in savings from 20 to 50 percent, occasionally as much as 80 percent. —SS

SHOESTRING MULTIMEDIA

San Francisco: 1500 Twentieth St, SF (415) 920-6920.
Mon–Fri 8 am–5 pm.
Checks accepted
Parking: Street

CD-ROMs provide an excellent medium for archiving large bodies of data and for recording interactive presentations. Like audio-CDs, they are compact, reliable, and easy-to-navigate. Until very recently, however, mere mortals could not afford to have their digital information encoded on the shiny discs.

Shoestring Multimedia is a pioneering company that for as little as $150 will transfer up to 650MB of data from a client's large hard drive or stack of SyQuest storage disks to a CD-ROM. (A hard drive that holds this much data costs $500 to $800.) If you press a thousand CD-ROMs instead of one, the price drops to under $14 per disc; ten thousand discs can run a mere $2.50 apiece. Prices vary according to how much design and programming the Shoestring Multimedia staff contributes. —*SS*

THE USED COMPUTER STORE

East Bay: 2440 Shattuck Ave, Berkeley
(510) 548-8686.

Mon–Sat 10 am–7 pm, Sun noon–5 pm.
MasterCard, Visa
Parking: Street

If your computing needs are modest—fairly simple word processing and spreadsheet chores, for instance—you might consider purchasing a secondhand computer. It may not sport all the niceties of today's newest models, but it will perform the same tasks it did when its circuits were shiny and new. The Used Computer Store in Berkeley stocks many venerable oldsters and sells them at inviting prices. A somewhat used XT PC might run $100 to $200, and a Mac SE goes for $350 to $500. A full spectrum of Apple II computers are available, as well as a nice selection of software packages that run on all of these older machines. —*SS*

WEIRD STUFF WAREHOUSE

South Bay: 1190 Kern Ave, Sunnyvale
(408) 746-1100.
Mon–Sat 9:30 am–9 pm, Sun 10 am–6 pm.

Discover, MasterCard, Visa
Parking: Lot on premises

Not everyone is intrigued by bins of discontinued chips and shelves full of surplus computers, monitors, mice, keyboards and hard drives, but for those who revel in digital effluvia, there is no richer lode than the Weird Stuff Warehouse in Sunnyvale. Across the road from Fry's Electronics, this ten-thousand-square-foot scavenger's dream has been in business since 1986. Some finds are so esoteric even the salespersons aren't sure what they're good for. Others, like the six-month-old VGA color monitors that we saw selling for $150, are fabulously practical. Stock changes regularly, but check it out for the latest in trailing-edge technology. —*SS*

WINDOWS ONLINE

East Bay: (510) 736-8397, fax (510) 736-8397, modem (510) 736-8343.
(Mailing address: PO Box 3487, Danville 94526)

 ALPHABETICAL STORE LISTING

American Express, MasterCard, Visa

Windows OnLine bulletin board service (BBS) boasts 25,000 free or nearly free shareware programs for the Windows platform—more than any other online source. In addition, you can find more than 35,000 OS/2 files and 34,000 DOS files. To help sort through all these options, two online electronic magazines, *WinOnLine Review* (updated monthly) and *WinOnLine Review, Shareware Edition* (updated three times a month) offer enhanced descriptions for each file and many software reviews. To subscribe, you can sign up for three months with nearly unlimited online time for $39.95; for a year with somewhat more limited access for $69.95; or for a year with virtually unlimited access, plus a CD-ROM filled with the most popular programs, for $109.95. Eight thousand members worldwide regularly log onto the eighteen telephone lines (at speeds up to 14,400 bps), but most must pay long-distance fees. Lucky Bay Area residents need only set their modems to dial (510) 736-8343 for a free tour. —*SS*

ELECTRONICS

Walking into an electronics showroom can intimidate even the most seasoned of shoppers. Hundreds of makes and models, each with an array of puzzling features, line the walls and overwhelm the senses. The more you prepare yourself in advance of stepping into this confusing atmosphere, the better chance you stand of walking away with a good deal on a model that meets your needs.

CALIFORNIA DISCOUNTS

North Bay: 9550 Main St, Penngrove (800) 866-1222.
Mon–Fri 10 am–7 pm, Sat 10 am–6 pm.
American Express, MasterCard, Visa
Parking: Lot on premises

Don't be fooled by this store's small showroom. California Discount has three warehouses filled with all the major makes and models of stereos, televisions, and video equipment. With a low overhead and volume-purchasing practices, the store is able to offer prices that are very close to cost. Its nonaggressive sales staff know the ins and outs of the electronics business and will help you select a model that meets your needs and fits your budget. Special orders are welcome, and all in-stock merchandise can be shipped within twenty-four hours. —*MS*

CLYDES CORNER ELECTRONICS

East Bay: 15796 East Fourteenth St, San Leandro (510) 276-8739.
Mon–Sat 9 am–5 pm.
MasterCard, Visa
Parking: Lot on premises

This small, somewhat rickety-looking shop offers great deals on select models of CBs and radar detectors. By purchasing by the crate load, owner Cliff Welch is able to save customers 25 to 30 percent over department store prices. For example, a Uniden 40 channel CB that usually goes for $60 at department stores recently carried an everyday price of $40 at Clydes. The store also offers in-house service on all the products it sells. —*MS*

EPIK AUDIO

East Bay: 129 Woodsworth Ln, Pleasant Hill
(510) 682-1711.
Daily, by appointment only.
Checks accepted
Parking: Street

For customized sound systems at discounted prices, EPIK Audio is the place to go. In addition to serving a loyal local following and mail-order customers, owner Bob Pickard has designed and built audio systems for Hollywood's elite. Working from a studio adjacent to his home, Pickard avoids expensive markups by purchasing components directly from the factory. While EPIK speaker systems range from $695 to $25,000,

the average consumer can expect to save from 30 to 45 percent off comparable models. —*MS*

THE GOOD GUYS

San Francisco: 1400 Van Ness St, SF
(415) 775-9323.
Daily 10 am–midnight.
Major credit cards
Other stores: Eighteen Bay Area stores; check telephone directory for nearest location.
Parking: One hour free parking at Holiday Inn, Van Ness and Pine St

Although all Good Guys products carry a low-price guarantee, the best deals at the Good Guys are on the wide selection of floor models and returned items.

For instance, during a recent visit to the Good Guys on Van Ness in San Francisco, a RCA 46-inch Projection TV was reduced from $1500 to $996. A Panasonic PV122 video camera was reduced from $795 to $299. And a Sony Sports Discman was

reduced from $289 to $209. Good deals can be found on open items throughout the year, but especially right after the holidays. —*MS*

INTERNATIONAL ELECTRONICS CENTER

San Francisco: 1163 Mission St, SF
(415) 626-6382.
Mon–Sat 10 am–6 pm.
Discover, MasterCard, Visa
Parking: Lot across the street

This is the place to go if you're looking for a good deal on a television set of any size. By not advertising, this independent store is able to undercut chain store prices by 5 to 10 percent. For example, a Toshiba 35-inch PIP Stereo TV, which usually retails for $1700, recently went for $1500 at the International Electronics Center. With its own in-store repair center, the store also offers fast, reliable service on all the products it sells. —*MS*

 ALPHABETICAL STORE LISTING

KUSTOM HI FI

Peninsula: 220 California Dr, Burlingame
(415) 348-3888.
Tues–Fri noon–8 pm, Sat 10 am–6 pm.
American Express, MasterCard, Visa
Parking: Street

For good prices on high-end audio components, Kustom HI FI is a one of the better places to go on the Peninsula. In business for over thirty years, the store offers some discounted prices on closeouts, discontinued models, and auctioned goods.

On a recent visit, a Yamaha CDX-920 Natural Sound CD player was reduced from $700 to $480; an AKAI four-channel stereo pre-main amp was reduced from $349 to $199; and an Onkyo TX-20 servo-locked tuner/amplifier was reduced from $429 to $234. The store also offers custom installation. —*MS*

LZ PREMIUMS

South Bay: 1162 Saratoga Ave, San Jose
(408) 985-9718.
Tues-Sat 10 am–6 pm, Fri 10 am–8 pm, Sun 11 am–5 pm.
MasterCard, Visa
Parking: Lot on premises

In the San Jose area, LZ Premiums is hard to beat for bargain prices on televisions and electronics. For about seventeen years, the store has demonstrated that low overhead can translate into low prices. On a recent visit, a Pioneer twelve-disc magazine CD player (that retailed for $375) was selling for $329, while a $600 JVC high-resolution VCR was marked $489. —*MS*

MARIN PHOTO

North Bay: 1425 Grant Ave, Novato
(415) 898-3456.
Mon–Sat 9:30 am–6 pm, Sun noon–4 pm.
Discover, MasterCard, Visa
Parking: Lot on premises

Although this camera store offers in-house service and competitive prices on new equipment, some of its best deals are on used cameras, lenses, and filters. Marin Photo has well over one hundred used lenses, which sell for half or more off their original prices. The store accepts trade-ins and most used equipment comes with a thirty-day warranty on parts and service. —*MS*

NOVATO TV

North Bay: 1305 Grant Ave, Novato
(415) 897-6217.
Tues–Fri 9 am–6 pm, Sat 9 am–5 pm.
Major credit cards
Parking: Street

For great prices on televisions in the North Bay, this independent store is hard to beat. A small shop loaded with a wide variety of makes and models, Novato TV matches or beats most department store prices while offering in-house service on all of the products it sells. Particularly negotiable are prices on higher-end televisions and video equipment. The store offers free delivery and setup on new equipment over $750 and also carries an assortment of reconditioned televisions and VCRs at discounted prices. —*MS*

OEMI INC

Peninsula: 102 Grand Ave, South San Francisco (415) 872-6668.
Mon–Fri 9 am–5 pm, Sat 11 am–3 pm.
MasterCard, Visa
Parking: Street

From typewriters to photocopiers to cash registers, OEMI sells and repairs just about any electronic business machine there is. The knowledgeable, nonaggressive sales staff will help you choose a quality make and model appropriate for your business or personal needs. Being in the repair business, the staff knows the difference between machines that stand up to heavy use and those that break

frequently. In addition to new models, the store also carries a large selection of used typewriters, photocopiers, and fax machines. Special business and quantity rates are also available. —*MS*

ORION BINOCULAR AND TELESCOPE RETAIL STORE

South Bay: 10555 South DeAnza Blvd, Cupertino (408) 255-8770.
Mon–Sat 10 am–5:30 pm, Sun noon–5 pm.
Discover, MasterCard, Visa
Other Stores: 2450 Seventeenth Ave, Santa Cruz (408) 464-0465; 3609 Buchanan St, SF (415) 931-9966; for free catalog call (800) 447-1001.
Parking: Street

Bay Area naturalists and astronomers are fortunate to have three Orion retail stores nearby. Although customers can find below-catalog prices on some items and avoid shipping costs, the real advantage in visiting the store is the ability to try out the various makes and

models in a pressure-free environment. Helpful trained experts at each store will go through the basics for the novice and dispel misconceptions about magnification and size. Whether you order by catalog or in person, you'll save 30 to 40 percent by buying directly through the company. —*MS*

REMINGTON RETAIL STORE

San Francisco: 86 Second St, SF (415) 495-7060.
Mon–Fri 8:30 am–5:30 pm.
Major credit cards
Other Stores: Outlets at Gilroy (408) 847-3676; Factory Stores at Nut Tree, Vacaville (707) 447-6548.
Parking: Street

Owned and operated by the parent company, these outlet stores offer great prices on their entire Remington line of men's and women's electric shavers. In addition to the newest models, the store also carries older Remingtons such as the XLR-3000, which,

ALPHABETICAL STORE LISTING

at $50, continues to be one of the best sellers. Discounted prices can also be found on a wide selection of knives and travel accessories.

For current Remington electric-shaver owners, the store offers tune-ups by factory-trained repairpeople for $13. —*MS*

SANFORD'S TV/VIDEO/STEREO

**East Bay: 1509 Shattuck Ave, Berkeley
(510) 845-0400.**
**Mon–Fri 10 am–7 pm, Sat 9 am–6 pm, Sun
noon–5 pm.**
American Express, MasterCard, Visa
Parking: Street

For over forty years, Dale Sanford has been offering good deals on a large selection of televisions and other electronics. As a member of the Associated Buyers Group, Sanford's carries billions of dollars in purchasing power, which is passed on as savings to its customers.

Unlike most electronics super stores,

Sanford's offers in-shop repair on everything it sells and free setup and delivery for TVs over thirty-one inches, as well as six months same-as-cash financing. —*MS*

SAN JOSE CAMERA & VIDEO

**South Bay: 1600 South Winchester Blvd,
Campbell (408) 374-1880.**
**Mon–Sat 10 am–6 pm (Thur until 8 pm),
Sun noon–5 pm.**
Discover, MasterCard, Visa
Parking: Lot on premises

In business since 1929, San Jose Camera and Video has a solid reputation among photo buffs throughout the Bay Area. Because this is a specialty store, dealing only in cameras, it feels little competition from electronics super stores. During a recent visit, the Canon Elan 35-105mm camera outfit (advertised at Good Guys for $699.99) was marked $589. In addition, San Jose Camera carries Nikon video cameras. Manufactured by Sony, the Nikon

clones retail for 10 to 15 percent less than those with Sony labels. —*MS*

SAN JOSE HONDA/SONY

**South Bay: 1610 South First St, San Jose
(408) 294-6632.**
**Mon, Wed, Fri 10 am–7 pm; Tues, Thur 10
am–8 pm; Sat 9 am–5:30 pm, Sun noon–5
pm.**
Discover, MasterCard, Visa
Parking: Lot on premises

If you're absolutely determined to buy a Sony, be sure to check out the prices here. Buying in large volume and dealing exclusively in the Sony line, this store has an austere showroom with stacks of televisions, stereos, and camcorders still in their crates. Overall, I found the prices to be $50 to $100 lower than at any of the electronics super stores. You can save an additional 1.5 percent if you pay using cash or check instead of a credit card. —*MS*

ALPHABETICAL STORE LISTING

SCANNERS UNLIMITED

South Bay: 1199-A Laurel St, San Carlos
(415) 573-1624.
Tues–Fri 10 am–5 pm, Sat 10 am–4 pm.
Major credit cards
Parking: Street

If you're looking for a scanner, CB radio, or radar detector, this small shop offers big savings and reliable service. Established in 1977, Scanners Unlimited is able to offer discounted prices throughout the year by employing volume-buying strategies. On a recent visit, the Uniden MR 8100 professional hundred-channel scanner was reduced from $650 to $400; the top of the line Cobra 148 GTL CB was reduced from $320 to $200; and the Bel 966 three-band radar detector (voted best by *Car & Driver*) was reduced from $280 to $130. The store also has bargains on used equipment, accepts trade-ins, and offers in-house service on all the products it sells. —*MS*

SOUND COMPANY

East Bay: 1500 Monument Blvd, Concord
(510) 825-0300.
Tues-Sat 9 am–5 pm.
Discover, MasterCard, Visa
Parking: Lot on premises

The owners of this independent store keep abreast of the discounts offered at electronics chain stores and adjust their prices accordingly. During a recent visit, we found that the majority of their prices matched or beat prices comparable on audio equipment found at Whole Earth Access and Circuit City.

What really makes the Sound Company a better place to shop, however, is the store's in-house, factory-authorized service center, which gives top priority to its own customers. Also available at the Sound Company is a wide selection of used, high-end audio components at significantly reduced prices. —*MS*

SOUND WELL

East Bay: 1718 University Ave, Berkeley
(510) 549-2126.
Tues–Sat 9:30 am–5:30 pm.
MasterCard, Visa
Parking: Street

The Sound Well is a crowded little shop with used high-end audio equipment especially from the seventies and eighties and from manufacturers such as Marantz and Kenwood. In the age of the compact disc, as phonographs become increasingly hard to find, the Sound Well offers a wide assortment of turntables ranging from around $95 to around $275.

Other used, top-of-the-line equipment we saw during a recent visit included a McIntosh C 28 stereophonic preamplifier (originally $650) for $450; a Nakamichi BX-2 two-head cassette deck (originally $450) for $225; and a pair of Bose 601 III two-way speakers (originally $999) for $400.

Most products come with a six-month guarantee on parts and labor. —*MS*

STEREO SHOWCASE

North Bay: 923 Tennessee St, Vallejo
(707) 552-1515.
Mon–Fri 10 am–6:30 pm, Sat 10 am–5 pm.
Major credit cards
Parking: Lot on premises

An annoying feature of most stores that deal in high-end audio equipment is the total absence of any price tags. This is not the case at Stereo Showcase—here discounted prices are proudly displayed. Since 1954, the store has earned a reputation for excellence. It now draws the majority of its business from outside of Vallejo. Examples of excellent deals that we found during a recent visit included a Macintosh MR 510 digital tuner, reduced from $1600 to $798; a Yamaha AVC-50 Natural Sound amplifier reduced from $569 to $248; and an NAD 5060 six-disc magazine–CD player reduced from $450 to $318.

The store also offers in-house, factory-authorized service on all products it sells. —*MS*

TELECENTER

Peninsula: 1830 South Delaware St, San Mateo (415) 341-5804.
Mon, Wed, Fri 9 am–6 pm; Tues, Thur 9 am–8pm; Sat 9 am–5 pm; Sun noon–5 pm.
Discover, MasterCard, Visa
Parking: Lot on premises

Purchasing direct from the factory through a national buying group enables the TeleCenter to go head-to-head with electronics chain stores and win.

Although we found all prices there to be competitive, the real deals were on high-end electronics such as a Sony forty-six-inch Videoscope TV that was reduced from $3200 to $2400. The variety of goods in its audio department is somewhat limited, but good deals can be had on speakers. For example, the Advent Legacy II was reduced from $450 to $280 a pair. —*MS*

UNCLE RALPH'S

East Bay: 2569 Telegraph Ave, Berkeley
(510) 841-5628.
Mon–Sat 10:30 am–7 pm, Sun noon-5 pm.
Discover, MasterCard, Visa; ATM
Parking: Lot on premises

Purchased by Whole Earth Access in 1993, Uncle Ralph's continues to offer low prices on an even larger selection of electronics. Although the store still carries exclusive product lines and remains in competition with Whole Earth, it is able to capitalize on the parent company's buying power and pass this savings on to its customers.

For consumers, the one drawback under the new arrangement is the elimination of in-house repair. Still, customers can expect to find 20 to 30 percent savings over regular department store prices. —MS

ALPHABETICAL STORE LISTING

VIDEO ONLY

San Francisco: 1199 Van Ness Ave, SF
(415) 563-5200.
Mon–Fri 10 am–9 pm, Sat 10 am–7 pm, Sun
11 am–6 pm.
Major credit cards
Other stores: 1801 South Grant, San Mateo
(415) 578-1212; 2404 Hesperian Blvd,
Hayward (510) 785-1470; 6920 Amador
Plaza Rd, Dublin (510) 829-2900.
Parking: Next door at Cathedral Hill Quality
Hotel

A small national chain with four stores in the Bay Area, Video Only is able to keep its prices low by avoiding expensive advertising. Prices on camcorders are consistently $50 to $150 lower than major electronics super stores. On a recent visit, a Hitachi VME55A 8mm Camcorder that Circuit City advertised at $999 went for $850 at Video Only. The store also offers 5 to 10 percent additional savings on floor models, which are continually being rotated. —*MS*

SUPERSTORES

The so-called superstores, shopping clubs, and warehouse stores are the embodiment of the volume-buying philosophy. Here, shoppers come to seek out bargains among tall racks of shelves lined with bulk-package products, closeouts, and overstocked items.

If there is a tip to pass on here, it's to listen to your wallet and not just your eyes. With all the bargains you're likely to see, it's easy to exceed your credit limit by purchasing items simply because they're a good deal.

If you're grocery shopping, buy in bulk only those items that you know you or your family will eat. You don't want to wind up with an eight-pound bag of onion rings in your freezer for months. If you're a disciplined shopper, you can save yourself a lot of money in these stores. If you're not, it might be better to leave the credit cards at home.—Michael Sharon

THE HOME DEPOT

Peninsula: 91 Colma Blvd, Colma (415)
992-9600.
Mon–Fri 6 am–9 pm, Sat 7 am–8 pm, Sun 7
am–7 pm.
Major credit cards
Parking: Lot on premises
Other stores: 40525 Albrae St, Fremont
(510) 657-8800; 1933 Davis St, San
Leandro (510) 636-9600; 1125 Old County
Rd, San Carlos (415) 592-9200; 680 Kifer
St, Sunnyvale (408) 245-3686; 30055
Industrial Pkwy, SW, Union City (510) 489-
9400; 1175 Admiral Callaghan Lane,
Vallejo (707) 552-9600.

If you had a big enough shopping cart, you could build a house and landscape a yard—literally—with all of the merchandise to be found at The Home Depot. The ultimate hardware store, The Home Depot has great prices, a knowledgeable sales staff, and all kinds of hard-to-find items for your home and yard. Among other things of interest to gardeners, you'll find an enormous selection of wood and ceramic planting pots, as well as below-list prices on Burpee vegetable seeds.

If you're remodeling your home, visit the interior-design center for a free consultation and great prices on brand-name carpeting, wallpaper, drapes, bedding, and vinyl and ceramic flooring. Visit the kitchen-and-bath center for free consultations and estimates on custom cabinets by Kraft Maid, Vantage, Schuler, and General Marble.

In each department you'll find helpful salespeople and displays offering tips on everything from potting a plant to installing a kitchen floor. For even more advice, stop by one of the weekly free home-improvement seminars. —*MS*

PRICE COSTCO

PRICE CLUB

San Francisco: 451 South Airport Blvd, South San Francisco (415) 872-2021.

Mon–Fri 11 am–8:30 pm, Sat 9:30 am–6 pm, Sun 10 am–5 pm.
Discover
Parking: Lot on premises
Other Stores: 2300 Middlefield Rd, Redwood City (415) 365-9384; 150 Lawrence Station Rd, Sunnyvale (408) 730-1575; 1111 Story Rd, San Jose (408) 286-6690; 2300 Bates Ave, Concord (510) 676-2535.

PRICE COSTCO

San Francisco: 450 Tenth St, SF (415) 626-4288.
Mon–Fri 11 am–8:30 pm, Sat 9:30 am–6 pm, Sun 10 am–5 pm.
Discover
Parking: Lot on premises
Other Stores: 2201 Vern Roberts Circle, Antioch (510) 757-7130; 40580 Albrae St, Fremont (510) 683-6707; 3150 Fostoria Way, Danville (510) 277-0407; 2800 Independence Dr, Livermore (510) 443-6738; 1021 Arnold Dr, Martinez (510) 372-3777; 1000 North Rengstorff, Mountain
View (415) 988-9766; 300 Vintage Way, Novato (415) 899-1331; 4801 Central Ave, Richmond (510) 526-9671; 1340 El Camino Real, San Bruno (415) 871-0460; 1900 South Tenth St, San Jose (408) 287-5530; 1933 Davis St, San Leandro (510) 562-6125; 198 Plaza Dr, Vallejo (707) 648-2245.

Frequent shoppers fortunate enough to be in one of the select groups eligible for membership can find some good bargains by joining one of these clubs. Price Club and Costco have recently merged, so members can now use their cards to shop at either store. Although much of the merchandise is the same, you might find some products at one store that are not available at the other.

In general, these clubs are not the place to go if your heart's set on a particular make or model. If you're hunting for a bargain on a sewing machine for instance, you might be able to save $50 or more by shopping here, but chances are your choices will be limited to one or two models. However, these clubs regularly make available a few products that can save you up to 50 percent and more than pay for your membership.

Price Costco Membership Qualifications:

Business Membership ($30 for primary card, includes free card for spouse; $15 for each add-on card.) All owners or managers of a licensed business or professional practice; directors and managers of nonprofit organizations and government agencies; farmers and ranchers.

Gold Star Membership ($35 for primary card, includes free card for spouse.) Current or retired employees of public or private schools, colleges, universities, government agencies, banks, savings and loans, credit unions, passenger airlines, railroads, public or private utilities, health-care facilities, the media, and approved employers; members of approved credit unions, unions, depositor clubs, professional associations, and community-service groups; state-licensed professionals.

What You'll Find:

Groceries If you like to buy bulk groceries, you'll love the savings you can find here. Examples of prices we saw recently include Minute Maid orange juice, two ninety-six-ounce containers, $5.69; Dreyers ice cream, one-gallon bucket, $6.99; Yoplait yogurt, twelve-pack, $5.49; Ore-Ida tater tots, eight-pound bag, $4.69; Dole California navel oranges, twenty-pound box, $5.99.

Wine, beer, and liquor If you're planning a party, you can cut the cost of spirits 30 percent or more by shopping here. We found Samuel Adams Boston Lager, twelve-pack, $9.59; Robert Mondavi Sauvignon Blanc, 1.5 liter $5.79; Tanqueray Gin, 1.75 liter. $19.99.

Office Supplies Price Club was originally started to cater to businesses, and both stores continue to have excellent prices on office supplies. Delivery is also available. Recently sighted bargains include Paper Mate pens, six twelve-packs, $4.79; Hi-Lighters, twelve-pack, $3.79; ten-by-fifteen-inch Manila envelopes, hundred-pack, $5.99.

Tires Perhaps the best deal to be found at the clubs is on automobile tires. Shoppers can expect to save from $20 to $30 per tire. Both clubs carry all the major brands including B.F. Goodrich, Michelin, Yokohama, and Goodyear.

Film Developing If you plan to shop for an hour or more, be sure to bring along any unprocessed film. On our last visit, both clubs' standard rate for twenty-four exposures was $4.99 for one-hour service, $3.99 for one-week home delivery, and $2.99 if you return to pick your photos up in one week.

Books The selection is nowhere near that of a normal bookstore, but both clubs carry some of the most current titles at up to 50 percent off their listed prices. During a recent visit, discounted titles included Rush Limbaugh's *See, I Told You So*, Margaret Thatcher's *The Downing Street Years*, Steven King's *Nightmares & Dreamscapes*, and Anne Rice's *Lasher*. Also available are a large selection of computer reference books, cookbooks, children's classics, dictionaries, and health guides. —*MS*

WAL-MART

East Bay: 30600 Dyer St, Union City (510) 475-5915.
Daily twenty-four hours.
Discover, MasterCard, Visa
Parking: Lot on premises
Other Stores: 2700 Los Positas Rd, Livermore (510) 455-0215; 2203 Loveridge Rd, Pittsburg (510) 427-2022; 5180 Sonoma Blvd, Vallejo (707) 557-4393.

You don't need to pay a membership fee to find bargains at Wal-Mart, the original super-department store. Overall, you'll find Wal-Mart's prices are significantly lower than those at smaller department stores and a few cents higher than at the shopping clubs. The store itself is truly colossal, incorporating a pharmacy, optical store, and photo department. You won't find the enormous bulk packaging that you do at shopping clubs, but if you don't enjoy lugging a two-hundred-ounce bottle of detergent to the laundry room, you'll appreciate Wal-Mart's prices on smaller containers. —*MS*

INSIDER TIP: SHOPPING THE SUPERSTORES

By Michael Sharon

Before leaving the house, read through the various consumer magazines to pinpoint two or three models in your price range that carry the features you want. Since you're likely to hang onto electronics purchases for several years, be sure the models you choose have reliable performance and repair histories.

COMPARE PRICES

Having narrowed the field a bit, it's time to start tracking advertisements and visiting stores. Electronics superstores, with their low-price guarantees, are sure to grab your attention. But be sure to check out specialty and independent stores as well. Smaller stores can often match or beat the biggest chains, and some provide better service. Specialty stores may also carry bargain product lines such as Quasar. Owned by the same parent company as Panasonic, Quasar models are made on the same assembly line with the same quality standards as Panasonic. However, comparably equipped Quasar models sell for between $50 and $150 less than Panasonic.

BARGAINING

Not everyone likes to bargain, but if you're serious about getting the best deal, a little haggling can go a long way. Once you've browsed in

INSIDER TIP

three or more stores, go back to the most convenient store and say that you are willing to buy today, provided the store can match the lowest price you've found. More than likely, the salesperson will agree to the deal. If not, ask for the manager or store owner. If for some reason the store is unable to match the price, a sales manager will likely offer compensation in the form of a free accessory such as an extra battery pack.

OPEN ITEMS

If you are shopping for a radio for the bathroom or a CD player for your teenager, you might want to consider open items. Because of their large inventories and liberal refund policies, electronics superstores carry a wide selection of floor models and returned goods. Although these items may not come in their original packaging, they carry the same warranty and can save you 20 percent or more. You can find a large selection of returned items year-round, the best time is just after the holidays. Deals on floor items are more common in October and November when product lines change. If there are no signs indicating a deal on floor models, ask anyway—and be sure to point out any scratches or nicks for additional savings.

DECLINE EXTENDED WARRANTIES

According to *Consumer Reports* and other watchdog publications, only stores are likely to benefit from extended warranties. No matter how convincing the salesperson is, *Consumer Reports* advises, "Don't believe it, and don't bite." ▥

INSIDER TIP

INSIDER TIP: EXTENDED WARRANTY WARNING

By Ginny Graves

It's the ultimate hard sell. And it doesn't begin until after you've chosen the brand new coffee-maker/tape player/radio/microwave/washing machine you've always wanted. Just as the salesperson is about to ring up your purchase, it happens. He or she looks very solemn and says something like this: "Of course this comes with a standard one-year warranty. But for real protection, we offer an extended warranty that provides you with much more security. It's a great deal because it covers all parts and labor for a full two-year period. Most of our customers agree it's the smart thing to do. It's only $39.95, and remember that if you need repairs without this protection, there's a minimum $50 service fee. Okay?"

It's cheap. It'll protect you and your purchase. Smart people do it. Right?

Wrong. Wrong, in fact, on all counts. Extended warranties, or service contracts, are not cheap. They offer, at best, only dubious protection. And, they are a risky investment—one in which millions of consumers have gotten burned.

"IT'S ONLY $39.95 . . ."

But what are they offering you for your money? In general, a service contract gives you coverage beyond the one- or two-year manufacturer's warranty. Most extended warranties are offered on a one- or three-year basis and can be renewed, at a higher rate. A typical contract covers the cost of most repairs, including parts and labor, and probably will provide for a replacement in the case of a chronically troubled product. But you might be required to maintain a certain servicing schedule to keep the contract in force.

The pitch makes service contracts sound cheap. In reality, the coverage is relatively expensive, when weighed against the cost of repairs. At Sears Roebuck and Co., a three-year service contract on a refrigerator costs $89 to $119; at home servicing without the contract costs $40 for the call plus $55 to $60 for parts and labor. At Radio Shack three-year contracts run as follows: $33 for a portable cassette deck; $139 for a twenty-inch stereo color TV; and $139 for a VCR.

Unless the parts were extremely expensive, you could take your VCR in for servicing three times in three years and come out almost even with the service contract price.

"BUT FOR REAL PROTECTION . . ."

When a salesperson begins the service contract spiel, his or her zeal may overwhelm you. "I should protect myself," you reason. "Better safe than sorry." Stop right there, and consider this: A retailer generally can make a 50 percent profit on service contracts, and the salesperson stands to score a healthy commission—sometimes 20 percent—as well. Don't mistake slick salesmanship for sincerity. The first thing to keep in mind is that extended warranties protect the pocketbooks of retailers, especially in the capital-starved audio-video industry.

"There are no restrictions on how much they sell these contracts for," says Herschel Elkins, senior assistant attorney general in California. "In many cases, companies can do quite well selling a product at cost if they sell service contracts, too."

"It's a big source of profits for many retailers," says Bill McGuire, assistant editor of *Consumer Reports*. Although he hasn't seen any recent industry-wide figures, McGuire says it's one of the few remaining ways that a retailer can turn a big profit. "Most retail operations have been cut pretty close to the bone."

The retailer's enormous markups notwithstanding, service contracts could be a worthwhile investment if the product you were purchasing was so inherently unreliable that you might have to have it fixed as many as three times in three years. By buying an extended warranty, you are, in effect, betting the machinery will break down and that it will do so within a certain amount of time. But most appliances and electronic equipment are likely to outlast the service contracts that cover them.

"In '91, we knew with some certainty that about 10 percent of the people who bought the appliance actually made a claim," says McGuire. "But the statistic could have included people who didn't know how to use the appliance in the first place. So the actual number of service calls could have been much lower."

The upshot? If you buy a service contract, you're buying protection for a product that probably won't need it.

INSIDER TIP

"IT'S THE SMART THING TO DO..."

Many consumers have learned the hard way that buying an extended warranty is the retail-industry equivalent of investing in oceanfront property in Iowa. The problem is that the companies that sell the contracts are often unreliable.

Service contracts can be handled in two ways. Either the dealer sells its own contracts, as is the case with most big-name stores; or the dealer buys the contracts wholesale from a third party, called a service-contract company. The service-contract company is then responsible for providing repair service. Unfortunately, these companies aren't always around when you need them.

"A couple of years ago, there was a real clearing out of service-contract companies in the industry," says Curt Augustine, chief of the Bureau of Electronic and Appliance Repair. When a company goes under, another company may pick up the client list in the interest of seeing their business expand. But more often, "the contract becomes worthless and the consumer is stuck," says Augustine.

That was the case when Extended Service of America closed its doors in May of 1989. With only a small percentage of its contracts insured, the company reneged on hundreds of thousands of dollars in claims from consumers nationwide.

Many service-contract companies are located out of state, making suing them impractical. You might be able to hold the retailer responsible in a situation like this, but no legal precedent has been set for that practice. The reason is simple: Most people just accept the loss.

New service contract legislation that was passed by Congress in 1993 states that anyone who sells a service contract must demonstrate financial viability. According to Augustine, extensive consumer information is also required.

Recently, a group of service-contract companies formed the Service Contract Industry Council to develop a higher set of standards for the industry. One of the requirements for membership is that the company report its insurance status to the National Association of Retail Dealers, where the information is kept on file and made available to the public. But since the service-contract pitch begins at the cash register, the likelihood of a consumer ever checking the status of a company is almost nil. Besides, there is no way of knowing how many contracts the company is administering. If its insurance covers $10,000 and the company issued $20,000 worth of contracts, many consumers are still at risk.

The industry council is also drafting a dispute-resolution procedure for consumers, in which an arbitration panel will review complaints against members. Though a member is not bound by law to comply with the finding of the council's panel, a criteria for membership is to agree to follow the group's rulings.

Even if the dealer sells its own service contracts, you aren't assured of security. In 1990, three California operations—University Stereo, FedMart Stores, and Pacific Stereo—went out of business, and people who'd bought extended warranties at these stores were left with worthless contracts and no legal recourse. "There's no way of pulling teeth if you can't find a jaw," says Busman.

 INSIDER TIP

Your best bet when buying appliances and electronic equipment is to stick with trusted names. Shop at a store that has a good, solid reputation, and buy an established brand—you can even check *Consumer Reports'* annual survey to determine what companies have proven to be reliable. Then ignore the inevitable last-minute pitch—that $39.95 could be put to good use someday.

CREDIT CARD WARRANTIES

Need further proof that you probably are wasting your money on an extended warranty? Many credit card companies now offer them free with purchases made using their card. These warranties are available with all American Express cards, some standard Visas, and all MasterCard and Visa "gold" cards. It's worth checking out.

The deal generally works something like this: They double the product's original warranty if it is one year or less. If the manufacturer's warranty is longer than one year, you get an extra year for free. If a product is lost, stolen, or broken within ninety days of purchase, the credit card company will replace it or refund your money. Things such as furs, jewelry, and tickets, however, may be excluded from this part of the coverage.

Credit card companies are able to offer these generous warranties for the simple reason that they get very few claims.

To file a claim, you need the store receipt, the card receipt, and a copy of the original warranty.

TIP SHEET

A study conducted by *Appliance* magazine showed how long, on average, various appliances lasted.

- Color TVs: seven years.
- VCRs: six years
- Stereo receivers: eight years.
- Walkabout stereos: five years.
- Coffeemakers: six years.
- Dishwashers: twelve years.
- Air-conditioners: nine years.
- Microwaves: ten years.
- Washers (gas): fourteen years.
- Washers (electric): twelve years.
- Dryers: fourteen years.
- Freezers: fourteen years.
- Refrigerators: fourteen years.

Source: *Consumer Reports* ▪▪

INSIDER TIP

INSIDER TIP: CONSUMER RIGHTS

By Michael Sharon

Say you went overboard during the holiday shopping season. It happens. You overspent through mail-order catalogs, telephone solicitors, and even worse, signed up for ten weeks of dance lessons. Now you're wondering, is there any way out of these obligations?

The answer is yes. California has numerous laws designed to protect consumers from shoddy merchandise, unscrupulous merchants, and their own worst impulses. In the case of those dance lessons, California civil code 1812.54 allows you to cancel the contract within 180 days, although you must pay for any lessons you've already received.

Written contracts involving services such as weight-loss clinics, time-share agreements, job-listing services, telephone solicitations, and dating services, for example, can all be canceled within a specified "cooling-off" period, usually within three business days after the agreement is signed. If the seller fails to inform you of the cooling-off period in writing, you may request it at any time, after which you have three days to cancel the contract, even if several months have passed.

To cancel the contract, notify the seller by telephone, then write a letter stating your intentions. Cite the three-day cooling-off rule (specified by federal law 16CFR§429.1 and state civil codes 1694.1 through 1694.6). Be sure your letter is postmarked by midnight of the third business day after your purchase.

Other examples of consumer protections follow.

Warranties Many people believe that they cannot take advantage of a warranty because they failed to send in the owner registration card. Yet under California law, you are still entitled to the warranty, regardless of what the manufacturer's written policy might say.

If a product does not come with a written warranty, California's Song-Beverly Consumer Warranty Act provides for an "implied" warranty on almost every new product for one year. Items not covered by an implied warranty include food, personal-care products, clothing, and "as is" sales.

Mail-Order Merchandise If you order products by mail, the manufacturer must ship the product within the time promised or within thirty days. If the seller fails to do this, it must notify you of a new shipping date and offer you the option of canceling your order for a full refund. Products excluded by the law include COD orders, photo-finishing services, and plants or seeds.

Refunds and Exchanges Although many businesses offer refunds or store credit for returned merchandise, this is not required by California law. However, if a store does not give full cash refunds, store credit, or equal exchanges for products returned within seven days with a receipt, state law requires the store to post its policy. You should find clearly marked signs at either the cash register, on sale tags, or on the retailer's order forms. If the owner fails to do this, you are entitled to a full refund for up to thirty days following the purchase.

 INSIDER TIP

WHEN YOU REALLY NEED TO FIGHT

Go back to the store and ask to talk with the manager. Calmly describe the problem and what action you'd like taken. Keep a record of your efforts and note whom you speak with. If the store manager refuses to cooperate, your next course of action should be a complaint letter. If it is a relatively small store, the owner can be tracked down by writing to the Corporations Status Unit of the California Secretary of State, 1230J St, Sacramento, CA 95814.

If it is a large corporation, write to the president or top management. Your complaint will be forwarded to the appropriate department.

If a complaint letter fails to produce an adequate response, don't give up. There are a variety of federal, state, and local agencies to contact. The following organizations can help find solutions to a variety of consumer problems.

Better Business Bureau, 33 New Montgomery St, Suite 290, SF 94105 (415) 243-9999.

California Department of Consumer Affairs, (916) 445-0660.

Consumer and Environmental Protection Unit, SF County District Attorney's Office, 732 Brannan St, SF 94103 (415) 553 1814.

Office of the Attorney General, Public Inquiry Unit, PO Box 944255-2550, Sacramento 94244 (800) 952-5225; (916) 322-3360. ▪

INSIDER TIP

CHAPTER **6**

AUTOMOTIVE

AUTOMOTIVE

Buying a car doesn't have to be scary. Information is power and the more you have, the better you'll be able to negotiate a really good deal. Here you'll find a number of strategies for buying or leasing a new car, plus tips on where to find fair, low prices on car repairs throughout the Bay Area.

INSIDER TIP: HOW TO BUY A CAR

By Robert M. Krughoff

You've probably heard friends' accounts of their cunning and bravery on the car-buying battlefield. They tell about sitting eyeball to eyeball with an entire sales department, then finally emerging, victorious, with a $2000 or $3000 price reduction.

It's all nonsense.

The only leverage you have with a new-car dealer is the possibility that you will walk out and buy a car from another dealer or not buy one at all. All the back-and-forth posturing is either what the dealer thinks is necessary to keep you from walking away or simply a ritual dance that has been passed down through generations of car salespersons.

But there is a way to get the best price on a new car without all the hassles. The key is competition. You have to make car dealers bid for your business.

Bay Area Consumers' Checkbook has been using this strategy since February 1991 to help customers get good prices on automobiles. *Checkbook's* service, known as CarBargains, charges consumers $135, but you can use the same approach on your own. What follows are lessons that come out of the experience of the CarBargains service.

Make dealers bid for your business. To get a good price, set up a bidding process, as you might do if you were contracting for plumbing, roofing, or home-renovation work. Shop around to decide on the make, model, and style of car you want. Then get at least five dealers to bid.

Conduct the bidding by phone. If you try to do it in person, you'll waste hours of time, and you'll have a hard time persuading salespeople that you're serious about getting other dealers' prices.

Use the invoice price as the reference point. Get each dealer to bid an amount above or below the factory-invoice price, which is the same for all dealers. So if one dealer bids $500 above invoice and a second bids $500 below invoice, the second is $1000 lower than the first. You can get factory-invoice prices from books published by Pace Publications or Edmund's, available at most bookstores and libraries.

Talk only to a sales manager or a fleet manager. Here's the basic approach:

"I'm in the market for a (make/model/style) and I've made a list of dealers to call—including one that's out of the area. I've done some homework, and I know the approximate invoice cost of the car. What I'm doing now is calling each dealer on my list to find out what each wants as a markup or markdown from factory-invoice cost. I would expect to take my pick of any car on your lot of the make, model, and style I'm looking for at the markup or markdown you quote. I'm calling each dealer once, and I'm not saying what any other dealer is bidding.

"So that everyone is on a level playing field, I need to go over with you exactly what charges show up on your factory invoice. What is the destination charge? Is there a dealer advertising association fee? How much is that? Any other miscellaneous charges? I assume you will let me see a copy of the invoice for any car I pick out.

"Are there any charges you'll expect me to pay that are not listed on the invoice? Are there any dealer add-ons, like rustproofing, pinstripes, or wheel locks, that you put on all your cars and that I'll have to pay for whether I want them or not?

"Now, would you give me a commitment as to exactly how much markup or markdown you'll accept above or below all these costs we've just discussed?

"What if I don't see the car I want on your lot but I still want to buy my car from you? Will you honor the bid you just gave me if you have to get the car from another dealer? What if I want to factory-order a car? How will that affect your price commitment?"

Don't accept a runaround. Some dealers will give you responses such as:

"I'll beat any price you get. Call other dealers and then call me back."

"What do you think is a fair markup? You tell me."

"We don't quote prices over the phone. Just come in and I'll give you the best deal in town."

You have to make dealers understand that if they won't give you a bid, they have no chance at selling you a car. You will succeed if you're persistent. If a dealer won't give you a serious price, go on to the next dealer.

The factory-invoice price is theoretically what the dealer paid for the car. This is different from the window sticker, which lists the manufacturer's suggested retail price.

Almost all cars are sold below the sticker price, and some are sold below invoice as well, because manufacturers often give dealers allowances that reduce the cost below what the factory invoice shows.

Ford Motor Company, for example, gives back to its dealers a 3 percent holdback allowance several months after the dealer receives the car. Most automakers now have such holdbacks, although the amount varies. Ford also gives dealers an allowance equal to two months of financing costs and a modest payment for dealer preparation of each car—an amount that may or may not match the dealer's actual preparation cost. Ford also has been giving dealers a 5 percent end-of-year carryover allowance: As soon as the 1994 cars were introduced, dealers became eligible for a 5 percent payment—$1000 on a $20,000 car—for each 1993 car still in stock.

Most manufacturers also make factory-to-dealer incentive payments at certain times on certain models—$500, $1000, $2000, or more for every car the dealer sells.

Different automakers have different allowances for their dealers. The

INSIDER TIP

programs change constantly. Although the factory-invoice price is not the dealer's true cost, it is a useful figure because it is about the same for all dealers. That's why you can use it as a reference point for dealers' bids. The savings are large. How much you'll save depends on the car, and on supply and demand at the moment. But you are sure to save a lot of money.

Recently, for example, the CarBargains service used the bidding method to help a customer get a price for a '94 Mercedes Benz S320 sedan. The sticker price on the car was $71,105; the dealer paid only $55,351 to obtain the car from the factory. That was $4000 below the factory invoice price of $59,351. Through the bidding process, the dealer was forced to give the customer the benefit of a large factory-to-dealer incentive program.

Similarly, a '94 Nissan Maxima GXE four-door sedan with antilock brakes and automatic transmission had a sticker price of $23,724. The price the bidding process produced for the customer was $19,332, which was $1300 below the invoice price of $20,632.

And a '94 Ford Taurus GL sedan with a 204A package and antilock brakes was sticker-priced at $18,825, had a factory invoice price of $17,206, and sold for $16,606 (including a $500 factory rebate).

Keep the extras separate. Don't even discuss financing, trade-in, or extended service contract until you've settled the price of the car. If you do, the deal will get too confusing.

Check the competition for the extras. Before even going to the dealer where you'll buy your car, check available annual percentage rates (APR) at banks, S&Ls, and your credit union. Then ask your dealer what it will offer. If its offer is competitive, take it. Otherwise, go with an alternative source.

Do the same for an extended service contract. You can shop for this, too. For example, you can buy your new Ford at one dealer, buy a Ford extended service contract from a second Ford dealer, and get all your repairs at a third Ford dealer.

Check your trade-in's value. You can lose the benefit of a good price on a new car by settling for too low a trade-in allowance on your old car. But if you've gotten a rockbottom price for your new car, you can't expect to get more than the wholesale value for the old one.

You can check the approximate value of your used car in the *NADA Official Used Car Guide*, the *Black Book* guides, or similar publications available at libraries and banks. But these sources are only very rough guides. It's not unusual to find differences of $2000 or more from one source to the next for the exact same car.

The best way to find out the wholesale value of your old car is to visit several used-car dealers and used-car departments of new-car dealers. Ask each what it will pay for your car, explaining that you plan to visit a half-dozen used-car dealers.

You'll get more money by selling your car outright; you can check the prices in classified ads to determine whether the difference is worth the trouble of selling the car yourself.

Don't expect to guess the best timing. Guessing the car market is no easier than guessing the stock market. Prices respond to supply and

 INSIDER TIP

demand. Consider two examples. In April 1992, the best bids that *Checkbook*'s CarBargains service could get for a Nissan Pathfinder four-door automatic SE with four-wheel drive were at $300 above invoice; by September, bids for the same vehicle had dropped as low as $500 below invoice. In late July 1992, the CarBargains service's best bids for a Honda Accord two-door coupe LX automatic were at $1000 below invoice; by mid September, the best local bids for the same car were $200 above invoice—a $1200 increase.

But you generally are likely to get a better price if you can wait at least a month or two after a new model is introduced.

The Bay Area has bargains. For example, for most of the past year, CarBargains was getting Bay Area bids for the Chrysler Concorde at $200 below invoice—$500 better than the best prices in some other parts of the country.

You can get the information you need. Three good sources of comparative information on cars are *The Car Book* by Jack Gillis, *Consumer Reports'* April issue, and the December issue of *Kiplinger's Personal Finance Magazine*. For more information on *Checkbook*'s CarBargains service, call (415) 397-8305.

COMPARING REPAIR COSTS

When buying a car, many consumers take into account the cost of repairs. Here's a way to compare repair costs. Find out the price of an extended service contract for that car. The cost of the extended warranty will reflect the likelihood of that car's breaking down and, more importantly, the cost of parts and labor.

What follows are prices a dealer would pay for a six-year/100,000-mile extended service contract backed by Ryan Warranty Services, plus a $75 markup. Most dealers mark up these contracts $200 or more to calculate the price to the consumer, but a few dealers mark them up less than $100:

Mazda 929	$463	Pontiac Grand Prix	$811
Honda Accord	$517	Oldsmobile Cutlass Ciera	$811
Toyota Camry	$555	Oldsmobile Cutlass	
Acura Legend	$676	Supreme	$811
Lexus LS400	$676	Volvo 740	$812
Infiniti Q45	$676	Lincoln Continental	$815
Mitsubishi Diamante	$693	Lincoln Mark VII	$815
Hyundai Sonata	$706	Dodge Dynasty	$846
Nissan Maxima	$706	Dodge Monaco	$846
Chrysler New Yorker Salon	$741	Eagle Premier	$889
Ford Taurus	$802	Buick Riviera	$1022
Ford Thunderbird	$802	Oldsmobile Toronado	$1022
Mercury Cougar	$802	Audi 100	$1046
Mercury Sable	$802	Cadillac Seville	$1087
Buick Century	$811	Saab 9000	$1243
Buick Regal	$811	BMW 535i	$1718
Chevrolet Lumina	$811	Mercedes Benz 300	$1718

INSIDER TIP

INSIDER TIP: TOP-RATED REPAIR SHOPS

By Robert M. Krughoff

Once you buy a car, you can have warranty repairs done at any franchised dealership. The dealerships listed below are those that *Bay Area Consumers' Checkbook* has rated highest for car repair service. Their ratings are based on the following: A survey of more than ten thousand customers; a review of complaints on file with the Bureau of Automotive Repair; and other information. In a survey conducted from 1984 through 1990, some dealers were rated by fewer than ten customers and some by more than one hundred customers.

Audi
Anderson-Behel Imports, 3350 Stevens Creek Blvd, San Jose (408) 247-1655.

Buick
Don Collins Buick, 502 Francisco Blvd, San Rafael (415) 453-9180.
Herrera Buick, 3700 Geary Blvd, SF (415) 668-5656.

BMW
Weatherford BMW, 735 Ashby Ave, Berkeley (510) 654-8280.
Stanford BMW, 3045 Park Blvd, Palo Alto (415) 324-4488.

Cadillac
Marina Motor Company, 4100 Auto Plaza Dr, Capitola (408) 475-3500.

Chevrolet
Winter Chevrolet-Geo-Honda, 2101 Railroad Ave, Pittsburg (510) 439-8222.
Park Chevrolet-Geo, 1101 El Camino Real, Redwood City (415) 365-2200.
Redwood Chevrolet, 7123 Redwood Blvd, Novato (415) 897-2191.
Ellis Brooks Chevrolet-Nissan, 1395 Van Ness, SF (415) 776-2400.

Chrysler-Plymouth
San Leandro Chrysler, 232 E. Fourteenth St, San Leandro (510) 562-4871.
Cavanaugh Motors, 1700 Park St, Alameda (510) 523-5246.

Dodge
Butler-Conti Dodge, 3434 Mt. Diablo Blvd, Lafayette (510) 284-4491.
Valley Auto Center, 6015 Scarlett Ct, Dublin (510) 829-0800.

Ford
Bob Lynch Ford-Lincoln Mercury, 6290 Monterey Hwy, Gilroy (408) 847-1111.
San Bruno Ford, 601 El Camino Real, San Bruno (415) 952-0500.
Codiroli Motor Co, 3737 First St, Livermore (510) 443-1000.

 INSIDER TIP

Ed Chovanes Ford, 13889 E. Fourteenth St, San Leandro (510) 352-2000.

Geo
Park Chevrolet-Geo, 1101 El Camino Real, Redwood City (415) 365-2200.
Good Chevrolet-Geo, 1630 Park St, Alameda (510) 522-9221.

Honda
El Cerrito Honda, 11820 San Pablo Ave, El Cerrito (510) 529-1323.
Honda of Hayward, 24895 Mission Blvd, Hayward (510) 886 0777.

Hyundai
Boardwalk Auto Center, 1 Bair Island Rd, Redwood City (415) 364-0100.

Isuzu
Anderson Chevrolet, 300 El Camino Real, Menlo Park (415) 321-4280.

Jeep Eagle
Al Sanchez Volkswagen, 190 Welburn Ave, Gilroy (408) 842-9371.
Falore Sunnyvale Jeep Eagle, 776 E. El Camino Real, Sunnyvale (408) 732-7800.

Lincoln Mercury
Almaden Lincoln Mercury-Isuzu, 909 W. Capitol Expwy, San Jose (408) 267-8100.
Stanford Lincoln Mercury, 444 El Camino Real, Menlo Park (415) 321-8030.

Mazda
Richmond Mazda, 600 Twenty-third St, Richmond (510) 237-4700.
Al Sanchez Volkswagen, 190 Welburn Ave, Gilroy (408) 842-9371.

Mercedes Benz
Mercedes Centre, 2831 Soquel Ave, Santa Cruz (408) 462-4624.

Nissan
Forest Nissan Imports, 480 Veterans Blvd, Redwood City (415) 365-6390.
Valley Auto Center, 6015 Scarlett Ct, Dublin (510) 829-0800.

Oldsmobile
Groth Bros. Oldsmobile, 59 South L St, Livermore (510) 447-5161.
Kastner Pontiac-Oldsmobile-GMC-Honda, 282 Soscol Ave, Napa (707) 252-4011.

Pontiac
Marina Motor Company, 4100 Auto Plaza Drive, Capitola (408) 475-3500.
Kastner Pontiac Oldsmobile GMC Honda, 282 Soscol Ave, Napa (707) 252-4011.

Porsche
Claridge's Ltd, 44355 Auto Mall Circle, Fremont (510) 790-1111.

INSIDER TIP

Saab

B&B Saab, 2983 El Camino Real, Santa Clara (408) 246-6388.

Subaru

Carlsen Subaru-Volvo, 4190 El Camino Real, Palo Alto (415) 493-1515.

Suzuki

Bob Lewis Volkswagen, 911 W. Capitol Expwy, San Jose (408) 265-4400.

Toyota

Bob Reynolds Toyota, 3800 Geary Blvd, SF (415) 752-4111.
Fairfield Toyota, 1658 N. Texas St, Fairfield (707) 422-3060.
Novato Toyota, 7505 Redwood Blvd, Novato (415) 892-1501.

Volkswagen

Braner Sloane Motors, 1840 N. Main St, Walnut Creek (510) 934-8224.
Al Sanchez Volkswagen, 190 Welburn Ave, Gilroy (408) 842-9371.

Volvo

Continental Volvo, 4030 E. Fourteenth St, Oakland (510) 532-3778. ▪

INSIDER TIP: NEGOTIATING TACTICS

By Kevin Berger

Let's get right down to it: There is no reason not to pay the lowest possible price for a new car. Unlike, say, a new television, a new car does not have a set retail price. Three people could walk into a Toyota dealer and buy identically equipped Corollas, and one person could drive away with a month's worth of savings. Why shouldn't that person be you?

Of course, negotiating is never easy. It's a game that favors the experienced salesperson. Still, the Information Age is on your side. Based on the latest consumer research, the following questions and answers will help put you on a level playing field with the salesperson and boost your confidence in making the perfect deal.

What kind of car should I buy?

One you can afford. The average price of a new car is $16,000, so, like most people, you will probably finance it. But before you get anywhere near a car dealer, decide how much you can comfortably afford each month.

Should I finance my car through the dealer?

No. It's best to borrow the money in the low-stress environment of your own bank or credit union. Try to put at least 20 percent down and

INSIDER TIP

arrange to pay off a car within two or three years. If you stretch your monthly payments over four years, the substantial interest payment will negate any savings you negotiate. Having your own financing allows you to keep showroom negotiations focused strictly on the car's price, and keeps you from being confused by the dealer's complex loan plans.

Should I trade in my current car?

No. You'll get more money by selling it yourself. Determine a fair asking price by calling *Consumer Reports'* Used Car Price Service at (900) 446-0500 ($1.75 per minute). By selling your car yourself, you keep confusing "trade-in" schemes—designed to raise the dealer's profit—out of the negotiation process.

Where do I learn new car prices?

Newspaper ads, consumer publications, and auto-enthusiast magazines. However, regard these prices as ballpark figures only. Magazines such as *Consumer Reports* and *Motor Trend* also provide valuable information about safety, fuel economy, reliability, and driving comfort. They also point out a particular model's "trimlines"—its various body styles—and reveal other carmakers' sister models in a similar price range.

Does this information mean I don't have to take a test drive?

No. A car is not a toaster. You should feel comfortable, safe, and happy in your new car. Visit a dealer near your home or work. Plop yourself down in the car's front seat. When the salesperson approaches, tell him or her that you are interested in this car, but under no circumstances are you buying a car today.

Go for a drive. Tune out the salesperson and concentrate on how the car steers, brakes, and accelerates. Is your vision unobscured on all sides? Are the controls comfortably within reach? Will you feel at ease driving this car every day?

Upon returning to the dealer, thank the salesperson for his or her time and leave immediately. Test-drive the next car you are interested in. There is absolutely no need to feel guilty for taking up a salesperson's time. It is your $16,000 at stake.

Now that I've decided which car I want, where do I go?

To the telephone. Forget every price or clearance sale you've read about. What you need is the price that dealers themselves paid for the car. You can obtain this price by calling the Long Beach auto-consumer group, Fighting Chance, at (800) 288-1134.

For $19.95 you'll receive a detailed invoice that lists the dealer's cost and the manufacturer's suggested retail price (the "sticker price") for every trimline of the car you want, and each piece of optional equipment. Also included are tax and delivery fees, an analysis of the car's standing in the current market, and a list of price incentives that manufacturers offer dealers to sell certain models.

The Fighting Chance package allows you to see, as clear as day, how a dealer stands to make a profit off you.

INSIDER TIP

I realize the dealer has to make a profit to stay in business. So what is a fair price to pay over the dealer's cost?

First of all, you should realize that sales of new cars rank only third in the ideal dealer's annual profits, behind the sales of used cars and auto parts. The most profitable dealers plan to make more money on trade-ins and service bills than on sales of new cars. So don't feel even a moment's guilt for offering a low price.

For a domestic car, make your first offer $100 over dealer's cost. If you're buying a domestic car under $20,000, venture no higher than five percent over dealer's cost; set your maximum price at six percent over. For import cars under $20,000, begin slightly higher than $100 over dealer's cost. For a car over $20,000, set your maximum prices at six percent for a domestic car, and seven percent for an import.

What's the most important thing I can do during the negotiation process?

Act like Robocop. Salespersons will pull on your heartstrings without mercy. Expect to hear refrains like "You're taking food out of my family's mouth with that offer." Don't give in. The reason cars have negotiable prices is to keep competition healthy. And don't linger. If the salesperson rejects your offer, simply head for the showroom across town. Competition is positively seething in the Bay Area.

Is it a good idea to call a dealer first?

Only if you've studied your Fighting Chance material and are firmly set on the single price you want to pay. Then ask the sales manager if he or she will commit to your offer. Better yet, ask the dealer for his or her fax number. Then fax in your offer and ask the dealer to fax back a reply. This is a particularly good practice, because now you have a commitment on paper.

Are there certain cars I can't bargain for?

Afraid so. The law of supply and demand still holds. Certain trends make certain cars hot. For instance, you'll have a tough time getting a deal on a Chevy Suburban. When a salesperson knows a particular model is hot, he or she will tell you in no uncertain terms that the price is not going to budge. But don't take any one dealer's word on it. If you must have a Suburban, it still pays to shop around.

You also can't negotiate the price of a Saturn. In fact, Saturn's factory mandated "one-price" selling has been so succesful that various Bay Area dealers have adopted the strategy. Don't trust them. "No-dicker" prices favor the manufacturer or dealer over the consumer. If a non-Saturn dealer insists on the no-dicker price, quote that price to another dealer as a figure that is too high.

Negotiating is not for me. I'd rather spend an afternoon in a dentist chair than in a car dealership. What should I do?

You may want to look into Price Costco's auto-buying program. Price Costco has already negotiated with certain dealers to sell their cars for a pre-set amount—usually $300 to $400—above the factory invoice.

 INSIDER TIP

Dealers will not quote this price over the telephone. Members must set up an appointment, but no bargaining is necessary. A booklet with dealer listings is available at Price Costco outlets.

Another option for members of the California State Automobile Association (CSAA) is to use CSAA's Official Vehicle Purchasing Service (800/477-1222). This system is similar to Price Costco's, in which CSAA provides a list of dealers that have agreed to charge a specific percentage above the factory invoice. You must make an appointment; dealers will not quote prices over the telephone.

Also available is CSAA's Vehicle Pricing Service (800/272-2877) This service provides an information packet on the car of your choice that lists the dealer's invoice price, the manufacturer's suggested retail price, warranty, crash test results, estimated frequency of repair, and financing options.

What can I do if I don't belong to these organizations?

You can call the Consumer's Car Club at (800) 227-2582. Unlike private auto brokers who charge an upfront fee as high as $500, the Consumer's Car Club charges you $89 and insists it can get you the best current market price for any car. Located in San Francisco but national in scope, the Consumer's Car Club employs a staff of buyers who solicit bids from five or more dealers in your area. You are guaranteed to pay the best price. Also, because the Consumer's Car Club can sell numerous cars a week for a particular dealer, that dealer is anxious to keep the Consumer's Car Club's business by submitting a low price.

Can I beat the Consumer's Car Club's price on my own?

Yes, and you can have fun doing it. Treat the negotiation process like a game that only you can win. Get your loan. Sell your old car. Study your dealer's invoice. Stick to your low price in the showroom, and shop around.

As you drive away in your brand new car, you'll have only yourself to thank for making the perfect deal. ▪▪▪

INSIDER TIP: NEGOTIATING AUTO LEASES

By Michael Sharon
As the prices of new cars skyrocket, many consumers are looking into leasing as a worthwhile alternative.

But first, you must determine if leasing makes sense for your needs. Although personal finances and individual automotive needs can differ as much as fingerprints, leasing may be for you if:

— You tend to drive a car for a period of three years or less before trading it in.

— You can earn 15 percent or more on the capital you would use for a large down payment and higher monthly financing.

— You prefer to drive a status car, but want the lowest possible monthly payment.

— You want to know exactly what your car will be worth after a cer-

INSIDER TIP

tain number of years.

— You lack the immediate funds for a large down payment.

On the other hand, leasing is probably not for you if:

— You plan to keep a car for more than three years.

— You drive more than fifteen thousand miles per year.

— You have young children, pets, or a profession that causes excess wear and tear on a car.

— You like options, specific colors, or detailing.

If you have decided to lease, don't be tempted by the enticing advertisement that offers low monthly payments and no money down on a newly leased car. Get out your magnifying glass and examine the fine print. The key to negotiating a successful lease lies in understanding the lexicon of terms, conditions, and phrases used in the contract.

RESIDUAL VALUE

In leasing, knowing the car's residual value—the estimated worth of the car when the lease expires—is as important as knowing how much the dealer paid for the car. Your lease payments will primarily be determined by subtracting the residual value from the price you've negotiated for the car. A low negotiated price, combined with a high residual value, will give you a low monthly lease payment. "Typically," according to Bill McGuire of *Consumer Reports*, "the more expensive the car, the higher its residual value."

Because both price and residual values tend to fluctuate, it's useful to know the most up-to-date estimates. Santa Barbara–based *Auto-*

motive Lease Guide (which can be reached at 805/965-1403) puts out a bimonthly listing of factory-invoice and residual prices for new cars. The price for individual copies is $9, or $42 for a yearly subscription.

You should also negotiate the fair price of your car "as doggedly as if you were buying the car," says McGuire. One resource is the California State Automobile Association's Vehicle Pricing Service (see page 249). For $12.50, CSAA will send you a complete report on the car you're interested in; for $20, a report on two cars; for $25, a report on three.

OPEN- OR CLOSED-END LEASES

Open-end leases hold the consumer responsible if the car depreciates more than expected. In a closed-end lease, the residual value is determined beforehand. At the end of the lease, you can simply walk away or buy the car for the predetermined value.

RATE OR YIELD FACTOR

Besides the residual value, monthly payments are affected by what is known as the yield factor. This term refers to the interest rate charged by the leasing company, which is based on the money it paid up front to buy the car. The dealer is not required by law to reveal this interest rate, but if he or she refuses, you should take your business elsewhere.

CAPITALIZED COST REDUCTION

This is a fancy name for the initial payment, equivalent to a down payment on a new car. The average lease requires the first monthly pay-

INSIDER TIP

ment, including sales tax, in advance. It is possible, however, to negotiate paying off the sales tax over the life of the lease.

Although individual leases vary greatly, consider these added factors:

— Leases come with mileage restrictions, generally between twelve thousand and fifteen thousand per year. If you overshoot your allowance, penalties are charged, which usually range from eight to fourteen cents per mile. According to the Federal Trade Commission, if you purchase the car at the end of the lease, you probably won't be required to pay for excess mileage. As *Consumer Reports* points out, however, dealers have been known to use "end-of-lease" charges in order to pressure the lessee into buying the car.

— Many contracts also have travel restrictions. Some restrict the number of days a car can be out of state, and others prohibit travel outside of the United States, including Canada and Mexico.

— Last, beware of substantial penalties if you terminate the lease early. A 1989 survey by the New York Attorney General's Office found penalties ranging from $2000 to $11,000 on a forty-eight-month lease following twelve months of payments.

The best way to get the full value out of a car is to buy it outright and drive it for seven or eight years. "You'll have a much lower overall cost than you would with leasing," explains McGuire. But advocates of the practice say that financial concerns have led to leasing's increased popularity. According to Art Spinella, vice president and general manager of CNW Market Research, based in Oregon, "People have come to realize that putting $20,000 into a depreciating asset such as a car is crazy."

For a free booklet, *A Consumer Guide to Vehicle Leasing*, call the Federal Trade Commission's Informational Services at (202) 326-2222. ▪

INSIDER TIP: LOOKING UNDER THE HOOD

By Anita Amirrezvani

If you feel you've been ripped off by your auto mechanic, you're not alone. A recent survey by the National Association of Consumer Agency Administrators found that unnecessary, overpriced, and unauthorized car repairs top the list of consumer complaints.

The worst repair shops take advantage of consumer ignorance. Take Sears, Roebuck and Co, which runs seventy-two auto-repair shops in California. In June 1992, Sears was accused by the state's Department of Consumer Affairs of deliberately selling consumers unneeded auto parts and services. The agency's chief blamed Sears' policies, which included paying mechanics on a commission basis and pressuring them to meet high sales quotas.

To settle the lawsuit, Sears agreed to provide $50 rebate coupons to customers who were sold unnecessary parts and service and to finance auto-repair classes at California colleges to the tune of $8 million. Consumer advocates say the publicity surrounding the case has pressured other large auto shops to clean up their act.

INSIDER TIP

GET A SECOND OPINION

If you want hands-on diagnostic help for your car trouble, try one of the three fully equipped diagnostic clinics run by the California State Automobile Association (at 415/565-2012 in San Francisco, 408/ 247-5405 in San Jose, and 510/671-2708 in Concord). Clinics at AAA offices in San Francisco and San Jose will perform a hundred different tests on your car and eighty tests in Concord ($56 in San Jose and San Francisco, $46 in Concord). You get a written report, too, which you can take to your repair shop if a problem is diagnosed. Or try their Answer Van, a mobile unit that rotates among AAA offices and checks sixty separate mechanical and electrical systems in your car for $38.

FIGHT HIDDEN DEFECTS

If you have an ongoing or unexpected problem with your car, it may be suffering from a manufacturing defect. Groups like the Center for Auto Safety (at 202/328-7700) charge that the auto industry doesn't always admit to widespread problems after the original warranty has expired. Instead, manufacturers may only reimburse consumers who complain the loudest, says Debra Barclay, spokesperson for the Center for Auto Safety. Consumer groups call this the "secret warranty," because the warranties don't exist on paper.

To check the defect history of your automobile, write the Center for Auto Safety at 2001 S St NW, Ste 410, Washington, DC 20009. Enclose a SASE with two first-class stamps, and specify the make, model, and year of your car.

INSIDER TIP

FIND A GOOD MECHANIC

Another stumbling block for auto owners is finding a trustworthy mechanic. AAA helps by referring members to one of the 750 local auto-repair shops on its approved list (800/645-4288). To win approval, a shop must employ at least one mechanic certified by the National Institute of Automotive Excellence for expertise in one of eight service areas. AAA also surveys one hundred past customers and requires that shops have at least an 80 percent satisfaction rating. Shops agree to participate in an arbitration program if a AAA member has complaints.

Another source for auto-repair referrals is the *Bay Area Consumers' Checkbook* (at 415/397-8305), a magazine that publishes a report on auto repair every few years. The latest issue rated five hundred local repair shops based on extensive customer surveys conducted over a period of years. The magazine also contains thorough articles that help you understand how the repair industry works and how to get the most for your money. The 1991 issue on auto repair (Vol. 5, No. 3) is available for $6.95 plus $1.50 for postage from the Center for the Study of Services, 733 Fifteenth St NW, Ste 820, Washington, DC 20005.

If you can't resolve a complaint with your mechanic, you can always ask the Bureau of Auto Repair for help. Call (800) 952-5210 to get a complaint form, and the bureau will attempt to mediate the dispute on your behalf. You can also order a free copy of *A Consumer's Guide to Automotive Repair in California*, a booklet that informs you of your rights and provides tips for dealing with mechanics. ▪

CHAPTER 7

SPORTS & ENTERTAINMENT

SPORTS AND ENTERTAINMENT

Don't call it "leisure time." Today, many of us put as much energy into playtime as worktime. Our free time is spent jogging and aerobicizing, kayaking and camping, and planning weekend activities with the kids or an evening at the theater. What follows is a special section that takes a wide view of entertainment. We'll let you know where to find bargains on sports gear and we'll give you insider tips on discount entertainment prices for the whole family.

ENTERTAINMENT

AMERICAN CONSERVATORY THEATER

San Francisco: 420 Mason and 609 Sutter, SF. For information on special programs call (415) 749-2ACT; to usher, call (415) 749-2274.

Parking: Street and downtown garages

The Bay Area is blessed with some of the most respected regional theaters in the country, and thankfully they offer economical ways to appreciate their work. American Conservatory Theater (ACT) offers a 20 percent discount plus one free ticket for groups of fifteen or more. Students and seniors can also take advantage of rush tickets, which go on sale ninety minutes before each performance. Rush tickets for students are half-price and $5 for seniors.

TIX Bay Area, located at Union Square, sells half-price tickets for shows on the same day. If you're willing to work a little, you can see a show for free through ACT's ushering program. In addition, ACT offers several free programs that can enrich your theatrical knowledge. ACT Prologue, a discussion among designers, directors, and other theater workers involved in the production, takes place from 5:30 to 6:30 pm on the evening of each show's final preview. It's not necessary to buy a ticket to the preview to sit in on the Prologue, but previews, starting at $10, are a bargain.

Speaking Out is a similar program that takes place after a selected Sunday performance. It's free and open to the public, though discussions are specific to the show. The NEH Symposia Series, two-hour discussions with scholars, writers, and dramaturges from all over the world, is often, but not always, show-specific and takes place on selected Monday evenings. —*LJ*

BERKELEY REPERTORY THEATRE

East Bay: 2025 Addison, Berkeley. For information on group rates, call (510) 204-8901; to usher, call (510) 204-8910. Parking: Street

The East Bay's crowning theatrical force, the Berkeley Repertory Theatre, offers special rates to groups of fifteen or more, though the discount varies (usually 25 to 30 percent off)

ALPHABETICAL STORE LISTING

from show to show. Students and seniors over sixty-three can buy half-price rush tickets thirty minutes before the show. The Rep's Hot Tix program offers half-price tickets to the public on the day of the show, with a two-ticket limit per person. Those tickets go on sale at the theater box office at noon, Tuesday through Friday only (cash and checks only). —*LJ*

CALIFORNIA ACADEMY OF SCIENCES

San Francisco: California Academy of Sciences, Golden Gate Park, SF
(415) 750-7000.
10 am–5 pm, every day of the year, including holidays; open until 8:45 pm the first Wed of every month.
Parking: Lot on premises

Home to the Steinhart Aquarium, Natural History Museum, and the Morrison Planetarium, the Academy of Sciences boasts everything from black-footed penguins to a simulated earthquake. Admission on the first Wednesday of every month is free, and hours are extended from 10 am to 8:45 pm.

If you can't make it on the first Wednesday, keep in mind that the Academy offers a $2 discount on adult admissions to people who ride public transportation to the Academy (don't forget your Muni pass, bus transfer, or BART card).

The Academy's family membership has been rated among one of the best bargains around. For a family of four, $50 includes unlimited admission to the Museum of Natural History and the Steinhart Aquarium, eight passes to the Planetarium (admission to the Planetarium is not part of the Academy's general admission fee), a monthly newsletter, a quarterly magazine, a 10 percent discount at the Museum store, and reciprocal or discount admission to 140 museums and science centers throughout the country. —*LJ*

EXPLORATORIUM

San Francisco: 3601 Lyon St, SF
(415) 563-7337.
Tue–Sun 10 am–5 pm, Wed open till 9:30 pm; first Wed of every month free; unaccompanied youth up to age seventeen enter free; children under six always free.
Parking: Lot on premises

Newsweek once wrote, "There are two models for great American amusement centers: Disneyland and the Exploratorium." On the first Wednesday of every month, from 10 am to 9:30 pm, admission to San Francisco's famed hands-on science museum is free. In addition to its 650 interactive exhibits, the Exploratorium offers changing temporary exhibitions, craft demonstrations, and a sophisticated film program on the weekends—all for free with price of admission. So round up the neighborhood kids and set them loose on the museum that has been likened to a mad scientist's penny arcade. —*LJ*

ALPHABETICAL STORE LISTING

FORT MASON CENTER

San Francisco: at the intersection of Marina Blvd and Buchanan St near Marina Green, SF (415) 979-3010.
First Wednesday of every month.
Parking: Lot on premises

The historic Fort Mason Center, home to countless nonprofits, theaters, and cultural organizations, holds a free museum day on the first Wednesday of every month, from noon to 8 pm—quite a deal for five museums and two galleries. Museums include Mexican Museum, Museo Italo-Americano, San Francisco African American Historical and Cultural Society, San Francisco Craft and Folk Art Museum, San Francisco Museum of Modern Art Rental Gallery, Bayfront Gallery, and CCSF Art Campus. Book Bay Bookstore, which sells bargain books to help support programs of Friends of the SF Public Library, stays open until 8 pm on that Wednesday, too. —*LJ*

GOLDEN GATE PARK CULTURE PASS

San Francisco: The Culture Pass is available at the Asian Art Museum, the M.H. de Young Memorial Museum, the Conservatory of Flowers, the Japanese Tea Garden, the California Academy of Sciences, the Visitor Information Center at Hallidie Plaza and at TIX Bay Area. Call (415) 391-2000.

There's lots to see in Golden Gate Park. A $10 pass will get you into the Asian Art Museum, the M.H. de Young Memorial Museum, the Conservatory of Flowers, the California Academy of Sciences, and the Japanese Tea Garden. Though the pass offers admission to each location only once, you don't have to go to all of them on the same day. —*LJ*

KQED MEMBERSHIP, CHANNEL 9 AND 88.5 FM

San Francisco: 2601 Mariposa St, SF
(415) 553 2150.
Basic membership $40 contribution; Family membership $65 contribution.

Joining KQED not only allows you to support the kind of programming you see only on public television (documentaries, music, drama, current affairs) and to support the in-depth news coverage that KQED-FM provides, it also gives you easy access to the culture and community of the Bay Area.

BASIC MEMBERSHIP

This includes a subscription to the award-winning regional magazine *San Francisco Focus* (which provides the *Member Guide*—a directory of what's on KQED Radio and TV), or you can choose to simply receive *Fine Tuning*, the monthly radio and television program guide. In addition, membership offers discounts to over seventy Bay Area attractions, such as museums, music and dance performances, science and nature events, theater, and tours. KQED Special Events, such as the Annual Wine and Food Festival, Ice Cream Social and Dessert Tasting, Beer

Festival, and Cooking at the Academy Dinner, are also discounted for members.

The Annual Membership Appreciation Weekend offers cooking demonstrations by great chefs, *Sesame Street* Sing-Along for the young ones, and discussion panels. With a KQED membership, you also gain eligibility for a KQED Visa card, with its competitive interest rates and no yearly fee.

Other services include VideoFinders, a way for members to conveniently purchase their favorite PBS television programs at a 10 percent discount; tours of the KQED studios; VCR Member Request, the opportunity to vote for programs you wish to see repeated on Saturdays; and KQED Response Line, where you can offer your ideas about programming.

Fax on Demand gives members an easy way to get a variety of KQED information. Also available is the *Instructional TV Guide,* a comprehensive schedule used by over sixty-thousand Northern California teachers to record KQED educational programs. You also have the right to vote in the Board of Directors elections.

FAMILY MEMBERSHIP

A family membership offers all the same benefits as the basic membership, with added materials and activities aimed at family and children. A "Welcome Pack" provides materials about parenting as well as educational activities for families and children.

One of the family membership's most interesting benefits is the *Family Learning Guide*, a quarterly publication that covers topics like how to talk to your kids about making new friends at school, or about such difficult issues as homelessness and AIDS.

Book and video recommendations, and resource listings also appear regularly. The *ITV* schedule highlights KQED programming for kids. You'll be invited to a parents' workshop at KQED studios where experts will show you how you can use *Sesame Street* and other children's programs to help your child find excitement in learning.

Other workshops and field trips are available to members. The KQED Membership Discount Card entitles members to savings and special opportunities at participating Bay Area book, toy, and children's stores. —*LJ*

MIME TROUPE

San Francisco: Mission Dolores Park at Church and Eighteenth St and other parks throughout the Bay Area, SF.
July through Sept; for schedules and locations call (415) 285-1717.
Parking: Street

How often can you see a Tony award–winning theater company for free? Pretty often, thanks to the San Francisco Mime Troupe's long tradition of free performances in Bay Area parks. They perform their unique brand of political satire every summer in parks in San Francisco, Berkeley, and Oakland, kicking off the season July 4 in Mission Dolores Park, at Church and Eighteenth streets. Their season runs through Labor Day. —*LJ*

NOON TIME CONCERTS

San Francisco: 660 California St at Grant St, SF (415) 982–6666.
Tue 12:30.
Parking: Nearby garages

It's a heavenly reprieve from the hustle and bustle of the Financial District—free noon-time classical music at Old St. Mary's Church, one of San Francisco's historical landmarks. Weekly concerts feature local notables, and special annual events include a Fourth of July Pops concert, Bach's Birthday concert in March, and Dr. Martin Luther King Jr.'s Birthday concert in January. —LJ

OPERA IN THE PARK

San Francisco: Golden Gate Park, Sharon Meadow, SF (415) 861-4008.
Free
Parking: Street, in the park

San Francisco Opera kicks off its season each year with a free outdoor celebration in September at Sharon Meadow in Golden Gate Park. Past years have included the likes of Placido Domingo. Take a sweater—fog is a frequent guest. —LJ

SAN FRANCISCO SHAKESPEARE FESTIVAL

San Francisco: Golden Gate Park, SF
Call (415) 666-2222.
Sat and Sun 1:30 pm, Aug–Oct.
Free
Other Sites: St. James Park, downtown San Jose, First and St James Streets, San Jose; Lake Merritt, Oakland.
Parking: Street

Shakespeare in the Park is another long-standing San Francisco tradition. This inventive company utilizes its outdoor settings to the fullest, offering traditional and nontraditional interpretations of England's most famous bard. This is another popular event, so it's wise to get there early to claim a plot of grass and spread out your picnic. —LJ

SAN FRANCISCO SYMPHONY

San Francisco: Davies Symphony Hall, 201 Van Ness Ave, SF.
For information about center terrace seats or open rehearsals, call (415) 431-5400; to order student tickets, call the Howard Skinner Student Forum at (415) 864-6000; to usher, call (415) 552-8000, ext 325.
Parking: Nearby garages and lots

With a flexible schedule and a little spontaneity, you can see the prestigious San Francisco Symphony for a reasonable cost. Center terrace seats, located behind the stage, go on sale two hours prior to all performances for only $8 to $10 (except some that feature the SFS Chorus). There's a two-ticket limit per person, and there are only forty tickets available.

Open rehearsals, held on selected Wednesday mornings, offer an economical, behind-the-scenes glimpse at the Symphony.

Tickets for selected dress rehearsals cost $14 and include complimentary coffee and doughnuts in the Orchestra lobby at 8:30 am, a pre-rehearsal talk at 9:15 am, and the rehearsal at 10 am. Full- and part-time students can buy tickets at up to 50 percent off on selected Wednesdays, Thursdays, and Fridays of the subscription series. Like most major arts organizations, SFS uses volunteer ushers, which is one way to hear the Symphony for free. —*LJ*

SAN JOSE MUSEUM OF MODERN ART

South Bay: 110 South Market St, San Jose
(408) 294-2787.
Arts Alive! First Wed of every month, 5–8 pm. Family Sunday, the first Sun of every month, 11 am–3 pm.
Parking: Nearby garages

The excellent San Jose Museum of Modern Art boasts several innovative programs that make art accessible and fun. Family Sunday, an afternoon of free performances, storytelling, live music, and hands-on art projects for kids that coincide with the Museum's current exhibition, is held the first Sunday of every month. For adults, Arts Alive! is held on the first Wednesday of every month from 5 to 8 pm. For $5, it's a wonderful way to end one's work day, listening to local jazz combos and other music, free munchies, and docent-led tours of the exhibitions. —*LJ*

SFMOMA

San Francisco: 401 Van Ness Ave, SF
(415) 252-4000.
First Tue of every month is free; every Tue free for students and seniors; Thur evenings are half-price.
Parking: Nearby garages

One night a month, you can take in Frida Kahlo, David Park, and Jasper Johns for free at the San Francisco Museum of Modern Art. The first Tuesday of every month is free, and Thursday evenings from 5 to 9 pm are half-price ($2 for adults, $1 for students and seniors). It's $2 especially well-spent if you go on a third Thursday, when you can view the Museum's exhibitions, take a docent tour, and listen to jazz by local artists. —*LJ*

STERN GROVE MIDSUMMER MUSIC FESTIVAL

San Francisco: Sigmund Stern Grove at Sloat Blvd and Nineteenth Ave, SF
(415) 252-6252.
Sun 2 pm, mid-June–mid-Aug.
Free; some seating is available, and if you reserve a week in advance, picnic tables are available
Parking: Street and small lot on Vale St off Sloat Blvd

Idyllic Stern Grove serves as the setting for this free concert series, featuring some of the best music around—ranging from San Francisco Opera to Flamenco to jazz. Get there early, because these high-profile musicians pack the place regularly. —*LJ*

TIX BAY AREA

San Francisco: Union Square, on Stockton St between Post and Geary, SF
(415) 433-7827.
Tue–Thur 11 am–6 pm, Fri and Sat 11 am–7 pm; closed Sun and Mon (tickets for these performances can be purchased for half-price on Sat).
Cash only
Parking: Nearby garages

Here's where a little spontaneity really pays off—TIX Bay Area on Union Square sells half-price tickets on the day of any show—however, there is a four-ticket limit per person and they must be paid for in cash. TIX offers about twenty-five shows daily—so if you can't get half-price tickets to one, find another that suits your fancy. Shows range from touring Broadway musicals to shows at nonprofits, such as Magic Theatre, Cowell Theatre, and Climate Theatre. Occasionally,

tickets are available for the long-standing San Francisco favorite, Beach Blanket Babylon, as well as an odd opera or symphony. —*LJ*

KIDS' TOYS

Kids can't help it. They see the latest toy, and they want it. If you're a parent, a doting aunt, uncle, grandmother or grandfather, this section will help you save money on the latest in kids' toys.

BASIC BROWN BEAR FACTORY

San Francisco: 444 De Haro St, SF
(415) 626-0781.
Mon–Sat 10 am–5 pm, Sun 1 pm-5 pm.
Factory Tours: Mon–Fri 1 pm, Sat 11 am and 2 pm, Sun 3 pm.
American Express, MasterCard, Visa
Parking: Street

Basic Brown Bear patrons can buy ready-made bears at factory prices, or they can have the unique experience of making their own. The stuffing machine and the bear bath are a big hit with young children. Both educational and fun, the experience yields a bear at 50 percent below retail cost. The least-expensive stuffable bear is Baby Bear, which we saw priced at $8.50. Schools and large groups should book tours ahead; other shoppers can walk right in. Soft, cuddly Bernard, Charlotte, and five-foot, five-inch-high Grandma, and many other bear relatives are ready to go, right off the factory belt. —*JA*

FOLKMANIS, INC

East Bay: 1219 Park Ave, Emeryville
(510) 658-7678.
Mon–Fri 9 am–4:30 pm.
MasterCard, Visa, American Express
Parking: Lot on premises

The second floor of this factory features plush puppet representatives of the animal

ALPHABETICAL STORE LISTING

kingdom available at prices 50 percent below retail. The outlet carries factory seconds with minor flaws, as well as some prototypes and discontinued lines. Made from the same soft, synthetic materials used for stuffed animals, these lovable, lifelike creatures are easily manipulated by small hands. When we visited, outlet prices ranged from $5 for black velour spider gloves to $25 for a fierce lion with whiskers and a movable mouth. Especially popular are the slightly flawed, $7 ladybugs that specialty gift and nature stores carry at double the price. —*JA*

TOY EXCHANGE

East Bay: 1224 Solano Ave, Albany
(510) 527-3737.
Mon–Sat 11 am–6 pm.
Cash only
Parking: Street

Children learn all about recycling cans, bottles, and paper in school. In this small snazzy secondhand toy store they can learn about recycled fun. Toy Exchange buys or trades with kids (and adults) in a straightforward, friendly, common-sense manner. Pre-teens upgrading from Nintendo to Sega Genesis can sell their old system and find secondhand games for half the price of new. Although merchandise is geared toward older children (comic books, sports equipment, video games, and GI Joe) they do have a nice selection of name-brand toddler toys like Brio, Fisher-Price, and stuffed animals. —*CA*

TOY SAFARI

East Bay: 1330 Park St, Alameda
(510) 522-0825.
Mon–Sat 10 am–6 pm, Sun 11 am–4 pm.
Checks accepted
Parking: Street

FAO Schwarz watch out! When a used toy store is as beautiful as this one with prices less than half of what you'd pay retail, there's no reason to shop at high-priced toy stores or even Toys 'R Us. In this delightful, well-organized store it's easy to find the perfect toy for every kid you know from toddlers to teens. Wooden puzzles that can run up to $12 are all 99 cents, My Little Pony costs 99 cents to $2.49, and books are half the cover price. Collectors love this place because all Hot Wheels are 50 cents, Happy Meal Toys 85 cents, and Barbies $3.95 to $6.95, regardless of collectibility. —*CA*

TOYS UNLIMITED

South Bay: Pacific West Outlet Center,
8155 Arroyo Circle, Gilroy (408) 848–5423.
Mon–Fri 10 am–9 pm, Sat 9 am–9 pm, Sun
10 am–6 pm.
Discover, MasterCard, Visa
Other Stores: (Toy Liquidators) Natoma
Station, 13000 Folsom Blvd, Folsom (916)
985-7127; Factory Stores at Nut Tree, 284
Nut Tree Rd, Vacaville, (707) 448-7314.
Parking: Lot on premises

Set alongside several other outlet stores, this

toy emporium carries discontinued items and over-runs from Wisconsin Toys, a major supplier for Toys 'R Us and other toy store chains. All the top name brands are represented, including Mattel, Sesame Street, and PlaySkool, with prices discounted 25 percent below retail. The selection changes frequently and slow movers get aggressive discounts of an additional 30 percent. Check preschool toys and children's board games for the best selection. If you just have to find an item no longer in stock anywhere else, or are a serious toy collector, this is the place to visit first. —*JA*

SPORTS GEAR

This is what we like to hear when we're shopping for sports equipment: that the store buys in bulk, offers at least a 20 percent discount over retail prices, and gives a low-price guarantee.

If you're a real sports nut or a true athlete, *you'll want to find bargains on sports gear that's constantly being improved and updated. We've searched for stores where we found low prices on high-quality, up-to-the-minute products and good customer service.*

ANY MOUNTAIN

North Bay: 71 Tamal Vista, Corte Madera (415) 927-0170.
Mon–Fri 10 am–9 pm, Sat–Sun 10 am–6 pm.
American Express, MasterCard, Visa
Parking: Lot on premises

Any Mountain is a full-service outdoor store with an extensive selection of new skis. Skis for all levels are proffered here, from a Rossignol 3ATL package, including mounting and tune up, for $269.99 on our last visit, to a high-end pair of Volkl VP 19 Varios, priced at $739. Other brands include Fischer, Kastle, K2, Atomic, Salomon, and Volant. —*PC*

BERKELEY WINDSURFING

East Bay: 1411 San Pablo Ave, Berkeley (510) 527-WAVE.
Mon–Sat 10 am–6 pm, Sun 10 am–4 pm.
Discover, MasterCard, Visa
Parking: Nearby lot and street

According to owner Pat Danly, this retail store discounts its seasonal windsurfing merchandise beginning July 1. Closeout sales offer 20 to 40 percent off regular prices—a significant amount, considering the pricey nature of the equipment.

For example, on a recent visit, Body Glove wetsuits cost $99.99, down from $149.99; a Bic Sport board cost $695, down from $995; and a Bic board and rig cost $999, down from $1399. Hint: The deals get better toward the end of the season, when manufacturers start discounting their wares as well. —*GG*

ALPHABETICAL STORE LISTING

DEMO-SKI

North Bay: 509-B Francisco Blvd, San Rafael (415) 454-3500.
Mon–Fri 10 am–8 pm, Sat 10 am–6 pm, Sun 10 am–5 pm.
American Express, MasterCard, Visa
Parking: Nearby lot and street

This tiny, hole-in-the-wall store has some surprising bargains for skiers. First of all, the store "sets the lowest price it is allowed to by the manufacturers," says Steve Merrifield, owner. Shoppers can expect to find prices here about 10 to 20 percent lower than many retail stores. In addition, the store has an annual demo ski sale on April 1. It starts compiling a purchase priority list on February 1, so consumers can sign up to buy the skis they want at prices that are below wholesale.

For example, Salomon 9000 Equipe skis with Salomon 997 Driver bindings sold for $395 at last year's sale—a savings of about $325; and the Burton Craig Kelly snowboard with bindings, which normally retails for about $580, sold for $325. "Most demo packages are between $295 and $395," says Merrifield. The equipment at the demo sale has likely been used a few times, but the store reconditions everything with its stone grinder and edge filer before the sale. Demo Ski carries Atomic, Dynastar, K2, Rossignol, Salomon, Volkl, and Olin. —*GG*

DOHERTY & DUNNE

East Bay: 1511 Park St, Alameda (510) 522-2345.
Open Mon–Fri 9 am–6 pm, Thur till 8 pm, Sat 9 am–5 pm, closed Sun.
American Express, MasterCard, Visa
Other Stores: 5100 Clayton Rd, Concord (510) 687-6800; 696 Rancho Shopping Center, Los Altos (415) 949-2331; 3230 Auburn Blvd, Sacramento (916) 488-3373; and 76 Camaritas, South San Francisco (415) 952-6060.
Parking: Street

Known for its discounts to teams and schools, Doherty & Dunne's everyday prices to individuals are about 10 to 15 percent below full retail as well, according to Adolph Adragna, manager. The best buys are on items such as baseballs, footballs, and basketballs, which start at about $12 for a high-quality rubber ball. Brands include Spalding, Rawlings, and Wilson. The store also carries tennis rackets, golf clubs, fishing rods, skis, apparel, and shoes. —*GG*

FRY'S WAREHOUSE GOLF & TENNIS

San Francisco: 164 Marco Way, South San Francisco (415) 583-5034.
Mon–Fri 9:30 am–6 pm, Sat–Sun 10 am–5 pm.
MasterCard, Visa
Parking: Lot on premises and street

With 16,500 square-feet of space, this store has the space to buy in bulk—and, as a result, pass savings along to consumers. "If some manufacturer has a good deal, we have the square footage to buy a lot of it and store it," says Don Hahn, manager. "For example, if we buy eight hundred to a thousand pairs of shoes, we can pass along a 35 to 40 percent discount to consumers." The store also keeps its overhead low thanks to its location in an industrial area where rent is cheap. The atmosphere at Fry's is warehouse-like, with one big difference: There are plenty of sales people—usually about ten to twelve on the floor at a time—so shoppers aren't left wandering aimlessly. Golfers will find Ping, Titleist, Lynx, and Cleveland Classics. Tennis rackets, clothing, and ball sales are backed up with stringing services. Players will be particularly pleased with the prices on Wilsons, Princes, and Dunlops. For example, we recently found a Fry's Prince Graphite racket (normally about $160) for $129, and a Wilson Profile 3.0 (normally about $189) was on sale recently for $79. —*GG*

THE GOLF MART

Peninsula: 4937 Junipero Serra Blvd, Daly City (415) 994-4653.
Mon–Fri 9 am–8 pm, Sat 9 am–6 pm, Sun 10 am–5 pm.
Major credit cards
Parking: Lot on premises

The Golf Mart works on a small margin and belongs to a twenty-nine-store buying group, enabling it to offer discounts from 5 to 50 percent off its name-brand merchandise, which includes Callaway, Lynx, Ping, Powerbuilt, Spalding, Titleist, and Wilson. The seven-thousand-square-foot store looks like a typical retail store in the front, where merchandise such as clothing and shoes are displayed, but it opens up into a big warehouse in the rear. We recently found a set of eight Titleist DCI irons for $459.99 (the suggested retail price is $640). Hint: The store has a mailing list that can alert you to its six or so sales per year—the best times to buy. —*GG*

GRAND AVENUE HARDWARE

San Francisco: 306 Grand Ave, South San Francisco (415) 588-3367.
Mon–Fri 8 am–6 pm, Sat 8 am–5 pm, closed Sun.
MasterCard, Visa
Parking: Street

Here fisherman can find a decent selection of gear (including fishing poles) at below-retail prices. The front portion of Grand Avenue Hardware is devoted to hunting and fishing. It's there that you'll find items such as Federal's package of twenty-five steel shotgun shells, a gun-cleaning kit, and a Redfield scope. The store also has a wide variety of fishing lines at about 25 percent off suggested retail and fishing hooks for 25 cents per package. —*GG*

HIRSCH & PRICE

San Francisco: The Chancery Building, 564

ALPHABETICAL STORE LISTING

Market St, Ste 214, SF (415) 781-1790.
Mon–Thur 9:30 am–5 pm, Fri 10 am–2 pm,
closed Sat–Sun.
Checks accepted
Parking: Nearby lot

The oldest and smallest sporting goods store
in San Francisco, Hirsch & Price has always
prided itself on offering reasonably priced
merchandise. It specializes in softball and
baseball, but it also carries a smattering of
basketballs and footballs.

Be warned: The store is only three hundred square feet—not enough space to test-
swing a bat. But if you know what you want,
you can probably find it here at a good price.
Some of the best buys are on gloves—which
ranged in price from $30 to $250 when we
were last there.

For example, a Rawlings Fastback baseball glove, which lists at $78.50, was going
for $55. Likewise, the popular Wilson
A2000, listing at $160, was only $120 at
Hirsch & Price. —*GG*

INTERNATIONAL DISCOUNT GOLF

**East Bay: 2066 Salvio St, Concord
(510) 689-4653.**
**Mon–Fri 9 am–6 pm, Sat 9 am–5 pm, Sun
12 noon–5 pm.**
American Express, MasterCard, Visa
**Other Stores: 2225 Plaza Parkway, P-3,
Modesto (209) 523-7888.**
Parking: Nearby lot and street

This neat, well-configured store offers good
deals on golf clubs, bags, clothing, and accessories. Its discounts work two ways. First, the
store is part of a large buying group, which
gives it the clout to get good deals from manufacturers on name brands such as Ping,
Wilson, Titleist, Callaway, and Spalding.
Second, the store designs some of its own
products and asks manufacturers to make
them for a certain price. As a result, golfers
who can live without name brands will find
even better deals, saving on average about 20
percent.

Some of the best bargains are on the store's
Palm Springs line. In addition, the store runs
regular specials. For example, on a recent
visit, a golf package that lists at $783 was
priced at $399.99. It includes eight cavity
irons, three metal woods (1, 3, and 5), a golf
bag, fur head covers, a putter, and a pack of
tees. —*GG*

LAS VEGAS DISCOUNT GOLF & TENNIS

**Peninsula: 38 E Fourth St, San Mateo
(415) 347-6200.**
**Mon–Fri 9 am–7 pm, Sat 9 am–6 pm, Sun
10 am–5 pm.**
Major credit cards
Parking: Lot on premises

Las Vegas Discount Tennis & Golf gets
good deals on its merchandise thanks to the
power of bulk buying. With eighty or more
stores in its buying group, the store is able to
pass along an average discount of 20 percent
to consumers. The best buys are on clubs,

bags, and shoes, according to Hans Janzen, manager. For example, a beginner to intermediate package, including eight irons, three woods, a putter, a golf bag, and head covers was recently priced $279. The fourteen-thousand-square-foot store carries brands such as Callaway, Wilson, Spalding, Taylormade, Powerbuilt, Yonnex, Lynx, and Ping. —GG

LOMBARDI'S

**San Francisco: 1600 Jackson St, SF
(415) 771-0600.
Mon–Wed 10 am–7 pm, Thur–Fri 10 am–8 pm, Sat 10 am–6 pm, Sun 11 am–6 pm.
American Express, MasterCard, Visa
Parking: Lot on premises**

This popular retail store recently moved to a new 65,000-square-foot site—plenty of space for its wide array of sporting goods. The store is reasonably priced year-round, but skiers and cyclists get the benefit of annual sales. Lombardi's holds its ski sale the first weekend in November, and anyone in the market for skiing equipment would be wise to check it out.

The store typically marks current merchandise down about 20 percent, and older stock is available at 60 to 70 percent off. Look for skis from lines such as Salomon, Rossignol, Dynastar, Head, and Hart, and boots from Technica, Nordica, Salomon, Lange, Raichle, and Rossignol. The only downside of this ski sale is the crowds: Be prepared to wait to get help from the overwhelmed sales staff. Lombardi's also has an annual bike sale the last weekend in March. Shoppers will find savings of 20 to 40 percent on this year's and last year's models from Giant, DiamondBack, Gary Fisher, and Schwinn. —GG

MAINE-IAC

**San Francisco: 2325 Third St, #202, SF
(415) 553-4529.
Mon–Fri 9 am–5 pm, Sat 10 am–4 pm, closed Sun.**

**MasterCard, Visa
Parking: Street**

This funky line of cotton workout clothing is popular with the skateboard crowd as well as mountain bikers—and any other active person with a penchant for cool, comfortable activewear. Maine-iac is sold in Cool World Sports, Rolo, and Marmot Mountain Works, but an excursion to the source will reap rewards. Last season's merchandise and seconds are sold at wholesale out of the designer's garment shop.

This is not luxurious shopping. The cutting table is often strewn with bits of fabric, and jars of dye line the desks and tabletops. But for fans of this small local company, its well worth the slight inconvenience. Maine-iac's popular long-sleeve tops and sweats were $25 on our last visit, and its berets were an affordable $10. —GG

MARIN SURF SPORTS

North Bay: 254 Shoreline Hwy, Mill Valley

(415) 381-9283.
Daily 9 am–6 pm.
American Express, MasterCard, Visa
Parking: Street

Serious surfers head to Marin Surf Shop, where they can find Rusty surfboards from about $305 to $405. According to those who know their boards, there is not a lot of markup on merchandise and the personnel provide excellent technical service. "They're interested in getting you on the right surfboard," said one shop fan. In addition to equipment, Marin Surf Shop has a wide variety of surfwear available. —PC

MOUNTAIN BIKE FACTORY OUTLET

North Bay: 400 W Francisco Blvd, San Rafael (415) 457-1222.
Mon–Fri 10 am–7 pm, Sat 10 am–6 pm, Sun 12 noon–5 pm.
Discover, MasterCard, Visa
Parking: Lot on premises.

This slick-looking store has capitalized on a tried-and-true method of discounting: It has cut out the middle man. By going straight to the factories in Taiwan where most name-brand mountain bikes are made, the factory outlet can pass along a 15 to 20 percent savings to consumers without sacrificing quality. The store also keeps costs low by offering limited models—consumers have a choice of three—and limited colors. When we last visited, the outlet's City bike cost $239, the Trail cost $369, and the Comp cost $499; all have Shimano components, Cro-moly tubing, and Araya rims, and the store offers a lifetime warranty on frames and forks. Buyers also receive a free year of tune-up service. Hint: Comparison shoppers will love the store's "spec" sheets, which contrast the outlet's bikes with name-brand versions. —GG

NEVADA BOB'S DISCOUNT GOLF

East Bay: 1500 Monument Blvd, Concord

(510) 680-0111.
Mon–Fri 10 am–7 pm, Sat 9:30 am–6 pm, Sun 10 am–5 pm.
American Express, MasterCard, Visa
Other Stores: 574 El Camino Real, Belmont (415) 593-2177; 4095 Mowry Ave, Fremont (510) 713-2177; 5430 Commerical Blvd, Rohnert Park (707) 584-4466; 14390 Union Ave, San Jose (408) 371-8544; and 2952 Alvarado St, San Leandro (510) 352-4653.
Parking: Lot on premises.

Nevada Bob's is a franchise with about 350 stores—which gives the chain optimum purchasing power. The name of the game here is volume, which enables the stores to work on smaller margins than most other places. "We discount prices and try to sell more to make up for it," says Tim Farrell, director of operations for five of the locations.

Most items are discounted between 20 and 40 percent, and the discounts are supplemented with occasional coupon offers or sales. Because of the small margin, however, prices don't fluctuate very much. The stores also take advantage of pre-pay or pay-on-time discounts offered by manufacturers. Every six months or so, the store will have closeout golf shoes, but most of the items are current.

For example, a popular Taylormade mid-size metal wood normally retails for around $290; Nevada Bob's recently carried it for $219.99. Among the other brands the stores carry are Wilson, Spalding, Titleist, Dunlop, Ping, and Callaway. —*GG*

NORTH FACE FACTORY OUTLET

San Francisco: 1325 Howard St, SF (415) 626-6444.
Mon–Sat 10 am–6 pm, Thur till 7 pm, Sun 11 am–5 pm.
Major credit cards
Other Stores: 1238 Fifth St, Berkeley (510) 526-3530; and 217 Alma St, Palo Alto (415) 327-1563 (clothes only).
Parking: Street

Bargain hunters looking for deals on this popular brand of outdoor equipment will be disappointed to know that the store is no longer manufacturing its special line of low-price gear made for the discount outlets. "The focus has been shifted to retail," says Pete Sayour, assistant manager. As a result, the discount stores carry primarily last season's merchandise, overstocks, and seconds, and everything is at least 20 percent off retail.

In addition, a bargain section in the rear of the store offers discounts on top of the initial mark-down. Items range from 25 to 75 percent off the original discount price, so it's still a great place to buy all the things that North Face is known for—backpacks, tents, sleeping bags, and outerwear.

Some good deals found in the store recently: A Goretex mountain jacket, which retails for $399, was offered for $299; and a Blue Kazoo sleeping bag, one of the store's most popular, was selling for $169 ($46 off its regular retail price). —*GG*

REI

East Bay: 1338 San Pablo Ave, Berkeley (510) 527-4140.
Mon–Tue 10 am–6:30 pm, Wed–Fri 10 am–6 pm, Sat–Sun 12 pm–5 pm; hours change throughout the year, so call ahead.
Discover, MasterCard, Visa
Other Stores: 1975 Diamond Ave, Concord (510) 825-9400; 20640 Homestead Rd, Cupertino (408) 446-1991; 5961 Sunrise Blvd, Sacramento (916) 965-4343; and 1191 Industrial Rd, San Carlos (415) 508-2330.
Parking: Located in a strip mall with ample parking

REI is the largest retail cooperative in the country and offers members first crack at sales as well as rebates at the end of the year based on the store's profits. The lifetime membership fee was $15 (at press time); last year the store made a profit of 10.35 percent, so members received that percentage back on merchandise they had purchased at full price throughout the year. Members also receive 20 percent off labor, such as ski tuning.

While prices are very competitive at REI, nonmembers aren't likely to see any great differences between here and anywhere else. "We offer competitive prices, but we don't try to undercut the competition," explains Sally McMillian, assistant manager at the Berkeley store.

Still, shopping is a pleasure at this nicely merchandised store, which specializes in muscle-powered outdoor equipment, including gear for climbing, backpacking, camping, biking, and hiking. However, it helps to know what you're looking for at REI; the nearly 30,000 square feet of retail space can be a little daunting to browsers. —*GG*

ROYAL ROBBINS

East Bay: 841 A Gilman St, Berkeley
(510) 527-1961.
Mon–Sat 10 am–5 pm, Sun 11 am–5 pm.
American Express, MasterCard, Visa

Parking: Street

This line includes active sportswear items such as stonewashed twill jackets and men's and women's flannel shirts. Prices are usually 30 to 50 percent off, with bins of clothing full of the real deals, such as slightly sun-damaged shirts. —*GG*

SCUBA UNLIMITED

San Francisco: 651 Howard St, SF
(415) 777-3483.
Mon–Fri 11 am–7 pm, Sat 10 am–6 pm, Sun 12–6 pm.
American Express, MasterCard, Visa
Parking: Street

Many downtown divers searching for more air stop here on their way out of town. Options include classes for the noncertified and first-timers, equipment sales, and service. It's an expensive sport, but it's also not the kind to fool around with using shoddy equipment. —*PC*

SIERRA DESIGNS

East Bay: 2039 Fourth St, Berkeley
(510) 843-2010.
Mon–Sat 10 am–6 pm, Thur till 8 pm, Sun 12 pm–5 pm.
American Express, MasterCard, Visa
Parking: Street

This second-floor store carries about half factory-outlet merchandise and half full-retail items. The merchandise is tagged to indicate the discounts. Most of the low-price gear is seconds or items that have been discontinued, and it sells for about 20 to 40 percent less than retail, and even larger discounts during annual spring and fall sales. However, some older merchandise can go as low as 60 percent off retail, according to Fred Dieter, manager.

The store carries outerwear, backpacks, and sleeping bags, but tents are the biggest sellers, Dieter says. For example, the popular Half Moon tent—a two-person, three-season style that weighs four pounds, six ounces—

regularly retails for about $230. We found it here for $180 on our last visit. —*GG*

SKATE PRO

San Francisco: 2549 Irving St, SF
(415) 752-8776.
Mon–Fri 11 am–7 pm, Sat 10 am–5 pm, Sun
11 am–4 pm.
Major credit cards
Parking: Street

If you're one of those skilled in-line skaters seen sailing through traffic in the Marina, or a member of one of the packs that cruise Golden Gate Park, then you probably know all about what's developing under your feet. Weekend skaters, many of whom are still renters, should check out the pros for advice and training, however. At Skate Pro, state-of-the-art equipment is available, with top-notch service. In addition, and perhaps more importantly, they provide a free two-hour lesson with every skate purchase. Skate Pro sells what they believe are the sturdiest of in-lines—Rollerblades. Roller hockey, previously known as street hockey, is becoming a new urban rage, and today's players are outfitted with helmets, padding, and of course high speed in-line skates. Skate Pro can handle those demands as well. —*PC*

SKATES ON/OFF HAIGHT

San Francisco: 384 Oyster Point Blvd, Unit
5, South San Francisco (415) 244-9800.
Mon–Fri 10 am–6 pm, Sat 11 am–4 pm,
closed Sun.
Major credit cards
Other Stores: 1818 Haight St, SF (415)
752-8376.
Parking: Lot on premises

This warehouse is a find for anyone who likes skateboarding, snowboarding, or in-line skating. It offers prices at least 10 percent below its nearest competitor and 20 to 30 percent lower than many retail outlets. Skateboarders will find decks from names such as Girl, Think, Acme, and Blind. On our last visit, decks were $39.90 for wood and $43 for slick. Better yet, house-made blank decks of the same quality cost $19.90 for wood and $26.90 for slick. Wheels were priced at $15 and up for a set of four, as compared to $19 at most other places. Van Half Cab shoes were selling for $45.90, about $5 less than other stores.

In addition, the store carries snowboards from Santa Cruz and Avalanche, and in-lines from Roces and Bauer. Hint: Roces used to make Rollerblade, so they have nearly identical skates for much more reasonable prices. For example, the Roces Moscow, recently priced at $140, is basically the same as the Rollerblade TRS, which usually retails at $200. Even better news: The store carries good, solid skates for children for around $75. —*GG*

SOMA SKI & SPORTZ

San Francisco: 601 Brannan, SF
(415) 777-2165.

Mon–Wed 10 am–8 pm, Thur–Fri 10 am–9 pm, Sat–Sun 11 am–7 pm.
American Express, MasterCard, Visa
Parking: Nearby lot and street

Skiers and snowboarders will be thrilled with this new south-of-Market shop, which offers all the hot brand names at an average of 20 percent off retail. It's not technically a discount outlet, but sales director/owner Ernest Schlobohm has set very competitive everyday prices. "Many shops keep prices as high as possible and then have preseason sales to get rid of the old stuff," Schlobohm says. "I took an average of other stores' pre- and postseason prices and went with that."

As a result, shoppers will find Nordica and Dolomite ski boots for as much as $100 less than usual. We found ski boards with bindings in the $450-$500 range, White Fir ski suits at $100 off, and skis, like Atomic Synchros, at $199 (at least $50 less than other stores). The store carries other top brands, such as Hooger Booger, K2, and Avalanche snowboards, and Elan, Head, K2, Olin, and Pre skis. This second-floor shop is small, and could get extremely crowded once it is discovered; still, snowboarders will be happy about the separate room for their equipment, and a rental and tuning space downstairs will give skiers a good one-stop shopping outlet on the way to the Sierra. *—GG*

SPORT SHOE OUTLET

East Bay: 2433 Durant Ave, Berkeley (510) 843-8500.
Mon–Sat 10:30 am–6 pm, closed Sun.
American Express, MasterCard, Visa
Parking: Nearby lot

Last season's shoes and manufacturer's close-outs are sold in this small store near the UC campus for 20 to 30 percent off retail. The store specializes in running shoes, and carries a good selection of Saucony, Avia, Asics, Brooks, Etonic, and Converse; it also stocks a smattering of Nike and Reebok. For example, we found Saucony's Jazz for $45 here, and Brooks Gels were $40. In addition to good prices, the outlet offers great service. Owner Cliff Brown, a long-time runner, is extremely conscientious about fitting runners, and will give interested shoppers tips on injury prevention. A year-end clearance starts in mid-November, and Brown usually knocks an extra 10 to 20 percent off the already low prices. *—GG*

START TO FINISH

San Francisco: 599 Second St, SF (415) 243-8812.
Mon–Fri 10 am–7 pm, Sat 10 am–6 pm, Sun 11 am–5 pm.
Major credit cards
Other Stores: 2530 Lombard St, SF (415) 202-9830; 672 Stanyan St, SF (415) 221-7211; and 1619 Fourth St, San Rafael (415) 459- 3990.
Parking: Small lot on premises and street

At the end of every bicycle "model year," which can be anywhere from November through January, this great bike shop offers the current year's versions at a notch or two above wholesale. "We need to make room for the new bikes, so we cut the prices drastically," says Jan Bass, assistant manager. Since the delivery date fluctuates annually, there is no telling exactly when this blow-out will happen, but if you start checking in early November, you'll catch it.

Start to Finish also offers thirty-day price protection, so if you buy a full-price bike on October 15, say, and the sale starts November 1, the store will refund the difference. But the sale is worth waiting for. The 1993 sale featured bikes such as a Trek 7000, which normally retails for $729, for $490; and a Bridgestone MB5 with rapid-fire shifting, normally $600, for $420. The store also offers one year free maintenance and one major tune-up. —*GG*

TIGHT END

San Francisco: 434 Ninth St, SF
(415) 255-8881.

8 am–4 pm.
Checks accepted
Parking: Street

You might have seen this brand of exercise clothing in stores such as Nordstrom, Macy's, Ross, and Marshall's, but you've never seen it priced like this. We found this tiny wholesale factory outlet offering cotton/lycra T-shirts for $9, leotards for $12, tights for $12, shorts for $9, and unitards for $15. Its hottest seller, however, is its line of prewashed, preshrunk thermal active wear. These sweats, oversize tops, and shorts ranged from $10 to $25. —*GG*

T. L. BRODERICK

South Bay: 2605 Lafayette, Santa Clara
(408) 748-0880.
Mon–Fri 10 am–8 pm, Sat 10–6, Sun noon–5 pm.
MasterCard, Visa
Parking: Lot on premises

First-quality, in-season skiwear sells here

from September until the end of ski season with supplies dwindling until the new season begins. October and November are the best months to find the widest selection of Columbia, Medalist, and other nationally known brands at 40 to 60 percent off retail. This family-owned store has very low overhead, a no-frills operation, and a friendly approach. Along with ski clothing, this outlet sells gloves, mittens, goggles, sunglasses, scarves, socks, and more, but no skis. —*PL*

WALLIN DIVE CENTER

Peninsula: 517 E Bayshore Rd, Redwood City (415) 369-2131.
Mon–Fri 11 am–7 pm, Sat 10:30 am–6 pm, Sun 11 am–5 pm.
Major credit cards
Parking: Small lot on premises and street

If it's lessons, equipment, and exotic locales you need, look no further than Wallin Dive Center. Their enormous stock selection, various instruction options, rental equipment,

 ALPHABETICAL STORE LISTING

maintenance, and in-house travel agent provide a full spectrum of dive services. —*PC*

WILDERNESS EXCHANGE

**East Bay: 1407 San Pablo Ave and 1730
San Pablo Ave, Berkeley (510) 525-1255.
Sun–Wed 11 am–6 pm, Thurs–Fri 11 am–8
pm, Sat 10 am–6 pm.**
MasterCard, Visa
**Parking: Lot on premises (1407 San Pablo
Ave location)**

Used equipment that has been reconditioned accounts for about 20 percent of these stores' inventory, and the other 80 percent is irregular, overstocked, or closeout new merchandise from manufacturers. Used items are typically sold at about 50 percent of their original retail price, and new stock is discounted between 15 and 50 percent, according to Kelly Keith, manager.

The stores specialize in mountaineering, rock-climbing, cross-country skiing, backpacking, and camping. Some sample prices:

New Trak Nova cross-country skis with last year's graphics were going for $99.95, when the suggested retail price is $175; a new Goretex jacket from Moonstone sold for $207.95, when the suggested retail price is $259; and a new Kelty Tioga women's backpack sold for $109.95, when the suggested retail price is $135.

The 1407 location carries smaller merchandise, such as clothing and hiking boots, and the 1730 address stocks larger items, such as tents and sleeping bags. The inventory changes frequently, so it pays to check in regularly. —*GG*

WINDSURF BICYCLE WAREHOUSE

**San Francisco: 428 S Airport Blvd, South
San Francisco (415) 588-1714.
Mon–Sat 10 am–6 pm, Thur–Fri till 8 pm,
Sun 11 am–6 pm.**
Major credit cards
Parking: Lot on premises

Buying in bulk allows this 7200-square-foot store to offer good prices on retail products such as bicycles, windsurfing equipment, snowboards, and in-line skates. The tactic is given added muscle with a low-price guarantee, which says that if you buy something at the warehouse and then find it cheaper at another store, the warehouse will refund the difference between the two prices, plus 10 percent.

The savings here aren't huge—you can expect to see prices about 10 percent lower than many places—but the excellent service offered by the knowledgeable staff makes it a good value. "Our philosophy is that we don't sell something because it's in the store; we sell it because it's what the customer really needs," says Alan Schacter, marketing manager.

We found complete snowboard packages, from names like Burton, Sims, Morro, and Nitro, ranging from $380 to $650; bikes, including Trek, GT, Diamond Back, and Bianchi, started at $259; a complete beginner's windsurfing package cost $599; and in-line skates from manufacturers such as Bauer and Rollerblade started at $109. —*GG*

WISE SURFBOARDS

San Francisco: 3149 Vicente, SF
(415) 665-7745.
Daily 10 am–5 pm.
American Express, MasterCard, Visa

In the city, downtown surfers find most of their gear at Wise Surfboards, where a vast inventory provides surfers with not only a complete selection of the tried-and-true equipment, but with what's hot as well.

Prices here are pretty standard most of the year (boards usually start around the mid-$300s); however during the annual "weekend of the equinox" summer sale you'll find some of the best bargains in the area. —*PC*

YOUNG'S BACKPACKS

East Bay: 2508 Telegraph Ave, Berkeley,
(510) 548-7463.
Mon–Sat 10:30 am–6:30 pm, Sun noon–5 pm.
American Express, MasterCard, Visa
Parking: Street

Young's Backpacks has one of California's largest selection of travel bags, backpacks, and day packs—all at 5 to 8 percent below retail—including Lowe, MEI, and Jansport. Young's own Cordura shoulder bags, travel bags, and day packs (some of which are manufactured in Korea by the company that makes similar goods for L.L. Bean) cost 25 to 30 percent less than comparable merchandise. Outdoor wear and camping gear (Eureka tents, Kelty sleeping bags) and a large selection of hiking boots (Hi-Tec, Timberline, Nike) are also 10 percent off. —*GG*

ALPHABETICAL STORE LISTING

INSIDER TIP: BAY AREA HIKES

By Barbara Tannenbaum

Many Bay Area walkers were disappointed when Margot Patterson Doss retired her *Chronicle* column. But Doss still has advice for the intrepid walking enthusiast. Taking into account the summer fog that envelops San Francisco and the North Bay and the scorching rays of the sun that heat up the Peninsula and the East Bay, here are some of Doss' favorite walks to take in June, July, and August.

BAY AREA RIDGE TRAIL

In 1987, the National Park Service, in association with Golden Gate National Recreation Area and the Greenbelt Alliance, mapped out an ambitious four-hundred-mile-long Ridge Trail along the mountains ringing the Bay. Today only 168 miles of this trail are under public ownership and open to walkers.

Doss recommends hiking the Peninsula section of the Bay Area Ridge Trail. "Head down to the open-space preserves that are strung like diamonds along Skyline Blvd," she says. "Once you make the ascent, it's mostly level with stunning views of both the bay and the ocean." Trails in the Monte Bello Preserve, Purisima Creek Redwoods Preserve, or Edgewood Park afford cool walks through fern-filled canyons, shady oaks and redwoods, and rolling grasslands.

"We call these preserves 'Stegner country,'" says Doss, "because Wallace Stegner was the first president of the Mid-Peninsula Open Space District. He pioneered the idea of setting aside these lands for the public's enjoyment."

BLACK DIAMOND MINES REGIONAL PRESERVE

While the west winds blow smog across some areas of the East Bay in the summer, Black Diamond, in Antioch, has a cool alternative. The four-thousand-acre park boasts a mile-long underground trail and museum (both currently closed) that runs through an old sand mine, and forty-four miles of trails. Formerly a coal mine from the 1860s to the turn of the century, Black Diamond turned to sand mining by the 1920s. The museum displays mining equipment and a naturalist displays the art of turning sand into glass. The underground trail and the museum are expected to reopen within six months to a year. Call (510) 757-2620 for complete details.

"There are forty-eight parks in the East Bay, plus more in their land banks that they haven't even opened to the public yet," says Doss. "That's more acres of preserved land in one park district than has been set aside in eight Eastern states."

STEEP RAVINE TRAIL

An easy, three-quarter-mile walk downhill from the ranger station, Steep Ravine is completely sheltered by Douglas firs, California laurels, and deep redwoods. It descends with Webb Creek along a series of well-made switchbacks to the seashore. With our late spring rains, the

INSIDER TIP

creek should still be flowing, says Doss, but the waterfalls won't return until next winter.

Since you don't want to make such a strenuous hike back that's uphill all the way, work out a shuttle arrangement with a friend: Drive together to your final destination, park one car, then drive back to the trail's origin and begin the hike. "Better yet," says Doss, "walk the length of the Steep Ravine trail, turn right onto the Dipsea trail, and head into Stinson Beach. There you stop in the bookstore, get a snack at the grill, then catch the Golden Gate Transit 63 bus back to the Pantoll Ranger Station." Call (415) 332-6600 for bus schedule information. For park information, call (415) 388-2070.

GOLDEN GATE PROMENADE

Popular with joggers, bicyclists, kite flyers, and strollers walking their dogs, this promenade runs from Fort Mason, along the Marina, through the Presidio, all the way to Fort Point. The summer fog burns off by 11 am and returns by 3 pm. The views—Marin and the Golden Gate Bridge on one side, and the city's northern skyline on the other—are spectacular. But Doss puts this walk on her summertime list because former Mayor Joe Alioto gave her this trail as a birthday present on August 22, 1971.

Before the GGNRA was passed into law in 1973, Fort Mason and surrounding areas were not under federal protection, and Doss awoke one morning to read in the *Chronicle* that developers, with Mayor Alioto's approval, planned to build luxury housing out on the Marina

Green. "I called Mel Wax, the head of KQED's old *Newsroom*," Doss remembers. "He sent me and a cameraman out to do a story extolling the virtues of Fort Mason. Then Wax aired it minutes before Alioto's live press conference on Channel 9. Well, the mayor blew his stack live on camera and challenged me to a debate about the appropriate use of this land. I accepted his challenge but I sent Willie Brown to debate the issue for me.

"Needless to say, the threat of development died down. Then a few months later, I got a call from the mayor asking me to accompany him on a chartered harbor tour. I tried to decline, explaining that it was my birthday. But he said, "Come along and I'll give you a birthday present you'll never forget." The boat was full of public dignitaries and we headed out to Fort Point. When we debarked, there was a podium, microphones, and the media laying in wait. Alioto stepped up to announce a new trail, the Golden Gate Promenade, in my honor. It was a wonderful way to make up with me." ▥

INSIDER TIP: SUMMER STREET FAIRS

By Leslie Plummer Clagett

UNION STREET SPRING FESTIVAL ARTS & CRAFTS FAIR
Weekend after Memorial Day. Union between Steiner and Gough.

 INSIDER TIP

All waiters should be as sprightly as the ones who race up the Laguna Street hill in the kick-off event at this festival, where—rest assured—there is an abundance of self-service food and drink available. Living up to its billing as San Francisco's most elegant street fair, neighborhood boutiques host a fashion show and tea dance. Show-offs can step out in the afternoon swing dance contest. For information, call (415) 346- 4561.

BLUES & ART ON POLK
Weekend in mid-July Polk between Bush and Pacific.
Blues fans will find plenty to feed the soul and the stomach at this venerable street fest. Two music venues facilitate a friendly battle of the bands, and a bounty of tasty food fuels the most enthusiastic dancers. Less active attendees can find fulfillment browsing through one of the city's oldest shopping districts. For information, call (415) 346-4561.

HAIGHT STREET
Weekend in mid-June. Haight between Masonic and Stanyan.
If you're in the market for a flashback, put some flowers in your hair and head for the annual Haight Street Fair. Its six blocks of funky crafts, ethnic foods, transcendental vibes, and the most colorful crowd in town makes Berkeley's Telegraph Avenue look like a musty counterculture diorama. Call (415) 661-8025 for more information.

NORTH BEACH FESTIVAL
Father's Day weekend. Grant between Columbus and Filbert, Green between Columbus and Grant, Washington Square.
There's more than palate-piquing food and drink here. Touches of authentic Italian culture—Venetian mask painting, commedia dell'arte performances, and bocce ball games—elevate this gathering above the typical fair. Plenty of kids' activities (including a petting zoo) make this festival an appropriate Father's Day outing. Call (415) 403-0666 for complete information.

SAN ANSELMO ART & WINE FESTIVAL
Mid-June weekend. San Anselmo Avenue between Tumulpuis und Mariposa.
The relaxed, rural feeling of small-town Marin is an ideal refuge for those seeking a respite from summer in the city. At San Anselmo's "Function in the Junction," cool jazz wafts through the tree-shaded streets, fine wines are poured, and gourmet tidbits are served in a truly sybaritic setting. Call (415) 346-4561 for more information.

NOVATO ART & MUSIC FESTIVAL
Last full weekend in June. Old Town Novato.
All the senses are satiated at this festival in the hills of Marin. Highlighting the gustatory pleasures: Over forty California wineries will be uncorking select vintages to sample. Crafts and classic cars delight the eye. And for music aficionados, a roster of noted artists will provide a diverse repertoire. For information, call (415) 897-1164.

INSIDER TIP

DANVILLE SUMMERFEST

Last weekend in June. Hartz between Diablo and School.

Visitors to this sunny enclave in the San Ramon Valley can wile away the afternoon in outdoor cafés, peruse the creative efforts of an array of artisans, and take in a variety of musical presentations. A stroll down historic Hartz Avenue will reveal many well-preserved turn-of-the-century buildings, certain to appeal to vernacular architecture buffs. For more information, call (415) 346-4561.

JAZZ & ALL THAT ART ON FILLMORE

First weekend in July (including Fri). Fillmore between Jackson and Post.

Three days of continuous jazz performances commemorates Fillmore Street's heritage as a musical hotspot in the forties, fifties, and sixties. In a visual counterpoint to the auditory entertainment, more than two hundred craftspeople display their wares, from fine art to functional pieces. Home cooking and hauté cuisine will satisfy all appetites. Call (415) 346-4561 for information.

NIHONMACHI

First weekend of August. Post between Laguna and Webster.

As much a community celebration as a cultural one, Nihonmachi focuses on the contributions of Asian Americans to San Francisco. At Children's World, youngsters can try their hand at origami and fish printing, as well as the Daruma ring toss. More mature fair-goers will enjoy the edibles from all around the Pacific Rim. There's also lots of music, featuring local Asian bands, as well as bands of other cultures. For information, call (415) 922-8700.

LOS GATOS FIESTA DE ARTES

Second to last weekend of August. Old Town Los Gatos.

For over twenty-five years, local chefs have served up a feast of secret recipes and house specialties at this festival, held in the downtown gardens of this quiet South Bay burg. Custom designed wine glasses are available to taste the fruits of the vine and toast the fair's talented performers and exhibitors. For more information, call (415) 346-4561.

OAKLAND CHINATOWN FAIR

Fourth weekend of August. Seventh to Eleventh streets between Webster and Broadway.

For a weekend in August, the Far East is as close as the East Bay. Two stages feature traditional Chinese, Japanese, Vietnamese, and Hawaiian theater and music, and contemporary music. Central to the fair is the Cultural Village, where demonstrations of many Asian arts can be observed close-up, among them Chinese calligraphy and brush painting, mask making and fortune telling. For information, call (510) 893-8979. ⅲ

 INSIDER TIP

CHAPTER 8

TRAVEL

TRAVEL

There are more ways to save money on travel than just accumulating frequent-flier miles. Our handy insider's travel guide will give you the latest strategies for saving big travel dollars on airline tickets, hotel rooms, rail passes, and more—so you can travel more often for less.

INSIDER TIP: THE SAVVY GLOBE-TROTTER'S GUIDE

By Judy Jacobs

AIR DISCOUNTS

Ten or fifteen years ago, charter flights were the cheap way to go. Now, travelers seeking the best bargains usually turn to consolidators. Don't overlook charter operators, however. Consolidators sell mainly big-city destinations. Charter operators specialize in resort areas, mainly Mexico and Hawaii. And their prices are usually about 10 to 20 percent less than flights booked directly through scheduled carriers, and sometimes the discounts are even better.

Suntrips of San Jose (408/432-1101), for example, charters Leisure Air, with daily flights from San Francisco to Hawaii during the summer and flights six days a week the rest of the year. Suntrips' weekly sched-

ule for Mexico is three times to Cabo San Lucas, once to Mexico City, and twice to Cancun, Puerto Vallarta, and Guadalajara. **Sky Tours** (415/777-3544) sells charter seats on American Transair to Hawaii and Condor to Germany, with varying schedules.

CHARGE CARD BONUS

Frequent-flier **credit cards** are about as close as you'll come to getting something for nothing. Charge daily purchases on one of these cards, and every dollar spent adds one mile to your frequent-flier mileage bank. It's amazing how quickly those miles accumulate, especially when some airlines give bonus miles just for signing up. The only hitch is that all cards have a yearly fee.

Here are the details:

Airline	Yearly Fee	Sign-up Bonus	Bank Contact
Alaska Airlines	$45	1000 bonus points	(800) 552-7302
America West	$35	2500 bonus points	(800) 242-5722
American	$50	None	(800) 359-4444
Northwest	$55	1500 bonus points	(800) 948-8300
TWA	$50	3000 bonus points	(800) 322-1418
United	$60	$25 discount plus 1 upgrade certificate	(800) 537-7783
USAir	$35	1500 bonus points	(800) 732-9194

 INSIDER TIP

TRANSPORT PASSES

Are you the "If it's Tuesday, this must be Belgium" type, someone who likes to cover a lot of territory? Do you want to see four South Pacific islands in four weeks, or travel from one end of a country to the other and hit everything in between? Then an air or rail pass might offer great savings.

Take **Air Pacific's** Air Pacific Pass, for example. It costs just $449 for thirty days of travel to Western Samoa, Tonga, and Vanuatu from Fiji. **Varig Brazilian Airlines** sells a twenty-one-day pass for $440 that covers five flights within Brazil.

If you prefer to see the countryside as it passes by, consider a **railway pass**. Twelve European countries have their own passes, several nations combine for regional passes, and there's the old standby Eurail Pass, which includes seventeen countries. If you aren't traveling far, however, it may be cheaper to buy individual tickets. **Rail Europe** (800/438-7245) can help you decide.

There is one place where a rail pass is always a bargain: Japan. The one-week **Japan Rail Pass**, priced at $268 when we called, is about the same price as a round-trip bullet train ride between Tokyo and Kyoto. You can spend a few days in Tokyo, travel around Japan (the two-week pass is $425), stay in Kyoto, and fly home from Osaka, where the new Kansai International Airport opens in fall 1994.

SAILING TRIPS

Gather a group of friends together and take off on a vacation you'll never forget. Slow down, kick off your shoes, and leave your worries behind while you explore the Caribbean, South Pacific, or Mediterranean beneath the sails of a **chartered yacht**.

What a way to travel—and it's not as expensive as you might think. The more people you take, in fact, the cheaper the charter becomes. If you know how to sail, you can charter bareboat (without crew). You can also charter a boat with just a skipper, or with a full crew, including chef. A week of sailing in the Caribbean will average $400 and up, per person, on bareboat, or from $1200 per person with all meals and drinks on a fully crewed boat.

One of the most popular places for boat chartering is the British Virgin Islands. The winds are steady, the seas protected, and the islands are within an hour or two sail of each other.

Ocean Voyages in Sausalito (415/332-4681) can help you make the arrangements. So can the **Moorings** (800/437-7800 for crewed yachts; 800/535-7289 for bareboat yachts).

HOTEL DISCOUNTS

Never again pay the "rack rate," or published price of a hotel room: Join a **hotel discount club** or make your reservations through a discount service. The clubs require a yearly membership fee, for which you get a directory of participating hotels. **Entertainment Publications** (415/873-1975) sells localized discount books that include not only 50 percent off

INSIDER TIP

hotel rates at about eighteen hundred hotels in the US, Europe, Caribbean, and Australia, but also markdowns at restaurants and shops, and discounts on entertainment of all kinds, including sporting events, amusement parks, and activities for kids. And the profits go to a local organization, which usually sells the memberships as a fundraiser. There are books for nearly all Bay Area communities, and they are priced at $40 or less. Another company, the **ITC-50** (International Travel Card, 800/342-0558), also offers 50 percent discounts at hotels in the US and abroad for $36 per year.

If you'd rather not pay a yearly fee—or any fee at all—you can go through a discount hotel reservation system, which offers corporate-style discounts. **Quickbook** (800/789-9887) has hotel rooms in twenty cities at 40 to 60 percent off rack rates. **The Central Reservation Service** (800/548-3311; 800/950-0232) gives up to 40 percent off rooms in about two hundred hotels in San Francisco, New York, Miami, and Orlando, plus discounts on rental cars. This agency has twenty-four-hour "white courtesy" airport telephones for on-the-spot bookings in those cities.

HOUSE EXCHANGES

Want all the comforts of home when you travel—and a place to stay for free? How about a French farmhouse, a cottage in the Scottish country-side, or an apartment along the Thames in London? For a modest membership fee, you can join an organization that arranges **house-exchanges,** and will include your listing in its directory.

You give the details about your home or apartment, where you want to travel, and roughly when. A directory, usually published three times per year, guides you to potential households in the country that you wish to visit. Or someone may contact you. If you're flexible, and you want to stay in one place for a while, you will save hundreds of dollars. And you'll get to know a place as a temporary resident rather than as a tourist.

There are only a handful of house exchange agencies in the US, but two of them are in the Bay Area. **Intervac** (800/756-4663) has homes in thirty countries and three yearly directories with about nine thousand listings. The annual membership fee is $62. **The Invented City** (415/673-0347) also publishes three directories each year and has about two thousand active members in twenty countries. The annual membership fee is $50.

FAMILY DEALS

If your household includes young travelers, the hotel companies and cruise lines are out to get you. And they've got some great bargains. Most hotel chains have **"kids stay free" programs** for minors who stay in the same room as the parents. **Holiday Inn** goes even further. At about half of its hotels, children twelve years and under eat for free.

It's not just bargains that hotels are offering these days. More and more chains are setting up children's programs so that mom and dad can have a vacation themselves. Take your kids to a Hyatt resort that has a **Camp Hyatt** program and really relax. Or try one of Holiday Inn's

 INSIDER TIP

six new **SunSpree** family resorts, such as the Camelview Resort in Scottsdale, Arizona. At **Westin's** recently inaugurated Kids Club, your children will get special amenities and activities planned just for them. Even **Days Inn** is luring little travelers, with a special Flintstones family package that gives special room rates and a Flintstones Fun Days travel pack full of games and toys for each child at check-in.

Many hotels have family bargains in Hawaii, one of the best family vacation destinations around. Perhaps the best Hawaiian bargain, however, are the **Aloha Festivals**, which take place from mid-September through late October. For $3, you can see a week's worth of cultural events on the island of your choice. The festivals travel from Island to island—one week on each.

If you'd like to see Hawaii in a more leisurely way, take the kids on a one-week cruise aboard one of **American Hawaii Cruises'** two ships. Special onboard activities introduce children to Hawaiian culture, and what's even better, kids age sixteen and under whose parents buy a certain cabin category cruise for free (except during Christmas and New Year's). Single parents who pay the single supplement rate can also take their kids along at no extra charge.

BUDGET ROOMS

To a big degree, a hotel room is a hotel room is a hotel room. What you pay for at upscale properties is fancy lobbies, convention facilities, restaurants, and room service—all things that many people never use. Why stay in an expensive hotel when many moderately priced, and even budget, hotels offer a totally acceptable room at a fraction of the price? Many even throw in continental breakfast and let kids stay free.

Check into one of the 220 nationwide **Courtyard by Marriott** hotels for only $50 to $80 per night, or try one of the company's **Fairfield Inns,** where for $30 to $45 you get a complimentary continental breakfast and free local phone calls along with your single room. Currently, a room at a **Days Inns** will cost you between $39 and $79, depending on the hotel and season; a room at the **Super 8** chain averages $38.

LOCAL HOTEL SPECIALS

Grab your honey and head for one of San Francisco's top hotels for a weekend of luxurious abandon. It's a mini-vacation with a moderate price tag (less than rack rate) with all sorts of extras that the regular guests never receive.

Take advantage of the **Huntington Hotel's** Romance Package any night and get either a park-view or city-view room, a bottle of sparkling wine, tea and sherry service, and the use of the limousine during the day—all at a price 20 percent below regular rates. **The Sheraton Palace** offers weekend rates and even better deals if you book at least fourteen days ahead. Its *Phantom* package comes with deluxe room, dinner in the Garden Court, opera tickets, and limousine transport to and from the opera house. Stay at the **Ritz-Carlton** any weekend and save up to 26 percent, or buy one of its packages for some added amenities. Escape to the sunny East Bay hills and luxuriate in the **Claremont Resort's** spa, with a package that includes a full-body massage, facial,

INSIDER TIP

fitness classes, and spa gift.

These aren't the only deals in town. Nearly every hotel offers them, so check with your favorite before you make your plans.

TRAVEL EXCHANGE PROGRAM

This may be the best bargain of all. Travel the world without leaving your living room by becoming a **Servas host**. Servas is an international travel exchange program that was founded after World War II to restore peace by encouraging people from different countries to get acquainted. Now there are Servas hosts in more than a hundred countries, with more than two hundred hosts in the Bay Area alone.

It works like this. Everyone who participates in the organization (both host and traveler) goes through an interview process in his or her own country, to ensure an understanding of what Servas is all about. Then, travelers receive a letter of introduction to show to their future hosts, and hosts are listed in a directory that travelers carry along. The directory describes each host and tells how many people live in the household, their ages, professions, and interests. Hosts also state the number of days advance notice they require and whether or not they are willing to host families and/or disabled visitors. Travelers contact hosts directly by mail, fax, or phone. Stays are limited to two nights (four for families traveling together), unless a longer visit is arranged. No money is exchanged, but host families are asked to make a voluntary yearly donation (suggested $25) to help run the Servas office in New York and pay for publication and distribution of the host directories.

Servas travelers can stay with hosts throughout the world. All you have to do is go through the interview process and pay a fee of $55, plus a $25 refundable deposit for host lists. For more information, contact US Servas, Inc, 11 John St, Rm 407, New York, NY 10038; (212) 267-0252. ▥

INSIDER TIP: AFFORDABLE LUXURY CRUISES

By Judy Jacobs

If you think cruising is an expensive vacation only the wealthy can afford, you might need to reconsider that notion. With more than one hundred ships and five thousand cruises marketed in the US and Canada, there's at least one cruise tailored to every type of person.

When compared to a land-based resort vacation, a cruise may be a better deal. There are no hidden costs, and you can closely estimate the exact costs of a cruise before departure.

Prices will fluctuate according to the type of vessel and size of its cabins, although rates usually include airfare, accommodations, meals, on-board activities, and entertainment. The only extras are alcoholic drinks, optional shore excursions, and gratuities. And if you follow these tips, you won't have to pay the full price published in the cruise company's glossy brochure.

 INSIDER TIP

EARLY BOOKING PROGRAMS

Several lines, such as **Regency Cruises** (212/972-4499), offer discounts of between 35 and 50 percent to passengers who book trips several months to a year in advance. Such deals come with "price-float guarantees." If the company drops the price after you've booked a particular cruise, it automatically adjusts your fare.

SHORT TRIPS

As more Americans cut their vacations down to one week or less, the cruise industry has responded by offering short trips lasting two or three days. **Carnival Cruise Lines** (305/599-2600) sells three-day cruises to the Bahamas from Florida aboard the *Fantasea*, starting at $499 including airfare from San Francisco. **Royal Caribbean Cruise Lines** (305/539-6000) operates three-day weekend cruises on its ship the *Viking Serenade* from Los Angeles to Baja California starting at $545 including airfare from San Francisco.

OFF-SEASON CRUISING

If you can take your Alaskan cruise in late May instead of summer, or visit the Caribbean in September instead of winter, for example, you will save several hundred dollars.

CRUISE CONSOLIDATORS

These companies sell unsold cabin space from cruise lines, passing substantial discounts on to passengers. While some trips can be booked a year in advance, the bulk of their inventory is usually available one to two months prior to sailing.

One consolidator, **Spur of the Moment** in Los Angeles (800/343-1991), publishes a monthly fourteen-page newsletter listing the cruises it is currently selling. **South Florida Cruises** (800/327-7447), a cruise discounter, employs counselors who match vacationers with the appropriate ship. Although price is an important consideration, don't pick a cruise based on price alone. Cruises provide a wide range of activities. Choose a ship that matches your interests.

Travel agents and cruise-only agencies, such as **Cruise Holidays** with locations in San Francisco (415/550-1899) and Emeryville (510/596-4090), can explain the personalities of each cruise line. For more information, contact the **Cruise Lines International Association**, 500 Fifth Ave, Suite 1407, New York, NY 10110; (212) 921-0066. ▪

INSIDER TIP: STRETCHING YOUR TRAVEL DOLLARS

By Ginny Graves

Whether you are suddenly struck with a case of wanderlust or you're a frequent business flier, here are some quick and painless tips for getting out of town without paying a fortune.

INSIDER TIP

DISCOUNT TICKETS

The easiest way to get free flights is with **frequent-flier mileage.** You build the most miles by selecting hotels and car rental firms that participate in a mileage program (see page 284). "About 30 to 40 percent of frequent-flier mileage comes from flying," says Randy Petersen, editor of *InsideFlyer* magazine. "The rest comes from travel partners."

For more tips and information on travel partners and special mileage promotions, subscribe to *InsideFlyer*, $33 per year, 4715-C Town Center Dr, Colorado Springs, CO 80916; (800) 333-5937.

If money is an object when you're making travel plans, think about signing on as an **air courier.** Couriers give up their checked baggage space on international flights in exchange for deeply discounted tickets (usually between 30 and 60 percent less than the unrestricted coach fare). The disadvantages? Only carry-on luggage is allowed, and flights tend to be limited to major gateway cities. The advantages? You have the opportunity to walk down the streets of London, Singapore, or Sydney on a whim, at a fraction of the usual price.

Several air courier companies are located in the Bay Area. They include **Jupiter Air** (415/872-0845), **Polo Express** (415/742-9613), **TNT-Skypack** (415/692-9600), **UTL Travel** (415/583-5074), and **Way to Go Travel** (415/864-1995).

For more details on becoming an air courier, contact the **Inter-national Association of Air Travel Couriers** (IAATC) at 8 South J St, Box 1349, Lake Worth, FL 33460; (407) 586-0978. Or consult the *Courier Air Travel Handbook,* by Mark I. Field (Thunderbay Press, $9.95).

BOOKING YOUR FLIGHT

There are around thirty thousand travel agents in the United States who sell roughly two-thirds of all airline tickets annually. According to George Albert Brown, author of *The Airline Passenger's Guerrilla Handbook* (Slawson Communications, $14.95), the majority of agents subscribe to only one of the five industry-wide, computerized reservation systems. Brown tips us off to **Traveltron,** a division of Associated Travel Services, Inc, based in Santa Ana, CA, which subscribes to four of the five systems. This multiple capability enables Traveltron to find listings for second-tier airlines that participate in only one reservation system, and to overcome delays in receiving information as it's transmitted between systems.

In addition, Traveltron has a unique computer auditing program that continues to search airline schedules for lower fares as well as seat assignments even after you've purchased your ticket. That alone is worth the long-distance call to Southern California. Traveltron, 1241 East Dyer Rd, Suite 110, Santa Ana, CA 92705; (714) 545-3335 or 300 Ocean Gate Blvd, Suite 115, Long Beach, CA 90802. ▥

 INSIDER TIP

INDEX

SUBJECT INDEX

To make your bargain shopping research easier, we've organized this index into three parts—you can find great bargains by chapter and category, geographical region, or alphabetically (by name of store).

This first index lists stores by subject: Look up men's clothing, electronics, kids' toys—or any other shopping category—and you'll find extensive listings of stores in that category throughout the Bay Area.

APPAREL

CLOTHING

FACTORY

OUTLET CENTERS

HOUSE AND GARDEN

FLOOR COVERINGS

FURNITURE

HOME ELECTRONICS

REGIONAL INDEX

If you know which city in the Bay Area you'll be shopping in, this index will help you find great deals. First locate the region you're interested in—North Bay, South Bay, East Bay, and San Francisco—then look up a city, such as Alameda or Sunnyvale. You'll find all the stores, regardless of category, that are located in that city.

EAST BAY

ALPHABETICAL INDEX

If you know the name of a store with great deals (but you don't know exactly where it is in the Bay Area)—this index is for you. These listings are arranged alphabetically, by name of store.

MORE BARGAINS!

As a KQED member, you'll receive

- A 10% discount on videotapes of thousands of PBS shows.
- Discounts on admission to *Fog City Radio*, KQED's famous Wine & Food Festival, and other popular special events.
- An opportunity to tour the KQED studios.
- Discounts on admissions to more than 70 museums, theater companies, performing arts centers, and other cultural attractions, including:

ART AND CULTURE

- ALLIANCE FRANÇAISE, San Francisco
- ARTSPAN/OPEN STUDIOS, San Francisco
- CALIFORNIA HISTORICAL SOCIETY, San Francisco
- FRIENDS OF THE SAN FRANCISCO PUBLIC LIBRARY, San Francisco
- MUSEO ITALO AMERICANO, San Francisco
- NEW LANGTON ARTS, San Francisco
- SAN FRANCISCO HISTORICAL SOCIETY, San Francisco
- SAN FRANCISCO & MARIN CHILDREN'S ART CENTERS, Mill Valley
- SAN FRANCISCO PERFORMANCES, San Francisco

MUSEUM & TOURS

- AMERICAN HERITAGE MUSEUM, Palo Alto
- AMERICAN MUSEUM OF QUILTS AND TEXTILES OF SAN JOSE, San Jose
- BAY AREA DISCOVERY MUSEUM, Sausalito
- BEHRING AUTO MUSEUM, Danville
- CARTOON ART MUSEUM OF CALIFORNIA, San Francisco
- COYOTE POINT MUSEUM FOR ENVIRONMENTAL EDUCATION, San Mateo
- CROCKER ART MUSEUM, Sacramento
- DASHIELL HAMMETT TOUR, Glen Ellen

- EGYPTIAN MUSEUM & PLANETARIUM, San Jose
- HELEN'S WALK TOUR, Berkeley
- JEWISH MUSEUM SAN FRANCISCO, San Francisco
- MEXICAN MUSEUM, San Francisco
- PHOEBE A. HEARST MUSEUM OF ANTHROPOLOGY, Berkeley
- ROARING CAMP & BIG TREES NARROW GAUGE RAILROAD, Felton
- SAN FRANCISCO MARITIME NATIONAL HISTORICAL PARK, San Francisco
- SAN FRANCISCO PERFORMING ARTS LIBRARY & MUSEUM, San Francisco
- TRITON MUSEUM OF ART, Santa Clara
- UNIVERSITY ART MUSEUM & PACIFIC FILM ARCHIVE, Berkeley
- UC BERKELEY MUSEUM OF ART, SCIENCE AND CULTURE, Danville
- USS PAMPANITO, W.W.II SUBMARINE, San Francisco
- VALLEJO NAVAL AND HISTORICAL MUSEUM, Vallejo
- WESTERN RAILWAY MUSEUM, Suisun City
- WOK WIZ CHINATOWN TOURS, San Francisco
- YOSEMITE MOUNTAIN SUGAR PINE RAILROAD, Fish Camp
- YREKA WESTERN RAILROAD, Yreka

MUSIC & DANCE

- AUDIUM, San Francisco
- BACH DANCING AND DYNAMITE SOCIETY, El Granada
- BERKELEY MOVING ARTS, Berkeley
- DANCERS' GROUP, San Francisco
- MASTERWORKS CHORALE, San Mateo
- NEW CENTURY CHAMBER ORCHESTRA, Mill Valley
- NOVA VISTA SYMPHONY, Sunnyvale
- OAKLAND SYMPHONY CHORUS, Oakland
- PACIFICA ARTS AND HERITAGE COUNCIL, Pacifica
- PALO ALTO CHAMBER ORCHESTRA, Palo Alto
- PALO ALTO PHILHARMONIC ASSOCIATION, Palo Alto
- PENINSULA SYMPHONY, San Mateo

- SAN JOSE CLEVELAND BALLET, San Jose
- SAN JOSE SYMPHONY, San Jose
- THE WINIFRED BAKER AND SAN FRANCISCO CIVIC CHORALE, San Rafael
- THE WOMEN'S PHILHARMONIC, San Francisco

SCIENCE AND NATURE

- CALIFORNIA ACADEMY OF SCIENCES, San Francisco
- CALIFORNIA STATE PARKS FOUNDATION, Kentfield
- EXPLORATORIUM, San Francisco
- LAWRENCE HALL OF SCIENCE, Berkeley
- LINDSAY MUSEUM, Walnut Creek
- MENDOCINO COAST BOTANICAL GARDENS, Fort Bragg
- NATURE CONSERVANCY OF CALIFORNIA, San Francisco
- SAN FRANCISCO ZOOLOGICAL SOCIETY, San Francisco
- TECH MUSEUM OF INNOVATION, San Jose
- TERWILLIGER NATURE EDUCATION CENTER, Corte Madera

THEATER

- BERNARD OSHER MARIN JEWISH COMMUNITY CENTER, San Rafael
- CALIFORNIA THEATRE CENTER, Sunnyvale
- CAPUCHINO COMMUNITY THEATRE, San Bruno
- CENTER REPERTORY COMPANY OF WALNUT CREEK, Walnut Creek
- KIDSHOWS, Oakland
- SAN JOSE STAGE COMPANY, San Jose
- THEATER OF THE BLUE ROSE, Berkeley
- THEATRE RHINOCEROS, San Francisco
- YOUNG AUDIENCES' ARTSCARD PROJECT, San Francisco, (Participating organizations subject to change)

Complete details are in the Member Benefits Guide you'll receive on joining.

KQED - THE BEST ENTERTAINMENT AND EDUCATION BARGAIN IN THE BAY AREA!

Mystery... Masterpiece Theatre... MacNeil/Lehrer News Hour... Nova... Great Performances... National Geographic... Sesame Street... Ghostwriters... "Tales of the City"... This Week in Northern California ...

AND ON AND ON—

KQED/Channel 9 brings you so many of your favorite, best remembered television shows.

And for unparalleled depth of news and information, you rely on *Morning Edition, All Things Considered, Forum, Fresh Air with Terry Gross,* and all the other great features on 88.5 KQED FM.

All of this exceptional programming comes to you *free,* just because you live in the Bay Area.

But for less than the cost of a night at the movies, less than a couple of months of a daily paper, less than a month of your cable TV bill, you can help make all this and more possible.

Become a member of KQED and do your part. You'll gain all the great member benefits described on page 258 of this book—a free subscription to *Fine Tuning* or the award-winning *San Francisco Focus* magazine, member discounts at more than 70 Bay Area cultural attractions, discounts on videos and on special events.

But best of all, you'll keep great programming coming on *your* station— KQED TV (Channel 9) and KQED FM (88.5)

Return the coupon today.

KQED MEMBERSHIP FORM

Enroll me immediately as a KQED Member! Send me my KQED Membership Card, my first of 12 issues of *Fine Tuning* or *San Francisco Focus,* and information about the additional benefits I am entitled to as a KQED Member.

Enclosed is my contribution of:

$40 ___ $65 ___ $120 ___ Other $___

_____
NAME

_____
ADDRESS

_____
CITY, STATE, ZIP

_____
DAY PHONE #

___ My check is enclosed.
___ I prefer to charge my:
    __ American Express __ Discover
    __ MasterCard __ Visa

_____
ACCT. #   EXP. DATE

_____
SIGNATURE

I would like a subscription to: (Check one)

___FINE TUNING. Member magazine provides station news, events and TV and Radio program information.

___SAN FRANCISCO FOCUS. The city magazine of San Francisco, "smart reading for the Bay Area." Includes KQED's Member Guide, with complete TV and Radio program information.

MAIL TO: KQED,
              PO Box 44235,
              San Francisco, CA 94144-4235

UA4EZ000